Elementary School
Administration
and Supervision

Elementary School
Administration
and Supervision

WILLARD S. ELSBREE *Professor of Education*
TEACHERS COLLEGE, COLUMBIA UNIVERSITY

HAROLD J. McNALLY *Associate Professor of Education*
TEACHERS COLLEGE, COLUMBIA UNIVERSITY

AMERICAN BOOK COMPANY NEW YORK

CINCINNATI   CHICAGO   BOSTON   ATLANTA   DALLAS   SAN FRANCISCO

PREFACE

The many changes which have taken place in educational thought and practice in the past few decades have had considerable effect on school administration. The increasing size of the educational enterprise, the sharp upgrading in the qualifications of teachers, and broadened concepts of the role of leadership are a few of the forces which are causing a newer definition of the administrative function, and a re-thinking of the role of the principal in the elementary school. The trend toward differentiation among schools in school systems, and toward greater autonomy for individual schools has placed the principalship in a position of key importance in the educational picture. Furthermore, forces have been at work in the world which have broadened and deepened our conception of the functional meaning of democracy, and have added urgency to the job of educating for it. Concurrent with this there has been a rapidly growing recognition that democratic administration is necessary to the development and operation of democratic education. This recognition of the need for democratic administrative practices has been evident not only in educational administration; it has left its mark on administrative theory and practice in business, industry, and the operation of public enterprises as well.

Throughout this volume, the authors have attempted to indicate some of the implications of these forces and trends for principals and supervisors of elementary schools. It has been the purpose of the authors to provide a broad overview of the kinds of problems faced by principals and supervisors, and to develop guidelines to action. The emphasis throughout is upon co-operative endeavor for the achievement of modern educational objectives by means of modern educational methods. There is an attempt to place the practical, everyday aspects of the job on a sound theoretical base.

The topics discussed have been grouped into seven major sections.

Nevertheless, there is an explicit recognition of the interrelationships between and among these aspects of the elementary school. The authors have attempted to indicate that consistency in educational practice can be achieved better when the principal and his staff clarify their understanding of the fundamental reasons for, and objectives of, each policy and practice; and appreciate the relationship of those policies and practices to the basic aims and beliefs of the school itself.

The material has been developed as a result of the needs the authors have identified in their educational experience in elementary school classrooms, in supervisory and administrative positions, in intensive studies of schools and school systems, and in their work as college instructors of prospective elementary school leaders. It is as truly a product of their students as it is their own. It is hoped, therefore, that it will be found to be a valuable adjunct to the instruction and orientation of elementary school workers of all kinds, but particularly for principals and supervisors.

The authors wish to express their indebtedness to their students, to the other authors of texts in the field of school administration and supervision, and to several of their colleagues who offered constructive criticisms and suggestions on the manuscript. A number of individuals and school systems supplied information and record forms for inclusion as illustrative material. To them we are most grateful. Special acknowledgement is due to Professors A. Wellesley Foshay, Paul W. F. Witt, Alice Miel, Henry H. Linn, and Miss Alice N. Fedder for advice and assistance in their areas of special competence.

WILLARD S. ELSBREE

HAROLD J. MCNALLY

TABLE OF CONTENTS

vii

Contents   ix

FIGURES

TABLES

Elementary School

Administration

and Supervision

Part I THE PRINCIPALSHIP

The position of elementary school principal has undergone significant changes during the last century. Many forces have combined to broaden the scope of the principal's work and to challenge his imagination and ability. Among the influences which have conditioned the nature of the principal's duties are many legal requirements bearing directly on the administrative and supervisory procedures of the school principal.

In the three chapters which follow, the factors influencing the development of the elementary school principalship are identified and appraised, the current responsibilities of the modern principal are analyzed and his legal rights and liabilities are discussed.

CHAPTER I

FACTORS INFLUENCING
THE DEVELOPMENT OF THE
ELEMENTARY SCHOOL PRINCIPALSHIP

The elementary school principal today holds a position of unusual importance in the typical public school system. Not only does he have wide latitude with respect to administrative policies and procedures relating to his school, but more and more he is being asked to assume the leadership responsibility for curriculum improvements and for school-community relationships. This condition arises from the fact that boards of education and superintendents of schools rather generally are according a degree of self-government to individual school units far in excess of the powers commonly given in the past to principals and their staffs.

Needless to say, the elementary school principalship in America has undergone considerable change since its inception in the early part of the last century. During this relatively short period in educational history notable improvements have been made in the status of the principal. The forces which have affected public education generally have also given direction and momentum to the professionalization of the principalship, and have helped to determine the nature and status of this position as it has finally emerged. While it is difficult to identify all the influences over the years which have left their imprint on the elementary school principal's work and standing, there are several which are clearly discernible.

Urbanization

Perhaps the most observable factor leading to the inauguration of the office of school principal was the *urbanization* that took place in America during the nineteenth century, particularly between the years 1830 and 1860. During this period the proportion of people living in communities of over 8000 population rose from 6.7 per cent of the whole to 16.1 per cent—this despite the fact that the West was being opened up largely to rural population. Experiments in educational procedure in the United States were a phenomenon of the cities, not of the rural areas. As Reisner so effectively pointed out, *it was in the urban districts where innovations and improvements first appeared in the development of the common school.*[1] This is understandable since the needs were most obvious in the congested areas, and the numbers of pupils and teachers made experimentation more feasible in city schools than in the schools of the rural districts.

The rapid increase in city population which characterized this period led superintendents of schools who had heretofore graded the schools themselves and supervised the teachers, to delegate these responsibilities, in large part, to subordinates. The sheer size of the task made this necessary. It was logical to relieve the principal-teacher, the forerunner of the school principal, of some of his teaching activities and hold him primarily responsible for pupil classification, for supervision, and for the general administration of individual school units. To some extent the principal-teacher, despite heavy teaching assignments, had always been responsible for classifying pupils and for the general conduct of the school. But with the increase in size of schools, principal-teachers could not give adequate attention to their manifold duties, and hence were more and more relieved of teaching responsibility. By 1870, several of the large cities had freed principals of all classroom teaching duties. Yet this reform was not universally adopted. Even today, there are head-teachers whose assignments resemble, in many respects, the duties of principal-teachers in the middle decades of the nineteenth century. But the number of these positions is declining rapidly with consolidation and with the gradual elimination of small urban schools. That the principal-teacher arrangement is one practical answer to the leadership problem in certain sparsely settled districts must be acknowledged. But in urban centers it is highly unsatisfactory since it restricts too greatly the scope of the principal's activities, preventing him from devoting adequate time to professional leadership.

[1] Edward H. Reisner, *The Evolution of the Common School,* The Macmillan Company, New York, 1930, p. 324.

The Graded System

A second influence which hastened the advent of full-time principal-ships was the introduction of the graded system of schools, involving, as it did, the attempt to sort pupils into classes according to attainment. The implications of this innovation were far-reaching. The graded system led to the unification of all departments or classes under one head. It encouraged careful prescription of the work to be done in each grade and produced extensive revisions in courses of study. As the need for co-ordinating the work of several teachers within the building be-came apparent and the administrative tasks inherent in the graded ar-rangement were understood, boards of education and superintendents of schools saw the necessity for freeing principals of classroom teaching duties.

The graded system still poses vexing problems for administrators. Promotion procedures, grouping plans, marking arrangements, and curricular adjustment devices—all inherent features of the graded scheme—join to challenge the judgment and imagination of the modern elementary school principal.

Poorly Qualified Teachers

A third factor which strongly affected the establishment of the posi-tion of elementary school principal and left its mark upon the work and status of this school officer was the unpreparedness of early teachers for the tasks confronting them. When Horace Mann and Henry Barnard made their heroic fight for public education, they were confronted with the almost unanswerable argument that qualified teachers were not available, and that there were no facilities for training them. How then could schools be maintained for all children? Two answers were consist-ently given to this basic question. First, that even granting the dearth of competent new teachers, there were enough women interested in teach-ing and gifted by nature in the art of instructing young children to fill the teaching posts required to make public education a reality. This sug-gestion, that women should "take over," constituted an "about face" for many leading educators who, steeped in the tradition of the times, be-lieved that woman's place was in the home; that women were not suited to teaching, save possibly children of tender years. The second reply to those who said public education was an impractical dream was that the school principal could train his teachers on the job and could add greatly to their efficiency through supervision. After long and bitter debate these answers were tentatively accepted by the people, and the great venture of free public schools was launched. The pattern of school administration which logically followed called for a male principal, with duties resembling somewhat those assigned to a foreman in industry. A primary task was to supervise the work of the less adequately qualified employees.

It is significant and unfortunate that this early emphasis on teacher training as an important phase of supervision survived its usefulness and persisted beyond the period when teachers as a class were inadequately prepared for their jobs. In fact, supervisory practices today in many communities still reflect the point of view prevalent in 1840. Probably the greatest good arising from the early practice of holding the principal responsible for the results of his teachers, beyond meeting the immediate problems of the times, was the increased stress given to the leadership function of the principal. In addition to training his teachers, he was expected to inspire them, to enlist their co-operation, and to call forth their best efforts. Though the methods of approaching this problem were often highly undemocratic and unsound psychologically, the responsibility for leadership was at least fixed. Moreover, as a result of study and experimentation, superior techniques have been developed which over the years have come to supersede the rather crude supervisory methods employed during the last century.

Increased Prestige of Elementary Teachers

The fourth and one of the greatest factors in determining the status of the elementary school principal has been the gradual elevation of the position of the elementary school teacher in the minds of the profession and the public. Senior high school teachers until recently enjoyed a prestige far in advance of that accorded those teaching in the elementary schools. This fact grows out of the time-worn belief that the older the child, the more difficult and important the task of instructing him. The result of this early attitude was the development of something resembling a caste system. High school teachers were more generously paid; they had more education—in fact many of them studied at liberal arts colleges; their cultural background was substantially higher than their counterparts in the elementary school; their parents had more money; in short, they were blessed with superior opportunities in nearly every aspect of living. This situation carried over, in large part, to principalships in the two divisions of the school system. The high school principal always stood above the elementary principal in the hierarchy. While the effects of this may not always have been bad, it unquestionably did harm the personalities of many elementary school principals. Until recently they have tended as a group to be more timid and less articulate than high school principals. This is quite understandable in view of the relatively low esteem in which elementary principals as a group have been held.

The state of affairs just described is gradually being improved. It would be inaccurate, however, to claim that the two positions today are equal in prestige in the eyes of the taxpayers or, for that matter, in the minds of the profession itself. There is still a disparity, as is evidenced in most cities by wide differences in salary and by the views commonly expressed by both laymen and professional educators. Great progress, however, has been made in correcting the erroneous impressions regarding the nature of the two positions. Today the elementary school is coming into its own. Research findings, coupled with philosophical and psychological theories, have laid stress on the importance of education in early childhood. Moreover, the personal requirements, together with the fund of information necessary for successful teaching in the early grades, are deemed to be equivalent in every respect to those essential for success in working at the upper rungs of the school ladder—a contention which was not seriously viewed before the turn of the century. Obviously, if these arguments are upheld, the qualifications of principals whose major task is to give leadership to the instructional staff should not vary from division to division. Rather it seems apparent that only gifted persons should be appointed to principalships whether elementary or secondary. The profession and the public are gradually becoming aware of the importance of this fact and are, more and more, according the elementary principalship the status which it deserves.

Predominance of Women

Closely related to the prestige problem growing out of the association of elementary principals with young children and the teachers of young children, is a fifth influence which has affected the position of the elementary school principal. Boards of education have been readier to appoint women to this post than to the high school principalship. In fact, at the present time approximately half of the elementary principals in the United States are women, whereas the number of women high school principals is relatively negligible.[2] It is too early to assess the full effects of this policy. It is certain that until recently a large proportion of women in any vocation has spelled low salaries and limited prestige. Society, during the nineteenth century and for the first two decades of the twentieth century, reserved the better paying positions for men. Arbitrary restrictions were commonly applied and only when the supply fell short of the demand were women welcomed. Public school teaching is an illustration in point. So long as men were available, women were discouraged from teaching. When men teachers became scarce, public opinion was modified and classroom doors were thrown open to women. The wages of the latter, however, for many decades were decidedly lower than those commonly received by men. It seems likely that the increase in the proportion of women teachers during the last century was one factor, although by no means the only one, in keeping teachers' salaries relatively low. Elementary principals have experienced similar obstacles in their struggle for financial recognition and professional prestige. Fortunately, the battle to emancipate women has been practically won, even if the inequalities have not yet been entirely eradicated. Woman suffrage, industrialization, and two major wars have combined to remove most of the discriminatory practices unfavorable to women. Equal-pay laws are but one evidence of this generalization. Hence, despite the lower prestige and salary produced by the predominance of women principals in the public elementary schools, there seems to be reason for believing that a new era is at hand. Women today have achieved a position of great power, and stand to influence administrative policies as never before. That unwarranted sex discrimination in salaries will not be tolerated in the future seems certain.

Another consideration that is coming to weigh heavily with school boards is the effect that keeping the door to promotion open has on the morale of the masses of women teachers. Of all the administrative posts, the elementary principalship offers the best opportunity to teachers for advancement and is without doubt a powerful motivating factor in the

---

[2] In the case of supervising elementary principalships, men outnumber women three to two but in the case of teaching principalships the ratio in 1947–48 was four men to five women. Department of Elementary School Principals, *The Elementary School Principalship—Today and Tomorrow*, Twenty-seventh Yearbook, National Education Association, Washington, D. C., 1948, pp. 19–20.

lives of many of the teaching personnel. Whereas there is often only one high school principalship in a school system, there are likely to be ten or a dozen elementary principalship posts.

Expansion of the Curriculum

Sixth among the influences which have helped to define the responsibilities of the elementary school principal is the expansion of the common school curriculum. State legislatures have tended to prescribe subjects to be taught in the elementary schools, the curriculum items ranging from manners to the Constitution of the United States.[3] Overzealous pressure groups commonly originate curriculum change and influence legislators to prescribe courses to be taught in the public schools. Much of this prescription has been unwise and ineffective. Some of the expansion in the program of studies, however, has come from local surveys of needs, and includes among the areas added such practical subjects as manual and household arts. This extension of the traditional curriculum has compelled principals to inform themselves with respect to visual aids and materials of instruction, and to become conversant with current methodology in fields not formerly included in the school curriculum. The effect of this change has been to broaden the perspective and knowledge of principals. It has also added to their supervisory responsibilities. Moreover, the pressure from many sources to add new subjects and areas of instruction to the school curriculum has stimulated principals to weigh values and has encouraged them to develop a well-rounded philosophy of education. Hence, the pressure for curriculum change over the years, despite the unfortunate prescriptions of state legislatures, has had (in the main) a salutary influence on the work and effectiveness of the elementary school principal.

State Legislation

A seventh important factor in the history of the elementary school principalship relates to the action of state legislatures beyond the curriculum prescriptions just described. This branch of the government has devoted much thought and consideration to school problems. All of the states, for example, have passed education laws compelling the attend-

[3] Included among the curriculum prescriptions in some states are physiology and hygiene, the nature and effects of alcoholic drinks and narcotics, American history, civics, citizenship, state history, patriotism, forestry and allied agricultural subjects, and humane treatment of animals.

ance of most children of elementary school age. While the laws permit parents some choice in the matter of how and by whom their children may be taught,[4] in actual practice at least 90 per cent of the children who attend school go to public schools. Thus, legislative action has tended to increase the stability of the principal's position. Children are always on hand to be taught, with the result that changes in economic conditions, while reflected in the financial support of schools, have had little effect on the number of principalships. One other observable influence of compulsory education has been the challenge which it has carried with it for principals to be imaginative and creative in planning with teachers how best to meet the needs of such a widely varied school population.

Not only have the states dealt directly with the matter of pupil attendance, but most states have specified the minimum qualifications necessary for appointment to an elementary school principalship. This action has served, in a number of commonwealths at least, to restrict appointments to trained and experienced persons. In many states the days when a high school teacher without any experience or training in the field of elementary education could be appointed to a principalship are gone forever. Today new elementary principals in several states[5] must have a master's degree or the equivalent, including some training in administration and supervision. Two or three years of teaching experience are also commonly required. In this manner, children and the teaching staff are now given some protection against the appointment of wholly unqualified principals. These minimum safeguards, although still inadequate, have already had a wholesome effect on the profession and on the public attitude toward it, and are indicative of the direction in which the elementary principalship is moving.

While the state has not ordinarily prescribed the minimum salary status of principals, it has indirectly influenced it through salary legislation for teachers, and through tenure laws. Communities often use teachers' salaries as a basis for establishing the salaries of supervisors and principals. Tenure laws make it difficult for local communities to lower existing salaries. City school systems have played a major role in improving the salary status of principals everywhere. A few boards

[4] Parents may, if they prefer, send their children to private or sectarian schools, or under some laws provide instruction at home.

[5] See *The Elementary School Principalship—Today and Tomorrow,* National Education Association, 1948, pp. 301–310; also Robert C. Woellner and M. A. Wood, *Requirements for Certification of Teachers and Administrators,* 15th ed., 1950–51, University of Chicago Press, Chicago, 1950 (Mimeographed).

of education, notably Oakland, California, and Baltimore, Maryland, have adopted single salary schedules for principals, removing the pay differentials which formerly existed between elementary and secondary positions. Schools in these districts are classified according to size, but the division of the school system to which a principal is assigned has no bearing upon his salary. Whether or not this policy constitutes the wisest answer to the salary problem has not yet been determined. The action of these communities does suggest, however, that the day is not far distant when the work of the elementary school principal will be assessed at a value more nearly comparable to that now placed upon the efforts of high school principals.

It is altogether probable that the existing numerical ratios between teachers' and principals' salaries will undergo some modification favorable to elementary principals. Present ratios do not allow adequately for the larger responsibilities assumed by elementary principals, nor are they defensible when compared with the ratios which obtain between teachers and high school principals. The future hope of principals for an improved economic status lies in persuading laymen of the importance of the elementary school principal's job and in securing the active support of teachers' organizations for adequate salaries. Principals working alone will find it difficult to improve their economic position significantly. Only through the co-operative efforts of the whole profession can the salary problem be wisely resolved.

The Influence of State Education Departments and the Federal Office

Any discussion of the elementary school principalship which failed to include the influence of state departments of education and the work of the Federal Office of Education on the development of the elementary school principalship would be inadequate. Several of the states have provided genuine leadership to school principals and have helped to build in the minds of local boards of education and, to a lesser degree, the public generally some appreciation of the importance of the principal's job. This has been achieved through school visits, the preparation and distribution of special bulletins, and through group conferences. In a few states, of which New York is a notable example, the research activities of the headquarters staff have been fruitful in bringing about improvements in the practices and procedures of school principals. It must be admitted that some state departments in the past have supplied little leadership to local school administrators and can therefore claim little credit for whatever progress this group of professional workers has made.

It is important, in assessing the influence of state departments of education on the status of school principals, to remember that official recognition itself from an agency of the state has had significance. It has contributed to the public acceptance of the office of principal and has also influenced the attitude of the teaching profession toward the job.

Students of education would undoubtedly differ as to the importance of the role played by the Federal Office of Education in defining the work of the elementary school principal, and in influencing the achievements of this group of administrators over the years. The Office has maintained a staff of approximately fifteen members including specialists in health and physical education, science, fine arts, social studies, physically handicapped, nursery, kindergarten, and primary levels, upper grades, rural schools, extended school services, and research.[6] The work of these specialists has filled a real need in providing school systems with information and counsel and in bringing to the attention of principals the data bearing on countrywide conditions. Numerous pamphlets and bulletins dealing with nearly every phase of elementary education, including the status of the elementary principalship itself, have been issued.

Graduate Schools of Education as a Factor

Included also among the agencies and institutions which have helped to mold the elementary principalship are graduate schools of education in American universities. Their influence has been confined to the last fifty years, since no comprehensive program of training existed for this group of workers prior to the turn of the century. Universities in planning their curricular offerings for the preparation of principals have been guided somewhat by state certification patterns. This emphasis has been unavoidable in light of the practical needs of students. But preparing students to meet certification standards has not constituted the universities' major contribution. Schools of education have provided a broad background of subject matter, including the psychological and philosophical foundations, curriculum materials and procedures, supervision,

[6] U. S. Office of Education, *Educational Directory,* "Federal Government and States," U. S. Government Printing Office, Washington, D. C., 1948–49.

and administration. Moreover, in recent years some graduate schools of education have developed internship programs which promise to enrich the background of those entering this phase of school administration. University professors have also played an active role in the activities of principals' associations and in the development of the literature bearing on the principal's work. It seems probable that the university will continue to exercise significant leadership in the improvement of this position.

The Principal's Contribution to the Job

Finally, the principals themselves, through their professional associations, have played an important role in determining the nature of the position and work of the elementary school principal. During the latter half of the nineteenth century, local principals' associations became very active and there is evidence that during this period the principals in New York City, Chicago, Detroit, and Cleveland, as well as those in smaller urban centers, gave serious thought to the professional status of the school principal and to the curriculum and organizational problems related to the elementary school. State principals' associations, in recent years, have made significant contributions both to the literature of elementary education and to the development of the principalship. It is hard to appraise the relative influence of these associations. They are still in their infancy, and the full impact of their efforts has not yet been felt. That they have inspired some young principals to grow and have served as a goad to the run-of-the-mill administrator is certain. Their forces are relatively small in number, but when merged with teachers' organizations and friends of education, they promise to exert great influence for good in improving both the quality of their own service and, indirectly, public education.

A national organization of principals, the National Department of Elementary School Principals, was created in 1921 and has experienced a steady growth during its brief history. It had, in 1950, a membership of approximately 10,000. The Department has shown great vitality and has exercised leadership among principals generally in the United States. It has issued a series of yearbooks and bulletins. The former have dealt with a variety of topics including teaching methods, supervision, administration, curriculum, and the status of elementary school principals. The Department also publishes a professional bulletin, *The National Elementary School Principal*. This is issued five times a year and is an effective medium for keeping members up to date on recent trends. Several monographs have also been published containing extensive reports of study committees on topics of vital concern to elementary school principals.

Through its publications, its working committees, and conferences, the National Department of Elementary School Principals has performed a significant service not only to its members but to the entire profession of education. That it will continue to be a powerful force in fashioning the position of the elementary school principal and in establishing standards for the profession appears certain.

Conclusion

Undoubtedly, there are other influences which have helped to form the general pattern of the elementary school principalship as we know it today. They are so interwoven, however, with the warp and woof of our American civilization that it is difficult to isolate them and give them their proper weighting. Business and industry, for example, have left their imprint on school organization; economic and political forces have undoubtedly touched the office of the principalship at various points. Their influence, however, is too intangible to assess.

The ten factors emphasized in this chapter, namely urbanization, the graded system, the unpreparedness of early nineteenth century teachers, the gradual elevation of the position of elementary school teachers in the minds of the profession and public, the predominance of women in the elementary principalship, the expansion of the common school curriculum, state legislation, the leadership exercised by state education departments and the Federal Office of Education, the contribution of faculty members in graduate schools of education, and the professional activities of principals' associations—these have been especially significant influences in determining the status of the position of the elementary school principal as it exists today.

As for tomorrow, no one can speak with certainty. But the forces which give promise of elevating the position of the elementary principalship to still greater heights than those yet attained are operating with considerable strength. Setbacks are possible should new influences appear which counteract the effectiveness of the more favorable ones enumerated earlier. That there is justification for optimism, however, seems clear.

SUGGESTED READINGS

Department of Elementary School Principals, *The Elementary School Principalship*, Seventh Yearbook, National Education Association, Washington, D. C., 1928.

————, *The Elementary School Principalship—Today and Tomorrow*, Twenty-seventh Yearbook, National Education Association, Washington, D. C., 1948.

Pierce, Paul Revere, *The Development of the Public School Principalship*, University of Chicago Press, Chicago, 1935.

Reisner, Edward H., *The Evolution of the Common School*, The Macmillan Company, New York, 1930.

Woellner, Robert C. and Wood, M. A., *Requirements for Certification of Teachers and Administrators*, 15th ed., 1950–51, University of Chicago Press, Chicago, 1950 (Mimeographed).

CHAPTER II

RESPONSIBILITIES OF
THE MODERN PRINCIPAL

Many of the duties of the modern elementary school principal have been mentioned in the foregoing discussion of influences that have played a major role in the development of the principalship over the past century. Here an attempt will be made to classify the principal's functions as they exist today, and to relate them to the qualifications which principals need if they are to measure up to their responsibilities.

The principal's duties will depend somewhat upon the size of the school and the type of community in which the school is located. A large school with many pupils, parents, and teachers necessitates a more complex administrative organization than is required in a relatively small school. The principal's task will also vary according to whether or not he is organizing and administering a new school or taking over one which has been operating for several years. Starting from scratch presents some organizational problems which many principals never experience simply because the major job was done by one of their predecessors when the school was first established. Principals seldom have complete freedom to set up a record system for their school, to establish a new curriculum, or to revamp the office arrangements thoroughly, including the filing system. There will undoubtedly be occasions when existing plans and provisions can be revised and modified, but often it is impractical to scrap them and make a completely fresh start. The recurring or ever-present responsibilities of the principal are the ones with which school administrators need to be especially familiar. Among these, personnel leadership deserves to be ranked first.

Personnel Leadership

This responsibility has been the most neglected, and it is the point at which principals are likely to be weakest in their preparation and personal fitness. The elementary school principal has duties that are related to the central office staff, teachers, parents and other lay citizens, the custodian in his school, the school secretary, and finally to the children attending the school. The manner in which he meets his obligations to these groups and individuals will condition his success. The modern school requires democratic leadership. Democratic leadership implies co-operation on the part of all members of the team. It assumes that the employees will identify themselves enthusiastically with the school enterprise, that their efforts will be respected and will bring satisfaction, and that group planning and decisions will be the rule rather than the exception. To develop a democratic atmosphere and to bring about a co-operative method of meeting problems is the principal's responsibility. Moreover, his job is to stimulate staff members and parents to think co-operatively on the real problems confronting the school, and his leadership must ultimately be weighed against the frequency with which sound solutions are reached.

Supervision, as it relates to classroom teaching efficiency and growth of teachers in service, is one aspect of personnel leadership. Much has been said and written about this phase of the principal's work; unfortunately, tradition has left its imprint so deeply upon supervisory practices that a thoroughly rational approach to influencing the modern teacher's behavior is difficult to achieve. As was mentioned earlier, many supervisors and administrators are operating under the assumption that theirs is a job of teacher training, a function which at one time in our history properly belonged to the principal because other agencies had not yet been created to meet that need. But today, teachers, for the most part, are not dependent upon the principal for advice as to how to perform the usual tasks assigned them. Hence, classroom supervision, *as it was developed in the nineteenth century* and carried over to the twentieth, has no real reason for existence. Instead, the principal's basic supervisory task is to set up environmental factors that are conducive to the continuous growth of the staff, to provide for exchange of views and information among them, and to encourage them to help one another by capitalizing on their own resources. The combined wisdom of a staff of teachers is obviously much greater than the wisdom of a single principal. The process of discovering and utilizing the talents of staff members is the function of the principal and this poses a more challenging problem than giving direct counsel to teachers on how to improve their instructional methods. The latter procedure may be defended upon occasion, but as a general practice it has little to commend it.

Teachers grow most when they become enthusiastic about improving something which they themselves feel needs to be improved. Problems which teachers identify, therefore, are better areas for study than those which the principal may consider to be important. Through co-operative attacks on real problems of concern to teachers, attitudes are modified, teaching efficiency improves, and everyone involved learns. Giving leadership to efforts of this character is the principal's primary responsibility.

In addition to his work with teachers, the principal also has a responsibility for bringing parents into a constructive relationship with the school program, thus helping to insure more sympathetic and intelligent guidance on the part of both home and school than is likely to result if parents are not made real partners in the task of education. This involves parent-teacher planning based on a thorough understanding and an acceptance of the goals of the school, on the part of both teachers and parents, together with an appreciation of the methods employed in achieving these goals. Unless children are treated with some consistency in their learning experiences both within and outside the school, the results are likely to be sadly disappointing. Most parents, if given an opportunity, can become acquainted with the philosophy underlying classroom procedures in a relatively brief period of time. Helping teachers and parents to see the need for such understanding, and devising means of achieving the desired co-operation, are essential features of the principal's job. In dealing with parents, as in dealing with members of his staff, the principal should employ the democratic principles implied earlier.

Enough has been said above with respect to the manner in which the modern principal exercises his leadership function with the teaching staff and parents to indicate the general pattern he should employ in dealing with the custodian and the school secretary. These latter employees are often ignored when educational matters are being considered. This policy is unfortunate because it tends to reduce the effectiveness of the school program. Both the school secretary and the custodian influence the behavior of pupils for good or ill. If these workers understand the goals of the school and are in sympathy with them, they can be a positive force in promoting the welfare of pupils. The elementary school principal who senses the importance of capitalizing the resources of all the workers in his building will take steps to bring the school secretary and the custodian into close relationship with teachers. All employees in the building should be included in the school's social life and should be made active participants in the formulation of those policies which relate to their spheres of work.

The implications of personnel leadership for the preparation of principals for their work are tremendous. Knowledge of theory alone is not sufficient. Admission to the elementary principal's profession should imply successful experience in leading people to work together cooperatively. There should be evidence procured also to show that the new principal possesses sufficient personal magnetism to work effectively with teachers and parents. He should be friendly and approachable. Basic to everything is a dedication to the education of children themselves. There is a type of principal whose apparent love of children stems out of a starved and emotionally unsatisfied personal life. This is not a healthy condition. A normal respect and affection for "youngsters" is what is required, together with a conviction that the education of children is important for the welfare of democracy. Qualifications for the principalship, therefore, cannot be met solely by a formal college education. They should encompass skills in human relationships, an understanding of social trends and forces, educational vision, and capacity for democratic leadership.

Leadership training is important. Unfortunately, few colleges and universities have done more than to treat this area rather superficially. Internship programs (although as yet few in number) seem very promising; when adequately supervised and related to the other graduate study efforts of students, they should substantially improve the quality of preparation. Moreover, it appears likely that present college programs for the preparation of school principals can be modified and enriched so as to contribute more significantly to the leadership phase of the elementary principal's work. As was indicated above, however, no amount of formal training by itself will suffice. Principals should be selected on the basis of demonstrated aptitude for working with people, either as teachers in the classroom or as workers in some other vocational field.

Plant Management

A second, though less complicated function of school principals than personnel leadership, is plant management. The principal is responsible for seeing to it that the building is safe, that sanitary conditions are maintained, and that acceptable standards of heating, lighting, and ventilating are observed. This duty may be light or heavy for the principal, depending upon the interest and knowledge of the custodian. As was indicated earlier, the leadership function of the principal has pertinence for all employees; if he is skillful in working with people, the morale of the school custodian is likely to be good and his efficiency correspondingly high. If the principal is weak in his ability to lead, then there is considerable likelihood that the custodial work will reflect this inaptitude.

Included under plant management are a number of duties that relate to playground organization and supervision. Here again, safety is an important consideration. But over and beyond the protective aspects of the principal's work in relationship to the management of the plant is his responsibility for furthering the educational aims of the school. Making the plant serve the needs of children should be a primary objective. There is a substantial body of subject matter in the field of school building operation and maintenance with which principals should be familiar. Recent developments in heating, lighting, and cleaning have implications for the efficiency of the educational program.

Business Management

A third function of the principal is business management. In addition to the cost of a school building which represents a sizable investment, hundreds of dollars worth of supplies, books, and equipment are entrusted to the care of the principal as head of the local school unit. With the exception of the school plant, the principal commonly has a major responsibility for ordering and distributing these valuables and has a duty to account for them. Moreover, there are usually activities within his school which require the handling of moneys. Among these are cafeteria services, parent-teacher association projects, and entertainments. Unless a careful accounting system is developed and the management of business activities thoroughly supervised, serious embarrassment can arise. In fact, carelessness and indifference with respect to business management have, in some instances, cost the principal his job. This responsibility need not be as time-consuming as some other duties, but it is very important that it be handled efficiently.

Public Relations

Public relations is a fourth large category pertaining to the work of the modern principal. Education, to be effective, must be administered in an atmosphere of sympathy and understanding. Public relations has, as its aim, the creation of this atmosphere. Ideally, the principal should share the responsibility with his staff and with other persons associated with the school. But the job of seeing to it that a positive program of public relations is evolved, that it functions, and that its importance is duly appreciated, cannot be delegated. It belongs logically to the school principal.

Educators are gradually awakening to the fact that the school program itself is the biggest factor in building good public relations. The product, as in the business world, eventually conditions the attitude of the public. If the people are satisfied that children are getting an excellent education, their enthusiasm will be great. No amount of propaganda can serve as a substitute for a school program of "quality." While admitting the truth of the above generalization, that the best school publicity stems from a strong school program, it is still possible to extend the influence of the school somewhat more widely than otherwise through planning and organization.

It is a known fact that schools located in communities where laymen participate actively in the formulation of school policies enjoy greater support than do schools which encourage little or no lay participation. The average citizen should be made to feel that he has a genuine stake in the educational program in his school district, and such resources as he possesses should be utilized in the interests of children.

Public opinion polls are being used by some administrators to discover what the layman's attitude is toward various aspects of the school program and what he knows about his school. If they are well conducted, polls will reveal to the principal how the public views existing and contemplated practices and can serve to arouse public interest in vital school questions. Newspaper articles, radio programs, parent-teacher association meetings, special bulletins to parents, active participation of staff in community organizations, are some other important means of informing the public regarding school needs and school opportunities.

Other Functions

Besides the four major functions just discussed, there are several miscellaneous duties which, while not comparable in scope to those already enumerated, are inherent in the principal's work. *Record keeping* is one. The school principal is the custodian of important records dealing with the background and progress of children. He should also be concerned with the improvement of record forms. The efficiency with which data are recorded and made available when needed is of considerable importance in providing adequate guidance to children and parents. On certain occasions the court makes demands on the schools to furnish reliable information on children's behavior. Moreover, the state requires that attendance records be kept accurately and that regular reports be made. This record-keeping function, then, cannot be taken lightly. It has significant implications for the welfare of children.

In a similar category is the principal's responsibility for *providing guidance* to individual children. This duty is sometimes deemed to be identical with handling disciplinary cases referred to the principal by classroom teachers. The latter interpretation is entirely too narrow. The good principal establishes friendly relations with pupils generally and he strives to exercise a positive influence on them. Pupils who are referred to him by teachers because they are troublesome or maladjusted naturally will receive his sympathetic guidance and counsel. This will often tax his imagination and patience. But this phase of his guidance activities must not be allowed to overshadow his responsibility to children whose behavior is normal. The Department of Elementary School Principals of the National Education Association, in a little pamphlet entitled *And Proudly Serve,* has expressed a sound point of view with regard to the principal's relationships with individual children and has suggested areas which principals might well explore. The author of this bulletin points out that:

> Many principals set aside a part of each day for conferences with children. Much understanding and guidance may result from a few minutes of

personal counselling. It may be to admire a dress, to recognize a birthday, or to give a compliment for work well done. It may be an occasion to comment on a child's service to the school, to share in a family joy, or to help with a personal problem. Principals, no less than teachers, come to know children at first hand. From close observation of child behavior they learn to identify the facets of child nature upon which more technical knowledge can be built.

The professional principal seeks to discover why children are slow or fast, lazy or energetic, fat or thin, aggressive or timid and studies all of the variations between these extremes. He comes to know their homes, companions, hobbies, interests and skills.[1]

It is only from such close daily associations with children that the principal can fulfill his guidance responsibilities.

Still another function of the principal is *curriculum improvement*. This obviously overlaps with his responsibilities for personnel leadership. Giving leadership to curriculum planning and revision involves working effectively with teachers, parents, and children. It is basically a group process, and its success rests upon the participation of many individuals. Hence, while engaged in curriculum building activities, the principal should be serving as a leader of personnel. But beyond this function, there is a sphere of activity in which he alone can operate. He should be informed on curriculum experimentation and trends; he should have a well-thought-out educational philosophy of his own (subject, of course, to modification when facts and logic warrant it); he should take the initiative in collecting curriculum materials, and should sense the administrative implications of various types of school curricula.

There are many minor duties which belong to the school principal, and there are responsibilities that defy detailed classification. The obligation of the principal to participate in community activities will vary widely, depending upon local conditions. He may feel it wise to accept an office in a service club if invited, even though the time expended will have to be borrowed from some major school project. In making personal decisions of this character, he will have to weigh carefully the relative advantages of various alternatives for the school program. There is also an over-all co-ordination function, inherent in an elementary school principalship, similar to that of any important executive. The

---

[1] Department of Elementary School Principals, *And Proudly Serve . . . as a Principal*, The National Education Association, Washington, D. C., 1947, p. 4.

work of teachers, the projects of parent-teacher associations, and the activities of social agencies are only a few of the many educational forces that affect the lives of children. The importance of working in harmony toward the achievement of common goals is so clear as to require no elaborate argument. That these various groups often work at cross-purposes in ignorance of the program and plans of other agencies must be acknowledged.

The good principal takes steps to co-ordinate the efforts of all the agencies that affect the education of children, or at least to see that they are co-ordinated. Moreover, he is interested in the articulation of class groups within the school itself. The kindergarten program should not be divorced from first-grade activities; artificial hurdles must not be allowed to impede normal progress; skills and subject matter should be taught and emphasized at the age levels where experimentation suggests they are most easily and efficiently learned. Ironing out inconsistencies and bringing about greater teacher understanding of the logic behind a comprehensive school program are worthy objectives for the school principal to work toward.

Summary

A principal must be a versatile individual to fulfill all the responsibilities demanded of him. He must be skillful in the realm of personnel management; he must understand the school plant and know how to operate and maintain it efficiently; he must be conversant with modern school business practices; he must know how to work with the public and he must be able to give leadership to his staff in curriculum improvement. These combined functions constitute a tremendous challenge to the elementary school principal; they demand a higher and more professional type of leadership than ever before, and offer him a great opportunity to serve the children of his district.

In the chapters which follow, the foregoing responsibilities of the elementary school principal in today's schools are elaborated, and methods and principles for carrying on the work of this important school official are discussed.

SUGGESTED READINGS

Committee of 14, *Public Action for Powerful Schools,* Metropolitan School Study Council, Bureau of Publications, Teachers College, Columbia University, New York, 1949.

Department of Elementary School Principals, *The Elementary School Principalship—Today and Tomorrow,* Twenty-seventh Yearbook, National Education Association, Washington, D. C., 1948, Part II, pp. 85–132.

————, *The Public and the Elementary School,* Twenty-eighth Yearbook, National Education Association, Washington, D. C., 1949.

Hand, Harold C., *What People Think About Their Schools,* World Book Company, Yonkers, N. Y., 1948.

Koopman, G. Robert, Miel, Alice, and Misner, Paul J., *Democracy in School Administration,* D. Appleton–Century Company, New York, 1943.

Linn, Henry H., Helm, Leslie C., and Grabarkiewicz, K. P., *The School Custodian's Housekeeping Handbook,* Bureau of Publications, Teachers College, Columbia University, New York, 1948.

Yauch, Wilbur A., *Improving Human Relations in School Administration,* Harper and Brothers, New York, 1949.

CHAPTER III

THE LEGAL RESPONSIBILITIES
AND RIGHTS OF THE ELEMENTARY
SCHOOL PRINCIPAL

Most state laws have little to say directly about elementary school principals. Yet it can logically be contended that the school principal is constantly bound by legal responsibilities and restrictions. In fact, he is confronted with legal hurdles in the form of certification requirements when he first enters the profession, and he cannot usually make his exit at the end of a life career without fulfilling certain legal provisions relating to his retirement. It is in his everyday work, however, that the principal needs to be alert to his legal responsibilities as well as to those relating to the members of his staff. A knowledge of the school laws of his state, and particularly those provisions which have significance for him as principal, is essential if he is to perform his duties efficiently and measure up to his responsibilities as a school administrator. Since there are forty-eight separate school codes differing widely in their provisions, it is beyond the scope of this discussion to attempt an exhaustive analysis of the principal's rights and liabilities. There are certain facts and principles, however, which have rather general application, and there are a few problem areas where considerable litigation has occurred and where a body of legal opinion exists.

It is perhaps most important for the principal to recognize that his position constitutes an important link in a long chain of responsible school officials and leaders employed to carry out the education laws of the state; and that by virtue of his position he must perform certain duties to insure that the intentions of the people, as reflected in state

26

legislation, are satisfied. A principal cannot depend upon specific mandates in the law in assessing his duties. Responsibilities and ways of
behavior are often implied or are to be found in the rules and regulations
of the local board of education, whose rules, incidentally, have the
force of law when not inconsistent with statutory provisions.

Implied Obligations

One area where there is an implied obligation for the principal is the
legal provision commonly prevailing that certain specified subject matter shall be taught in the elementary schools of the state. Sometimes
these prescriptions stipulate the minimum amount of time per week
that shall be devoted to instruction in the subject under consideration.
Health education, for example, together with thorough and scientific instruction in the subject of alcoholism and narcotism are matters on
which several states have passed legislation. Instruction in the humane
treatment of animals is another illustration of a state prescription that
calls for action by the elementary school principal. As the responsible
head of the school the principal must see that these subjects are taught
in conformity with state law.[1]

Daily Bible-reading may be required of teachers, together with
monthly reports showing that this provision of the law has been complied with. Where such laws exist the principal is expected to supervise
the activity specified and to see that it is carried out.

The above are but a few of the legal duties involved in carrying out
the state's requirements with respect to instruction. A principal is also
under obligation to co-operate with the superintendent of schools and
other officials in many different ways. In North Carolina, for example,
the county superintendent is required by law "to advise with teachers,
principals and supervisors as to the best methods of instruction, school
organization, and school government, and to that end he shall keep
himself informed as to the progress of education. . . ."[2] But even more
pertinent to this discussion is the specific mention in the law that "teachers, *principals,* and supervisors shall co-operate with him in putting into

---

[1] In Alabama the law specifies in the case of instruction in humane treatment of
animals "it shall be the duty of the principal . . . to see that there is devoted at
least twenty minutes each week. . . ." and in addition there is an added requirement that the principal or teacher shall state in the monthly reports that this provision has been complied with. *Alabama School Laws,* 1941, Title 52, para. 546.

[2] *School Laws of North Carolina,* 1943, para. 114–115. State Superintendent of
Public Instruction.

use the best methods of instruction, school organization, and school government."[3]

Even if the law failed to specify as directly as it does in the North Carolina statute that principals shall co-operate, there is little reason to doubt their legal obligation to do so. Co-operation is essential for the realization of the purposes of the law and for a principal to act in a fashion that can be interpreted as failing to co-operate, is to be derelict in his duty.

School Board Rules

Not only should the principal examine the provisions of the state laws which have both specific and implied legal obligations for him, but he should also familiarize himself with the detailed rules and regulations of the local school board. When not inconsistent with or in opposition to state laws, these local rules have the weight of law just as certainly as if passed by the legislature. Hence they must be observed. Some of the rules relate to reporting on the condition of school property, the handling of school moneys, on pupil absenteeism, on staff efficiency or conduct, on school accidents, and on numerous other items bearing on the operation of the school enterprise. Rules and regulations vary widely among school systems and it is not safe for a principal to assume when appointed to a new position that his legal obligations are identical with those which obtained in his previous post.

What Constitutes Negligence

The old adage that "ignorance of the law is no excuse" applies to the principal who fails to act in accordance with the law. The prudent individual will analyze his obligations before assuming his duties and will act in accordance with them. A copy of the state law and the book of rules and regulations of the local board of education are primary sources to be studied by the principal. But even when the contents of these two documents have been mastered the principal may find himself in legal difficulty, for not every contingency is provided for in the statutes. There is no escaping the fact that a principal or teacher in carrying on his work must behave as a reasonably prudent person would under similar circumstances and with comparable responsibilities. Otherwise he may be judged guilty of negligence. To be negligent one must have a duty

[3] *Ibid.* Italics ours.

implied or expressed toward the person harmed, which duty is disregarded. An important test of negligence is *foreseeability*. When in the judgment of the court a "reasonably prudent" person could have foreseen the harmful consequences of his act, the actor in disregarding the foreseeable consequences is liable for negligent conduct. In testing the behavior of the principal then, the basic question to be answered is, Did he, in carrying on his supervisory activities, subject pupils or other persons to unreasonable risks? If so, he is in a vulnerable position. This fact alone, however, does not make him guilty in the eyes of the law. A second condition must also be present, namely, that his negligence was a proximate cause of whatever injury was suffered by the pupil or person involved. The injured party may have contributed to his own misfortune; and if it can be demonstrated that the harm sustained was caused as much by the failure of the person suffering the injury to exercise reasonable caution as by the carelessness of the accused, then the courts will rule that recovery of damages is barred since there was evidence of contributory negligence.

In determining whether or not the conduct of the injured party was below the standards to which he should conform for his own protection the courts will take account of the age and maturity of the injured individual. Minors are not expected to exercise as much judgment and care as adults. The standard obtaining in the case of a child is that conduct which can rightly be expected of other children of comparable age, intelligence, and experience. In some states the law specifies that children under certain ages cannot be guilty of contributory negligence.

The Principal and Accidents to Pupils

There is much greater likelihood of the principal's running afoul of the law in the matter of pupil accidents than at any other point, and the wise principal is the one who organizes and administers his school in such a fashion as to safeguard himself and his teachers as much as possible against negligence.

Accidents to school children are most likely to occur when the activity engaged in is carried on outside of the building where it is more difficult for teachers and principal to control the possible dangers to life and limb than is the case when children are at work in their regular classrooms. Shops and the gymnasium offer certain hazards beyond those found in typical classrooms, and the principal should provide adequate supervision to pupils when engaged in shop and physical education activities.

Field Trips

Field trips present certain risks which deserve the thoughtful consideration of the principal. A modern program of education cannot be housed within the four walls of a classroom, nor can it be limited to the school building or the school grounds. A good education is dependent upon the utilization of many resources, including museums, industrial plants, farms, the post office, the fire house, and a wide variety of other institutions and agencies. Since these cannot be brought to the school the school has to go to them. If class trips are to be exploited for their fullest benefit in children's learning, a great deal of planning and supervision will be necessary. Safety is a primary consideration. From the legal standpoint there are no barriers to taking children on trips except that in case of injury to a pupil the principal and the teachers involved are likely to be called upon to defend themselves against charges of negligence. And since trip conditions are so much more hazardous than those commonly found on the school grounds or within the building, more than ordinary care should be taken in preparing for and carrying out trips.

Some principals have been operating trips under the illusion that a waiver signed by a parent relieves teachers and principal of any possible liability for pupil accidents occurring on trips. The difficulty here is that a parent cannot legally sign away the rights of his child to collect damages. In other words, a principal or teacher cannot escape the penalty for his own negligence even when a parent voluntarily waives his right to sue for damages.

There is, however, a good reason for getting parents' permission for their children to be taken on field trips. It is one bit of evidence that can be presented later in court in case of a mishap to show that thoughtful consideration was given to the added dangers of taking children on the trip in question, and it serves to inform the court that parents were apprised of the plan and consented to it.

But a still more important step for the principal to take is to provide enough qualified supervisors so that it is apparent that the increased hazards were anticipated and as adequately prepared for as was reasonably possible. It is obvious that one teacher assigned to supervise thirty children does not constitute adequate protection on most field trips although in the classroom this would be deemed sufficient as far as physical hazards are concerned. It is better to err on the side of having too many qualified adults accompany children on class trips than to provide too few. The matter of qualifications of the adult also deserves consideration. Experience in working with children of the ages and maturity of those registered for the trip is certainly one essential qualification. Good judgment and character are other traits to look for. Being a parent is a factor worth considering, but is not in itself evidence of being qualified to supervise children.

There has been some intimation by the courts that where a pupil is injured in the course of a visit to an industrial plant, the teacher could be held liable for taking children to a dangerous place and that the owner of the plant was under no obligation to provide special safeguards. This suggests that thorough investigation be made of the hazards involved in visiting a plant before taking children there for educational purposes.

A still further step to insure adequate protection to the school staff against a charge of negligence is to have the board of education formally accept class trips as an integral part of the educational program of the schools, and in no sense extracurricular in character. This brings trips clearly within the scope of the school enterprise and they then become a part of the regular business of principal, teachers, and pupils.

From the standpoint of the courts, evidence showing that the board of education took action of the character just described and that careful preparation was made in planning trips and in providing supervision will undoubtedly carry weight in determining the presence or absence of negligence.

Errands

Some principals are prone to send pupils on errands beyond the confines of the school. Occasionally the purpose is related to an educational aim, but often it is a matter of convenience to teacher or principal. Whatever the objective, the practice is fraught with danger. Pupils cannot be regarded as messengers and if some injury befalls them while running an errand for the school the principal or teacher responsible can be held liable for negligence. While court rulings have apparently not been handed down on this particular activity, the opinion of the city solicitor of Wilmington, Delaware, clearly brings out the issue involved. He ruled, in an opinion rendered to the superintendent of schools in 1936, that "the sending of children on errands for the teacher or principal is not an act of the Board in its public or governmental capacity and in the event of negligence on the part of the Board liability would attach both to the one who sends the pupil on the errand and to the Board."[4]

Since, in addition to the legal questions involved, there are other good reasons for not using children as messengers, principals will do well to heed the warning of the Wilmington city solicitor quoted above.

Safety Patrols

When the automobile replaced the horse-drawn carriage and became a fairly common means of transportation, school administrators became increasingly aware of the need both for safety education and for some additional protective schemes to safeguard children against accidents while in the school's immediate neighborhood. One organization which was created to accomplish these ends was the school safety patrol. While in the beginning, educational values to the pupil were less commonly stressed than now, the safety patrol has always been viewed by alert principals as having real educational significance.

From a legal standpoint the major question for a principal to consider is how to organize safety patrols so as to safeguard the school staff and the board of education against liability for accidents. Apparently court decisions have not been handed down and one is compelled to draw his conclusions from opinions of law experts and from legal principles.

It seems clear that the board of education has the right to control to some extent the conduct of its pupils off the school grounds and to make rules for the good order and safety of the school and the students. Moreover, legal opinion supports the thesis that student safety patrols are a part of the physical and health education of children and can be used as a means of inculcating principles of safety and discipline.

Despite the opinions upholding the rights of boards of education to create safety patrols, the school principal will do well to establish a number of safeguards and to administer safety patrols in such a manner as to leave no doubt as to the thoroughness of his supervision. This conclusion is supported by the opinion of the attorney general of Wisconsin

[4] Opinion of the city solicitor, Wilmington, Delaware, August 7, 1936.

who holds that principals, superintendents, and teachers may be personally liable if the pupils participating in safety patrol activities are not properly instructed and if the system is established in a careless manner or if irresponsible students are appointed as patrols.[5]

Rosenfield, who has devoted considerable attention to this problem, suggests four specific steps for school systems to take with respect to school safety patrols if they wish to avoid charges of negligence.[6] School principals should give careful thought to these in directing and supervising their own safety patrols. Rosenfield advises that first the school safety patrol system be officially adopted by the board of education so that its organization cannot be held to constitute a voluntary act of the school principal.

"Second, the scope, operation and limitations of the plan must be very clear in the minds of all concerned." It is agreed that the school district has no police power and cannot therefore direct traffic or make arrests.

Third, responsible and reliable students, not the "bad" boys, should be selected for patrol activity.

Last, the whole scheme, including the plan of operation, schedules of conferences with patrol officers, announcements to the pupils enrolled in the school of the plan approved, and their relationship to it, should be worked out in advance. A principal will need to make sure that proper instruction is given with regard to the duties of patrol members, that parents' consent is secured, and that competent adults are assigned to supervise the patrol activities of the pupils selected.

If the precautions just outlined are taken by principals, there should be little occasion for concern with respect to legal violations and possible charges of negligence.

Other Accident Hazards

It is normal behavior for young children to be somewhat careless in their activities within a school building or at play on the school grounds. Whereas a typical adult may move about the school premises with relative safety, elementary school children require some supervision. Experience has demonstrated that the greatest number of school accidents

[5] Opinion of attorney general addressed to Hon. John Callahan, superintendent of public instruction, February 24, 1939.
[6] Harry N. Rosenfield, *Liability For School Accidents,* Harper and Brothers, New York, 1940, pp. 101, 102.

occur in athletic and playground activities. Since elementary children do not commonly participate in athletic contests and their games are somewhat less rugged than those engaged in by children in the upper divisions of the school, the proportion of accidents occurring on elementary school playgrounds or in gymnasiums is undoubtedly considerably smaller than for the school system as a whole. But it still behooves the principal to take stock of the condition of the school building and equipment as it relates to safety, and in fact to make a periodic study of other environmental factors which bear on the physical welfare of the pupils.

Slides, ladders, fire escapes, swinging gates, ramps, loose floor boards, slippery playgrounds, poorly operated or supervised elevators, insecure flag poles, protruding objects in corridors or classrooms, oiled floors, and worn steps are but a few of the items of equipment or conditions which may produce accidents. While the principal may not always be held responsible when accidents occur as a result of defective equipment, he is clearly obligated to report dangerous conditions to a responsible administrator in the central office. Moreover, he should make a practice of putting his report in writing and retaining a copy for his files. He may be required to testify in court, and written evidence showing that he has fulfilled his duties may save him from public criticism as well as legal liability. It is true that individual teachers also have an obligation to report dangerous conditions within their respective classrooms. But the principal is responsible for the building and grounds as a whole and he cannot afford to delegate this responsibility to others. Special mention is due the operation of a cafeteria or lunchroom. Negligence can easily arise in connection with the food served and in the use of equipment. Systematic checkups are needed here to insure protection against carelessness and indifference on the part of employees.

Transportation problems fall for the most part outside the domain of the principal and hence need little emphasis in this discussion. It is pertinent, however, to note that the principal should be thoroughly familiar with the rules and regulations of the board of education relating to pupil transportation and that all transportation activities occurring on school grounds be carefully planned and supervised. As mentioned earlier, the courts have held that the principal's rights and to some extent his liabilities extend beyond the school premises and while, perhaps, in the case of transportation he need have little anxiety beyond the loading and unloading of school buses, he nevertheless cannot afford to be indifferent to the problem of pupil transportation as it relates to safety.

First Aid

The matter of first aid has received considerable attention in the courts and, because of the immunity of school boards, is a problem of considerable importance to the school principal. Failure on his part or on the part of one of his teachers may result in damages for negligence as well as in a loss of public confidence in his administrative competence.

The issues in first aid briefly are twofold:

1. Is there a duty to render first aid in case of an injury to a pupil?
2. If there is a legal duty to render first aid, what are the permissible limits of the aid to be rendered?

The answer to the first question is in the affirmative. There is a duty on the part of teachers and principal to administer first aid.

The answer to the second question as to how far the aid should go is that no aid can legally be administered beyond first aid. While this is a well-established principle, it requires some explanation. The qualifications of the person giving the aid will determine to some extent the scope of the treatment which can safely be given. A nurse, for example, could legally provide first aid services beyond those administered by a layman or a teacher. The definition of first aid is *emergency* treatment, and all other treatment, according to the courts, must be provided by a trained physician.

Meeting an Emergency

As the reader will have probably concluded from the preceding discussion, regarding negligence, there is no escape from liability except as one exercises good judgment and organizes and plans his supervisory and administrative activities intelligently and thoroughly. Thoughtful consideration of what steps to take to safeguard pupils, staff and himself against negligent conduct will go a long way toward resolving the problems raised in this chapter. Planning what to do in advance is a good precautionary measure to take. There is also much to be learned from the experience of other administrators. A report of how one school principal and his staff met a serious emergency is reported below. This report summarizes the thirty steps taken in dealing with a tragic accident and shows the efficiency and dispatch with which a school staff met a very difficult situation.

*Principal's Report of a School Accident Showing
How the School Personnel Dealt with the Situation*

On Monday, March 14, 1948, at 3:35 P.M., a boy, Charles Barth, was run over by a backing bus on the school grounds of the Mahopac Central School, Mahopac, New York. He had stepped into the roadway to walk beside the bus as it backed into position to load for the second afternoon trip. Apparently his right foot became caught under the front right wheel, and he fell nearly parallel to the bus and with his head to the rear. He did not cry out, nor did anyone realize what was happening until the wheel rolled onto his head. He was crushed and died within a few minutes.

The following thirty steps listed under four headings were taken following the accident:

Immediate Steps

1. *Alarm and First Aid*—A student who saw the accident rushed into the building and reported it to the office and to the nurse. The principal, nurse, and two teachers arrived on the scene within a minute or two at the most. It was apparent that on the spot first aid was out of the question.

2. *Patient to the Hospital*—The bus driver, Mr. Miller, first realized what had happened when he completed backing—some ten feet from the point of the accident—and saw the boy lying in front of his bus. He jumped from the bus and called to another driver, Mr. Williams, who had driven up at about the same time. They ran for a fire department ambulance which we store in the school garage. Miller moved another car and Williams rushed the ambulance to the spot. The ambulance was beside the boy by the time I arrived—a matter of not more than two minutes. These two drivers, the teachers, nurse and I lifted the boy onto the ambulance stretcher, placed the stretcher in the ambulance, and they were off. The nurse and teachers rode in the back with the boy. Williams drove the ambulance. Miller, the driver, and I stayed on the scene.

3. *Notifying the Doctor*—As soon as the accident was reported the office secretary called the school physician. As soon as we had the ambulance off I sent another teacher who had arrived on the scene to phone again to the doctor and direct him to the hospital instead of to the school. They were fortunate enough to catch him before he had left his office. The doctor arrived at the hospital almost as soon as did the ambulance. Charles was still alive at this time but died within the next few

minutes. All of this had taken from ten to fifteen minutes after the accident.

4. *Notifying the Police*—As soon as the doctor had been phoned the second time, the secretary in the office called the police. The local force consists of two patrol cars with two-way radio connection to headquarters. The Chief, Wallace Barrett, received notice of the accident in his car at 3:38—about three minutes after the accident. He asked headquarters to phone the fire department and have the "resuscitator" sent to the hospital. He went there himself.

5. *Notifying the Priest*—In most cases I believe parents should be called after the doctor and the police, but in a case like this, particularly if the patient is a Catholic, it might be wise to call the priest. We did not think of this, but fortunately the Catholic Church is near the hospital, and Father Herrick, who happened to be out for a stroll, heard the ambulance siren and arrived at the hospital at the same time as did the doctor. He was in time to anoint the boy before he died.

6. *Notifying the Parents*—As soon as the ambulance left I told all who had seen the accident to stay around, and then I went to the office to call the parents. It was only a matter of a few moments for the secretary to complete the calls to the doctor and police, but since the Barths have no phone, it took some time to get in touch with Mrs. Barth by way of a neighbor. When I finally did get Mrs. Barth on the phone I told her what had happened and asked her if she would be able to get to the hospital. She said the neighbor whose phone she was using would take her. We could not locate Mr. Barth until about an hour later because he was out on a truck.

7. *First Account of Witnesses*—I next went outside again and took down the names of those who had seen any part of the accident—five boys and one girl. I asked each of them to show me just where he had been and to describe in full what he had seen. Naturally they were shocked by the experience, but it seemed necessary to get their accounts while they were still free from the confusion that sometimes occurs after witnesses have talked with others. We found that all six were in very close agreement as to what had happened.

8. *Report to the President of the Board*—We were still waiting for the police to arrive at the school, so I took the opportunity to call the office of the Board President. He was not in, but another Board member was there and promised to locate him. Both of these men arrived at the school within the next fifteen minutes.

Secondary Steps

1. *Arrival of Police*—Chief Barrett arrived from the hospital at about 3:55. He took down a brief account, names and addresses, and asked a few questions. Due to the limits of his force he could not make a complete investigation at the time, so he told all witnesses to be on hand at the

school in the morning. He released the driver and bus and returned to the hospital. Later in the day he made a careful examination of the bus and the scene. He also took the driver's statement later in the day.

2. *Children*—Two bus loads of children were still to be taken home. Williams returned from the hospital about 4:00 P.M. and took out his bus load. The other load was sent out in the bus that had been in the accident after Chief Barrett released it.

3. *The Mother*—At about 4:05 I went to the hospital to see Mrs. Barth and her nine-year-old daughter, Beth. Although Charles had been dead some fifteen minutes she did not fully realize that it was all over. The priest and I spent some time getting her to understand that Charles was gone.

4. *The Father*—At about 4:30 I took Beth to the home of a friend and on the way we saw Mr. Barth unloading his truck. I had to tell him of the death of his son and I took him back to the hospital. Mrs. Barth went home with friends about 5:30 but Mr. Barth and I stayed at the hospital until the funeral director arrived about 6:00.

The Next Days

1. *Assemblies*—At 8:30 Tuesday morning we had a high school assembly and at 12:50 we had a similar meeting with the grade children. In each case the students were told that before the next day we would review the whole transportation arrangement. For the one day minor changes were announced and previous rules repeated. The students were told that they would be kept posted on funeral arrangements. I also asked if there were any witnesses that we had missed the day before. There were none.

2. *Written Statements*—After the brief assembly I asked each of the six witnesses to write in his own words a simple statement of what he had seen. We drew a diagram of the accident and each student placed himself by marking the diagram at the proper point.

3. *Police Questioning*—Chief Barrett arrived about 9:00 and took down a more detailed account of the statements of witnesses.

4. *Coroner's Inquest*—At 10:00 we went to the Coroner's Office and each witness told his story. The Coroner declared that in his opinion there was no criminal negligence involved and instructed his secretary to give a statement to that effect to the police and to the driver.

5. *Motor Vehicle Report*—With the help of Chief Barrett the secretary in the school office filled out a complete Motor Vehicle Report.

6. *Public Service Report*—We found out that the bus should not have been moved before a Public Service Inspection. On Tuesday afternoon we had the inspection and filed a report to that Commission as required by law.

7. *N. Y. State Education Dept. Report*—A one-page report in duplicate was filled in and filed with the Bureau of Field Services—State Education Department, Albany, N.Y. The forms are furnished by the Bureau.

8. *Insurance Report and Investigation*—The investigator for the in-

surance company arrived about 11:00 A.M. and spent the rest of the day interviewing all concerned. With his help we filled out a complete insurance report.

9. *Conference with Drivers*—The drivers, Chief Barrett, and I met at 1:30 to review the whole transportation system. We found a number of ideas that might contribute to greater safety—particularly with reference to routing vehicle traffic on the school grounds.

10. *Faculty Conferences*—Meetings were held during the next two days with faculty groups for the purpose of reviewing suggestions and formulating policies about loading at the new loading point which the rerouting makes necessary.

11. *Student Discussion*—In one of the faculty groups it was mentioned that the grade students would like to review the rules of conduct on the bus in so far as the rules applied to them and not to the high school students. The Pow-Wow (grade school council) discussed these rules on Thursday, took them back to their own rooms for discussion on Friday morning, and made a final report in a regular assembly on Friday afternoon.

12. *Board Action*—Board members were kept informed at every step and on Friday afternoon held a special meeting to take official action on changes of policy, rerouting of traffic, posting of signs, and the like.

13. *Publicity on New Policies*—Final revision of new and revised policies were mimeographed and distributed to each student. A complete statement was issued to the local paper covering all changes.

14. *The Funeral*—A number of us were in close touch with the Barth family. It became apparent that a large number of students wanted to attend the funeral and that the church would not be able to take care of such a crowd. The family was consulted and we agreed to ask all students to stay away except those in the boy's class and such other close friends as the Barths might stipulate. In addition we required all who came into those categories to bring notes from home asking that the children be excused. Those who were allowed to go were taken from the school to the funeral in a group under the supervision of a teacher. The school was also represented by three Board members, the two drivers—Miller and Williams —and myself.

15. *Flowers*—Charles' friends brought money to school for flowers and soon there was too great a sum to be used for that purpose. The money was finally given to the Barths with the suggestion that it go toward the purchase of some lasting memorial for Charles.

Still to Be Done

1. *Review*—All groups concerned—students, teachers, drivers and parents—will be asked to re-evaluate present policies from time to time. The Board will receive reports of these reviews and will be asked to act if necessary.

2. *Hearing*—Chief Barrett informs us that a court hearing may not be necessary since the matter of criminal negligence has apparently been cleared up in the Coroner's Report. Such a hearing is usual, however, in cases of this sort.

This is submitted merely as a report of what was done in a specific case and not as a guide for other cases. In all probability each reader of this report will think of other things that might have been done or things that could have been done better.

I want to apologize for the excessive use of the personal pronoun in my account, but I do not know how to tell the story except as I saw it. It should be recognized that many people had to act quickly and decisively. Some of those deserving credit include the student who gave the first report, the nurse, the driver, Mr. Williams who drove the ambulance, the secretary in the office who made the reports to the doctor and the police, the doctor who came so promptly, the police who were on the job quickly and efficiently, the priest who came without being called, the witnesses who gave a clear and accurate account of what happened, and others.

Report submitted by:
Philip B. Langworthy, Principal
Mahopac Central School[7]

Legal Privileges of the Principal

While the legal responsibilities of the elementary school principal are numerous and not to be treated lightly, his legal privileges must not be forgotten when assessing his position. For a principal has certain peculiar rights which stem from the nature of his responsibilities. He can speak and write and make judgments about the pupils and employees within his jurisdiction which are denied to teachers, parents, and the lay public generally. He enjoys what is legally termed "qualified privilege." This privilege relates to all communications made *bona fide* upon any subject matter in which the party communicating has an interest or in reference to which he has a duty. So long as a school principal acts in good faith, he has wide latitude in what he can legally say and write. He is privileged, for example, to criticize and pass judgment on teachers and others employed in his building. He is permitted to write letters to the superintendent of schools expressing his views on the competency and efficiency of individual members of his staff.

Cases involving slander or libel are therefore seldom proved against

---

[7] The authors are indebted to Dr. Langworthy for permission to reproduce his report in full.

school administrators because, while not completely immune, these officials do have exceptional privileges. If it can be proved, however, in the case of defamatory statements that the principal knew the words to be false, he could not hide behind his rights to "qualified privilege." Whenever there is evidence of malice he can be charged with slander or libel depending upon whether or not the words were spoken orally or written.

Unfortunately some principals have abused their legal privileges and have been indiscreet in their oral and written comments relating to their employees and pupils. A principal should be most careful how and when he exercises these special privileges which were given him in order that he might perform his duties more efficiently. To misuse or carelessly use his legal privileges is to be guilty of unprofessional conduct and to prove himself unworthy of the public trust assigned him.

The Principal and Corporal Punishment

The alert elementary school principal seldom if ever resorts to corporal punishment in dealing with pupils exhibiting undesirable behavior. Psychologists and mental hygienists have repeatedly frowned upon the once commonly held notion that schoolmasters who spared the rod spoiled the child. Vastly superior substitutes for physical punishment have been used by creative teachers for years, and today schools have progressed so far in their thinking about this problem that corporal punishment in school is prohibited by law in one state, New Jersey, and by local school board regulations in several school systems in other states.

Legally, however, except where the legislature expressly prohibits, teachers have certain well-defined privileges with respect to punishing pupils for misbehavior. The public school teacher stands *in loco parentis* and except where specifically prohibited by state law may administer corporal punishment when occasion demands. The court cases to date suggest that the only limitations to the teacher's right are that the cause shall be sufficient and the punishment inflicted shall not be unreasonable, excessive, malicious, or given in an improper manner. In short, wide discretion is allowed the teacher in the matter of disciplining the pupil. By inference principals have similar rights to punish pupils, although a Texas case involving a superintendent of schools raises some question about the legal status of administrators. A Texas ruling held that since teachers do stand *in loco parentis* they are permitted to inflict corporal punishment but since the superintendent enjoyed no such status he was therefore liable for assault and battery.[8]

A pertinent question would therefore seem to be, "Do principals stand *in loco parentis?*" If not, they have rather generally exceeded their authority in the past. It seems probable that the courts would rule that principals have equal rights with teachers in the matter of administering corporal punishment since in the law "teacher" by and large includes principal and superintendent.[9]

The school principal is a key person in the maintenance of a good learning atmosphere. To this end he should think through with his staff and with the pupils in the school the factors that make for a wholesome school climate. Once these have been identified he should try to operate the school in such a manner as to take full advantage of all the favorable elements. Except in very unusual circumstances, a principal is not justified in exercising his rights to inflict corporal punishment; nor will he encourage his teachers to use their full legal powers in maintaining discipline.

Protection Through Insurance

The employees of a board of education are in some respects in a less favored position legally in carrying on their daily work than are employees in industry since the dominant principle of law in the United States is that the state or any of its agencies (including the school board) in performing its governmental functions is immune from liability for the negligence of its employees or for its own negligence unless it consents to such liability. This is derived from the old English theory of the divine right of kings and governmental sovereignty. The state can do no wrong. The board of education is an agent of the state. Hence a board of education can do no wrong.

However sound or unsound this theory of law is, it has marked implications for public school employees generally. A few exceptions, of which New York and New Jersey are the most noteworthy, deserve mention. These two states have so-called "save harmless" statutes which in effect insure school board employees when on duty against financial loss for negligence. But employees in most states are not so fortunate and hence

[8] *Pendergrass* v. *Masterson,* 196 S. W. 246 (Texas 1917).
[9] Rosenfield, *op. cit.,* p. 42.

must provide their own protection or assume whatever risks are involved.

One possible step for principals and teachers to take is to purchase individual or group insurance. This has merit if adequate protection is guaranteed in the policy purchased. In light of the exclusions and exceptions set forth in many of the policies written in the past it would be well to consult the state insurance commission or seek the help of an expert before entering into insurance arrangements. Certainly some protection should be sought against financial loss resulting from a judgment against an employee while on the job.

It may appear to some readers as they assess the principal's liabilities and privileges that the legal risks involved make the position of elementary school principal an unenviable one. But there is nothing alarming in the facts on negligence for reasonably prudent school administrators. In fact, relatively few principals have been charged with negligence, and still fewer have been found guilty. Careful planning and systematic supervision are the basic factors in eliminating "negligence." Nor can one justifiably find in the discussion of the principal's legal liabilities an excuse for limiting the elementary school program to the traditional three R's. The horse-drawn carriage was a much safer vehicle to operate than the automobile which replaced it and those who drive cars run much greater legal risks. But only the reactionaries and the timid want to return to the good old horse and buggy days. And so it is with field trips, school patrols, shop activities, food services, and bus transportation. These go along with this new generation. They present certain problems for the school principal. They are neither so complicated nor so hazardous as to warrant any hesitation on the part of a well-trained principal about including them in the school program.

SUGGESTED READINGS

Hamilton, Robert R. and Mort, Paul R., *The Law and Public Education*, Foundation Press, Chicago, 1941.

National Education Association, *Pupil Patrols in Elementary and Secondary Schools*, Research Bulletin, vol. XXVIII, no. 1, February 1950.

———, *Teacher Liability for Pupil Injuries*, 1940.

———, *The Legal Status of the Public School Pupil*, Research Bulletin, vol. XXIV, no. 1, February 1948.

Rosenfield, Harry N., *Liability for School Accidents,* Harper and Brothers, New York and London, 1940.

———, *Liability for School Accidents—High Points* (Reprint), June 1939.

Weltzin, Frederick J., *Legal Authority of the American Public School,* Midwest Book Company, Lincoln, Neb., 1932.

Part II

ORGANIZING FOR TEACHING AND LEARNING

Relation of Organization to Educational Purposes

One of the most important tasks of the elementary school principal is that of providing leadership in the area of curriculum organization and development. The manner in which the school program is planned and administered will be strongly influenced by the conception held by him and his staff of what a desirable educational program should be. It is the principal's responsibility, therefore, to develop with teachers an increasingly unified educational point of view, and to evolve patterns of organization which will help achieve the educational goals inherent in that viewpoint. Too frequently the relationship of organization to educational beliefs is not appreciated. The principal and the teachers should understand clearly that a given type of school organization will help in achieving the goals of one type of learning program, but may present great obstacles to the development and operation of another. This might seem to be obvious; yet it is true that many educators in the elementary school have never thought through the reasons why they have one type of organization rather than some other. The tendency is to accept the plan in operation when the principal comes to the school, and to make modifications only when the need for them can no longer be ignored.

Practical realities often make it difficult to be consistent in carrying out policy in action. Demands of parents and other community members, inadequacies of plant and instructional materials, oversized classes, remote and too rigid central office administration and supervision, legal requirements, poorly qualified teaching staff, or ineffective leadership are illustrative of conditions which may dictate something less than consistency in school policy. In the following four chapters, therefore, plans and methods of organization will be discussed in relation to major educational viewpoints or philosophies.

CHAPTER IV

SCOPE OF THE ELEMENTARY SCHOOL

Before discussing "internal" organizational features, some attention should be given to the range of ages of children whom they are planned to serve. At what age should public school education begin? Are "nursery schools" properly a part of the school? Should children complete the elementary school at age eleven, twelve or fourteen? Has the transition from childhood to adolescence any bearing on the question? What are the trends?

The usual public school system in the United States provides facilities for children from ages five or six to about age eighteen. It is with reference to this entire age range of children to be educated that we must consider the ages to be included within the elementary school. Ideally the best organization would be one which best facilitated the continuous growth of children throughout the entire span of their public school experience. This would seem to favor a school which houses all grades, from the earliest to the highest, within one building, or at least in one location. There are other arguments for such an arrangement, notable among which is that it has the advantage of providing for frequent contact among children of all ages, thus helping each child achieve better self-understanding. If these were the only criteria by which organization were to be appraised, one might accept this conclusion without further question. However, such factors as size of school population, educational costs, and the provision of specialized facilities to serve the expanded educational program in the later school years have almost universally resulted in the upper grades (the 4-year high school, or the junior high school and 3-year high school) being housed in separate buildings. Because of this, some decision must be made as to the upper age limit of the children to be housed in the elementary school building.

Upper Age Limit of the Elementary School

For many years, public schools in the United States tended to set this upper limit at grade 8, or about fourteen years of age. Children who continued formal education above this level attended the 4-year high school. The reasons for this pattern are obscure. It has been claimed by some that it was a transplantation from Europe, whereas others have maintained that it was indigenous to this country. Certainly, the 8-grade school did fit the once widely held conception that age fourteen or fifteen is the proper age at which formal education should end; that education beyond that should be specialized, and designed only for those preparing to enter college.

With the raising of the upper age limit of compulsory formal public education, the resultant increasing high school enrollments, and the steadily broader definition and diffusion of facts and implications of child growth and development, the validity of the 8-year scope of the elementary school was brought sharply into question. As a result of many factors, most of which do not warrant discussion here, the 6-year elementary school grew in favor, until today such schools constitute a steadily increasing majority. This trend is documented in the Twenty-seventh Yearbook of the Department of Elementary School Principals.[1]

The chief variations which have replaced the old 8-4 plan are the 6-6 and 6-3-3 plans of grade groupings.[2] Whereas one of the chief reasons for the rapid growth of these plans, particularly the 6-3-3 plan, was financial, the chief argument used to defend them was that they were more consistent with factors of child growth. It must be agreed that if it is in fact true that a 6-year elementary school (or at least one which terminates with about age twelve) is most consistent with the facts of child growth and learning, then other factors would have to be weighty indeed to justify another type.

---

[1] Department of Elementary School Principals, *The Elementary School Principalship—Today and Tomorrow,* Twenty-seventh Yearbook, National Education Association, Washington, D. C., 1948, p. 44.

[2] See *The School Executive,* vol. LXVIII, October 1948, pp. 63–76, for discussions of these plans by R. T. Gregg, R. Cherry, A. B. Shaw, J. W. Edgar, L. Wilborn, D. R. Davies, R. T. Ross, and A. A. Hanson.

It is true that prepubescent children are different in important physical, emotional, and social respects from pubescent children, and that pubescent children differ likewise from those undergoing the changes of adolescence. It is important to note, however, that one can seldom draw a sharp dividing line between these differences, even in the case of a single child, let alone a large group. Growth is a constant, continuous process, making it difficult to make sharp time differentiations between one "stage" and the next.

Studies of adolescent boys and girls indicate clearly this fundamental truth. There has been found a range of as much as nine years in the age of sexual maturing among children,[3] so that Dimock concludes: ". . . to assume that most boys become pubescent at whatever is considered or established to be the average age would be to miss reality in nearly 75 per cent of the cases."[4]

The Relativity of the "Best" Upper Age Limit

The foregoing seems to stress the fact that there is no single answer upon which we can pin our faith. This, the authors believe to be true. Many small school districts as now constituted can neither justify nor afford a 6-3-3 plan, and even some schools in larger cities face important practical difficulties in achieving this type of organization. Furthermore, even if all schools could change to a plan which set the upper limit of the elementary school at approximately age twelve, the facts of child growth do not point to that (or any other age) as the "best" time for all children to terminate the elementary school.

This simply emphasizes the fact that no plan of organization can solve the problem of educating children. It can solve some problems in providing education for children, however, as illustrated by the fact that in many places the erection of junior high schools has helped alleviate overcrowding in both high and elementary schools, whereas new elementary or new high schools alone could not have helped matters at both levels. The administrator must be alert to such problems, and to the possibilities for organizational plans to help in their solution. To the extent that such plans help provide the conditions for good education, they are desirable, but plans of organization cannot themselves do the job of

[3] L. Cole, *Psychology of Adolescence*, 3rd ed., Rinehart and Company, New York, 1948, pp. 55–56.
[4] H. A. Dimock, *Rediscovering the Adolescent*, 2nd ed., Association Press, New York, 1941, p. 209.

educating children. That can be done only by a dedicated staff, possessed of a sound philosophy and effective methods of teaching.

Lower Age Limit of the Elementary School

Decision as to what should be the lower limit of the elementary school is another question upon which general agreement has not yet been reached. Until the early part of the present century, it was accepted without much question that the elementary school should begin with grade 1, and that the entering age for grade 1 should be about six years. During the nineteenth century, the work of Froebel aroused the interest of many American educators in the education of children below six years of age, and kindergartens were established in several places. The kindergarten was accepted only slowly, however, as a part of American free public schools. It is only since about 1925 that any considerable progress has been made in adding kindergartens to the schools.

Although recent figures are not available, it is unquestionably true that kindergartens are now an established part of the American public school system, despite the fact that there are still many persons (including some educators) who are opposed to them. The Bureau of the Census figures for 1940 indicate that 69.1 per cent of all six-year-olds and 10.5 per cent of children two to five years old were attending school. A far larger percentage of urban children under seven are in school than is the case in rural areas.[5] This latter fact is strongly reflected in a study of the Department of Elementary School Principals of the National Education Association.[6] Davis quotes 1945 figures of the Bureau of the Census, released in 1946, which indicate ". . . general changes for the United States as a whole in percentage of five- and six-year-old children attending school and, in particular, a high increase for children of these ages who live in rural areas."[7]

The growing acceptance of this idea is also reflected in recent legislation. Numbers of states have passed enabling measures encouraging the provision of public education for children under six.[8]

[5] U. S. Department of Commerce, Bureau of the Census, *Sixteenth Census of the United States: 1940, Population,* vol. IV, Part 1, "Characteristics By Age," Table 14, p. 39.

[6] Department of Elementary School Principals, *op. cit.,* Twenty-seventh Yearbook, "Organization," Tables 7 and 8, pp. 43, 45.

[7] Mary D. Davis, *Schools for Children Under Six,* Office of Education Bulletin 1947, no. 5, U. S. Government Printing Office, Washington, D. C.

[8] National Society for the Study of Education, *Early Childhood Education,* Forty-sixth Yearbook, Part II, University of Chicago Press, Chicago, 1947, p. 15.

Strong resistance to this trend has been met from several sources. "Economy" groups object to the increased expenditures. Those who conceive of "learning" in terms of subjects and subject skills consider the time wasted. Finally, some uninformed sentimentalists decry the removal of children so young from their mothers' arms, claiming that mothers are thereby encouraged to shirk their responsibilities, that they know best how to raise their young, and that mothers will look on this as only an opportunity to "park" their children while they shop, play bridge, or otherwise occupy themselves in pursuits in which children would be a handicap.

These arguments are, of course, quite flimsy. A child attending nursery school or kindergarten two or three hours daily is not being deprived of adequate maternal care, nor will such attendance break down family structure and ties. Norton observes that these same arguments were earlier used in opposing the establishment of our free public school system.[9] In fact, in many cases it is probably desirable for mother and children to be apart from each other for brief periods. Furthermore, it is a known fact that mothers do not instinctively know the best means of raising their children. Nursery schools can perform a real service in parent education.[10]

Since it appears from all indications that public education for children below six "is here to stay," it behooves the administrator to consider the relation of that part of his school to the rest. In all too many cases kindergartens (and later nursery schools) were "tacked on" to the existing grade organization (as is evidenced by the term "pre-school"), and what went on in them was considered to be relatively unrelated to the "education" dispensed by the grades above. Such a point of view is understandable if one conceives modern education to mean simply an expanded and enriched program of teaching the three R's, plus some other things the schools "ought to teach," such as atomic energy facts, the United Nations, and conservation.

For those who view education as the enlightened guidance of children's all-around growth in socially desirable directions, however, this schism between kindergarten-nursery and the grade school is deplorable. In addition to helping fight the battle for these educational services,

[9] John K. Norton, "The Place of Nursery Schools in Public Education," *Childhood Education,* vol. XXI, January 1945, p. 215.
[10] Davis, *op. cit.,* pp. 43–44; Educational Policies Commission, *Education for All American Children,* Washington, D. C., 1948, pp. 253–254.

there is the great opportunity for forward-looking principals to integrate these educational levels into the public school pattern. It seems likely that this will not be fully and effectively accomplished until educators and the public cease thinking of the six-year-old grade level as being "grade 1." Indeed, until we free our minds of the shackles of the "grade" concept many desirable changes are likely to be delayed.

From all that is known of children's growth and development, it would seem to be desirable to establish age three as the beginning school age for most children, particularly where population, geographic, and financial factors contribute to the feasibility of such a plan. The three-year-olds would then constitute the first "grade" or level or group, and should be thought of as such. The education of three-, four-, and five-year-olds should be closely integrated with that of all other age levels in recognition of the continuous nature of growth and learning.

The most feasible immediate goal in most school systems, however, is to work for a one-year downward extension of the present elementary school. The authors suggest calling this "Year One" of the elementary school, or the "Four-Year-Old Group," or "Five-Year-Old Group" (whichever it may be), with other age levels named accordingly. A student of one of the authors has suggested naming classes by their expected year of completing the high school, so that the Four-Year-Old Group in 1952 would be "Class of 1966"!

Ultimately, then, we shall have an "elementary" school enrolling children at three years of age, which will do its level best to foster their optimum growth for nine years, then send them to another unit for continued guidance in succeeding years.

SUGGESTED READINGS
See pages 109–110.

CHAPTER V

THE CURRICULUM

Whatever the age range included in his school, the principal is faced with problems of instructional, pupil, and staff organization in his efforts to develop and carry out an effective learning program. This is clearly one of the most challenging and important of his numerous responsibilities, for the manner in which it is done influences strongly all other aspects of the school's operation.

Whereas a school has, or should have, an essential unity in its organization and operation, there are a number of kinds of organization within it. There is organization for fire drills, organization of the staff for playground, lunch or bus duty, organization of the learning program, organization for the ordering and distribution of books and other supplies, and many other working arrangements within the major framework of the school. In this and the next two chapters, three major aspects of a school's organization are considered: (1) curriculum issues and organization; (2) organization for instruction, frequently called pupil classification; and (3) organization of the staff for school improvement.

ISSUES IN CURRICULUM ORGANIZATION

There are a number of different theories and practices in curriculum conception and development. Whereas most educators agree on the goals to be sought, there is considerable difference of opinion as to how the outcomes are to be achieved. It would be impossible to consider these differences of opinion in detail in a volume of this nature, but there are seven major categories which seem to encompass most of them.

1. What is the curriculum?
2. What should be taught?
3. Should the demands of society, or the nature and needs of the individual determine the curriculum?
4. How much should the curriculum vary from school to school?
5. When and by whom should the curriculum be planned?
6. How should the curriculum provide for individual differences?
7. What is the relative importance of process and content?

The answers given to these questions have a direct bearing on the type of organization adopted by the school.

What Is the Curriculum?

In the past, the prevailing tendency in American schools has been to conceive of the curriculum as a collection of courses of study in the different subjects. Some school activities and child experiences do not fit into these courses of study. Consequently, they have been called *extra*curricular activities—outside the curriculum—while others (school lunch experiences, recess, etc.) were conceived as noncurricular—not consciously considered as learning experiences.

Most contemporary authorities in education stress the fact that learning for each child is a 24-hour-a-day process. They are pointing out that so-called "extracurricular" or "noncurricular" experiences (e.g. cafeteria experiences, playground experiences, school clubs, plays) are all rich learning situations. For this reason they are insisting that the curriculum consists of *all* the experiences the child has under the direct influence of the school; no such experiences are "extra" curricular. In the eyes of those who view the curriculum in this light, the curriculum is more than a program of learning facts and skills; it is a program of learning better how to live. The school, then, is responsible for guiding all aspects of the growth of children while it has them under its jurisdiction, and these experiences are the curriculum.

Thus there are two broad definitions of the curriculum. On the one hand it may be viewed as a collection of "courses" or written "courses of study," and no more than that; on the other hand, it may be considered to be *all* of the experiences the child has under the influence of the school. In the latter definition there are different interpretations of what "under the influence of the school" means. The school's influence

can be considered to be limited to the hours the child is in school, or—
as in extreme interpretations of the "community school"—it may be interpreted much more broadly, so that one hardly knows where to draw
the line.

Most teachers and principals find themselves somewhere between
these extremes. In fact, it would be difficult indeed to find any exponents
of either extreme in its pure form. The curriculum in the vast majority
of schools is still thought of as comprising the various "subjects," but
teachers commonly recognize their educative responsibilities in the so-
called "extracurricular" experiences of the children while they are in
school.

The authors prefer to think of the curriculum in terms of children's
growing experiences, rather than as a collection of "subjects." Properly,
they believe, it includes all the experiences of children while they are
under the direct and legal jurisdiction of school authorities. Children's
experiences during out-of-school hours are not a part of the school's
curriculum, although they influence, and are influenced by, the school's
learning program.

What Should Be Taught?

Much disagreement centers around the content of the curriculum.
Many educators claim that the curriculum of the elementary school
should be organized around the three R's, plus certain "basic" learnings
in history, geography, civics, health, art, and others, and that these
learnings should be arranged in logical sequence, and specified in detail. Others believe that the curriculum should comprise a specified series
of broad problems relating to the culture, or to commonly persistent
living problems. Still others believe that the learning program should be
built around the day-to-day living problems of the children, differing,
therefore, with every group. Others have convictions which are modifications or variations of these points of view.

Another aspect of the problem is the order in which learning experiences should be introduced. Many still are of the belief that the
sequence should be determined by the logic of the subject. In reading,
start with the simplest units—letters and phonograms—and "build" from
there; in social studies, organize according to the chronology of history;
in arithmetic start with the 100 basic number facts and build sequentially
from there. Others point to the fact that children do not learn that way,

and that there are scientific studies whose findings indicate how best to teach arithmetic, or reading or spelling. Still others maintain that the sequence and organization are to be found, not in the subject, but in the learner, and that they should be determined by the needs of the children maturing in the culture.

There is also a difference in point of view as to the degree to which the curriculum should consist of firsthand experience. Some would rely almost entirely on books and teacher explanations, with some objective illustrations now and then. Others would build the curriculum around book materials, and supplement the book learnings by frequent excursions and class "activities." Still others claim the curriculum should consist primarily of problems from the children's experience, using book materials largely to help solve those problems.

Should the Demands of Society or the Nature and Needs of the Individual Determine the Curriculum?

Each of these beliefs as to the content of the curriculum relates to certain viewpoints as to what should determine the curriculum. Basically, there are three different points of view. The first holds that since the schools are established by a society to serve its needs, the content of the learning program should deal primarily with the nature, background, and needs of that society.[1] The second maintains that since the business of education is to educate the individual, the curriculum should be built around the nature and needs of the individual.[2] As the reader can readily see, the first orientation is primarily social, while the second is primarily psychological. It should be pointed out that probably no person would defend either premise in its extreme form; every socially oriented learning program considers individual needs to some extent, and every psychologically based curriculum necessarily has some social orientation. The issue centers around the relative emphasis to be accorded the needs of the individual and those of society in achieving a unified curriculum which will meet both types of need. A third group takes the viewpoint that there is no essential conflict between these two points of view. They maintain that it is not only unnecessary to take an "either—or" stand; it is downright unrealistic. The individual, they point out, can realize

[1] John L. Childs, "A Student of Public Affairs Views the Problem of Curriculum Development," *Teachers College Record,* January 1949, pp. 232–240.
[2] Lawrence S. Kubie, "The Psychiatrist Considers Curriculum Development," *Teachers College Record,* January 1949, pp. 241–246.

himself as an individual *only in relation to the society in which he lives*. The content of the curriculum, therefore, should deal with the individual-in-society. In this orientation both the needs of the individual and of society will find their proper emphasis. The authors believe this latter approach to be most consistent with modern educational philosophy and the psychology of growth and learning.

Another aspect of this issue is the question as to whether the curriculum should be determined by adult needs (preparation for adulthood), or by children's immediate needs. Those who advocate a predominantly subject-centered curriculum determined by society's needs usually maintain that education's job is to prepare children for adult living. Much of the curriculum, then, consists of learnings which will be useful at some future time. An opposing school of thought maintains that children must be considered as children in their own right, not as miniature adults, and that the curriculum should therefore concern itself exclusively with the children's problems. Again, others claim that essentially there is no conflict here, that there are enough concerns common to both children and adults to provide a series of learning problems and experiences that will at the same time have immediate significance in the lives of children and prepare them for adult responsibilities. It is also pointed out that the older "preparatory for life" point of view implied a static society in which the adult needs of today's children could be predicted. The modern point of view, in stressing the solution of children's immediate and significant problems, makes for *flexible use* of intelligence, preparing the child to adapt to the dizzying changes of today's kaleidoscopic world. To do this, the curriculum is built around the developmental needs of children and persistent life situations found in the culture. This latter viewpoint seems to provide a sound basis for building a flexible, yet stable, framework for curriculum planning.

How Much Should the Curriculum Vary from School to School?

Closely allied to the foregoing is the problem of uniformity versus diversity. Is it desirable, for example, for all schools in a system to have the same scope, content, and sequence in their learning programs? Many believe that it is, particularly those who are partial to a subject curriculum, determined by the adult needs of the culture. Others, stressing that each community is in many respects culturally unique, and that children exhibit wide individual variations, maintain that each school's learning program should be unique in marked degree. These two view-points are, of course, different emphases, not pure extremes. The former group would grant the necessity of somewhat modifying a school's program because of community and pupil-population differences. The latter group, in turn, does not advocate complete uniqueness; there must be much that is common among American schools.

It would seem almost self-evident that a learning program which is uniform from school to school is not consistent with the American tradition, but is more compatible with the philosophy of those countries which make a shibboleth of uniformity. Furthermore, any program which purports to be derived from and geared to the community living and problems of the pupils must vary somewhat with the type of community. There are, of course, broad unifying themes, needs and problems which should strongly influence the learning program in American schools, and which can serve as part of the framework for a curriculum which will help children to live and grow as Americans, as well as citizens of specific and varied American communities. A defensible position, there-fore, would seem to be one which calls for a broad curriculum frame-work consistent with universal cultural and psychological needs and con-ditions, within which a local school can vary its program sufficiently to adapt it to the unique requirements of the pupils in its community.

When and by Whom Should the Curriculum Be Planned?

The fifth major issue centers around the problem of the responsibility for determining what the learning program shall be. Who shall plan it, and when? Some believe that such planning is a specialized job, and should be done by "experts" in curriculum planning. In such case, the curriculum is planned (often in detail) well in advance of the learning situation, and all children in all the schools in the system at a given level have approximately the same curriculum. Among those who would dis-agree there are different opinions concerning the degree of pre-planning. Some few believe that *no* aspects of the curriculum should be planned prior to the learning situation. Arranged on a scale, these beliefs might follow the pattern illustrated at the top of the opposite page.

There are evidences of a strong trend away from detailed, pre-planned courses of study toward the right end of the scale. However, the great majority of American elementary schools are still best described by categories 1 and 2 at the left end of the continuum; the trend consists

1	2	3	4	5
Curriculum entirely pre-planned in detail by "experts," and embodied in "Courses of Study."	Curriculum pre-planned in detail by teacher committees and embodied in "Courses of Study."	Curriculum planned in broad outlines by teacher committees, embodied in "resource guides." Individual teacher determines details in terms of pupil needs.	Curriculum planned in broad outlines, enlisting wide teacher and community participation. Details determined by teacher-pupil planning.	Curriculum planned by teacher and pupils on the spot, without any pre-planning.

simply in the fact that the minority which is moving away from those positions is increasing appreciably. The major problem posed is to determine the optimum position between the extremes of 1 and 5.

The authors believe that numbers 1, 2, and 5 are the least desirable situations; some plan approximating number 4 provides for stability and continuity, guards against crystallization and stagnation, and assures considerable flexibility and adaptability.

How Should the Curriculum Provide for Individual Differences?

The sixth group of issues centers around the problem of adjusting the learning program to the differences among children. The subject curriculum had its origin at a time when the present knowledge of the individual differences in abilities among and within children was still to be discovered. At that time it was assumed that everybody (with the exception of the feeble-minded) could master all school subjects equally well, provided they tried hard enough; that the level of achievement in those subjects depended only upon the amount of effort the learner exerted. This general belief is epitomized in the words of Disraeli in 1870: "The secret of success is constancy of purpose"; and of Samuel Johnson: "Few things are impossible to diligence and skill." McGuffey's Readers, used so widely during the latter part of the last century, are sprinkled with such expressions as: "Where there is a will there is a way"; and "The road to wealth, to honor, to usefulness and to happiness is open to all, and all who will, may enter upon it with the almost certain prospect of success."

The findings of psychology in the past three decades have emphasized the unwitting naïveté of these statements. It is now commonly recognized that human beings vary widely in their ability to succeed. This has moved educators to devise means of adjusting educational practice to these differences in ability. Here again there are different beliefs as to how this should be done. The first, which is now largely a "straw man," is the concept of a curriculum established in its minimum essentials. The problem is to adjust individuals of varying learning rates to this "reality." Whereas practically all educators repudiate this point of view intellectually, most educational practice (such as nonpromotion, acceleration, and prevailing marking practices) indicates that it is by no means extinct.

Another viewpoint is that children should be grouped according to their ability, on the assumption that such grouping will reduce the ability range in each group to such a degree as to simplify considerably the job of individualization. In the "slow" groups, only the "minimum essentials" are taught, while the "fast" groups cover these quickly and go beyond them in an "enriched" learning program. A third point of view is that a problem-centered, experience-type curriculum permits the group to work together on a common problem in which they are interested while permitting each class member to work at his level of academic, social, and emotional development, yet be able to contribute to the group enterprise. While the first two viewpoints are at the moment the most prevalent in school practice, the third seems to be growing in acceptance. This is probably because it appears to be more compatible with democratic principles, and because of the growing conviction that individualization must deal with *quality* as well as *rate* of learning.

What Is the Relative Importance of Process and Content?

Finally, there is the question of whether process or content is the more important in the learning program. In its present guise, this is a comparatively new issue, introduced by the recently recognized implication that children and adults both "learn to do by doing." Some educators, in stressing the importance of "activity" and "experience" in the curriculum, have gone so far as to belittle the importance of *what* is studied, so long as the kinds of experiences that children have are conducive to the social, esthetic, intellectual, and moral learnings they, the educators, deem important. This seems interestingly akin to the faculty psychology viewpoint of yesteryear, which maintained that such traits as will, perseverance, and determination could be developed by studying any one of a number of subjects, so long as the subject was sufficiently difficult and unpleasant. Content is certainly important. The modern viewpoint is different from the usual subject-content approach in its emphasis that the content be related to children's true needs and interests at their level of maturity.

In contemporary situations the specific subject matter has often been subordinated to the use of group planning, democratic procedure, independent research activities, and the like, with the justification that such methods are themselves content, and that the important things to learn are not facts, but patterns of behavior, such as democratic human relationships, constructive group participation, methods of independent inquiry, and critical-mindedness.

The authors would agree wholeheartedly that the means of learning are most important, that process is content in a very real sense, and that it most certainly is a highly important ingredient of the learning situation. However, one must be careful lest he throw out the baby with the bath. A sound approach will recognize that learning is the interaction of the learner with a situation, which includes (among other things) a problem, materials to help solve that problem, and—in the case of children—an adult to help and guide. In this situation, factual knowledge is placed in a new focus. Instead of being important *per se,* or in relation to its possible usefulness in the remote future, it has value because it contributes to the improved quality of present living of the learners, which is—as Dewey has stated—the best preparation for living in the future.

The foregoing groups of issues do not exhaust all those being debated. They do include the major factors determining curriculum organization, however, and the position concerning them taken by a principal and his staff (or by the administrative authorities of a larger system, or by the lay board of control) will determine to a great extent the type of curriculum operating in a given school, and in turn will dictate to some degree the over-all plan of school organization.[3]

[3] For similar, but somewhat different and more extended analyses of curriculum issues, see L. Thomas Hopkins, *Interaction: The Democratic Process,* D. C. Heath & Company, Boston, 1941, pp. 19–40; and F. B. Stratemeyer, H. L. Forkner, M. G. McKim, and others, *Developing a Curriculum for Modern Living,* Bureau of Publications, Teachers College, Columbia University, New York, 1947, pp. 1–24.

CURRICULUM DESIGNS

The Subject Curriculum

As a result of the differences of opinion represented in these curriculum issues, there are widespread differences in curriculum among American schools. Whereas differences among our schools have always existed, the areas of controversy have been greatly widened since the second decade of this century.

From their earliest times our schools have operated what is now termed a "subject" curriculum, organized basically around the teaching of reading, writing, arithmetic, history, geography, and English grammar. This type of curriculum is still operating in some American schools. It is based upon the belief, or philosophy, that it is possible and desirable to determine in advance what all children should learn; that it is feasible and necessary to determine minimum standards of achievement in those learnings; and that the important goal of education is to bring about mastery of the specified skills and knowledges, in the belief that such mastery insures the type of person necessary to the operation of American democracy. Like our early American society, this curriculum is highly individualistic (but not individualized) and avowedly competitive. It had its foundations in several beliefs:

1. Fundamental among these beliefs was the theory of mental discipline, a part of the faculty psychology which was widely accepted in the nineteenth century. This theory held that the mind is made up of "faculties," which, like the muscles, can be trained through exercise; the more rigorous the exercise the better the training. Formal grammar; ridiculously lengthy, difficult, and complex mathematical computations; meaningless drills; and otherwise useless rote memorization were all justified largely by this doctrine.

2. Closely allied to the first belief (indeed, a part of it) was the theory of transfer of training. This held that faculties trained by the study of one subject carried over to other areas. Rhetoric, grammar and mathematics, for example, were held to teach disciplined, orderly thinking. The memory training obtained in memorizing lists of prepositions, state capitals, boundaries, and the like was thought to improve memory proportionately in its other functions.

3. Also widely accepted was the idea that any accomplishment is

possible provided one strives hard and long enough. "Little by little does the trick," and "Plodding wins the race," were favorite precepts. Failure to achieve, therefore, was considered evidence of lack of application and effort, and was punished as such.

4. There was strong belief in the value of a competitive method of teaching and learning. Our early culture was a highly individualistic frontier society, often fiercely competitive. It was natural that its education should reflect this.

5. It was generally accepted that learning should progress according to an Aristotelian organization of neat logical and chronological sequences. A natural outgrowth of this was a graded school, which assigned segments of these sequences to different grades, each grade representing a year of "learning."

Educational experimentation into the nature of learning during the past few decades has exploded the theories of faculty psychology, with its tenets of mental discipline and transfer of training. It has been emphasized that learning is largely specific to the task. The actor who commits entire plays to memory with dispatch is no more likely than the usher to remember his wife's injunction to bring a pound of butter on the way home from rehearsal. It is true, of course, that there may be *some* transfer, proportional to the degree to which there are identical elements in the old and new tasks.[4] Investigation has also sharply revealed the fact of wide individual differences in learning capacity and rate of mental growth. It has indicated clearly that learning does not take place in the logical pattern of the neat progressions found in most earlier courses of study. Furthermore, the nature of our society has changed markedly. Instead of being an intensely individualistic culture, it has become a culture which is highly interdependent. From a culture that was sharply competitive in nature, it has changed to a culture that is now realizing that its continuance and improvement—its very survival—depend on co-operation.

The "Scientific Subject Curriculum"

These changes have been somewhat reflected in the curriculum of modern schools, and strongly reflected in the thinking of many educational authorities. Among the first modifications to be made were changes

[4] Arthur I. Gates and others, *Educational Psychology*, The Macmillan Company, New York, 1942, p. 513.

in the organization of courses of study, growing out of the findings on the nature of learning. The orders of learnings were rearranged, so that the teaching of reading, for example, was revolutionized. Instead of progressing "logically" from alphabet to phonic families and then to words, sentences and paragraphs, beginning reading now starts with words and phrases, words and phrases the children know, words and phrases about their everyday experiences. These are now taught as "wholes" rather than by parts, and the skills of word analysis are postponed until later, when they are more easily and effectively learned. This is illustrative of changes initiated in spelling, composition, history, geography and other subjects. The resulting curriculum has been called "the scientific subject curriculum."[5] This is probably the most prevalent type of curriculum in American elementary schools today.

The "Correlated" Curriculum

Over the years, many educators (laymen as well) criticized the subject curriculum on the grounds that it "fragments" learning. This fragmentation can be illustrated by considering a hypothetical case. In a subject-centered classroom, children might be studying Africa in geography, the medieval period of Europe in history, and in reading be perusing a story about Eskimos. The remedy for this, it was proposed, was to "correlate" the subjects. When studying European history, European geography should also be studied. In reading, the stories should be related to the historical period under study. Composition topics should be related to the historical or geographical matters under discussion. Spelling words should be derived from the terms used in the history and geography study. Work in science, drama, physical education (dance), art, and music should be similarly related to the history study. It was argued that the result would be a greater unity in children's learnings; learnings in the subjects would reinforce and supplement one another, and the whole thing would be much more meaningful to the children. The idea has had considerable acceptance, and the practice has spread through many school systems.

Whereas there is no doubt that it has done much to vitalize the subject curriculum, and make it more meaningful and interesting, some of the correlation is so far-fetched, and some of the "related" learnings so

[5] Hollis L. Caswell and A. Wellesley Foshay, *Education in the Elementary School*, 2nd ed., American Book Company, New York, 1950, pp. 236–238.

"dragged in by the ears" as to be amusing. For example, a group study-ing the history of New England finds that at one point the chief industry of several of the states was fishing. Correlation in geography is achieved by studying fishing the world over: kinds of fish caught, the quantities, the by-products, and the value. In nature study, they get a goldfish bowl and some goldfish, and study the life habits of goldfish, where they come from, what species of fish they are. In music they sing sea chanties and songs about fish. In art they draw and paint fish and pictures of fishing. Arithmetic problems are fish-oriented, as: "If a fishing vessel caught a half-ton of fish and the fish averaged 2.5 pounds in weight, how many fish did the fishing vessel bring back?" In English they write compositions about fish and fishing. When the teacher's ingenuity in finding "fish cor-relations" finally is exhausted, she and the youngsters thankfully leave their piscatorial problems and hopefully turn to another topic. At its best, however, a *good* correlated program (particularly in a self-con-tained classroom) has considerable vitality and appeal. It is nevertheless subject to the criticisms and weaknesses of any subject curriculum, of which it is simply a modification.

The "Fused," "Integrated," "Core," or "Broad-Fields" Curriculums

Some educational leaders felt that correlation was but a halfway step. Carrying the idea further, they proposed a genuine "merging" or "fus-ing" of related subjects. As a result, many schools have combined the study of geography, history, and civics into a broader subject called "social studies." Reading, spelling, composition and grammar have been "fused" into the "language arts."

The degree of "fusion" practiced varies widely among schools claim-ing to use this plan. In some schools, much the same original subject curriculum is carried on, with history, geography and civics, for ex-ample, simply grouped together and called social studies. Other schools have achieved a thoroughgoing merging, so that history, geography, and civics are not taught as separate subjects, but are interrelated in the study of a social problem which cuts across centuries and cultures. Examples of such a problem would be "The Development of Transportation," or "What Caused Some Peoples to Become Seafarers?" In some schools the broad central problem is called the "core," and most other school activities are related to it during the period of its study (which might be weeks or months, or a semester or year).

Many schools and writers have termed this a "broad-fields" curriculum, for obvious reasons.[6] It is to be noted, however, that this is still one type of subject curriculum, as the "cores" or "units" or "problems" to be studied during the year tend still to be organized within subjects, and are determined in advance, as are the materials of study and the conclusions or generalizations to be reached.

The foregoing has been a very sketchy presentation of types of curriculums which have as their major emphasis the learning or mastery of a predetermined body of subject matter and skills. This emphasis becomes less pronounced as we move from the separate-subject curriculum toward the broad-fields curriculum. The constant broadening of areas of study, the breakdown of hard and fast subject lines, the flexibility introduced by means of "cores" and "problems," all resulted from recognition of the inadequacies of the classical subject curriculum. They are evidences of a constant and commendable striving on the part of educators to develop a learning program more nearly recognizing the needs of pupils and the culture, more in harmony with the manner in which children really do learn, more meaningful, more useful and more interesting.

Criticisms of the Subject-type Curriculum

The foregoing curriculum types: subject, scientific subject, correlated, fused, integrated, core and broad fields, represent a range of subject-type curriculums. The latter of these types are more flexible than the former in their organization and permit of more pupil planning and initiative. Even of these latter types, however, there are numerous criticisms. Without pretending to be exhaustive, the following are representative of major points.

1. *The subject curriculum is authoritarian in its conception.* It assumes that some person or group other than the learners can prescribe the "best" learning program for all children. The fallacy of such a concept is well illustrated by the fact that "authorities" or "experts" cannot agree upon what *is* best for any given grade level. The curriculum which is "best" for any learner should be designed specifically to meet his needs and those of the culture in which he is growing. These needs will vary from time to time, place to place, and person to person, although there

[6] Hopkins, *op. cit.,* pp. 60–69; Caswell and Foshay, *op. cit.,* pp. 239–240.

will naturally be many common elements. Only those close to the learning situation can decide what learning experiences will be most profitable. A democratic culture is not well served by a curriculum determined in an authoritarian manner.

2. *The subject curriculum tends to be competitive and individualistic.* Since it emphasizes the learning of facts and skills, and awards honors in proportion to the quantities of them which are learned, children strive to outdo one another, often resorting to unethical practices to do so. Whereas such an education may have served nineteenth century America, it is not only anachronistic, but dangerous for the world of today.

3. *The subject curriculum emphasizes intellectual growth at the expense of other aspects of growth.* Psychological investigation has indicated that we react as "wholes," that the entire organism is involved in any experience. Any learning has its emotional, physical, and social as well as its intellectual aspects. Furthermore, psychologists and sociologists tell us that these other growth aspects are of tremendous importance, for (they ask) what good is intellectual development if the individual becomes unable to use it constructively because of social, emotional, or physical maladjustment or disability?

4. *The "compartmentalization" of learning which naturally results is artificial, and prevents the meaningful integration of knowledge.* Children frequently fail to see the relationships between the school subjects; indeed many teachers fail to do so. Poetry is dissociated from social studies, music from science, and the integration of arithmetic and reading skills with other subject areas is seldom realized. A genuine learning experience calls on all pertinent areas of knowledge to aid in the understanding or solution of a problem. The organization of the subject curriculum prevents this.

5. *Such a curriculum emphasizes fact-learning rather than meaning-getting.* True education is far more than the memorization of history or geography facts, or spelling words, or lines of poetry. It is largely a matter of expanding meanings, of seeing broader and broader relationships, of arriving at generalizations, insights, and understandings which give us greater control over our actions and environment, of learning better human relationships, and effective techniques of working with others. This the fact-learning nature of the subject curriculum not only does not foster; it actually hinders such a process.

6. *The emphasis is too exclusively on the future, too little on the*

present. There is too much concern to prepare the child for adulthood by teaching facts and skills which may be useful at a future time. Too little concern is given to meeting the needs he is facing daily at his particular growth stage. John Dewey expressed this well in saying:

> When preparation is made the controlling end, then the potentialities of the present are sacrificed to a supposititious future . . . We always live at the time we live and not at some other time, and only by extracting at each present time the full meaning of each present experience are we prepared for doing the same thing in the future. This is the only preparation which in the long run amounts to anything.[7]

This is not to imply that the future is to be ignored, of course; it is simply to assert that in planning education for the future adjustment of pupils we should assure that their learning experiences also have meaning and utility in their present growth and life.

7. *It is not conducive to attention to individual differences.* All pupils are required to study the same subject matter, usually at the same time and in the same way, and there are uniform minimum standards which all are expected to meet. Extensive investigations have revealed the wide range of differences among individuals. To expect children whose abilities, needs, and backgrounds differ so widely to fit into such a uniform program is unrealistic. Furthermore, the setting of uniform minimum standards puts "success" completely out of reach for some children while making its achievement too easy for others.

8. *It is not consistent with the nature of the learning process.* Psychological research within the past few decades has indicated that children do not learn by the logic of a subject. The logic of thinking is not that of a file drawer, or of a table of contents, or of a neatly patterned course of study. Learning, we are told, is a process of complete and progressive reorganization resulting from new experiences, much as the chemical reorganization brought about by the introduction of a reagent. Consequently, psychologists and educators are substituting the logic of learning for the logic of the subject as the desirable basis of curriculum organization.

It must be noted that all these criticisms do not apply with equal force to all types of subject curriculums. The chief reason for this is

[7] John Dewey, *Experience and Education,* The Macmillan Company, New York, 1938, p. 51.

that modifications of the "classic" curriculum came about because of recognition of the validity of one or more of these arguments. In fact, some of the more extreme departures of the core or broad-fields types almost succeed in meeting the conditions implied as good in the condemnations detailed above. Such curriculums seem to avoid all the characteristics denounced in the subject curriculum save two: (1) that their emphasis is *primarily* on the acquisition of facts and skills through vicarious experiences, and (2) that the learner and teacher have too little part in determining what the learning experiences shall be.

These appear to be sharp issues, and they are. However, we find that in practice the horse is very seldom all of a color. Many "subject" curriculums, particularly of the broad-fields and related types, provide much firsthand experience, and emphasize the development of meanings and generalized understandings. Many also determine only broad outlines of the curriculum, and allow considerable latitude to the teacher and learner in deciding the specific experiences of which the learning program will consist. Carried far enough, these programs are difficult to classify as "subject" or as "experience" curriculums, for they shade into one another as colors in the spectrum.

The Activity Movement and the Experience Emphasis

It is unfortunate that the terms "activity" and "experience" have been used to characterize types of curriculums emerging in the past few decades. It cannot be denied that learners have experiences in the subject curriculum and that they engage in activity of a sort. As a matter of fact, it is fair to say that there is no such thing as an "activity curriculum" which is clearly definable. It is more correct to speak of the *activity movement* or the *experience emphasis,* for they are not types of curriculum organization. As Freeman has stated, "Whether or not education depends on activity does not, for example, seem to determine whether the curriculum shall be worked out in advance, nor whether it shall be organized into large units, nor whether it shall be planned by the teacher or worked out by the pupils, nor whether it shall be organized in subjects, nor whether the pupils' work shall be evaluated in terms of standards, and so on."[8] Activity can be used, then, to vitalize and enrich a subject-centered curriculum, although its characteristics in such

[8] F. N. Freeman, in National Society for the Study of Education, *The Activity Movement,* Thirty-third Yearbook, Part II, Public School Publishing Company, Bloomington, Ill., 1934, p. 90. Quoted by permission of the Society.

situations differ from those it has as a part of currently advocated "life-centered" curriculums.

In applying or interpreting the principles of the experience emphasis, however, it must be remembered (for it has sometimes been forgotten) that the experiencing engaged in is but a means of achieving educational goals, not an end in itself. Furthermore, the *kinds* of experiences children have should be given close attention. Dewey emphasizes that good learning experiences are worth while not only for the present, but should grow directly and meaningfully out of past experience and lead to further fruitful and creative living.[9] This is also expressed in Kilpatrick's famous catch-phrase, "Activity leading to further activity." Dewey and Hopkins both differentiate the types of experiences in the subject curriculum and in the experience program primarily in terms of the *nature* or *quality* of the experiences. Good quality in experiences is evidenced by such characteristics as the following: unity, promotion of future desirable experiences, meeting of individual needs, and high level of co-operativeness.[10]

Extreme interpretations: the child-centered school. In the revolt against the restricting uniformity of the traditional subject curriculum, some educators erroneously concluded, *à la Rousseau,* that the child's natural interests and needs alone should determine the curriculum. In a few schools such a program was actually attempted, and in them there was an abundance of activity and "experiencing." Because of their almost exclusive interest in and emphasis on the nature, needs, wishes, and preferences of the children, these schools were termed "child-centered schools." Few educators were satisfied with this viewpoint, however, which made for a chaotic, unintegrated curriculum. The few schools which attempted such an extreme program soon abandoned it, usually reverting to a more subject-oriented program. It is unfortunate that the publicity given these few experiments should have resulted in the public's identifying them with "progressive education." The stereotype they have implanted in the public's mind has severely hampered the efforts of many other schools to develop soundly progressive methods. "Progressive" is, of course, a perfectly good word, meaning to progress toward an improved situation, but it is now in undeserved disrepute.

[9] Dewey, *op. cit.,* pp. 16–17.
[10] Dewey, *ibid.,* ch. III; Hopkins, *op. cit.,* pp. 41–44.

Curriculums of the Experience Type

In a very real sense, then, the "activity movement" was a bridge by means of which we have made a transition from a formal, subject-centered, study-and-recitation type of program to something else. The curriculums which are emerging from this newer emphasis are widely known as "experience-type" curriculums. In these sounder interpretations of contemporary progressive theory, a number of characteristics are discernible, which distinguish this type of learning program from the subject-centered curriculum.

1. *The nature of curriculum experiences differs.* In the subject curriculum the experiences are predominantly those of reading and listening, followed by written or oral reciting. It is true that great improvements have been made in these methods, so that pupils not only use more than one text, but often make extensive use of the library and other book facilities, and that the reciting may take the form of varied kinds of individual and written reports, but the experiences are still predominantly those of the reading, listening, and reciting type. In many cases the activity emphasis has caused the introduction of "enrichment" in the form of excursions, construction of models, related art work, and the like, but this is far from being central in the program, and seldom is the content or organization of the learning program appreciably affected by the needs or purposes of the learners.

In the experience-type program, on the other hand, there is an attempt to provide for far more lifelike and "real" experiencing. Since children's experiences outside school are strongly influenced by their own purposes and needs, it seems logical that their in-school experiences should be a product of those purposes and needs *in relation to needs imposed by society.* Learning, then, will take place through the definition of problems to be solved and the experiences undertaken to solve the problems. Hence, the experiences have far more of the ingredients of *pupil purpose,* evidence more *overt activity,* are *more varied,* and are *more related to one another* than the predominantly passive, adult-determined and unintegrated experiences of the subject-type curriculums.

2. *The selecting agents of curriculum experiences are those in the learning situation.* In the subject curriculum, the learning experiences

are determined primarily by agents outside of the learning situation (curriculum experts, state department officials, administrators, supervisors, textbook writers, teacher committees). In the experience curriculum, as we noted above, pupil purposes are enlisted in the determination of problems for study; hence, while the broad framework of goals and desirable areas of experience may be adult determined, *the specific learning experiences are selected primarily by those in the learning situation*—the pupils and teacher.

3. *The continuity of curriculum experiences is a function of the learner's growth.* In the subject curriculum continuity is primarily in terms of chronological sequence or of progression from simple to complex. In the experience-type curriculum, on the other hand, the continuity derives largely from the growth and stages of development of learners, and the nature of the problems they are facing, under the guidance of the teacher. The sequence is primarily psychological, rather than logical or chronological.

4. *The purpose of curriculum experiences is the improvement of the present living of the child.* Preparation for adult living by the acquisition of facts and skills deemed essential (by authorities or experts) for such living is the major purpose of the subject curriculum. Improvement of the quality of here-and-now living is the focus of the experience curriculum, founded on the belief that the best preparation for the future is successful solution of the living-problems of today and, through such solutions, the development of controlling generalizations, abilities and skills.

5. *The individualization of curriculum experiences is qualitative rather than quantitative.* The emphasis in the subject curriculum usually is to bring everybody up to the minimum acceptable standard, which is primarily quantitative in conception. Individualization is in terms of *rate* and *quantity* of learning. Emphasis is on learning the common cultural heritage. In the experience curriculum, individuality is highly prized. While attempting to insure common understandings and skills, *emphasis is placed on helping each learner to extend and improve his personal uniqueness,* so that instead of all engaging in the same kinds of experiences, all have unique experiences while co-operatively attacking common problems. Emphasis is on *quality* of learning.[11]

[11] Harold Benjamin, *The Cultivation of Idiosyncrasy,* Inglis Lecture, Harvard University Press, Cambridge, Mass., 1949.

Few clear-cut formulations of curriculums of the experience type have as yet been developed. For this reason, one cannot designate "types" as clearly as can be done with the more crystallized subject curriculums. There are several approaches which have been used, however, having an emphasis on here-and-now problems of living, so as to provide more "real" and lifelike experiences for learning. To many persons these curriculum organizations seem to be logical next steps beyond the core or broad-fields curriculum plans of the subject-type curriculums, but go much further in encouraging real pupil planning, purposing, executing and evaluating.

The "modern-problems" or "areas-of-living" approach. In an effort to provide a broad, guiding framework for the curriculum, without undesirably restricting the freedom of pupils and their teachers to plan and select "real" and purposeful learning problems and experiences, several proposals have been developed. One of these is that we use as the organizing principle broad problems of living which affect all of us. From within these broad problems, individual learning groups select experiences appropriate to their maturity, needs, and interests. Caswell and Foshay describe this type of curriculum as follows: "In the areas-of-living approach, the primary orientation becomes the broad areas within which social arrangements and individual activities tend to cluster. The areas selected for study tend to differ somewhat among schools which have planned curriculums on this basis, but the basic conception is the same. Areas frequently employed are maintaining health, making a home, making a living, and getting an education . . . The analysis of problems and needs of individual children indicates the immediate basis upon which the curriculum may be developed."[12]

The persistent-life-situations curriculum. Similar in some ways to the foregoing is another approach, in which the basis for curriculum organization is an analysis of "persistent life needs," or "persistent life situations." An interesting example of this approach was developed by members of the Horace Mann-Lincoln Institute of School Experimentation as a result of their work in member school systems. After making an analysis of persistent life situations of human beings, they grouped

[12] Caswell and Foshay, *op. cit.,* p. 240; see also W. S. Monroe, ed., *Encyclopedia of Educational Research,* rev. ed., The Macmillan Company, New York, 1950, pp. 310–312.

them into the following three major categories: (1) situations calling for growth in individual capacities, (2) situations calling for growth in social participation, and (3) situations calling for growth in ability to deal with environmental factors and forces.[13]

This orientation is proposed as the *organizing principle* for learning experiences selected co-operatively by the teacher and pupils. One such "persistent life situation," for example, is "respecting property rights." This is then analyzed into kinds of experiences in respecting property rights which are typical of early and later childhood, youth and adulthood.[14]

The modern-problems, areas-of-living, and persistent-life-situations curriculums are frequently termed "life-centered" learning programs, to distinguish them from the subject-centered, book-centered, and child-centered programs.

The reader will note that all of these "life-centered" approaches deal with problems of immediate concern to any person living in contemporary America. In working upon the problems selected, pupils must become facile in skills of number and quantity, and of communication and the language arts. History, science, the arts, sociology, and other "subjects" furnish the resources for solving problems, but are not treated as subjects. The belief is that knowledge in these areas is better and more functionally learned when it is learned for vital purposes related to problems of living. In addition, it is claimed that such a curriculum develops better skills of social living, of critical thinking, of leadership, of research and the like. Evaluative studies tend to support this point of view.

Summary of Curriculum Designs

Whereas this discussion may lead the reader to believe that a curriculum must be either a subject *or* an experience curriculum, the differences actually are largely a matter of emphasis. One would look long indeed to find a "pure" subject curriculum, which totally disregarded the problems and needs of the learners. Likewise, it would be difficult to find an experience curriculum which was entirely derived from such

[13] F. B. Stratemeyer and others, *Developing a Curriculum for Modern Living,* Bureau of Publications, Teachers College, Columbia University, New York, 1947, pp. 106–118.
[14] *Ibid.* An extensive analysis of this nature for a large number of "persistent life situations" will be found on pp. 126–289 of this reference.

needs and problems, and which was entirely free from subject emphasis.

Hopkins has tried to express this by placing different types of curriculums on a scale. This serves to highlight a fact which has caused confusion: a subject-oriented and an experience-oriented curriculum may both be labeled with the same name. Some "core" programs have as the core the "essentials," usually meaning language-arts and number skills; these are subject-oriented "core curriculums." Others use a major area-of-living problem as the core, drawing upon the "subject fields" for its solution; such are experience-oriented "core curriculums." As Hopkins observes, the only safe way one can conclude which emphasis is predominant is to observe the program in operation.[15]

The trend in curriculum change, while slow, has been away from the subject-type toward the experience-type, and has been more rapid in the elementary than in the secondary school. The slowness of the change has puzzled and exasperated many educational workers, but reasons for the lag are not far to seek. The subject curriculum is the educational expression of faculty psychology. It is founded on the belief that the mind can be trained like a muscle through exercise on subject matter. Most educators will now grant the fact that the concepts of faculty psychology are false. Yet, for practically every educational worker in the schools today, the subject curriculum is the only curriculum he has ever known; and he is reluctant to abandon the known, despite its admitted faults, for something unknown and untried. Undoubtedly this same factor operates in the case of parents and other laymen. There are many other factors, such as inadequate teacher training; large classes; timid or uninformed leadership; inadequate or inappropriate materials; restrictive school buildings; legal prescriptions; and vested interests in textbooks, subject-oriented learning materials and equipment.

An increasing number of elementary schools are moving toward an experience-type curriculum, however. In those schools which have made appreciable changes in this direction, there has almost always been able, well trained and energetic leadership. In numerous cases the leader in the change has been the elementary school principal, and to the writers' knowledge, no such significant change has taken place without at least the principal's active co-operation. This emphasizes the responsibility of the principal; as the professional leader in the school, he is expected— by staff and community alike—to set the pace for change. If he is com-

[15] Hopkins, *op. cit.*, p. 19.

placent and uninterested in bringing about fundamental improvement, it is very likely that little change will take place. Some schools have been operating the same curriculum for twenty-five or more years, the only "basic" alteration being the addition of some new subject and some slight modification of those being taught. This has been the situation in the face of social changes which one would think could not be ignored (atomic energy, air travel, World Wars I and II, the critical challenge to democracy, and the like). It is probable, therefore, that if any significant reforms are to be made—and they are sorely needed—principals will have to assume actively their share of the leadership.

Organization of the School Day

Each major type of curriculum demands a different organization of the school day. Consequently, the principal, by insisting upon a given type of school day organization, can prevent the effective development of curriculum designs which do not fit that plan. The typical subject curriculum, for example, divides the day into numerous periods of varying length for each subject. Thus the day may be broken up into ten or more periods daily. Frequently these are tightly scheduled, and administrative emphasis is placed upon adherence to the schedule. Whereas creative teachers can do much within this rigid framework to relate the learnings to one another and to life, this kind of daily organization will serve effectively as an obstacle to those who try to develop a core or broad-fields kind of program of learning, moving in the direction of a life-centered curriculum.

Curriculums of the fused or broad-fields types require larger blocks of time; consequently there are fewer "periods" in the day. In such situations the time limits usually are more flexible than in the subject-curriculum time schedules, although there are exceptions. There is less flexibility, for example, when the program is departmentalized than when the children stay with the same teacher through virtually all of the day.

The daily organization pattern of the experience-type curriculum is difficult to indicate in detail because it is characterized by large time-blocks and flexibility to an even greater extent than the subject-oriented fused curriculum. The organization, instead of being in terms of subject fields, is in terms of activities relating to the projects under way at the moment. An initial period may be set aside for planning, and during

FIGURE 1. Daily Organization for Three Curriculum Types

SUBJECT TYPE	BROAD-FIELDS TYPE	EXPERIENCE TYPE
8:45– 9:00: Opening Exercises	8:45– 9:15: Planning Period	8:45– 9:15: Planning Period
9:00– 9:40: Arithmetic	9:15–10:25: Language Arts	9:15–11:40: Time Used as Planned
9:40–10:00: Music		
10:00–10:15: Recess		
10:15–10:45: Reading	10:25–10:40: Recess	
10:45–11:00: Handwriting		
11:00–11:40: Social Studies	10:40–11:55: Social Studies	11:40–12:00: Evaluation Period
11:40–12:00: Spelling		
12:00– 1:00: Lunch	11:55– 1:00: Lunch	12:00– 1:00: Lunch Hour
1:00– 1:20: Current Events	1:00– 2:00: Arithmetic and Science	1:00– 1:15: Plan Modification Period
1:20– 2:00: Composition & Grammar		1:15– 2:40 Time Used as Planned
2:00– 2:15: Recess → REST ROOM	2:00– 3:00: Creative Activities (Art, Music, Construction, Poetry, etc.)	
2:15– 2:35: Health		2:40– 3:00: Evaluation and Cleanup Period
2:35– 3:00: Reading		

77

the rest of the morning or afternoon different pupil committees and individuals will be doing different things at the same time. One group may be in the library, looking for authoritative or illustrative material relating to the project under way; another group may go to interview some individuals or group in the community; another group may be planning or working on some construction related to the project, while a fourth group may be working on a written committee report. There are many times when the group works together as a class, of course, for there are times when the teacher and pupils will decide that they need to improve certain skills if they are to be successful in their project or in similar projects in the future. These skills might include such abilities as working together as a group, arithmetical computation, improved oral and written expression, general or specialized reading abilities, organizing into groups for work, and other abilities necessary to successful living. It should be obvious, therefore, that no two days will be alike; each day's organization is determined by the jobs to be done, just as in life outside the school. There may be some constants, dictated by other factors. Definite scheduling may be necessary for activities in the gymnasium, or auditorium, or shop, or library, or for the use of a part-time special consultant in art or music or science. These facts are taken into account in the planning.

Figure 1 is an oversimplified but illustrative comparison of three contrasting organizations of a school day. Note the trend toward broader, more flexible blocks of time as one goes from the subject toward the experience (life-centered) type of curriculum.

PRINCIPLES OF CURRICULUM ORGANIZATION

As we have seen, there are several distinct types of curriculums, and each has its own philosophy and methods of development. Principles of curriculum development will necessarily differ, therefore, with each curriculum type. It is perhaps trite to remark that a school's curriculum should be suited to the school's educational philosophy. That this is not always true is attested by beautiful statements of philosophy in the introductions of many courses of study, statements which apparently commit the schools to a thoroughgoing life-centered type of curriculum. The remainder of the course of study, however, is frequently a more or less detailed guide for the teaching of a subject through the study of textbook materials. It may be true, of course, that such a course of study has been a step forward by a staff in the development of a learning program more consistent with what they believe to be good education, in which case the staff should be conscious of that fact, and continue to modify their learning program in the direction indicated as desirable by their statement of philosophy. A learning program changes only as the people who operate and administer it change, and people—especially groups of people—change but slowly.

Furthermore, each curriculum type has a number of important implications which are frequently not recognized. There are implications for the time schedule, for the process of curriculum development, for the instructional materials used, for the teaching methods and kinds of teachers, for the grouping of children, for evaluation procedures, for the policy of pupil progress (promotions), for the philosophy and practice of discipline, for the nature of staff relationships, and for home-school-community relationships. These implications are pointed out throughout this volume, for it is of paramount importance for the principal to understand them.

Since it would be tedious to enumerate principles for each type of curriculum, and since the authors are convinced of the validity of the life-centered experience curriculum, the following principles are formulated with that type of curriculum in mind. They are treated separately for purposes of discussion, but it should be kept in mind that in operation they are inseparable parts of a whole. They overlap considerably, and are permeated and integrated by the goals of a life-centered program of learning.

1. *The curriculum should be interpreted to mean all the experiences that the children have under the direct jurisdiction of the school.* Under this definition, there can be no such thing as an "extracurricular" or "cocurricular" experience in school. *All* experiences are curricular, and should be part of the school's program of observing and guiding the learning and growth of the children toward the goals deemed desirable. Experiences at the lunch table, at recess, in celebrations, in community projects, in student council, on the safety patrol and the like, all are packed full of meaningful, life-centered learning situations. The modern school staff weaves them all into an articulated and integrating learning program.

2. *In school systems, the schools should work to develop a common educational philosophy related to the needs of individuals in the local, city, regional, national, and world communities, but individual schools should be encouraged to develop learning programs unique to the needs of their pupils and their communities.* One of the problems which has vexed many educators in school systems in which there are several schools is that of uniformity versus diversity. To what degree should the program of a local school be permitted to be different from that of other schools in the system? Pertinent to this issue, of course, are the problems of pupil transfers, of common evaluative systems, of economical central purchasing of materials, and the like. Actually, the degree of uniqueness to be encouraged within the system is a matter about which we cannot generalize for all schools. Local conditions such as the community's educational viewpoint; poor or capable school leadership; background, training and ability of the staff; finances; and community variability will influence the answer to the question.

Nevertheless, one can generalize to the extent of saying that the school system should certainly take steps to try to develop a unified viewpoint concerning the goals, methods, and organization of education. This should be a co-operative venture, in which all the staff, and desirably many community members, should participate in some degree. Co-ordination should be provided for among the schools so that, while the administration of education is facilitated, the learning program not only is not hampered but is actually enhanced.

Whereas a unified system viewpoint is desirable with respect to the broader aspects of policy and administration, individual schools should not be bound to uniformity in the specifics of their learning programs. Consequently, it is important for the school administration to give attention to the development of that nice balance between system-wide co-ordination and local school autonomy which will best contribute to a flexible and functional curriculum devoted to the improvement of the quality of living of the pupils and of the community at large.

3. *Participation in the planning of the general policies and framework of the curriculum should be broadened to include teachers, parents, and other community members.* In developing a life-centered curriculum increasing attention should be given to community conditions and problems which are important in the learning and growing of children. It is around many of these problems and conditions that the curriculum of

the school is organized. Such a program is naturally the concern not only of the school staff and the pupils, but also of the parents and other citizens of the community. For this reason, the broad policies and goals of the educational program cannot be left to the discretion of any one individual or small group; particularly can they not be determined by agents outside the community. Provision should be made, therefore, for representative parents and nonparents of the community to participate at the policy level in the planning of the educational program. An important contribution to thinking in this respect is a recent volume of the Metropolitan School Study Council, in which the following five patterns of public participation in educational planning are discussed. These are patterns which have been used successfully in a number of communities.

1. Administration Initiated Groups
2. The Unmet Needs Pattern of Development
3. The Educational Interests of Organized Groups
4. Individuals as Contributors to Educational Planning
5. Special Purpose Groups[16]

4. *The principal and his staff should work co-operatively toward the development of a unified philosophy of education.* A football team whose members were divided in their opinion as to whether the single-wing-back, the double-wing-back, the T-formation, or the winged-T-formation is the best offensive formation, and each of whom played accordingly without relation to what the others did, would be a sorry team indeed. Yet that situation is far too common in our elementary schools. The teachers and principal of an elementary school (yes, and the secretary and the custodians!) should constitute a team which co-ordinates its efforts for the co-operative improvement of the learning program. This is not to imply that all the teachers must think alike, but there should be discussion and group study by the staff with the objective of developing common objectives, some reasonable consensus concerning the type of curriculum which shall be developed, and some agreement concerning the kinds of methods which shall be employed. Some such over-all plan and principles are necessary to provide guidance. A truly life-centered curriculum cannot be developed by one teacher apart from the others; the school must be organized for it and,

---

[16] *Public Action for Powerful Schools,* Metropolitan School Study Council, Teachers College, Columbia University, New York, 1949, Part III.

as is suggested above, practically all other aspects of school operation have to be consistent with it if it is to be successful. It is important, therefore, that the principal be or become skillful in the processes of group leadership. This aspect of the principalship is discussed at greater length elsewhere in this volume.

5. *The framework of the curriculum should be such that the selection of specific learning problems is left to teacher-pupil planning.* The day of the detailed course of study which spelled out the learning program down to such specifics as the exact topics to be studied, the amount of time to be devoted to each, and sometimes even the textbook pages to be used, is passing with the two- and three-year teacher training institution. It is still far from gone, however. This type of course of study is not only inconsistent, but downright impossible in a life-centered curriculum. The staff should plan together a broad framework of areas to which attention shall be given; types of skills, competencies, knowledges and understandings to be developed; illustrative types of learning experiences; and suggestions as to sources of materials. But much beyond that, pre-planning cannot go. Opportunity should be left for teachers and pupils to learn together through practice the ability to identify problems for study within this framework, and to organize themselves for their study and solution. In this way, originality, initiative, judgment, and skills of co-operative human relationships are given an opportunity to be developed by the pupils far more than is possible under the more rigid and formal types of courses of study.

6. *The focus and source of the curriculum should be the nature and needs of the child in the contemporary culture.* This has been said so often as to have become almost meaningless. One reason for the fact that it has not been translated into fact too successfully in many schools is that we have not realized how fundamental a change in the approach to teaching and learning it implies. In most cases we have simply tried to find ways in which the old curriculum, organized around subject learnings, could be stretched and strained and squeezed and reshuffled to meet certain common needs of childhood. What this principle actually implies, however, is *that those needs are primary, that they serve as the organizing principle.* Instead of starting with subjects, and trying to make them meet children's needs, one starts with the problems of children growing up in today's world, and particularly the problems they face in their own communities. This is the fundamental difference be-

tween the subject curriculum and the life-centered curriculum, and unless it is understood we work in confusion.

It is to be noted that it is not the needs of the child alone that are important; it is the needs of the child related to the culture. Children and adults face the same kinds of problem situations; it is only that in childhood they have a different emphasis and some different characteristics. In the emerging type of American school, these problems are the foci of curriculum organization, and information that can be found in books and other sources gains its importance from its ability to throw light upon and help solve these problems.

7. *The school staff should become closely acquainted with the pupils and their home and community conditions and problems.* This principle follows logically from the premise proposed in number 6 above. Certainly if the problems of the children-in-their-communities are to become the stuff of the educational program, the school staff will have to be conversant with the community and with the backgrounds of the children. Administrative attention will have to be given to facilitating this. The learning program itself, by making investigation of the community a part of its activity, will accomplish it in some degree. Joint school-community planning, resource use of the community, community surveys, and home visits all can help. The entire topic of school-community relationships is discussed at length in Chapters XXIV and XXV.

8. *Curriculum experiences should be so planned as to enhance the desirable uniqueness of individuals.* In our emphasis upon community problems, and on the problems of *children* in society, we must not forget that each child is unique, and that his needs and problems are different than those of his peers. The "progressive school" of the late 'twenties and early 'thirties tended to glorify the needs and interests of each individual to the extent that the learning program sometimes lost all semblance of pattern. In a life-centered program we can give attention to common "persistent" life needs of all children, and yet keep the methods of studying them flexible and broad enough that each child has the opportunity to develop his abilities to suit his needs and interests. Emphasis should be placed *not* upon bringing all children up to some mythical standard, but upon helping each child to develop his unique abilities to the utmost while gaining reasonable command of the necessary skills of human intercourse in today's world. One is moved to wonder how many potential Einsteins, or Kreislers, or Edisons, or Whitmans,

or Hawthornes, or John Deweys have been lost to society because, instead of encouraging the development of their unique abilities, we have insisted that they memorize the rhyming scheme of the Elizabethan sonnet, or the export products of Brazil, or study history which glorifies war and military "heroes," or spend dreary periods on meaningless drill to bring them "up to standard." In developing our curriculums and our methods, therefore, (and in a functional curriculum method is part of the curriculum) we should take care to provide an atmosphere hospitable to originality and consistent with democracy, rather than one which emphasizes uniform grade standards—a practice which is characteristic of an autocracy and hostile to creativeness.

9. *The curriculum should be designed specifically to develop those abilities necessary to successful living together in a modern world.* Our final principle is a recognition of the fact that since human beings are social beings, one of our major problems in life is that of learning how to live and work harmoniously and constructively with one another. Heretofore we have not attached too much significance to this fact in our educational planning. Education has been largely a non-co-operative affair. Children did not have to co-operate with each other to achieve the goals of the curriculum. In fact, such co-operation was frowned upon and penalized in most schools, and still is in many. Each child was expected to work alone, and progress was stimulated by making learning competitive to such a degree that jealousies and antagonisms were aroused, and many pupils were led to employ unethical practices in order to gain artificial honors, to satisfy parents that one was doing as well or better than the Jones's boy, or to "pass." The belief was implicit that knowledge itself was moral, and that given a "good" education a person would automatically become a good citizen. This point of view is still widespread.

Yet the problems the world is facing today are not problems demanding simply more knowledge of the technical kind. They are *moral* problems, problems of human relationships. Man knows well enough how to make gadgets, instruments of war and work-saving machines. The crying need is for greater ability to live together at peace, ability to discuss differences of opinion reasonably and without rancor, ability to conceive "the good life" in terms of constructive human relationships rather than in terms of more material goods. This premise seems incontrovertible when we look upon the problems of labor-management, of race relations, of religious prejudice, or of international conflict. Yet these moral problems cannot be solved by teaching platitudinous precepts, for morals are not isolated from and somehow "above" life, but are the product of human association. They are not given in original "human nature."[17]

This emphasizes something mentioned earlier: that *process,* or method, is not apart from, but a part of the curriculum. Children learn by the way they do things and from the way people about them do things. The curriculum should be planned and operated in such a manner, therefore, that the pupils will grow in their ability to plan and work and play constructively and happily with others, and in their consideration and respect for the rights, abilities, contributions and shortcomings of all other human beings, as well as to insure important fact and skill learnings. Unless we make progress in the solution of these problems of human relationships the future presents a dreary prospect. Education can play an important and decisive part in fostering such progress if we plan specifically for the solution of human problems to be one of the ends education shall serve.

SUGGESTED READINGS

See pages 109–110.

[17] John Dewey, *Human Nature and Conduct,* Carleton House, New York, 1922, pp. 296 and 329.

CHAPTER VI

ORGANIZING FOR INSTRUCTION

The foregoing discussion has emphasized that the educational beliefs of the principal and his staff will strongly influence curriculum organization and the organization of the school itself. It has been suggested that there is a relationship between subject types of curriculum and the graded-school type of organization, and that the graded school is not the best pattern for learning programs which are not primarily subject-centered.

In the following pages, a number of organizational plans for instruction will be described and examined, with attention to their relationship to curriculum philosophy; and principles of instructional organization will be proposed.

THE GRADED SCHOOL AND THE SUBJECT CURRICULUM

American public schools have always taught, virtually without exception, some form of subject curriculum. As was pointed out, such a curriculum is founded upon the belief that there is a body of "essential" fact and skill learnings which it is highly desirable that everybody should learn. In our earliest schools, which usually had but one teacher and few pupils, little attention had to be given to the school's organization in order to carry on this learning program. It was possible for the teacher to take each child at his level of learning, and to extend it as far as he was able. With the advent of free public education, however, the increasing number of pupils attending school required more teachers per school, with the consequent problem of how to divide the children for instruction. The graded school, which still is accepted (with some spirited exceptions) as the basic form of organization for our schools, was the solution to this nineteenth century problem.

A few moments' reflection will enable one to see that the philosophy of the subject curriculum and that of the graded-school form of organization are both of the same cloth. Advocates of the subject curriculum have maintained that the learnings they deem essential are best learned in logical sequence, beginning for the most part with that which is least intricate and proceeding in the direction of increasing complexity. In a given school situation children will have progressed in this sequence in varying degrees. It was logical to assume, then, that the learners can be divided into groups of similar levels of achievement, so that the teacher will not have to teach all levels within his group. This is exactly what the graded school purported to do. If the subject curriculum has a logical sequence, it can be assumed that we can determine how much of that sequence the average child can learn in his first school year, and call that part of it the curriculum for grade 1. The same can be done for grades 2 through 12. All the children in the elementary school can thus be divided into graded groups on the basis of their levels of achievement. This will have the advantage of placing all children with similar levels of achievement in the same grade, and make instruction easier for the teacher. The plan certainly has appeal for the logical mind, *provided its underlying assumptions are valid.*

This latter point is the joker in the scheme. The findings of psychological research with respect to the nature of learning during the first part of the twentieth century have indicated that learning is not a "logical" affair in the usual sense of that term. It is now known that learning is as frequently a matter of proceeding from the complex to the simple as it is the reverse; in fact, it is a relatively unorganized process, in the Aristotelian sense of organization. What organization learning has is in terms of the purposes of the learner (not the logic of the subject), and its sequence is a function not only of increasing difficulty and complexity, but also of the learner's growth, needs, and experiences. Furthermore, children's learning rates differ so widely that it has proven a vexing problem to attempt to "grade" pupils into learning levels; they just will not seem to fit, or if they do, they will not stay there!

For these and other reasons, the graded-school organization never has worked as well as the theory assumed it would. In order to try to make it fit the theory, a number of interesting practices were developed. The almost universal practice of grade failure (failing to promote those children who do not learn what the theory postulated they should learn in the allotted year's time) is one of these. As is pointed out elsewhere, however, this "patchwork" practice has failed of its objective, which is the maintenance of the gradedness of the graded school. The whole system of marking in the elementary school is also an administrative device used to help make the graded school work. The child is given a mark to indicate the degree to which he achieves or exceeds (or fails to achieve!) the learnings required in his grade. These marks then enable the teacher to decide which of the children merit promotion to the next higher grade. Other devices born of the failure of the common school to maintain its gradedness are homogeneous grouping, "opportunity classes" (in which pupils are given the opportunity to "catch up" with the established pattern of standards), remedial work, "acceleration," multiple-track plans, and "special classes" of various types.

The chief difficulty of the graded school is that it is basically Procrustean in nature; it is an attempt to fit the child to a preconceived pattern, to screen out children who do not learn at the rate adults have decreed to be the proper rate, rather than an attempt to help all children to grow at the rate which is best for them. Hence, the facts of individual differences have always been embarrassing to proponents of the graded school, and are responsible for the fact that this type of organization never has really "worked."

A number of educators who have believed basically in the subject curriculum have recognized this fact and have attempted to do something about it. Whereas most of their plans are now "on the way out" in education practice,[1] they were sincere, interesting, and often ingenious efforts to improve the education of children.

GRADED SCHOOL PLANS OF ORGANIZATION

One Teacher per Grade-Class

By far the most prevalent type of internal organization in larger American elementary schools over the past hundred years has been the

---

[1] National Education Association, *Trends in City School Organization, 1938 to 1948*, Research Bulletin, vol. XXVII, February 1949.

plan which assigns a given graded class to one teacher, who is responsible for the teaching of all, or virtually all, the subjects. Caswell and Foshay call this "the self-contained classroom."[2] The consistency of this organizational plan with the graded-school philosophy should be obvious. Each teacher can "specialize" in the subject matter of his grade level and become familiar with the characteristics of children of the age level usually associated with that grade. In a subject-matter oriented program, the teacher maintains a daily schedule of time allotments for each subject.

While this plan was developed to serve a graded-subject curriculum, its flexibility makes it adaptable to other educational plans. For example, it is well suited to both the broad-fields type of curriculum and to the life-problems-centered program. (See Figure 1, page 77, for differences in the daily schedule under these three plans.) In addition, it has the advantage of enabling the teacher to see the interrelationships between the different topics or problems in the learning program, so that he may provide a more integrative learning program. Since he is with the same children for all of every school day, he can get to know their problems, needs, interests, and individual characteristics more intimately than under other plans, and thus is better enabled to develop a learning program suited to individual differences of children. This latter value has been largely vitiated in many school systems because of the large numbers of children assigned to single classes.

The one teacher per grade-class plan has been criticized by subject-minded educators on the grounds that the teacher, being expected to teach every subject, can become really competent in none of them. Some also see advantages in having the children meet several different teachers each day, and thus learn to adjust to different types of adult personalities. This argument is urged as being particularly pertinent in situations where the teacher in the one teacher per grade-class is incompetent or strongly disliked by the pupils.

In this, as in other organizational plans, one's educational point of view is a determining factor. It is to be noted, however, that this type of internal organization is adaptable to any of the curriculum philosophies discussed earlier. Within it the organization of the school day will differ with each point of view.

[2] Caswell and Foshay, *Education in the Elementary School,* 2nd ed., American Book Company, New York, 1950, pp. 315, 323–326.

Departmentalization

In attempting to operate graded schools, educators became aware of the fact that not only do children differ among themselves in their rates of growth and learning: each child seems to have different growth rates within himself. Thus a child may be making excellent progress in reading, but be doing poor work in arithmetic and English grammar. Assuming that the child is doing satisfactory work in all his other subjects, should he be promoted? Most educators in graded schools answered this negatively. They decided that failure in two "major" subjects would be adequate cause for grade failure. Some schools worked out elaborate weightings of subjects to help them in determining when a child should "fail." Such practice disturbed many who questioned whether a child should be made to repeat all the work he had done satisfactorily simply because he had failed some other part. Out of this concern was born the practice of departmentalization.

Departmentalization is a plan of teaching and promoting by subjects. Under this arrangement a child need repeat only those subjects in which he did unsatisfactory work. It has had very wide acceptance in American schools, and has been applied even in the primary grades. In recent years, however, the trend toward departmentalization halted and has begun to reverse. A study by the Research Division of the National Education Association in 1947–48 indicated that of cities of over 2500 population, 51 per cent still had departmentalized organization in one or more elementary schools. Of this 51 per cent, 35 per cent said that departmentalization is on the way out in that system, while 12 per cent stated that it is on the way in.[3] The U. S. Office of Education, in a study of organizational practices in the elementary schools of 100 cities, found that "not 1 of the 100 cities uses departmentalization as a basic plan of organization. Five cities report that none of their schools is departmentalized. Others indicate that departmentalization is present in some degree, in certain schools, grades, or subjects, chiefly in intermediate or upper grades; but that the school system as a whole is moving away from the plan."[4] It is likely that the trend away from departmentalization will accelerate during the present decade.

[3] *Op. cit.,* p. 16.
[4] U. S. Office of Education, *Organization and Supervision of Elementary Education in 100 Cities,* Bulletin 1949, no. 11, U. S. Government Printing Office, Washington, D. C., p. 37.

One's opinion concerning the advantages or disadvantages of the departmental type of school organization depends largely on one's educational philosophy, for departmentalization is clearly a plan designed to fit a subject-centered school. If one is a firm believer in a curriculum of pre-established essentials, the plan has the advantage of being designed specifically to teach those essentials. Furthermore, the teachers will each be specialists in a given subject and, therefore, presumably able to make that subject richer and more meaningful for the pupils.

Currently, however, the majority of elementary school educators are not in accord with that point of view. If one holds an organismic point of view with respect to learning, and believes that education should be life-problems centered rather than subject centered, a considerable number of objections will be raised against departmentalization. It will be pointed out, for example, that its approach to learning is fragmentary and disintegrative, discouraging of unity and wholeness in the learning program. Even with sincere attempts at "integration" the separate subjects will tend to be discrete and relatively unrelated in the minds of pupils. It is also claimed that such an organization tends to encourage teachers to be teachers of subjects rather than teachers of children. The teacher who must meet five classes of thirty pupils each every day (150 pupils daily) is prevented, by their very numbers, from knowing the children well enough to suit his instruction to their individual needs, except in the most superficial manner.

In addition, it is pointed out that this organizational plan sets up a relatively inflexible time schedule. A class may have reached a stage of excited interest in a social studies or science problem, in a situation rich with learning possibilities *at that moment,* and be interrupted by the tyrannical bell commanding them to stop their fruitful activity and progress to their next teacher and subject.

These are probably the major reasons for the decline in the popularity and practice of departmentalization, although it is still the prevailing pattern in many of our largest cities.

The Platoon Plan

A variation of departmental organization is the plan introduced in 1900 at Bluffton, Indiana, by Superintendent William A. Wirt, and developed further by him at Gary, Indiana (hence, often called "The Gary Plan"). Wirt's original plan divided the curriculum into two major divisions: the academic subjects and special "laboratory activities," comprising such activities as weaving, woodworking, metalwork, printing, art, and the like. The student body was likewise divided into two sections called "platoons." One half of them spent the first part of the morning with the academic subjects while the other half was engaged in the laboratory experiences. In the midmorning the two platoons exchanged places. A similar process was followed in the afternoon.

Whereas Wirt developed the plan to fit a specific industrial town situation, it was widely adopted and adapted in other school systems. Its expansion and popularity were probably due more to a physical situation, however, than to the appeal of its philosophical base. Since the platoon organization is probably the most efficient organizational scheme in the utilization of space, the crowded school conditions following World War I lent it great practical appeal. Consequently, it was primarily for its space utilization features that it became popular.

The platoon organization is subject to the same criticisms as is the departmental plan, of which it is a variation. For this and other reasons, it has been declining steadily in popularity. The National Education Association study on school organization referred to previously indicates that only 8 per cent of city school systems are now using the platoon plan, and of that 8 per cent, 55 per cent report that in the system the plan is on the way out, while only 12 per cent report that it is on the way in.[5]

Plans of Individual Instruction

Other educators have devised different schemes for individualization of instruction in the graded school. Their recognition that all children do not learn at the same rate resulted in plans providing for varying degrees of individualization in instruction.

Ability grouping. Illustrative of such plans was the Detroit "X-Y-Z" Plan. In this plan, pupils are divided according to some criteria of achievement and learning ability into three groups labeled X, Y, and Z, comprising fast, average, and slow pupils, respectively. According to the plan, the curriculum in these groups, and to some extent the materials of instruction, were differentiated; the slow groups got a program of "minimum essentials," while the superior pupils had a greatly enriched learn-

[5] National Education Association, *op. cit.,* pp. 17–18.

ing program. Modifications of this plan used more or less than three groups. This idea of grouping children by ability has had wide acceptance, and was still in use in over half of American city school systems at the end of the past decade.[6] This represents an appreciable decrease from the 67 per cent found by Otto in 1929,[7] although the figures are not strictly comparable. Ability grouping, as an organizational plan for individualization, has a number of undesirable features, which are discussed on pages 120–127.

Multiple-track plans. Similar to the Detroit Plan, but different in important respects, are other plans which group pupils on the same general bases as in Detroit, but in which each group takes a different length of time to complete the elementary school. Such schools permit superior pupils to complete the elementary school program in less than the usual amount of time, while requiring the slow pupils to spend more than the usual length of time there. Plans of this type were applied in the school systems of Pueblo, Colorado; Norfolk, Virginia; Portland, Oregon; and Cambridge, Massachusetts. It should be obvious that these organizational plans were designed to facilitate a learning program based on the belief that there is a given body of learning to be mastered in the elementary school, which some children can master in a shorter time than can others. It is also worth mentioning that such plans are feasible only in schools with a large enough pupil population to enable them to form more than one group at each grade level.

Although features of these plans were adopted widely, such grouping schemes have been losing favor in latter years. What they do, in effect, is to set up three sets of grade standards. But alas, there are more than three levels of difference among children.

Another type of organizational plan for individualization of instruction is that typified by the so-called Winnetka and Dalton plans. Actually it is more just and more accurate to refer to these plans as the Washburne and Parkhurst plans, since they were the respective authors of the plans. Furthermore, the school systems of Winnetka, Illinois, and Dalton, Massachusetts, where the plans were worked out by Dr. Washburne and Miss Parkhurst, have modified their school organizations considerably,

---

[6] *Ibid.*, p. 17.
[7] H. J. Otto, *Current Practices in the Organization of Elementary Schools*, Northwestern University Contributions to Education, no. 5, Evanston, Ill., 1932, ch. III.

so that they no longer resemble their former famous selves. It should be said that—in the opinion of the authors, at least—the changes have been improvements.

Although there are important differences in the details of the Washburne and Parkhurst plans, their distinguishing feature is common to both: each plan purports to allow each child to progress through the prescribed course of study at his own rate. These organizational plans are designed to facilitate the teaching and learning of a subject curriculum, but they also recognize more fully than any of the plans thus far discussed the significance of individual differences in the learning of facts and skills.

The plan developed by Miss Parkhurst divides the learnings in each subject into a series of "contracts" which the child completes at his own rate of speed. Washburne's plan features a series of "goal cards" in each subject, which outline in specific detail the objectives to be learned. Here, too, the pupils progress at their own rate. Both plans also include activity periods of different types for social and cultural learnings. The philosophy underlying these plans is well summed up by Washburne:

> Under the old regime, in the effort to give different children the same subject-matter in the same length of time, the quality of the children's work, the degree of their mastery, varied from poor to excellent, as attested by their report cards. But under the Winnetka technique of individual education, instead of quality varying, time varies: a child may take as much time as he needs to master a unit of work, but master it he must.[8]

Neither of these plans gained any wide acceptance in elementary education in the United States, although Miss Parkhurst's plan was widely applied in Europe.[9] It is to be noted, however, that such plans make the same basic assumptions as do other subject-oriented plans, plus a few more. Faith is still placed in a preconceived body of subject matter to be learned, and it is assumed that everybody should "master" it. It is also to be noted that the provision for individual differences is primarily in terms of time, a concept of individualization which many educators today

[8] C. W. Washburne, "Burke's Individual System as Developed at Winnetka," *Adapting the Schools to Individual Differences,* Part II, Twenty-fourth Yearbook, National Society for the Study of Education, Public School Publishing Company, Bloomington, Ill., 1925, p. 79. Quoted by permission of the Society.

[9] The descriptions given here do not provide the reader with enough detail to make a critical judgment of the plans. For more adequate descriptions of these plans the reader is referred to *Adapting the Schools to Individual Differences,* Part II, Twenty-fourth Yearbook, National Society for the Study of Education, 1925.

would maintain is too narrow. Finally, it is argued that these plans prevent adequate integration of learnings for the individual.

The organizational plans discussed in this section all are plans developed to serve the philosophy of a subject curriculum in a graded school. Some of the plans are interesting attempts to overcome the weaknesses of the graded school, weaknesses which became evident even to advocates of that point of view. All of them have failed to solve these weaknesses, primarily because they did not deal realistically with the basic inconsistency of the graded school idea: children who vary widely within and among themselves, and who have imperative and individual needs and purposes, cannot be forced into an adult-decreed pattern of a graded subject-matter curriculum. When the latter is attempted, the ensuing problems of failure, maladjustment, and rebellion are inevitable.

PROPOSED PRINCIPLES OF ELEMENTARY SCHOOL ORGANIZATION

In this all too brief discussion and evaluation of the foregoing organizational plans it is implied that certain values and features of them were undesirable. By implication, then, there are other values and characteristics which are more consistent with present day educational philosophy. The writers have attempted to embody these in the principles of school organization which follow:

1. *The organization should facilitate intimate knowledge of the pupils by the teachers through extended association.* A modern educational viewpoint holds the school responsible for gearing its program to the needs, problems, purposes, and abilities of the pupils. It would seem obvious that the greater the opportunity afforded a teacher to know these characteristics of his pupils, the better he will be able to adapt his learning program to them.

2. *The organization should provide for the grouping of children in relation to the educational objectives to be sought.* The manner in which the pupils are grouped reflects, to some degree, educational beliefs of the administration. Ability grouping, for example, emphasizes ability to learn subject matter. Belief in a high degree of individual independence and initiative is reflected in Miss Parkhurst's plan of highly individualized learning experiences. Conviction of the primary importance of the

learning of co-operative skills of living with others is evidenced in plans of heterogeneous grouping, particularly in the interage grouping such as was tried at the Horace Mann-Lincoln School of Teachers College, Columbia University.[10]

3. *The organization should be designed to attain greatest flexibility in the use of time, space, staff, and field resources.* One of the difficulties of some types of organization has been that they are so rigid that they prevent the capitalization of learning opportunities which arise unexpectedly, or sacrifice the best utilization of time and resources to a system of fixed assignments, periods, and time allotments. A modern program, however, demands flexibility. While certain organizational plans and features are necessary, they should be set up in such a fashion that the teacher and pupils may use them to assist in the learning program, rather than have them tyrannize their use of time and frustrate learning activities. Even in a subject-centered school many a fine learning situation has been cut off in mid-air by the signal bell for change of classes.

Time is not the only factor involved in this consideration of flexibility. The most fruitful use of space, of the resources on the staff, and of the learning opportunities in the field should be encouraged by the organization. Without flexibility in the organization it is unlikely that these will be adequately exploited for their learning possibilities.

4. *The organization should promote unity and continuity of the learning program.* This principle verges on being self-explanatory. In recent years there has been a growing impatience with the "fragmented" learning program which tends to separate learnings into discrete categories. This trend toward greater unity is reflected in plans of "integration," and "correlation" with respect to the subject curriculum, and in the trend toward core and problem-centered curriculum plans. The plan of organization should not only provide for such unity, but should also encourage it.

5. *The organization should be in harmony with known principles of psychology, mental hygiene, and child development.* Recent writings in the field of child development, mental hygiene, and psychology have stressed the importance of emotional factors in the growth of a child. It follows that the school's organization should be designed to promote

[10] A. Wellesley Foshay, *Interage Grouping in the Elementary School,* unpublished Ed.D. project, Teachers College, Columbia University, New York, 1949.

emotional security. The graded school, with its constant threat of failure for many children, and the departmental plan, with its constant changes of teachers and classrooms throughout the day, would seem to violate this principle. Another fact of child development which has a bearing here is the continuity and inexorability of child growth. Again, the graded school is not in harmony with this factor.

6. *The organization should be simple and administratively feasible.* It would do little good to develop a theoretical plan of school organization which would prove so difficult to administer as to be impracticable. Some systems, for example, have tried quarterly promotion plans (one small system even resorted to promoting every six weeks!). Even if such plans were desirable (the authors do not consider them to be so) the amount of time and effort necessary for their administration would call their justification sharply into question. Other systems have learned the force of this principle through experience with complicated systems of ability grouping, which proved to be almost impossible to administer satisfactorily.

7. *The organization should be consistent with democratic principles and processes, and should facilitate the learning and operation of them.* Current conceptions of democracy tend to emphasize the importance of the individual's participation in the formation of the decisions and policies which are to govern his living. Organizational features of the school should, therefore, provide for the participation of the staff and pupils, and where feasible and logical, the parents, in the formulation of school policies and decisions. This is not to say that everything should be discussed and decided by everybody. It is simply to emphasize that the organization should be such that it makes possible and encourages participation where such participation is sensible and valuable.

Another aspect of this principle relates to one's concept of leadership. If one believes that democracy implies that an intellectual elite shall be facilitated in its efforts to assume positions of influence and leadership, one will support certain organizational and grouping procedures in the elementary school. However, if one believes that democracy implies responsibility for all, respect for the abilities and personalities of all, and that leadership is a shifting function demanding the joint participation of all, a different plan of organization is indicated.

8. *The organization should be sensibly and efficiently related to local conditions.* Recent studies of the factors influencing the quality of educa-

tion in the community have emphasized that the school must be closely related and sensitive to local conditions.[11] Writers in the field have emphasized that the school cannot get too far "ahead" of its community's wishes and beliefs in the matter of school policy and practice. This is not to say that an administrator should resign himself to the status quo. As one of the community's leaders, he should be helping the community to extend its educational vision, and to want something better than it already has. If he develops school practice beyond the point which the community is willing to support and sanction, however, he is likely to lose more than he gains, for experience has been that the resulting reaction is likely to lead to return to the old, and to become a strong deterrent to further progress.

ORGANIZATION OF THE MODERN SCHOOL

An examination of the principles of organization, and assessment of graded-school organization plans against them will indicate that the graded-school plans do not meet these specifications. The type which apparently comes closest to measuring up is the one teacher per grade-class. In a subject orientation, however, even this type is too rigid and undemocratic to satisfy the conditions of the foregoing criteria.

It is the opinion of the authors that the one teacher per grade-class nevertheless has the greatest possibilities for a contemporary educational program. If we eliminate the rigid time scheduling of the usual subject-centered school, this plan enables the teacher to become acquainted with the pupils, provides great flexibility, permits and encourages unity and continuity, is consistent with psychological findings, is simple and administrable, and can be most democratic. Most communities would not consider it radical, for in many communities the elementary schools are already operating under this plan, and in the others the change would probably not be difficult to make, provided the community were enlisted in the study of the problem. Under this plan time can be used as the teacher and his class deem best, and there is a maximum of flexibility possible in the use of staff members.

With such a plan of organization there should be provided those auxiliary services which are coming to be recognized as not only desir-

[11] T. R. Pierce, *Controllable Community Characteristics Related to the Quality of Education*, Bureau of Publications, Teachers College, Columbia University, New York, 1947.

able to a good learning program, but almost necessary to it: library, crafts, art, music, physical education, audio-visual services, and health. Care must be taken in the administration of these auxiliary services. Many schools have permitted them to slip into a kind of departmentalization, wherein the "special teacher" in some of these areas makes the rounds of classes (or they go to him) teaching his subject. A better arrangement is to have the personnel of these special services cast in the role of service personnel and consultants to the teachers and pupils. They should be services in fact, not subjects to be taught. As an illustration, a group of pupils may become interested in Scandinavian mythology, and decide to develop a pageant around the Siegfried Saga. They may use the librarian as consultant in finding the facts they need. The music and physical education consultants can be called in to assist in the learning of Scandinavian songs and dances to be used in the pageant. The art consultant and the crafts consultant may work together with the teacher and class in the making of the stage props and the costumes. In this situation these people are not "teachers" in the usual sense of the word: they are resources to be called upon to assist in the solution of problems important to the group.

Furthermore, the teachers in the school can use these specialists to assist them to become more proficient in these areas. Some school systems have found that it is feasible to share such resource people among two or three schools, although schools which have learned to use them to best advantage will find that they need all of the time of specialized personnel.

There are a number of school systems which have modified the one teacher per grade-class type of organization in the direction of even greater flexibility by eliminating grade lines and classifying pupils by divisions. The most common form of this is the primary unit. The basic idea of such an organization is to conceive of several "grades" (as: K-2, K-3, or 1-3) as a unit of continuous growth. Within the unit the usual concept of promotion and nonpromotion is abandoned, and teachers take children as far as they can in their growth in the three or four years the children are in the unit. In many cases the same teacher stays with a class for two or more years. There seems to be much to commend in this plan, but unfortunately the promotion concept, which is in conflict with the point of view underlying the primary unit, confronts teacher and pupils at the end of the three or four years of the unit. Nevertheless, such units are one step toward a schoolwide educational program soundly based on a valid philosophy of growth and development. This practice has arisen in the attempt to break away from the stereotype of the graded school. The study of school organization already referred to several times previously in this section indicated that 17 per cent of city school systems have at least part of the pupils in one or more schools classified in this manner. Of this 17 per cent, 76 per cent report that the practice is on the way in in that system, while but 8 per cent report that it is on the way out.[12] This is indicative of a very strong trend, which may well herald the end of the traditional graded-school organization.

Simply naming the first three grades the "primary division," however, does not constitute true reorganization. If the staff truly recognize the facts of child growth, and modify their learning program accordingly, they are likely to come to the conclusion that grade failure in the primary grades is indefensible. A conception of the first three years of school (or four, if the kindergarten is included, and it should be) as a period of continuous growth, uninterrupted by grade promotions or failures, is entirely consistent with current best educational thought. In such plans, it is not unusual for a teacher to stay with the same group for two or more years, thus providing for continuity of guidance by one who knows the characteristics, needs, and progress of the children. At this writing, such plans have been almost entirely confined to the primary grades. If successful there, it is likely that they will be tried increasingly in the intermediate grades as well.

WHAT IS AHEAD?

The past thirty years in American public education have been exciting years of educational change and experimentation. Yet there is much to indicate that we are still only in the very early stages of the transition from the graded, subject-oriented school of the century just past to a school which will serve American democracy much more functionally and effectively. If this is true, it means that the future is to be even more challenging and exciting than the past.

The trends are becoming clearer in recent years. Educators are realizing the inadequacy of the subject curriculum to meet today's needs, realizing that a more dynamic, functional, realistic, and practical learn-

[12] National Education Association, *op. cit.,* p. 19.

ing program is necessary to help children learn the technique of living in today's challenging world. Out of this realization has been slowly evolving, over the past few decades, a learning program which is coming to be more and more centered in the here-and-now living problems of children.

Because the function of school organization is to enable schools better to achieve educational objectives, the changes occurring in the nature of goals and program are slowly affecting organizational practices. The trend is toward greater flexibility; greater participation of teachers, pupils, and parents in establishing or modifying organizational features; and elimination of the graded concept in our elementary schools, with its machinery of promotion, marking, ability grouping, sets of textbooks, graded courses of study, honor awards, and the like. There is a noticeable trend to assign teachers for longer periods of time with the same group of pupils, and to classify children within "divisions" rather than in grades. Correlatively, there is a trend away from the daily time schedules so characteristic of the subject curriculum, and toward the use of class periods of indefinite length,[13] which are planned jointly by teacher and pupils.

Whether the promise of these trends will be realized relatively soon— or at all—will be decided largely by the vision, courage, and intelligence of school administrators. It is probably no exaggeration to say that the responsibility and the opportunity rest more in the hands of elementary school principals than they do in those of any other persons in our educational system. If creative innovations are to be made, it is they who must initiate them and work co-operatively with parents and teachers to carry them through. Only time will tell how that challenge will be met.

SUGGESTED READINGS

See pages 109–110.

[13] *Ibid.*, p. 22.

CHAPTER VII

ORGANIZING THE STAFF FOR SCHOOL IMPROVEMENT

A principal who is professionally minded and alert will not be satisfied to ride along with the status quo in his school. He will wish to engage in activities which will be aimed at improving the teaching and learning process, at improving the manner in which the school meets the needs of the pupils, at improving the relationships between the school and its community.

It is possible for these improvements to take place in at least three different ways. Improvements can be devised by the principal (or the central office), and put into effect by administrative edict; this is the authoritarian approach. Or, the principal can simply wait until a need for change becomes so obvious that it cannot be ignored before he takes any action; this is the laissez-faire or "crisis" method. Principals who like neither of these approaches are likely to recognize that such an important matter as curriculum change cannot be left to chance. They may know, also, that institution of change by administrative edict usually results in only superficial change, and that it rarely solves problems in a satisfactory manner. Such principals realize that long-range planning is necessary, and that if effective change is to be made, the teachers and the community will have to understand the changes by having had a part in bringing them about. To achieve these conditions creative administrators are devising organizational features to facilitate the process.

Too frequently, the charge that "democratic" administration is inefficient has arisen from a misunderstanding of what democratic administration is, how it operates. Democracy in school administration does not imply that everybody helps decide everything in a series of town-meeting-like gatherings. Certainly this would be a most inefficient manner of going about administering. Understanding of the kinds of organization best designed to facilitate democratic administration is at the present time in an early stage of development, largely because of the fact that concepts of what democratic administration is in practice are themselves not yet mature, although they have recently been broadening and deepening. Even so, there has developed considerable understanding of factors and procedures characteristic of good democratic administration, despite the fact that these procedures have yet to be widely applied in our schools. The authors have summarized these in the following characteristics of staff organization to improve the functioning of the school, and to facilitate curriculum development. Note that these are *organizational* guidelines; co-operative *methods* of improving the school's program are discussed in Chapters XXVII and XXVIII.

Characteristics of Effective Staff Organization

1. *The local school is the key unit of participation.* In school systems having but one elementary school this will be obvious. In larger urban systems, however, the policy frequently has been to make changes and policies on a system-wide basis. Their experience has indicated that this is not an effective method. The practice of having new procedures and practices developed by the central office, or by small teacher committees, and then applying them throughout the system fails to develop, on the part of the teachers who are expected to put the newly developed policies and practices into effect in their classes, those insights and understandings necessary to do this effectively. Each school, even in a large city, has its own community, and a staff and student body different from other schools in the system. For these reasons it will have its own problems, which will parallel those of the other schools in some degree, but which often are quite different and peculiar to the local school. If change is to be truly effective, it should arise from a felt need for change, deriving from the local staff's recognition of the problems it is facing. For these and other reasons, school policy-making should be of the grass roots variety, and logically should start with the local school.

2. *There should be provision for relating the work and problems of the local school to the work and problems of the system as a whole.* While the local school should be the unit of participation, it is important

that its efforts be functionally related to the system as a whole. This is not to say that there should be uniformity of practice throughout the schools of the system. There are, however, respects in which uniformity is desirable and makes for greater efficiency or economy without having adverse effects upon the individual learning programs of the several schools. Furthermore, channels of intercommunication with the other schools will enable each of the schools to know what the others are doing, and encourage the diffusion, throughout the system, of new ideas and better practices as they are developed in the individual schools.[1]

3. *The organization should encourage close interrelationships between school and community.* Because of their isolation from their communities, American public schools are constantly vexed with the problem they term "public relations." The authors firmly believe that involvement of the community in the planning, policy-making and problem-solution efforts of the school will go far to help solve this "problem." The organization developed to facilitate school improvement should therefore make provision for community participation in the process.[2]

4. *The organization should provide every staff member an opportunity to participate in making policy and action decisions.* This does not mean that all will participate in the same way. Nor, as we pointed out earlier, does it mean that all staff members must be consulted before any given decision is made. An organization which provides for committees, subcommittees, and study groups, with opportunity for the entire staff to review major proposals of these bodies, satisfies this condition.

5. *The organization should be functional.* This would seem to be obvious, but observations of the authors seem to indicate that it is honored more in the breach than in practice. A functional organization implies three conditions, at least. *First,* it deals with real problems, and does not engage in the play-acting, going-through-motions type of business so typical of student organizations. In addition to dealing with such relatively petty and superficial problems as hall monitoring, the chewing gum problem, and homework copying, it will deal with such basic issues as the development of a lifelike learning program, the place of textbooks in the school program, what to do about the promotion problem, the improvement of the system of pupil marking and evaluation, and the like.

---

[1] U. S. Office of Education, *Organization and Supervision of Elementary Education in 100 Cities,* Bulletin 1949, no. 11, U. S. Government Printing Office, Washington, D. C., pp. 13–14.

[2] See Chapters XXIV and XXV.

Second, the organization should be such that these problems can be dealt with efficiently and effectively. It is easy to sit around and talk about these problems day after day, but action will not result unless the organization provides the machinery for action. *Third,* the administration must give evidence that authority is truly shared, and that the decisions of the staff organization will have as full weight and consideration as the ideas or decisions of any administrator. The administrator who encourages staff groups to study these problems and to come to considered decisions about them after considerable time and effort, and who then reserves and exercises the right of veto over the group's decisions, demonstrates his lack of faith in democratic group procedures. Furthermore, the morale of the staff will be adversely affected, and there will develop among them a justifiable lack of confidence in the good faith of their administrators.

6. *Responsibility should be shared to avoid overloading of a few individuals.* In group activity there is an understandable tendency to let the able and willing (particularly the latter) "George" do the work. This frequently results in an unfair burden being carried by a relatively few individuals. The administrator should be alert to help his staff avoid the development of such a situation, and to develop nascent leadership ability as well.

7. *The number of committees should be kept to a functional minimum.* One of the death blows to morale is to be assigned to a committee only to learn that the committee has nothing to do or, perhaps, has only a trivial function. Standing committees should be kept to an absolute minimum, and temporary (*ad hoc*) committees should be assigned for a particular purpose when needed, to disband when their job is done.

8. *Responsibility should be voluntarily assumed, and should be delegated by the group.* There are undoubtedly many who would disagree with the "voluntary" part of this condition. However, enforced participation in the improvement program is likely to defeat its own ends. It has, first of all, an unpleasant and strongly authoritarian flavor not conducive to good staff morale. "Ah, yes," say some practical administrators, "but what are you going to do about those stubborn die-hards who disagree with 'progressive' ideas, and who will not participate voluntarily in a program of school improvement?" It is the experience of the authors that such enforced participation serves only to make these individuals even more entrenched in their conservative (if they are con-

servative) beliefs, and arouses resentment which does neither them nor the school any good. It would seem much better to proceed without them for the moment, and to seek ways by which their interests may be aroused, and their co-operation enlisted.

Although it is important that participation be voluntary, responsibilities must be delegated by the group; they should not be assumed at the will of individuals. The group should make the decisions as to who shall assume leadership for this purpose or that, and the responsibility should be terminated by the group when appropriate, or when the purpose for which it was delegated has been served.

There are undoubtedly other characteristics of effective organization, but the above seem to the authors to be of considerable importance, if not essential to success. Knowledge in this field is as yet largely empirical, and is based on relatively little experience. It awaits further analysis and research to establish more definitely those conditions which are essential.

Because the operating procedures implied in the foregoing characteristics have been clearly developed in practice in only a few situations, there are few examples reported in the literature which can be offered as illustrations. Some interesting patterns have been reported for system-wide organization,[3] but little has been written which discusses organization for growth and change within a local school.

Koopman, Miel and Misner describe an interesting organization, which is illustrated in Figure 2.[4] It will be noted that the individual school is the unit of participation. In each local school there are four major committees. The *Teacher Affairs Committee* deals with those problems which are peculiarly teachers' problems: security, professional organizations, personal and professional growth, recreational and social opportunities, and representation of the staff in school affairs. The *Curriculum Activities Committee* addresses itself primarily to the problem of the improvement of the school's learning program. The *Community*

---

[3] G. R. Koopman, A. Miel, and P. J. Misner, *Democracy in School Administration,* D. Appleton–Century Co., New York, 1943, pp. 76–119; Alfred H. Skogsberg, *Administrative Operational Patterns,* unpublished Ed.D. project, Teachers College, Columbia University, New York, 1948; Gilbert Willey, "Organizing for Curriculum Improvement," *Educational Leadership,* vol. VII, October 1949, pp. 43–48; U. S. Office of Education, *op. cit.,* pp. 11–12, and 18; H. L. Caswell and others, *Curriculum Improvement in Public School Systems,* Bureau of Publications, Teachers College, Columbia University, New York, 1950, ch. 3.

[4] Koopman, Miel, and Misner, *op. cit.,* pp. 78–92.

FIGURE 2. All-City Staff Organization Pattern

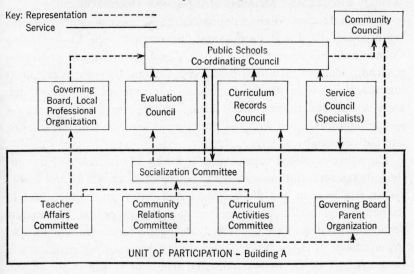

Relations Committee deals with the improvement of school-community relations, as the name would suggest. The *Socialization Committee* co-ordinates the work of the other committees, and deals with the over-all picture of the school's operation. An avenue of communication with the parents is provided by having the staff's *Community Relations Committee* represented on the *Governing Board of the Parents' Organization.*

In addition to the committee organization within the school, representation and participation in community and system-wide affairs is provided for primarily through the *Public Schools Co-ordinating Council.* Serving this committee are three councils. The *Evaluation Council* comprises representatives from each local building Socialization Committee. The *Curriculum Records Council* is made up of representatives of the local Curriculum Activities Committees. These two councils are known as the auxiliary councils. The *Service Council* includes service specialists, such as a psychologist, health workers, remedial specialists, guidance specialists, specialists in audio-visual aids, and the like. This council is headed by the Co-ordinator of Instruction, and serves all schools and the Co-ordinating Council. The membership of the central Co-ordinating Council is made up of: (1) One representative of each building Socialization Committee, (2) The superintendent of schools (who should *not* be chairman), (3) One representative of the *Governing Board of the*

Local Teachers' Organization, (4) One representative of each of the two auxiliary councils, (5) Members of the Service Council on call.

The local Teacher Affairs Committees are represented on the Governing Board of the Local Professional Organization. The Co-ordinating Council itself has representation on the *Community Council,* as has the governing board of each local parent organization. By such an organization machinery is set up for facilitating improvement activities of the local school, for relating local school activities to the entire school system, and for liaison with the professional organization, the parents, and the community at large.

The above-described organization is merely illustrative, and the authors do not set it forth as a model to be copied. Each school and school system will have to find the design of staff organization suited best to its nature and conditions. It can be said, however, that all too few schools and systems have deliberately developed functional and efficient organizations. It is the belief of the writers that such organization will be a hallmark of the well-administered school or system of the future.

Nevertheless, it must be recognized that there is a real danger of becoming so engrossed with the organization itself that one loses sight of the function. Numbers of staffs have discovered that a beautiful organizational pattern can formalize their efforts to an undesirable degree. This is likely to happen when organization gets ahead of purpose. For example, a principal may become convinced that a staff pattern of organization would be a good thing. His interest and enthusiasm may carry over to the staff (to put it euphemistically), and they may start planning an organizational pattern *before adequate consideration has been given to the problems they are organizing to study.* Organization is a tool, and the nature of the tool must be suited to the task.

It may be, therefore, that there are staffs which do not find the above-described type of organizational pattern to their liking, particularly in relatively small schools. Even in a school with a definite structure of faculty committees, there are times when different patterns may serve the purpose better. For example, there are problems which are of great concern to teachers of the youngest children, which may be of little concern to teachers of nine-, ten-, and eleven-year-olds. Problems of admission, of scheduling, of reading, of sharing of equipment, and discussion of the unique needs of children at the early childhood stage of development are a few examples of concerns which could bring such teachers together. Similarly, teachers of older children may wish to meet together to consider problems inherent in the teaching of the age levels with which they deal.

In addition, some teachers may wish to meet with specialists for different purposes. A group may wish to meet periodically with a specialist in art, or science, or music to consider the relationship of those areas or specialties to the classroom programs or to improve their own knowledge or skill in these specialized aspects of living and teaching. It is true, of course, that an over-all staff organizational structure should be flexible enough to include such activities. However, it could be unfortunate if a staff felt compelled to force their activities into some decreed—or even previously agreed-upon—pattern of organization.

This is simply to emphasize that the organization of a staff must be functional, that it can be effective only as it is developed to serve the staff's purposes. Its function is to facilitate constructive study, ready communication among members, and action. If the organization seems to "pinch" at any point, if one has to labor to fit purposes and activities into it, if it fails to provide for activity which is deemed necessary, it should be reviewed critically. Organization is justified only as it releases the creativity and energy of the staff for purposes of school improvement. When it gets in the way of that, it needs serious reconsideration.

SUGGESTED READINGS

Association for Supervision and Curriculum Development, *Fostering Mental Health in Our Schools,* National Education Association, Washington, D. C., 1950, Part I.

Caswell, Hollis L., and Foshay, A. Wellesley, *Education in the Elementary School,* 2nd ed., American Book Company, New York, 1950.

Caswell, Hollis L., and others, *Curriculum Improvement in Public School Systems,* Bureau of Publications, Teachers College, Columbia University, 1950.

Dewey, John, *Experience and Education,* The Macmillan Company, New York, 1938.

Educational Policies Commission, *Education for All American Children,* National Education Association, Washington, D. C., 1948.

Hopkins, L. Thomas, *Interaction, the Democratic Process,* D. C. Heath & Company, Boston, 1941.

Koopman, G. R., Miel, A., and Misner, P. J., *Democracy in School Administration,* D. Appleton–Century Company, New York, 1943.

Miel, Alice, *Changing the Curriculum,* D. Appleton–Century Company, New York, 1946.

Monroe, W. S., ed., *Encyclopedia of Educational Research,* rev. ed., The Macmillan Company, New York, 1950.

National Education Association, *Trends in City School Organization, 1938 to 1948,* Research Bulletin, vol. XXVII, February 1949.

Stratemeyer, F. B., Forkner, H. L., and McKim, M. G., *Developing a Curriculum for Modern Living,* Bureau of Publications, Teachers College, Columbia University, New York, 1947.

Teachers College Record, vol. L, February 1949. Entire issue entitled, "Toward Curriculum Improvement."

U. S. Office of Education, *Organization and Supervision of Elementary Education in 100 Cities,* Bulletin 1949, no. 11, U. S. Government Printing Office, Washington, D. C., 1949, pp. 8–14, 18–19, 22–23.

Part III ADMINISTERING PUPIL PERSONNEL

Some of the most perplexing problems in administering an elementary school relate to pupil personnel policies and procedures. A principal needs to be thoroughly informed on the issues involved in this phase of school administration, and in order to provide wise leadership he should develop a consistent philosophy with respect to pupil personnel practices. Moreover he should have a thorough understanding of child growth and behavior if sound personnel policies are to be formulated.

The administration of pupil personnel begins when the school makes its first contacts with preschool children; it involves admission practices and procedures; it relates to classification and grouping of children; it has to do with pupil progress and the evaluation of pupil progress; it is concerned with reporting pupil achievement and growth to parents; it includes the making and keeping of school records and it bears directly on the troublesome problem of school discipline. These topics are discussed in the pages which follow.

CHAPTER VIII

ADMISSION PRACTICES AND POLICIES

The elementary school principal has a unique opportunity and responsibility in the fact that he and his staff introduce children to their first school experience. Principals in the upper divisions of the school system receive pupils who have had six to nine or more years of schooling. In the case of these older pupils attitudes toward school have been formed, and various behavior patterns are rather well established. While it would be an exaggeration to suggest that children entering kindergarten or first grade have no strongly entrenched habits, teachers in the elementary school have the best opportunity to help the child realize his greatest potentialities.

The traditional attitude toward the problem of admitting children to school has been to establish policies that conform to the state attendance regulations and suit the convenience of the school administration. This is evidenced by the fact that rigid entrance requirements are fairly common, and that registration dates are often fixed with a very limited period of time set aside in which to provide children and parents with much needed guidance. Moreover, schools are doing very little to pave the way for richest possible experience for preschool children during their first year in school. The modern school principal takes a more enlightened view than this of the school's responsibility toward children whose formal education is still some distance away. Not only is it clear that early attention to the needs of these children and their parents will save time later for the school staff, by reducing the number of behavior problems, but what is even more important, it is considered educationally

113

sound to establish contacts with children prior to their entrance to school.

The School Census

Any thorough approach to the problem of school admission should start with a discussion of how to *find the children* who are likely to be the future pupils of the school. In a small school this problem is a fairly simple one, and the principal's knowledge of the school district may be sufficient to enable him to record the necessary data about children of preschool age, together with information relating to their parents, without a periodic house-to-house canvas. In urban centers, the problem of securing the information essential for wise planning is somewhat more complicated. States generally provide for a school census. The requirements are not uniform throughout the various commonwealths, and the results are not always satisfactory. The census is often taken in August, and since schools begin early in September, the data are not assembled in time to serve the immediate needs of the principal and his staff. Moreover, while most of the information collected has real value for the schools, the scope of the inquiries is limited, and many important matters are seldom treated. For this reason the legally required census needs to be supplemented. This can be done by employing qualified school employees to take the census and by adding to the regular census forms, questions which are designed to call forth responses on special matters of importance to the principal and staff of the local school. Skillful interrogators in the process of taking the census could also uncover lay reactions toward the school which, if dealt with early, might make children's lives happier. There is a great deal of misunderstanding in neighborhoods regarding the management and the program of the local school, particularly among those parents whose children are too young to attend school. Some of these parents have fears that are unfounded or notions that are highly unrealistic. Census takers, if composed of school personnel, could do a lot to allay parental fears and could establish a relationship with parents which, if followed up, would have real educational significance. The role of census taker should be expanded to include giving out, as well as collecting, information.

Some school systems permit upper-grade children to assist in keeping census data up-to-date, and in this way provide them with the opportunity to render important community service. At the present time, this procedure appears to be more practical in suburban districts than in large cities. It deserves the thoughtful consideration of school administrators since it offers one more opportunity of providing real work experiences for elementary school children. From the standpoint of future planning, it is important that census data be kept up-to-date and that the information be filed in such a manner as to be readily accessible to school employees who have occasion to use it.

Teacher-Parent Conferences

Finding and cataloguing data, however, are but the first steps in the school's effort to reach young children. The next job is to provide for conferences, visits, and other forms of communication so as to insure a continuing relationship between home and school. For the job of counseling parents and gaining insights as to the behavior, personality, and health of preschool children can be done adequately only through close association with the home over an extended period of time.

It is important that certain school employees confer with parents and come to know the children involved. Among these are the school nurse, whose early advice on immunization and other health measures will usually be welcomed. The kindergarten teacher and the visiting teacher, if one is available, should visit the home and establish friendly relationships—imparting information, learning something of the interests and aspirations of the parents, and coming to know the behavior patterns of children. It would be well if the principal would recognize this group of parents in planning his program of public relations and devote some time to discussing with them the organization and facilities of the school. Some explanation also of those school policies which are likely to be of most interest to parents should be made at this time. Parents of preschool children might be invited to spend an evening at the school to see the building and equipment, and to ask questions regarding the program of activities and studies.

Other Means of Informing Parents

Face to face contacts are, without doubt, the most satisfactory avenue of interpreting the school to the parents of preschool children and of collecting those facts about parents and children which it is essential for the school to have if suitable provisions are to be made for the pupils' first day at school. But personal visiting is time consuming and must therefore be limited. Other means of communication can be employed to supplement the scheduled visits of teachers and principal. Among these are bulletins, motion-picture films, specially prepared reading lists, parent-teacher association programs, and the school newspaper. Once the contact has been established, parents should be urged to take advantage of those resources which promise to make them better informed and wiser partners in the joint task of educating children.

Age of Admission

The question naturally arises as to when a child is ready for school, at what age and at what maturity level. This problem has been as perplexing to educators as the question of what education is of most worth. The states have not generally set the age limits below which communities are not privileged to go in providing education at public expense. It is true that the state has refused to provide financial support below certain age or grade levels, but it has left to the local school district the matter of how early pupils can be admitted to school. This has resulted in a wide variety of practices. A few school systems have extended the school program downward to care for children as young as two or three. Most school systems, however, provide for entrance to kindergarten or grade 1 somewhere between age four years seven months and six years.

The question of entrance age is closely related to the economic resources of school districts and the willingness of the public to support schools below the traditional age limits. Since nursery school provision usually implies the enlargement of school buildings and the employment of additional teachers, it is fought vigorously by taxpayers' associations and those who view increasing school budgets with alarm. Until greater public support can be won for the nursery school movement, school systems will do well to set the minimum age at five years by the opening of school. Since experience seems to indicate that children younger than five are generally too immature to profit from the typical school program, this admission age policy has much to commend it. Provision should, of course, be made for exceptions since, as far as resources permit, the welfare of children should be the governing principle underlying all school policies. A policy which would allow children of unusual maturity to enter school as early as four years nine months would add enough flexibility to care for most situations. In deciding on the admission of those children between age four years nine months and five years whose maturity is doubtful, appropriate tests should be given and several competent judgments should be secured. The California Test of Mental Maturity and the Binet are excellent instruments to use in discovering the readiness of children for kindergarten. When supplemented with the kindergarten teacher's observations of the child in group play, and with the psychologist's judgment after testing and interviewing the child, few mistakes will be made.

Need for Nursery Schools

The foregoing proposal will not alone satisfy the school needs of young children. Prekindergarten opportunities are badly needed throughout the United States, and the elementary school principal will do well to urge parents and other friends of education to support a program that would give children of three and four years of age the experiences and opportunities which have been found to be highly profitable in their growth and development. With the scientific knowledge now available in the child study field, teachers of young children are in a position to open up the major personality avenues of their pupils and pave the way for happier and more useful lives. Surely there is enough money available to achieve this goal, once the populace are aware of its benefits. The principal will have to judge for himself the readiness of his district for this downward extension of school opportunities. His leadership will in the long run have considerable influence on the community's decision to have or not to have nursery schools.

First Days at School

After the requirements for admission have been determined, the problem of how best to introduce children to this new experience of going to school presents itself. Traditionally, children without prior school experience have appeared at the school house with their parents on the first day of school or on a day specifically set aside for registration. But little thought has been given to their induction. Children in many schools are still left to "sink or swim." Some pupils make a good adjustment despite their early fears and the feeling of strangeness which a sudden and complete change of environment inevitably brings. It is not at all unlikely that the unfavorable reactions of many adults to their early school experiences are due to faulty admission procedures. In recent years, educators have become increasingly sensitive to the unfortunate effects of this traditional method of introducing children to school and have employed more humane and wiser means of acquainting children with the school program. In the first place, the process of entering school is more gradual than formerly. It is difficult, in a system that maintains a continuous contact with parents of preschool children, to know just when the shift takes place. To be sure, there is a day when school formally begins, but the activities are so in harmony with prior experiences that the child is not overwhelmed with the novelty and strangeness of the school atmosphere. Moreover, in the modern school, children entering kindergarten for the first time do not stay in school all day. On the contrary, they remain only a few hours each day for the first week, and fall into the class routine by degrees. Account is also taken of individual differences, with the result that some children are given more time to adjust to the daily schedule than others. In short, informality and flexibility are the basic elements in the program of induction. A small number of school systems are experimenting with a stagger system by which a few children appear the first day for a short time, with an equal number added on subsequent days, the whole process stretching out for a week or two. This gives the teacher and her assistants time to observe the behavior and needs of individual children. Since the problem of pupil adjustment is particularly acute in the kindergarten, the stagger arrangement is one way, at least, of partially resolving it.

Probaby the wisest approach to the whole admissions problem extending from census enumeration to the registration of pupils in school, is to invite teachers and parents to join with the principal in determining the procedures to be followed. Within the framework of the law and the local school board regulations, policies suited to the special needs of the district can be formulated. This process is almost certain to be an educative one for all parties concerned.

SUGGESTED READINGS

American Association of School Administrators, *Schools for a New World,* Twenty-fifth Yearbook, National Education Association, Washington, D. C., 1946.

Andrus, Ruth, "Next Steps in the Public Schools," *Progressive Education,* vol. XXIII, February 1946, pp. 135–138.

Association for Childhood Education, *Four and Five Year Olds at School,* Washington, D. C., 1943 (bulletin).

————, *What Is Happening to the Children,* Washington, D. C., 1946 (bulletin).

Baruch, Dorothy, *Parents and Children Go to School,* Scott, Foresman and Company, Chicago, 1939.

Frank, Lawrence K., "Community Planning for Children," *Journal of American Association of University Women,* vol. XXXIX, Winter 1946, pp. 77–80.

Hildreth, Gertrude, "Age Standards for First Grade Entrance," *Childhood Education,* vol. XXIII, September 1946, pp. 22–27.

Indiana Department of Public Instruction, *A Good Start in School,* Indianapolis, 1944 (bulletin).

U. S. Office of Education, *Legislation Concerning Early Childhood Education,* Pamphlet no. 62, Washington, D. C., 1935.

————, *School Census, Compulsory Education, Child Labor, State Laws and Regulations,* Bulletin 1945, no. 1, U. S. Government Printing Office, Washington, D. C.

————, "State Legislative Action for Young Children," *School Life,* vol. XXVIII, January 1946, p. 30.

CHAPTER IX

CLASSIFICATION AND GROUPING

ABILITY GROUPING

Classification of pupils has been an important responsibility of the principal since the graded school came into being in the early decades of the last century.

In schools which are relatively small the problem of classification is limited to sorting pupils into not more than eight or nine groups, the number depending upon how many grades there are in the school. In larger schools it is necessary to have more than one class in each grade, and the problem of grouping requires much more of the administrator's time and energy. These grade groups and classes within grades often represent the judgment of principal and staff as to the relative achievement, and sometimes the capacity of the various pupils in the school. The latter are assigned to the appropriate class on the basis of the amount of so-called essential knowledge which they are assumed to possess.

It would be misleading to suggest that school administrators generally classify their pupils with any such precision as is implied in the foregoing paragraph. They admittedly do not know how much knowledge Johnny possesses or how well prepared he is for the work of the next grade. Therefore, they compromise with the achievement standard and take account of effort, conduct, and age along with evidences of subject-matter mastery and acquisition of skills. But their thinking is still conditioned by the old grade-school philosophy.

Most of the attempts at grouping during the twenties and thirties were based primarily on intelligence and achievement test results (or a combination of them) with staff judgments being given some consideration. During this period fast, slow, and normal classes were organized and the work regulated according to the capacity of the pupils to do it. In some schools a few children spent eight or nine years in the six elementary grades, some pupils spent six, and a few spent less than six. In other schools, children were taught widely different subject matter but spent one year in a grade, the achievement standards being adjusted to meet the varying abilities of pupils. The chief emphasis in all these schools, though they attempted to recognize individual differences in learning capacity, was mastery of subject matter.

Educators in recent years have stressed the need for broadening the goals of education to include, among the aims, the development of skills in democratic living. Moreover, they have questioned the grouping arrangements employed in many schools because they did not minister to the needs of the child as a "whole." As Smith and Dolio have so well stated, the objective of grouping is to place "each individual within a group in which he will work better, where he will have a sense of belonging and status, where his mental health will be safeguarded and improved."[1]

To some degree then, similarity in intelligence or subject-matter mastery appears to be giving way to other traits as criteria in grouping. From the standpoint of a school principal who is faced annually (sometimes oftener) with the necessity of assigning hundreds of pupils to class groups, the problem is more than a theoretical one. Some practical procedures have to be adopted and a principal needs to be able to justify his policies.

The problem can be well illustrated and the alternatives appraised by assuming a situation in which chronological age is accepted as the basic criterion for determining grade status but where 75 ten-year olds have to be assigned to three groups. The principal is here faced with several possible choices, among which are the following:

1. He could give standardized achievement tests in the fundamental subjects and place the 25 most advanced pupils in group 1, the next highest 25 in group 2, and the balance in group 3.

2. He could give intelligence and achievement tests, get estimates

[1] Othanel Smith and A. J. Dolio, "Recent Developments in Grouping—A Minimum Bibliography," *Educational Leadership,* vol. IV, March 1947, pp. 403–411.

from the pupils' former teachers as to their future scholastic promise, and combine the foregoing information into a single score or rating for each pupil; rank the pupils from high to low; and divide them into three groups, placing the highest third in group 1, the next highest third in group 2, and the balance in group 3.

3. He could list the 75 children alphabetically by name, assigning the first 25 to one class, the next 25 to a second group, and the balance to a third class.

4. He could draw the pupils' names out of a hat (this good old American custom is employed frequently in other walks of life to avoid any show of favoritism), and assign the first 25 drawn to teacher A, the second 25 to teacher B, and the last 25 to teacher C.

5. He could secure detailed facts and judgments about pupils from teachers, parents, children, and from the pupils' cumulative record cards, and from sociometric studies. From an analysis of these data, assign pupils tentatively to the groups which seem to the teachers involved and to the principal to be the best classification.

Other alternatives (beyond those mentioned above) may occur to the principal when faced with the responsibility of pupil classification. His own philosophy regarding grouping, together with the point of view of the members of his teaching staff, plus perhaps the judgment of the superintendent of schools, will influence the methods employed. It is the opinion of the authors that the soundest grouping arrangement listed among the alternatives just described is number 5. According to this plan, a pupil would be assigned to a group and to a teacher which, in the judgment of the principal and his staff, were most likely to serve the pupil's interests best and enable him to measure up most nearly to his maximum potentialities. Moreover, the assignment would be tentative and subject to change if experience proved that the placement was less promising than was thought originally. Flexibility is a fundamental feature in a sound grouping plan. Not only must the needs of an individual pupil be assessed in placing him in a group, but the welfare of his classmates must also be considered. The public school has a first responsibility to the majority of pupils, and administrative policies including grouping, should be consistent with this general principle. Rarely, in classifying pupils, will it be necessary to choose between the welfare of the individual and the welfare of the group.

Advantages of Heterogeneous Grouping

No one can speak with certainty about the superiority of heterogeneous grouping over ability grouping or some form of so-called homogeneous grouping. But there is much to be said in favor of spreading intelligence and aptitude throughout each of the three classes as indicated in the illustration earlier. Each room should have its share of the bright, the average, and the slow learners. Moreover, in grouping pupils consideration should be given to the distribution of their interests and skills. If all the aggressive personalities are placed in one group and the timid, retiring children are grouped together, there is less chance, or so it seems to the authors, for "educational osmosis" to occur than in situations where a variety of personality types are housed in the same room.

Basic to the idea of distributing, rather than concentrating talent, is the belief that children learn from one another as well as from the teacher or from instructional materials. The less able learn from the more able, and strange as it may seem, the high I.Q. group often learn much from those with lower scholastic abilities, particularly in learnings which are not primarily intellectual, but are, nevertheless, highly important. Pupils who are gifted in intellectual matters do not have a corner on *all* knowledge and skill. Whereas good things may tend to go together, the exceptions are so numerous and the correlations so low as to invalidate the application of this generalization to grouping children in school.

The program of the modern school is not limited to teaching children academic knowledge and scholastic skills. Rather, it includes learnings and the development of appreciations in many areas not included in the old school curriculum. However true it may be to say that pupils of high intelligence tend to do well in arithmetic, reading, and the social studies, it is not valid to extend this generalization to include subjects for which standardized achievement tests have not been devised. Intelligence seems to play a much smaller role in achievement in such important areas of learning as esthetics and art, shop activities, musical skills, development of spiritual values, human relations skills, and certain other fundamental phases of a good school program.

From the standpoint of pupil achievement, then, there are advantages in grouping children in such a fashion that a cross section of the pupil population in each grade will be found in every class. Unplanned grouping, of course, is not so likely to result in a favorable learning situation as is the carefully studied arrangement recommended above.

Relation of Grouping Arrangements to Parent Co-operation

Other advantages not related directly to pupil achievement are present in heterogeneous grouping. Many parents hope that their children will enjoy a measure of success in life far beyond that which they themselves have experienced. Parents want their children to have at least equal opportunity with other children for social intercourse, and any grouping device which places their children in classes reserved for pupils of low ability and of low economic circumstances will constitute a barrier to developing good school relationships with many of the homes in the community. Not only will parents see in such a plan a threat to their hopes for their child's future, but what is worse, they will tend to nag the innocent offspring who had no voice at all in the placement decision. Parents prod in the hope that the child's achievement may be improved enough to warrant promotion to a faster learning group. Needless to say, this bodes ill for the child's adjustment. While proponents of homogeneous or ability grouping can point to questionnaire studies which suggest that parents, in general, appear to be satisfied when their children are grouped according to their aptitude or skill, it is a rare parent who really looks with favor upon a school that classifies his child as a slow learner. Naturally, many parents of children in "fast" groups are complimented by the placement policy. It is a reflection, as they see it, of their own aptitude and ability. But apart from parents of children in this high ability class, there is bound to be much unhappiness created through homogeneous grouping.

Social Implications

Not only is the cross-section plan of grouping more favorable than ability grouping for building constructive home-school relationships; it also promises more for democratic society generally. Basic to the American way of life is understanding and respect for the rights of the other fellow. Our society depends for its life blood upon co-operation, and while insuring a rich opportunity for individual accomplishment, it is imperative that our schools, as far as they have influence in the matter, should guard against the development of caste systems, whether economic, social, or intellectual. There is a tendency to forget the fact that the public elementary school is the one big melting pot into which 90 per cent of our children are placed. The organization of the school, and its policies and practices, should contribute to the attainment and preservation of our country's highest ideals, not merely those found in contemporary society. The school should be a model democracy, an example of corporate life at its best.

Even if one were to grant that ability grouping may not lead inevitably to class distinctions and heighten feelings of superiority or inferiority, there is in the arrangement, as it is commonly administered, the danger that these undemocratic results will follow. An aristocracy of brains is about as objectionable in its effects as an aristocracy of wealth. Intellectual snobbery creates rifts and is an obstacle in the way of co-operation. Segregation of children throughout the most formative period of their lives, according to some arbitrary criterion of ability, is likely to produce a hiatus in the sympathies and understandings of people later on in life.

The argument that good will, understanding, and co-operation are by no means characteristic of the products of schools where heterogeneous grouping is in vogue, is not an admissable argument against the use of this scheme in favor of some other brand. It is merely indicative of the need for greater stress on these objectives. A pattern of class organization which itself is consistent with the basic aims of democracy is certainly the most reasonable one to adopt. Harry Emerson Fosdick has expressed beautifully in another connection, the ideal which should stand uppermost in the minds of principals and their staff members in approaching the problem of grouping. Fosdick says:

> Primarily, democracy is the conviction that there are extraordinary possibilities in ordinary people, and if we throw wide the doors of opportunity so that all boys and girls can bring out the best that is in them, we will get amazing results from unlikely sources. . . . Beethoven was the son of a consumptive mother, herself a daughter of a cook and a drunken father. . . . Faraday, one of the greatest experimenters of all times, was born over a stable, his father an invalid blacksmith and his mother a common drudge. Such facts as these underlie democracy. That is why with all its discouraging blunders, we must everlastingly believe in it.[2]

Relation of Grouping to Individual Differences

Much of the argument about grouping has centered around the fact of individual differences. It is contended, and with some logic, that greater

[2] Quoted with the permission of Dr. Fosdick.

attention can be given to these needs if the variability in pupil ability and achievement is kept narrow. It is easier for a teacher to make the necessary adjustments to pupils who deviate in their achievement from the norm, both above and below, if they do not deviate too markedly. Students of this problem have reached widely different conclusions as to the differences found in teaching difficulty between classes where pupils are grouped heterogeneously, and those where the basis of grouping has been a measure of ability or achievement. Investigators have repeatedly reported wide ranges in achievement among so-called homogeneous groups of pupils.

It appears that the variability in achievement in ability groups in grades which have three sections each is about 83 per cent as great as in unselected groups.[3] While it could be argued that this is an indication that ability grouping facilitates teaching and provides greater opportunity for the consideration of individual pupil needs, there are other considerations inherent in the scheme of homogeneous grouping which have to be weighed in reaching a decision as to its efficiency.

It may be somewhat easier for a teacher to instruct a fairly "homogeneous" group (as measured by intellectual ability or achievement) where the curriculum consists largely of the traditional school subjects and where school objectives are narrowly conceived. A modern school which has the interests of the "whole" child at heart will find little evidence to support ability grouping when viewed from the angle of administering to individual needs of pupils or of making the teacher's task less arduous. In fact, as one examines the findings reported by students of the grouping problem, he is led inescapably to the conclusion that no final answer to the matter of classifying pupils is to be found in the statistical approaches to the problem. Therefore, the case must of necessity rest on the philosophical views of educators.

Trend Away from Ability Grouping

That there has been a gradual shift over the past few decades in the attitude of school administrators and teachers toward pupil classification seems rather certain.

Detailed statistics showing the prevalence of various grouping arrangements are not available, but there is some evidence pointing to the

---

[3] Henry J. Otto, "Organization and Administration of Elementary Education," in Walter S. Monroe, ed., *Encyclopedia of Educational Research,* rev. ed., The Macmillan Company, New York, 1950, pp. 377–378.

conclusion that ability grouping in the elementary grades is not as popular as it was two decades ago. In 1929 when Otto[4] made a survey of grouping practices, he found that approximately two-thirds of the city school systems of 2500 to 25,000 population employed some form of ability grouping. A recent study made by the Research Division of the National Education Association[5] of cities 2500 to over 100,000 population indicates that only about half (53 per cent) of the cities use ability grouping as an adjustment device. Since size of city appears to have direct bearing on grouping practices—the larger the city the greater the popularity of ability grouping—the above comparison is not entirely valid. However, an analysis of the data collected by the Research Division of the National Education Association shows clearly that the percentage of cities of less than 100,000 which now use ability grouping is consistently well under the proportion reported in the 1929 study.

Interage Grouping

A few students of the grouping problem are looking with favor upon an arrangement that insures even wider heterogeneity than that advocated by the authors. It is called "interage grouping" and is based on the assumption that the essential quality in a learning environment is *difference* rather than *similarity*. While in classifying pupils the advocates of this plan would undoubtedly place some limitations upon differences in age, physical development, and achievement, still the class group as finally established would be composed of children of different ages, interests, abilities and accomplishments. To date what little evidence there is regarding the effectiveness of interage grouping does not appear to support the claims and hopes of its proponents.[6]

While there is need for further experimentation and research before final judgments are passed on grouping schemes, the principal who is faced with the necessity of immediate action will do well to use chronological age as the basic factor and, as far as possible, take account of individual needs and requirements. The goal should be to place every child in an environment in which he can have a wholesome status and

[4] Henry J. Otto, *Elementary School Organization and Administration*, D. Appleton–Century Company, New York, 1944, p. 187.
[5] National Education Association, *Trends in City School Organization, 1938 to 1948*, Research Bulletin, vol. XXVII, no. 1, February 1949, p. 17.
[6] See A. Wellesley Foshay, *Interage Grouping in the Elementary School*, unpublished Ed.D. project, Teachers College, Columbia University, 1948.

where his relationships with other pupils and with the group as a whole seem most likely to contribute to his all-around development.

Grouping within the Class

No matter what plan of classification is adopted, there will be need for grouping within classes to meet the requirements of individual pupils. In fact, competent teachers have always employed this device to accomplish their aims. The task of the teacher is to provide an environment in which all children are profitably occupied. Sometimes, a third of the group may be reading under the direct guidance of the teacher, while the other two-thirds are elsewhere in the room or in the school building engaged in other tasks. Some of the latter may be employed in construction work on a class project; others may be doing number work at the board; still others may be drawing or painting. When the occasion suggests, these latter children will sit with the teacher, receiving her individual attention. An important feature of a modern school is that account is taken of the fact that children learn from other children through conversation and observation; that they also learn in the process of teaching other children; and that they learn from materials of instruction and from other environmental factors quite apart from the teacher. Understanding and acceptance of this fact will lead to markedly different practices in classrooms than those which too often obtain.

The fact that a cross-section type of grouping is adopted does not preclude, upon occasion, the grouping of children with special aptitudes and interests. School clubs are designed to meet this need and should be encouraged. There is also much to be said in favor of providing opportunities for children of different ages to associate with one another in constructive school experiences. Understanding and co-operation are fostered through these interrelationships. The auditorium program, the safety patrol activities, the work of clubs mentioned earlier, and student council responsibilities, provide a natural avenue for bringing pupils of various ages into group relationships that are essential for all-round development.

Some Conclusions and Suggestions

The school administrator faced with the practical problem of grouping children for instructional purposes can make certain logical conclusions from the foregoing discussion:

1. Some type of grouping is necessary, and a principal cannot escape making decisions with respect to pupil classification.

2. The criterion to apply in deciding on the adoption of a particular grouping arrangement is the effect it will have upon the welfare of the whole child, not just the promise it holds for his scholastic improvement.

3. Ability grouping is an appendage of the subject-centered curriculum and is inconsistent with modern concepts of education in which the all-round development of the individual pupil is central.

4. There is little evidence to support the claim that schools using ability grouping can deal more successfully with the problem of individual differences than where heterogeneous groups are used. This is especially true in schools having a modern program of education. Studies have shown that achievement ranges are wide under all grouping schemes. Individualization cannot be achieved through grouping but rests upon other considerations.

5. Planned heterogeneous grouping arrangements make for better parent co-operation; they promise more for democratic society; they are more consistent with the aims of modern education.

6. Grouping procedures should permit wide flexibility and pupils should be moved freely from group to group when circumstances warrant. The school should be organized so that ample opportunity is provided for older and younger children to work and play together. Special interest clubs, auditorium programs, and committee activities are but a few of the phases of school life where age and class barriers should be broken down.

7. Grouping within the class holds great promise for increasing instructional efficiency, and if wisely administered avoids the dangers inherent in most ability grouping devices.

MEETING THE NEEDS OF THE MENTALLY HANDICAPPED AND THE MENTALLY GIFTED

A special aspect of the problem of grouping is the question of how best to provide for the education of children who deviate markedly from the normal in intelligence. Advocates of grouping will maintain, of course, that these children should be educated in special groups. Even among those who do not advocate special grouping for the great majority of children, there are many who consider these children exceptions, and advocate placing them in special classes or schools. Finally, num-

bers of educators believe that none but those children who are so subnormal as to constitute special problems should be placed in "special"
classes. The elementary school principal should be acquainted with these
different viewpoints, with their reasons, and be able to assist his staff in
making intelligent decisions for the school.

Who They Are

Actually, there is no perfect consensus among educators as to the
limits of so-called "normal" intelligence. This is because of the fact that
in the population at large the range of intelligence is continuous; that is,
the differences are differences in *degree* rather than differences in kind.
Nevertheless, it is to be recognized that there are considerable numbers
of children who deviate sufficiently from the great majority to pose
significant problems for those responsible for their education. There are,
in particular, four such groups: "gifted" children, "slow-learning" children, "mentally retarded" children (sometimes called "mentally handicapped"), and "mentally defective" children (also sometimes called
"mentally handicapped," and popularly termed "feeble-minded").

Giftedness. The usual definition which seems to be used by most authorities for intellectual giftedness is in terms of the Stanford-Binet intelligence quotient, and ranges from I.Q. 120 to 130. In Los Angeles[7] and
Cleveland,[8] for example, the lower limit of such "giftedness" is I.Q. 125,
while in Birmingham, Alabama, the line is drawn at I.Q. 120.[9] In addition, most of those responsible for the selection of gifted children for one
purpose or another—usually grouping—take a number of other characteristics into account. In Detroit, for example, Baker considered ten
factors.[10] In Birmingham, ". . . candidates for these classes have been
selected from all schools in the city on the basis of teachers' and principals' recommendations, achievement test results, physical condition, and
psychological examination records indicating an I.Q. of 120 or above."[11]

One other type of giftedness is that expressing itself in special talents

[7] Department of Elementary School Principals, *Meeting Special Needs of the Individual Child,* Nineteenth Yearbook, National Education Association, Washington, D. C., 1940, p. 388.

[8] *Ibid.,* p. 398.

[9] *Ibid.,* p. 408.

[10] H. J. Baker, *Introduction to Exceptional Children,* The Macmillan Company,
New York, 1945, p. 283.

[11] Department of Elementary School Principals, *op. cit.,* p. 408.

in a given field, such as art, music, or mechanical skill. This may appear in children of otherwise mediocre attainments, although such talents are more common among children who are intellectually superior.

Subnormality. As in the case of giftedness, the limits of subnormality are not exactly defined. Most writers in the field define it primarily in terms of I.Q., and consider I.Q. 90 to be the dividing line between "normal" and "subnormal" intelligence, although other factors are usually considered. Children of "subnormal" intelligence are then further divided into three major categories: "slow-learning," or "mentally backward" (popularly termed "dull" children) fall in the I.Q. range 70 (or 75) to 89; those in the range of 50 to 69 (or 74) are termed "mentally retarded," "mentally handicapped," or "orthogenic backward"; those of less than I.Q. 50 are commonly known as "feeble-minded" or "mentally defective." These terms are used loosely, however, and one cannot be certain of their meaning unless they are defined by the person using them.

Educational and psychological authorities are agreed that children whose test intelligence is below I.Q. 50 are not educable in the usual school situation, and that institutionalization will serve them better. In fact, a number of states legally permit schools to exclude such children. The elementary school principal should know the relevant regulations and procedures in his state.

The great majority of educators are also of the opinion that children of the mentally retarded group (I.Q. 50 to 69 or 74) should be placed in special classes if at all possible. Since these children constitute less than 2 per cent of the total population, however, it is seldom possible to establish such classes in small school systems.

There is considerable difference of opinion concerning children in the "slow-learning" category. Some educators strongly advocate grouping them separately for instruction; others are equally emphatic that such separation is usually undesirable. Reasons for these viewpoints will be considered after a discussion of the problem of identifying mentally subnormal and superior children.

Identifying Mentally Atypical Children

If it is necessary, for any reason, to identify children of superior or subnormal ability, the principal should be acquainted with the methods commonly used. They will be sketched but briefly here, as detailed discussions can be found in the literature relating to the problem.[12]

The first step is usually a screening procedure, designed to select those children among whom true cases of mental retardation or giftedness may be found. Children overage or underage for grade, for example, will be candidates for further study. Group achievement and intelligence tests will also show up possible cases. It is to be stressed, however, that group tests have neither sufficient validity nor reliability to use them as the sole basis for making the decision. For example, a child of above normal intelligence, but with a severe reading handicap, is likely to do poorly on a group intelligence test, because such tests usually depend somewhat upon ability to read. They are nevertheless useful and economical means of screening, eliminating the necessity of administering individual intelligence tests to all children in the class, a time-consuming and costly process which is very rarely justified. When these "coarse" screening measures have been completed, there will have been selected a relatively small group of children, some of whom may be "gifted" or "subnormal" according to the local definition. To these children should be administered an individual intelligence test of the Stanford-Binet type. In the administration of these tests (usually given by a psychologist) the children suspected of being subnormal should be observed with particular care, for there are numbers of cases on record where the poor test performances were the result, not of mental retardation, but of emotional reactions to test situations. In one study, for example, it was observed that children from the homes of higher socioeconomic status tend to respond positively to test situations, try to make good, and generally do. Children of the lower socioeconomic levels, on the other hand, accustomed to "a family and class structure in which failure, worry, and frustration are common," and where academic success has often been abandoned as a goal not worth striving for, failed to do well on intelligence tests.[13]

It can be seen, then, that identification is not a simple procedure, and

[12] Baker, *op. cit.,* pp. 282–284; Herbert A. Carroll, *Genius in the Making,* McGraw-Hill Book Company, Inc., New York, 1940, ch. I; William B. Featherstone, *Teaching the Slow Learner,* rev. ed., Bureau of Publications, Teachers College, Columbia University, New York, 1951, chs. I and II; Henry H. Goddard, *School Training of Gifted Children,* World Book Company, Yonkers, N. Y., 1928, ch. 9; Arch O. Heck, *Education of Exceptional Children,* McGraw-Hill Book Company, Inc., New York, 1940, ch. 26 and pp. 360–361.

[13] August B. Hollingshead, *Elmtown's Youth,* John Wiley and Sons, New York, 1949, pp. 175–176.

must be done with care. Unfortunately, many schools and systems have not realized this, with the result that classes of mentally subnormal children, in particular, often have included not only children of low intellectual powers, but children of normal or above-normal intelligence who have emotional, social, and educational handicaps. The authors have observed such classes, in which were placed children who had been "discipline" problems in their regular classes; these children were somewhat retarded in their achievement, but were average or above in their test intelligence. It is most unfortunate to permit this to happen, for under such conditions the special class has become nothing but a "dumping ground" for the problems the regular teachers have been unable or unwilling to cope with. This frequently results in an almost impossible learning situation in the special class, with the special-class teacher hard put to maintain a semblance of order, let alone conduct a fruitful learning program.

One must be cautious against relying on test I.Q. alone. There are other factors which are most important in these children's learning. Sometimes such physical handicaps as poor eyesight or hearing cause poor learning and poor test performance. Glandular conditions, malnutrition, and emotional factors all should be carefully considered, as it is often they, rather than subnormal intelligence, which are responsible for the pupil's poor showing in school.

Shall These Children Be Segregated for Learning?

The development and wide application of group achievement and intelligence tests after World War I impressed upon educators the fact of individual variation in school accomplishment and intellectual ability. Growing out of this was a concern for the education of children who deviate markedly from the "normal" in the ability to master school subjects, and various grouping schemes proposed to achieve an education suited to the needs of all children were one by-product of this concern. As a result, many school systems now have a system of "special" classes for the subnormal and the gifted. New York has its "CRMD" classes—Classes for Children with Retarded Mental Development; Cleveland has its "Major Work Classes" for intellectually gifted children; Chicago has experimented with "rapidly moving" classes for superior children; Los Angeles has "opportunity rooms" for children of superior ability; Baltimore has its "Occupational Classes" for slow-learning children.

Practically every major city, and many smaller systems, have attempted provisions for intellectually subnormal and gifted children in sincere, commendable, and fruitful efforts to provide better education for all.

There are a number of educators, however, who have objected to separating slow-learning and gifted children from regular classes for learning purposes. They have pointed to the fact that there is no conclusive evidence of such a procedure resulting in better learning of subject matter; that it is conducive to conceit and snobbery on the part of the gifted and to feelings of inferiority and hopelessness on the part of the subnormal; that it may actually impede attention to individual differences; that it is unrealistic and unlifelike; and that it is in contradiction of the democratic philosophy as it is conducive to an aristocracy of the intellectually elite.[14] This is by no means an exhaustive listing of the objections which have been raised against the practice.

On the other hand, advocates of placing these pupils in special groups claim that instruction can thus be adapted to their ability; that they are less likely to be impressed with their difference from normal children when placed with groups of their intellectual peers than if left in regular classes; that in life we are likely to associate ourselves with others of like status and ability; that such grouping is democratic in that it provides intellectually exceptional children with better opportunities to realize their full development.[15] Again, these do not exhaust arguments for this point of view.

It is readily apparent, therefore, that the question of whether or not to place intellectually subnormal and superior children in special classes for instruction is still a moot one. The research evidence is inconclusive. The differences of opinion on the part of writers and administrators seem to be based primarily on philosophical considerations. Those who have organized and worked with such special classes are generally enthusiastic about them, and claim educational results beyond those which are ordinarily attained with these children in regular classes. Others, by differentiating instruction within regular classes, claim results just as

[14] See J. R. McGaughy, *An Evaluation of the Elementary School,* The Bobbs-Merrill Company, Indianapolis, 1937, pp. 247–275; and *The Grouping of Pupils,* Thirty-fifth Yearbook of the National Society for the Study of Education, Public School Publishing Co., Bloomington, Ill., ch. IV, by B. Raup; ch. V, by F. S. Chapin and M. I. Conway; and ch. VII, by H. B. Alberty and O. G. Brim.

[15] See *The Grouping of Pupils,* ch. XI, by Boyer; Department of Elementary School Principals, *op. cit.,* chs. V and VI; H. H. Goddard, *School Training of Gifted Children,* World Book Company, Yonkers, N. Y., chs. III, IV, and V; Arch O. Heck, *op. cit.,* pp. 398–403.

good, without the psychological ill effects they see inherent in special grouping.

Here again it seems to the authors to be profitable to consider the relationship of the problem to the general objectives and organization of our schools. If the objective of education is to be primarily the mastering of a basic minimum of a curriculum of essentials in the shortest amount of time, a grouping plan enabling children to proceed at their own rates seems reasonable. In the usual graded school, with a predetermined curriculum, with oversized classes, with a preparation-for-high-school viewpoint, and with the usual grade-standards promotion policy, it has not been common to find instruction differentiated so as adequately to meet the needs of the exceptionally slow-learning or the exceptionally bright. Harap points out, for example, that relatively few courses of study have had provisions or suggestions for the adjustment of the curriculum to the individual differences of pupils.[16] Such differentiation has apparently been left to the initiative and ingenuity of the teacher. In the classes of most teachers, the teacher has been expected to do the best he can to help each child achieve at grade level in the several subjects, rather than to help the pupil to achieve his best all-around growth. To most teachers, therefore, "differentiation" and "individualization" have meant giving special assistance to slow-learning children to improve their arithmetic, spelling, and reading skills; hence the intellectually superior children, who were probably at or above grade standard when they entered the grade, have received little additional attention to meet their unique abilities and needs. Furthermore, the often inordinate amounts of time demanded to bring the retarded children "up to standard" frequently caused the teacher to feel that he was prevented from doing the job he would like to do with the majority of "average" children in the class. Thus, the grouping of pupils into special classes can be seen for what it is: an attempt to make special administrative provisions to compensate for the shortcomings of the graded-school organization and the subject curriculum.

Suppose, for a moment, that the pressure were taken off the teacher to bring the class "up to standard." Suppose that the stereotype of a preconceived subject curriculum were put aside. Suppose that the objective of the school were *primarily* the promotion of the best living and growth

---

[16] H. Harap, "Differentiation of Curriculum Practices and Instruction in Elementary Schools," in *The Grouping of Pupils,* ch. IX.

on the part of each individual, not the attainment of a grade standard. Suppose that the teacher were permitted to organize his learning program around problems important in the lives of these children, and that the pupils could plan their work on those problems co-operatively with him. In this manner each child could find tasks suited to his ability, yet challenging to him. Each child would assume responsibilities or have them delegated to him by the group, responsibilities within his power to discharge. In such a program, every pupil would have an opportunity to develop resourcefulness, responsibility, and skill in the necessary basic processes *on his level of ability*. The teacher would be relieved of having to struggle mightily in a hopeless effort to bring slow learners up to standard, and would be free to give his attention equally to everybody and to help each at his level. Superior children would find as many tasks challenging to them as they could handle, and children of less than normal ability would be able to find opportunities for growth within their scope. "The activity curriculum presents the finest opportunity for individual adaptations, while maintaining the integrity of a desirable social grouping . . . In the child-centered situation, the teacher has intervals available for clearing up individual difficulties which may be obstacles to development."[17]

For large numbers of elementary schools the question of the segregation of intellectually atypical children for purposes of instruction will be an academic question, for small schools will be unable to muster a large enough group of such children to constitute a special class. In larger schools the decision as to whether or not to group such children separately should be a matter of staff discussion and decision, their attention being focused primarily on the question of the best manner of providing an educational program best suited to help children achieve their fullest and richest growth as persons.

Whatever the solution arrived at, it cannot be too strongly emphasized that organizational procedures will not of themselves do the trick. Special classes or no special classes, the teacher will still have to differentiate his program, and suit it to the needs, interests, and abilities of the pupils. One of the charges against special grouping is that it encourages teachers to ignore this fact, and to depend on the grouping to take care of it somehow. In all too many cases children have been divided into

---

[17] State of California, *Suggested Course of Study in Oral and Written Expression for Elementary Schools,* 1933. Quoted by H. Harap, *op. cit.,* p. 170.

ability groups, and that has been the extent of the provision made for individual differences, for the same curriculum was taught in all groups. The authors believe firmly, with Harap,[18] that ". . . no amount of classification will be of much worth unless the learning program for children is first made meaningful, until the learning activities are lifelike and varied, and until the learning environment is stimulating and satisfying."

In examining the nature of those programs of special classes which have achieved notable success, the reader or observer will find that in practically every case the learning program has been released from the requirements and conditions of the usual graded curriculum, that the pupils' interests have been used as fuel for learning, that the program is problem centered, that there has been much provision for enrichment in both slow-learning groups and groups of superior children, that the materials of instruction have been widely varied in both difficulty and subject matter, and that skill learning has been a function of the purposeful activities of the learners rather than the starting point and irreducible core of the learning program.[19]

To the authors this seems to point not to the superiority of special-class grouping for the education of these children, but to the superiority of a modern, problem-centered curriculum. Why not similarly release the *usual* classroom from the traditional inhibiting restrictions? It seems logical to assume that under such conditions slow-learning and superior children alike could find adequate work at their levels, suited to their interests, challenging their abilities, and teaching them better how to live and work co-operatively with their fellows of all intellectual levels, a far more lifelike situation than one finds in a segregated class.

Nevertheless, it is true that numbers of principals will have little to say about the organization for learning for these pupils, or will still believe in placing them in special classes. Under these conditions, care must be taken to provide for the association of those in segregated classes with those in regular classes, on the playground, in the auditorium, in school-wide activities, in art and craft work, and in any other respects in which their abilities do not range so widely.

---

[18] Harap, *op. cit.,* p. 172.
[19] W. B. Featherstone, "An 'Experience-Curriculum' for Slow Learners at Public School 500: Speyer School," *Teachers College Record,* vol. XXXIX, January, 1938, pp. 287–295; L. S. Hollingsworth, "An Enrichment Curriculum for Rapid Learners at Public School 500: Speyer School," *Teachers College Record,* vol. XXXIX, January 1938, pp. 296–306; H. H. Goddard, *op. cit.;* Department of Elementary School Principals, *op. cit.,* pp. 391–392.

Summary

1. In the majority of schools, the pupil enrollment will be so small as to make the question of segregation of mentally superior or mentally subnormal children an academic question. In such schools the only adequate solution to the proper education of these children is the development of a flexible, functional, problem-centered curriculum in which children of practically all intellectual levels can find challenge and success.

2. Where it is possible, children of 50 I.Q. and below should be placed in institutions specifically prepared to meet their unique needs and condition.

3. Children of 50-74 I.Q. can be educated effectively with other children, provided the curriculum is of the flexible, functional type, and the educational goals are broad enough, practical enough, and realistic enough to include the kinds of growth possible and desirable for pupils so handicapped.

Where the curriculum is primarily academic and subject-centered, however, it is likely that the "special class" will be the better solution for these children, particularly if the teachers of such classes are permitted—and able—to operate a functional program suited to the pupils' nature and needs. This latter condition is important, for a watered down curriculum of "essentials" is *not* what is needed for mentally handicapped pupils. They should be provided a learning program which will help them to improve the quality and success of their living at the moment and in the future.

4. Somewhat the same thing can be said for pupils of 74-90 I.Q., except that the arguments for their segregation have—to the authors, at least—considerably less force. If the school staff claims to give allegiance to such educational goals as growth in the quality of human relations, in emotional maturity, in effectiveness in dealing with persistent life situations, and in ability to contribute constructively and democratically to the improved quality of living of the group, it would appear to be indefensible to separate these children from their fellows simply because they differ somewhat in one aspect of growth.

5. Superior and gifted children can learn best and grow best in company with their peers in social, physical, and chronological maturity. This assumes, of course, that sincere efforts will be made to provide a

flexible learning program in which their abilities can be challenged. But it must be pointed out that what little research evidence there is on the topic indicates that segregated grouping is least effective for this group.

6. The problem of meeting the special needs of mentally atypical children will not be "solved," then, by administrative arrangements or organizational plans. It is basically a curriculum problem, and until it is conceived as such, and efforts are devoted to the development of a learning program focused primarily on improving the quality of living, mechanical grouping arrangements can give us only disappointing results.

SUGGESTED READINGS

Carroll, Herbert A., *Genius in the Making,* McGraw-Hill Book Company, Inc., New York, 1940.

Department of Elementary School Principals, *Meeting Special Needs of the Individual Child,* Nineteenth Yearbook, National Education Association, Washington, D. C., 1940.

Educational Policies Commission, *Education of the Gifted,* National Education Association, Washington, D. C., 1950.

Heck, Arch O., *The Education of Exceptional Children,* McGraw-Hill Book Company, Inc., New York, 1940.

Ingram, Christine P., *Education of the Slow-Learning Child,* World Book Company, Yonkers, N. Y., 1935.

Keliher, Alice V., *A Critical Study of Homogeneous Grouping,* Contributions to Education, no. 452, Bureau of Publications, Teachers College, Columbia University, New York, 1931.

McGaughy, J. R., *An Evaluation of the Elementary School,* The Bobbs-Merrill Company, Indianapolis, 1937, pp. 246–275.

————, *Classification of Pupils in the Elementary School,* American Education Fellowship Service Center Pamphlet no. 5, New York, 1941.

Martens, Elise H., *A Guide to Curriculum Adjustment for Mentally Retarded Children,* U. S. Office of Education Bulletin 1936, no. 11, U. S. Government Printing Office, Washington, D. C., 1936.

————, *Curriculum Adjustment for Gifted Children,* U. S. Office of Education Bulletin 1946, no. 1, U. S. Government Printing Office, Washington, D. C., 1946.

National Society for the Study of Education, *The Education of Exceptional Children,* Forty-ninth Yearbook, Part II, University of Chicago Press, Chicago, 1950.

————, *The Grouping of Pupils,* Thirty-fifth Yearbook, Part I, Public School Publishing Company, Bloomington, Ill., 1936.

Olson, Willard C., "The Improvement of Human Relations in the Classroom," *Childhood Education,* vol. XXII, March 1946, p. 317.

————, *Child Development,* D. C. Heath & Company, Boston, 1949, pp. 358–363.

"We Look at Grouping," *Educational Leadership,* vol. IV, no. 6, March 1947.

Wyndham, Harold S., *Ability Grouping,* Melbourne University Press, Melbourne, Australia, 1934.

CHAPTER X

PUPIL PROGRESS

At the close of every school year, with the inevitability of June weddings, principals and teachers are faced with the problem of whether or not to promote to the next grade that small group of pupils who, for one reason or another, fail to qualify for the happy estate. The problem is universal; there is almost no elementary school which is not plagued by it. In graduate college classes in education it becomes a topic of long and frequently heated discussion, and for these many years school staffs have struggled with it to little avail. Why should it be such a knotty problem? Why should intelligent people have had so little success in eliminating it as a problem?

Actually, the problem of school failure is only the symptom of more fundamental difficulties inherent in the graded-school subject-curriculum concept. Nonpromotion is clearly a part of the graded-school plan; it is one technique used in the attempt to sort pupils into achievement levels and to maintain the "gradedness" of the elementary school. As long, therefore, as we cling to our belief in the graded school as a desirable type of school organization, the "promotion problem" will remain. It is only indicative of the fact that current educational practice is failing to meet the needs of an appreciable portion of the children now in the schools.

Purposes Assumed To Be Served by Nonpromotion

If one believes that the graded type of school organization is desirable, it then seems logical to maintain that those who do not qualify for the next grade should "fail." Such failure has been justified on the grounds that it serves several "practical" purposes, chief of which are the following:

1. It maintains the standards of the graded school.

2. It reduces the variability in achievement levels within each grade, making instruction easier.

3. It serves as motivation to pupils to work harder and learn better the subject matter required for promotion.

4. It provides an opportunity for slow learners to bring their achievement levels up to standard.

5. Nonpromotion brings about better emotional adjustment by placing children in a grade most consistent with their achievement level.

If these assumptions are true, then it must be granted that there is considerable justification for the practice. Actually, there is convincing evidence that not one of the foregoing purposes is served by the graded-school promotional policy.

1. *Nonpromotion does not maintain graded school standards.* Teachers and principals have long labored under the illusion that nonpromotion is necessary to preserve grade standards. This assumption has not been borne out by careful investigation. One investigator, in fact, found that of the schools he studied, those which had the lowest rates of nonpromotion had the highest achievement levels.[1] Studies made in the Philadelphia schools led to the conclusion that "there is no evidence that rigorous achievement standards exemplified in low rates of promotion result in more rapid growth in achievement of school groups either through elimination of pupils or more effective instruction."[2] It can be seen then, that the evidence does not support the belief that high rates of nonpromotion serve to maintain standards.

2. *Nonpromotion does not appreciably reduce variability within grades.* At first thought it seems reasonable to believe that the practice of failing to promote those pupils who do not achieve the grade standard

[1] Hollis L. Caswell and A. Wellesley Foshay, *Education in the Elementary School,* 2nd ed., American Book Company, New York, 1942, pp. 349–357.
[2] *Report of the Division of Educational Research and Results for the Year Ended June 30, 1933,* Board of Education, School District of Philadelphia, Pennsylvania, 1933, p. 22.

would result in less variability in achievement level within each grade level. Again, however, the investigations which have been made do not bear out this assumption. In one study of schools relying on nonpromotion, Caswell found only a chance relationship between the rates of nonpromotion and the amount of variability in achievement level. Further analysis of his data resulted in the conclusion that ". . . a school with even a large amount of slow progress might be reorganized so as to eliminate retardation without materially affecting the variability of the instruction groups."[3]

In a study designed to examine whether nonpromotion reduces variability within grade groups, Akridge compared nine schools with low rates of nonpromotion and eight schools with high rates of nonpromotion. His data seemed to indicate that rather than *decrease* variability, there was a slight tendency for "irregular pupil progress" to *increase* the heterogeneity within a given group of pupils after they enter grade 1 together.[4]

Certainly more evidence is needed before a clear-cut and irrefutable conclusion can be reached on this matter, but it is clearly evident that nonpromotion is not as effective as its proponents have contended in making sure that the pupils in each grade group are at about the same achievement level. One doesn't need the evidence of scientific investigations to document this conclusion. Any teacher in any school with a grade-standards promotion policy knows very well that when a standardized test of achievement is administered in any of the subjects in his grade, the scores will range widely, and that the range will increase with each higher grade level. The writers have administered such tests in literally scores of classrooms in different parts of the country, and never, in any grade above three, have they found less than a five-grade range in reading, spelling, and arithmetic scores. In fact, the range was usually greater than that, sometimes being as much as ten grades. Nonpromotion is not serving the purpose of assuring narrow ranges in the achievement level of pupils within grades, despite popular belief.

Even if it were possible to arrange for all pupils at the beginning of a grade to be at the same achievement level in all respects (obviously an impossibility), they would not long remain so. Individual growth rates

---

[3] Caswell and Foshay, *op. cit.,* p. 360.
[4] Garth H. Akridge, *Pupil Progress Policies and Practices,* Contributions to Education, no. 691, Bureau of Publications, Teachers College, Columbia University, New York, 1937.

vary widely, and this factor, along with the many other influences which affect learning, would cause the variation inevitably to increase, resulting in the variability which is not only natural, but in many respects desirable. In a democratic culture individual differences should be neither deplored nor erased, but should be prized and capitalized for rich learning in living.

3. *Nonpromotion is not good motivation.* One of the strongest arguments in favor of the grade-standards promotion policy has been that it motivates pupils to work harder to avoid grade failure. This argument is vulnerable at several points. Three aspects of the argument should be considered:

Does nonpromotion motivate pupils to work harder?
Is fear of nonpromotion desirable motivation?
What are the effects of nonpromotion on children's personalities?

Several studies have been made to determine whether pupils do work harder because of nonpromotion. These studies have been of different types.[5] For example, some studies have divided a number of potential school failures into two groups equated on such bases as chronological age, I.Q., and reading score. One group is not promoted while the other is, and a comparative study is made of the subsequent achievement of the two groups. The results of such studies tend to indicate that those who are promoted show better subsequent achievement than those who are not. The evidence is clear that nonpromotion does not have the salubrious effects on achievement which commonly have been attributed to it, although most American schools are still operating as though it has. The old saw that "Nothing succeeds like success" is based on sound psychological principles, and these are violated by the traditional form of grade-standards promotion policy.

The second question relates to the desirability of fear of nonpromotion as a form of motivation. It should be obvious that any form of motivation in education which relies upon fear is not good. Teaching which has to depend upon fear as its chief motivation to learning is poor teaching in-

[5] G. Arthur, "A Study of the Achievement of Sixty Repeaters as Compared with that of Non-Repeaters of the Same Mental Age," *Journal of Experimental Education,* vol. V, December 1936, pp. 203–205; V. Klene and E. P. Branson, "Trial Promotion Versus Failure," *Educational Research Bulletin,* vol. VIII, January 1929, pp. 6–11; W. W. Cook, *Grouping and Promotion and the Elementary School,* University of Minnesota Press, Minneapolis, Minn., 1941.

deed; learning which takes place because of fear of the consequences is—in school, at least—poor learning. When learning takes place to serve constructive purposes of the learner, it is positive, integrating, and lasting; the "learning" which occurs because of fear of grade failure is negative, tends to be disintegrating, and tends to atrophy swiftly as soon as its purpose (promotion) is achieved. Yet many teachers still use grade failure as a motivation to achievement of pupils.

The motivating effectiveness of failure has been demonstrated by psychologists and mental hygienists to be puny in comparison with the motivating power of success. In the usual school in which academic achievement is the major criterion of successful living, there are a certain few pupils who will fail no matter how hard they try. After two or more years of such experience how much motivating power can one honestly believe these pupils find in further failure? Case studies have indicated that what actually happens is that the pupil resigns himself to his fate, concludes that he isn't worth much as this world's values go, and becomes apathetic and, perhaps, hostile. Certainly learning should be motivated by more constructive and defensible purposes than hope of promotion or fear of failure. The latter is neither good, desirable, nor effective.

Furthermore, psychologists have found that failure has motivating and learning value only when the pupil understands well the reasons for his failure, and can see clearly what he can do to avoid failing again in the same situation. These conditions seldom obtain in the case of grade failure. An extreme but common illustration is the six-year-old who fails grade 1 because he hasn't learned to read. He doesn't know why he failed to learn to read, and has little idea what to do about it. In fact, he may not even realize that the reason for separating him from his playmates and associates is his reading "failure." Perhaps it is pertinent to question whether it was the pupil or the school that failed.

A third question relates to an aspect of the problem which has been receiving increasing attention: the mental hygiene effects of nonpromotion. Failure implies frustration: it is, in effect, the thwarting of the pupil in the achievement of what he holds to be a desirable goal. Such thwarting can have two effects: either the pupil will abandon the goal as a desirable one (a "protection" reaction), or he will continue to hold the goal to be desirable, and suffer the effects of frustration. In either case, the effect on his personality has been undesirable. Psychological literature abounds with the evidence of the disintegrating effects of frustration upon personality. Carroll states:

> Failure is always at least temporarily disintegrating; persistent failure usually leads to serious behavior disorders. Success is a constructive experience; continued success usually leads to self-confidence.[6]

Frustrations are the roots of neuroses, and one is led to wonder how many extreme cases of adult neuroticism had their origins in the frustrating experiences suffered by large numbers of pupils in our elementary schools.

This is not pure surmise. Numbers of investigations have documented the belief that children suffer severe and adverse mental hygiene effects from school failure.[7] Perhaps the most thoroughgoing investigation of this factor to date is that made by Sandin,[8] who studied many aspects of the problem. His general conclusion was that nonpromotion clearly had strong adverse effects upon the adjustment and mental hygiene of the children studied.

Such a finding should not be surprising to teachers. Children who are not promoted become overage for their grade, become separated from the playmates and friends with whom they usually associate, are more mature than the children in their new grade, are looked upon as "dummies" by pupils and teachers alike, and frequently experience continuing disapproval and pressure at home. The question naturally comes to mind, "Is the maintenance of the school's gradedness more important than these factors?"

The avowed purpose of schools is to help children grow better in desirable directions. Any experience which is strongly disintegrative of personality is clearly in opposition to that purpose. This would imply that nonpromotion, on this criterion alone, is a most indefensible practice in modern schools.

4. *Slow learners do not "catch up" when not promoted.* One purpose

---

[6] H. Carroll, *Mental Hygiene,* Prentice-Hall, Inc., New York, 1947, p. 204.

[7] R. G. Barker, "Success and Failure in the Classroom," *Progressive Education,* vol. XIX, April 1942, pp. 221–224; C. Bassett, "School Success, an Element in Mental Health," *Journal of the National Education Association,* vol. XX, January 1931, pp. 15–16; A. Sandin, *Social and Emotional Adjustment of Regularly Promoted and Non-Promoted Pupils,* Bureau of Publications, Teachers College, Columbia University, New York, 1941; S. M. Stoke, "What Are the Effects of Frustration on Children?" *Progressive Education,* vol. XIX, January 1942, pp. 42–45.

[8] Sandin, *op. cit.*

of grade failure is to give the slow learner another year or semester to achieve the learnings he was unable to master in the "normal" time. If this result actually does occur, then the practice has some claim to justification. Here again, however, the searching light of investigation fails to bear out the assumption. Although the proportions vary in the different investigations, it has been found that only a small proportion of those who are failed do appreciably better work the second time in the grade. Most pupils do no better than before, and a sizeable proportion actually do worse the second time around.[9] On the basis of studies previously cited, it seems evident that the chances are brighter for a "failing" student to better his achievement the next year if he is promoted than they are if he is "flunked."

5. *Nonpromotion does not bring about better adjustment.* Proponents of the grade-standards theory of promotion maintain that it is harmful to a child's personality to place him in the next grade "if he is not ready for it" because he will find the work to be "above" him and be "out of his depth." They claim that it will provide for better adjustment if he is placed with a group of children whose achievement level is more nearly akin to his own.

This argument has at least the merit of going directly to the root of the problem. First, the reader will note that in it there is the assumption that there is an achievement level which is typical of each grade. Any casual student of elementary school education knows that this is not so. It was mentioned earlier that in any grade above 3 in any school (with perhaps an infinitesimal number of exceptions) the children will range over five or more "grade levels" in achievement in school subjects. Even in grades 2 and 3 the odds are heavy that one would find a range of four or more grades in reading level. In other words, if a teacher assumes that he is a "fourth-grade teacher" and teaches his subjects on a "fourth-grade level," *it is likely that the level of his teaching misses the achievement level of the pupils in the majority of cases.* This is the hard rock of fact upon which the graded school founders; the "graded school" is not graded at all, except in theory. It is dedicated to educating children in and into a common pattern, so that at the end of grade 6 it can be said with some certainty that all the pupils completing the grade have achieved a given level of learning and have "mastered" certain things.

[9] B. R. Buckingham, *Research for Teachers,* Silver Burdett Company, New York, 1926, p. 303.

Yet the facts of child development attest that children are born with differences, and that no matter what is done in school or out of it, these differences will become greater and greater with the passing years. The philosophy and efforts of the graded school fly in the face of this fact, having tried for these hundred years to *reduce* the differences among children, with results similar to those met with by Hercules in his encounter with the Hydra.

The concept, therefore, that failing a child is an effective method of placing him among his peers in achievement not only has little foundation in fact; it is based on a fallacious philosophy of education. Furthermore, the adverse mental hygiene effects of nonpromotion far outweigh any advantages which might accrue from failing a pupil to place him with others nearer his "achievement level." On the basis of intensive study of "failing" children, a psychiatric social worker states: "Constant failure, discouragement and unhappiness may not only result in a warped personality, but may push the child to the borders of mental disease."[10] Grade failure, then, in addition to being educationally ineffective, is miseducative and dangerous, and educators who practice it assume a frightening responsibility for its effects on children's personalities and maladjustments.

Attempts to Alleviate or Solve the Problem

To this point the discussion of this problem has been a destructive critique of the practice of nonpromotion as a device to bring about better learning on the part of children. Numbers of educators have recognized the validity of one or more of these criticisms, and have attempted to reduce the incidence of nonpromotion in their schools by various measures.

Semiannual promotions. On the theory that pupils who failed would lose less time, many schools adopted a plan of semiannual (some, even quarterly!) promotions. This, of course, does nothing to *solve* the problem of nonpromotion. It simply means that a pupil will repeat a half (or quarter) year instead of a whole year. Actually, studies indicate that more pupils are failed under such a plan (about twice as many), that its administration is more difficult, and that it has a number of other un-

[10] Bassett, *op. cit.,* p. 16.

desirable effects.[11] The growing realization of these results is reflected in the fact that the percentage of city school systems reporting semi-annual or quarterly promotions in elementary schools decreased from 27 per cent in 1938 to 7 per cent in 1948.[12] Apparently, then, changes in the length of the promotion period are not the answer to the problem.

Arbitrary reduction of the incidence of nonpromotion. Many schools and school systems which have become convinced of the undesirability of nonpromotion have sought means to reduce its incidence appreciably. A number of different plans have been used, some of which are discussed in another context in this book. Remedial teachers have been employed to bring failing pupils "up to standard." Curricula have been modified so as to require only "minimum essentials" for slower-learning children, while the "bright" children were provided with enrichment of the learning program. Multiple-track plans, such as the Detroit and Pueblo plans, were introduced, as were plans of "individualized instruction," like the Dalton and Winnetka plans. "Opportunity classes" were provided in many schools to give those who fell behind a chance to catch up. "Homogeneous" or ability grouping was resorted to, in an effort to give adequate attention to slow and faster learners, and to enable teachers of slow learners to concentrate on bringing these unfortunates up to standard. These are indicative of some of the original organizational features devised by creative administrators to try to do something about those pupils who, for one reason or another, failed to learn at the minimum rate that the graded school decreed was necessary and natural. None of them, however, has succeeded in solving the problem, and all have been the targets of severe and telling criticism.

In other schools a direct attack has been made upon the problem of grade failure. School staffs have studied the age-grade status of their pupils, and the percentages of nonpromotion in the various grades. Reasons for the failure of individual pupils were studied and the findings of other investigators of the problem were examined. As a result such schools usually revised their promotion policies so as to reduce the number of nonpromotions in their classes, but commonly did so within the

---

[11] H. A. Green, "The Effect of Semi-Annual Promotion as Revealed by Pupil Progress," *American School Board Journal,* vol. LXXVIII, May 1929, pp. 67, 86; Will French, *Promotional Plans in the High School,* Bureau of Publications, Teachers College, Columbia University, New York, 1933.

[12] National Education Association, *Trends in City School Organization, 1938 to 1948,* Research Bulletin, vol. XXVII, February 1949, pp. 29–30.

grade-standards framework. This was done by making "exceptions" and by liberalizing the standards for promotion. Children were promoted despite the fact that they had not attained the standard for promotion, because of a recognition that there are some factors in growth and development which outweigh the importance of attaining achievement standards.

Whereas all these attempts are commendable, and are efforts in a desirable direction, they are indicative of confusion as to the real issues at stake, and more or less beg the question, or skirt the issues. Within all of these "solutions" is the implicit assumption that although exceptions are made, still it is desirable for all pupils to achieve at grade level. Remedial plans, opportunity classes, and individualized instruction plans customarily have the objective of raising the level of achievement of the "laggards" to the desirable level, be it the standard for the grade, national test norms, or what not. They are props to the tottering structure of the graded school, when what is needed is a rethinking of that structure itself, and the building of a framework which is more functional, and geared to the realities of child growth, development, and learning.

The "no-failure" or "100% promotion" plan. As has been mentioned earlier in this discussion, a number of investigations have pointed out that failure does not result in improved learning, that it is not desirable or effective motivation, that it does not appreciably reduce the variability within grades, and that it frequently has harmful effects upon the personalities of those who suffer it. Numbers of schoolmen, therefore, have concluded that our best course is to abolish nonpromotion as a practice, and promote everybody. This, of course, is simply carrying to its logical conclusion the effort to reduce the incidence of grade failure in our schools. If the research evidence is valid, this plan should result in at least no worse a situation than now exists, and would seem to avoid the undesirable mental hygiene effects of the policy of nonpromotion.

The chief difficulty of this plan, which has been instituted by administrative edict in a number of our city school systems, is that it, too, begs the question, and fails to solve the educational problem underlying nonpromotion. The abolition of grade failure by such a method is akin to taking aspirin to eliminate the pain of persistent and severe headaches; it gets rid of the symptom without remedying the cause. As a result, teachers are likely still to teach in the same manner; the school and parents are apt still to cling to the illusion of the graded school; the same curriculum philosophy and content will probably continue to prevail; the community is likely to complain bitterly about "letting down the standards"; and teachers will complain about the incompetents who are getting into their classrooms, and about the fact that they can't be expected to teach to the wide range of achievement levels which they believe results.

The Theory of Continuous Progress

It is evident, then, that one's philosophy of pupil progress is part and parcel of one's educational point of view. As long as principals and teachers retain belief in the importance of maintaining minimum grade standards, they will inevitably be faced with the necessity of failing pupils, or of making "exceptions" in the interests of pupil adjustment. Schools will still face the dilemma caused by adherence to a philosophy and practice at variance with the realities of children's growth patterns, and the conditions and expedients engendered by this unrealistic approach will continue to characterize our schools: wide variation in promotion rates among teachers, subjects, schools and systems; "exceptions" who are passed and become the problems of subsequent teachers; cutting the flesh off the curriculum and offering the bare bone of "minimum essentials" to those unfortunates endowed with slower academic learning capacity; remedial classes; "opportunity" classes; and ability groupings.

If, on the other hand, teachers conceive of their function as that of accepting children at the age of five or six, and of helping each of them to grow to the best of the teachers' capacity to help, and of the children's to grow, for the six, seven, or eight years they are privileged to work with them, then one might well question whether the concept of "promotion" has any place in our schools. Children will grow, no matter what we do, and whether they are in school or out. It is the teachers' responsibility to help them to grow better. If a child fails to grow desirably in rate or direction, is it not possible—even likely—that the fault lies as much with the school as with him? Why, then, fail *him?* On the other hand, why promote the others? Because the misconception of common growth levels has been prevalent so long, it is hard to understand that each child has his own "timetable" of growth, and that in most cases, it does not conform to yearly or semiannual promotion periods. Olson, who has made extensive studies of children's growth patterns, states that:

> Instruction cannot make all children alike or bring them to the same point . . . at a given age. To understand this fully, one must appreciate that children, even with the same experiences, grow at different rates and have different aptitudes for learning.[13]

If this is so, why pretend that certain children have all reached the same point by May or June of each year, and certify to that by "promotion"? And why *promote* a child for *growing* anyway? Or fail him for not growing as much as some adults think he should grow? Recent studies in the field of child development have pointed out two facts which have profound implications for educational practice. The first of these is that a child's growth, like the sapling whose growing roots split a boulder asunder, is inexorable in its rate; it seems that little can be done either to hasten or to retard it. Education may modify its direction and influence its quality, but it is doubtful that it can accelerate its pace appreciably, despite "promotion," remedial classes, ability groups and such.

> It is probable that a growth pattern is hard to change. It was once assumed that diagnostic testing and remedial teaching could alter profiles in the field of achievement. However, Tilton reports that a deliberate attempt to change the achievement profile for low points in children in an experimental group as compared to a matched central group yielded inconsequential and inconsistent results.[14]

The second fact is highly significant when related to the foregoing. It is the conclusion that *achievement in school is a function of the total growth of the child*.[15] If these deductions are valid (and the evidence available seems to support them) it is foolish to attempt to force a child's growth; one can only pace it. Whereas educators have been becoming aware of this fact in the recognition of reading readiness, the generalization has not commonly been applied to all aspects of learning. Readiness applies in all learning areas at all levels. In other words, children will learn when, in their growth timetables, they are ready to learn and not before.

Further, it is now definitely established that children vary considerably

[13] W. C. Olson, *Child Development,* D. C. Heath & Company, Boston, 1949, p. 123.
[14] *Ibid.,* p. 183.
[15] *Ibid.,* p. 179.

in their growth timetables, so that it is not only unrealistic, but quite foolish, to expect all pupils to be ready for "fifth-grade level" at any given time (even if there were such a thing as "fifth-grade level"). A year of growth is a different thing for each child, and cannot be standardized.

With the foregoing in mind, it seems logical to suggest that our schools desist from placing such a premium upon *rate of learning* (a concern which seems almost to have reached the state of a compulsion), and devote their attention to improving the *quality of growth* of the pupils entrusted to their tender mercies. Under such an orientation, the six-, seven- or eight-year period of the elementary school will be considered as a period of *continuous progress* for each child, but at each child's individual rate. In the six-year elementary school, the staff will do all that it can for every pupil for six years, then send him to the junior high school without the unrealistic expectation that all will have achieved a "minimum level of achievement for the end of grade 6."

It must be clearly understood that one of our most vexing problems is that of meeting the range of needs which results from the factor of individual differences in growth rates, and that *no "promotion plan" as such, can solve that problem.* The problem can be solved only by a more realistic, practical and life-centered learning program operated in harmony with the facts of child development and geared to the needs and nature of the school's community. With such an approach, "promotion" ceases to be a problem because it doesn't exist. Perhaps a child may change teachers for the next school year (perhaps not) but he is not considered to have been promoted any more than he is considered promoted (or not promoted!) on his birthday. It is just something which happens as a part of his natural, continuous growth.

It is to be noted carefully that continuous progress is not synonymous with a 100% promotion policy, (sometimes known as a "no-failure" policy, or "forced promotion," or "automatic promotion"). The continuous progress theory is much broader in its conception than any mechanical plan of promotion. It is not a promotion policy, but a policy of individual and continuous progress in growth for each child. For this reason, it cannot be instituted by administrative edict, as can a 100% promotion policy, for it is a policy which must evolve out of the basic understanding of child growth and learning by the teachers. If it is to be developed successfully, the following conditions are necessary:

1. Together the school staff must study the total school learning program: learning experiences, teaching processes, evaluation procedures, and procedures of classifying and grouping pupils, to determine how it can be improved to do a better job of meeting the needs of pupils.

2. Together the staff must seek a more thorough understanding of the facts of child development and their implications for education in the elementary school. Individual teachers should study carefully the growth characteristics and needs of individual children in their classrooms, so that they may make suitable curriculum modifications.

3. Considerable flexibility must be provided and encouraged by the administration (principal and superintendent) so that teachers are free to modify their programs, materials, and methods of instruction to meet the needs and growth patterns of the pupils. Flexible grouping is necessary to allow for the readjustment of pupils, so that those who may have been misplaced need not wait until the end of the year for readjustment.

4. Parents should be involved in the development of the program so that they also may gain an understanding of the reasons underlying it. If possible, they should be involved in the planning *from the start*. Don't wait until the staff has "a bill of goods" to sell them.

5. Considerable flexibility and variation of materials of instruction in each classroom should be provided. Reading materials *in all the subjects* should range in reading difficulty over several "grade levels" of difficulty, and should challenge a wide range of interests.

6. Emphasis should be shifted from competition to co-operation in the learning situation. This is not to say that there will not be some competitive activities in the learning program, but that the major emphasis should be on learning to work together co-operatively, and on nurturing the finest quality of growth for each child.

7. There should be no expectation that the problem will be solved in a month or a year. Educators have been struggling with the "promotion problem" since the inception of graded schools one hundred years ago. Since the change proposed here first requires a change in people (their beliefs, attitudes, and the nature of their teaching) it is bound to be a slow process.

8. Small classes are desirable. They are desirable under any conditions, of course, but more urgently so under a plan which places such a high premium upon a thorough knowledge of the characteristics, needs and growth patterns of each child in the class.

Immediate Next Steps

Whereas this all sounds very well as a long-range program, the usual elementary school principal will undoubtedly wish to take some immediate steps to remedy his present situation. Some of these may be but stopgaps until better procedures are evolved; others will be steps in the progress toward an effective policy of continuous pupil progress.

Age-grade and grade-progress studies. One procedure which can be carried out with profit is the conduct of age-grade and grade-progress studies in the school. Some schools already make this standard practice yearly. The study simply involves plotting somewhat graphically the ages of the children in each grade in the school, so as to indicate clearly the extent of overageness and underageness for grade, and the years in school for all pupils, and for boys and girls separately. A valuable companion study is to determine the percentage of nonpromotion by grade and by sex over a ten-year period, to note any trends or interesting patterns.[16] Examples of forms for entering age-grade and grade-progress data appear in Figures 3 and 4. Such a study should raise interesting questions, which should be made the topic of staff discussion.

Extended teacher association with pupils. Numbers of schools have instituted the practice of having a teacher remain with a class for two or three years. It has been found that under such plans, teachers tend to fail fewer pupils at the end of their first year with the class, the teacher has a better opportunity to gain perspective with respect to the children's growth, and he is able to gain a greater understanding of the characteristics, backgrounds, and needs of the individual pupils.

Providing a wide range of instructional materials. One of the greatest handicaps to efforts to provide for individual differences is a dearth of instructional materials, particularly books, which range over several grade levels of difficulty. Since it is an established fact that the children in the usual grade show a range in reading ability, for example, of from five to ten years, it will facilitate their normal growth and continuous progress if each child can be using materials which are at approximately his stage

[16] See *The Survey of the Schools of Montclair, New Jersey,* Institute of Administrative Research, Division of Field Studies, Teachers College, Columbia University, New York, 1948, for an example of such a study on a system-wide basis.

FIGURE 3. Elementary School Age-Grade Table (Annual Promotions)

Grade	Kindergarten			Grade One			Grade Two			Grade Three			Grade Four			Grade Five			Grade Six			Summary		
Age[1]	B	G	T	B	G	T	B	G	T	B	G	T	B	G	T	B	G	T	B	G	T	B	G	T
4½ yrs.	6	5	11																			6	5	11
5 yrs.	21	13	34																			21	13	34
5½ yrs.	9	10	19		2	2																9	12	21
6 yrs.				8	10	18																8	10	18
6½ yrs.				6	7	13	2		2													8	7	15
7 yrs.				7	1	8	6	3	9													13	4	17
7½ yrs.				2		2	5	4	9	1		1										8	4	12
8 yrs.							6	1	7	4	7	11										10	8	18
8½ yrs.							6		6	7		7										13	1	14
9 yrs.							1		1	1		1	4	9	13							5	10	15
9½ yrs.							1		1	1	2	3	7	7	14							9	9	18
10 yrs.										2		2	1	3	4	3	7	10				6	10	16
10½ yrs.													3	3	6	3	9	12	1		1	7	12	19
11 yrs.													2		2	2	3	5	3	9	12	7	12	19
11½ yrs.																1		1	6	3	9	6	4	10
12 yrs.																3		3	5		5	8	0	8

12½ yrs.¹																						8	5	3	8
13 yrs.																						3	3	1	4
13½ yrs.																									
14 yrs.																									
14½ yrs.																									
Total	36	28	64	23	20	43	27	8	35	15	10	25	17	23	40	11	21	32	23	15	38	152	125	277
Normal age	30	23	53	21	18	39	17	8	25	11	8	19	12	19	31	8	19	27	14	12	26	113	107	220
Over-age				2		2	8		8	3	2	5	5	3	8	3	2	5	8	3	11	29	10	39
Under-age	6	5	11		2	2	2		2	1		1		1	1				1		1	10	8	18
% Normal age	83.3	82.1	82.8	91.3	90.0	90.7	63.0	100.0	71.4	73.3	80.0	76.0	70.6	82.6	77.5	72.7	90.5	84.4	60.9	80.0	68.4	74.3	85.6	79.4
% Over-age				8.7		4.7	29.6		22.9	20.0	20.0	20.0	29.4	13.1	20.0	27.3	9.5	15.6	34.8	20.0	29.0	19.1	8.0	14.1
% Under-age	16.7	17.9	17.2		10.0	4.6	7.4		5.7	6.7		4.0		4.3	2.5				4.3		2.6	6.6	6.4	6.5

¹To nearest birthday. E.g., 4½ yrs. includes ages from 4 yrs., 3 mos. to 4 yrs., 9 mos.; 5 yrs. includes 4 yrs., 9 mos. to 5 yrs., 3 mos.

of development. The principal should study with his staff the best means of providing such materials.

Formulation of "primary units." Numbers of schools have facilitated transition to a policy of continuous progress by considering the first three grades as a promotion unit. Children stay in the unit for three years before any consideration is given to promotion or failure. This has the effect of virtually eliminating promotion or failure in grades 1 and 2, and frequently reduces the number of nonpromotions in grade 3. Whereas this is certainly an improvement for the grades included, it should be noted that children still must meet the grade standards of the third-grade hurdle. For this reason, the primary unit is only a partial answer to the "promotion problem." Until the point of view it represents has permeated thinking and practice throughout, the school will have a sort of "split personality," and will face a number of resulting problems.

Study of failing pupils. An effective means of developing a point of view favorable to a continuous progress policy is that of making an intensive study of those pupils who fail. Study of their home backgrounds, relationships with their companions, the pattern of their play experiences outside school, of their personality and intelligence pattern, and of their problems, fears, and interests, coupled with a study of their progress during their repeating year, usually indicates clearly to teachers that nonpromotion is not the solution to the problems these children are facing. In fact, it frequently adds emphasis to the premise that nonpromotion serves only to make the situation worse.

Administrative encouragement to reduce the incidence of nonpromotion. One most important factor in the situation is what the teachers believe the administrator's point of view to be. In school surveys in which the authors have participated, it has been noticed with interest that the overall picture of promotion and retardation in a school is usually a reflection of the attitude of the administrator. Teachers tend to look to the principal for leadership in matters of policy, and give considerable weight to his opinion. In fact, many teachers (as well as principals!) want to be told just what their policy should be (a condition which the authors deplore). In any event, the knowledge that the principal is not in sympathy with the practice of nonpromotion is bound to have the

FIGURE 4. Record of School Grade and Progress

School _____   Year Beginning _____

No. Yrs. in School	Grade One			Grade Two			Grade Three			Grade Four			Grade Five			Grade Six			Total		
	B	G	T	B	G	T	B	G	T	B	G	T	B	G	T	B	G	T	B	G	T
Less Than One	39	32	71																39	32	71
One	1	1	2	19	22	41													20	24	44
Two				2	0	2	16	12	28										18	12	30
Three							4	3	7	14	12	26							18	16	34
Four							1	1	2	5	2	7	13	15	28				19	18	37
Five							1		1	1	1	2	3	2	5	11	16	27	16	19	35
Six										2		2	4		4	5	1	6	11	1	12
Seven													2		2	1		1	3	0	3
Eight																3		3	3	0	3
Total	40	33	73	21	22	43	22	17	39	22	15	37	22	18	40	20	17	37	147	122	269
No. Slow Progress	1	1	2	2	0	2	6	4	10	8	3	11	9	2	11	9	1	10	35	11	46
No. Normal Progress	39	32	71	19	22	41	16	12	28	14	12	26	13	15	28	11	16	27	112	109	221
No. Rapid Progress	0	0	0	0	0	0	0	1	1	0	0	0	0	1	1	0	0	0	0	2	2
% Slow Progress	2.5	3.0	2.7	9.5	0.0	4.7	27.3	23.5	25.6	36.4	20.0	29.7	40.9	11.1	27.5	45.0	5.9	27.0	23.8	9.0	17.1
% Norm. Progress	97.5	97.0	97.3	90.5	100.0	95.3	72.7	70.6	71.8	63.6	80.0	70.3	59.1	83.3	70.0	55.0	94.1	73.0	76.2	89.4	82.2
% Rapid Progress	0.0	0.0	0.0	0.0	0.0	0.0	0.0	5.9	2.6	0.0	0.0	0.0	0.0	5.6	2.5	0.0	0.0	0.0	0.0	1.6	0.7

effect of lowering the percentage of nonpromotion in the school. Ideally, of course, the policy concerning nonpromotion should be decided co-operatively by the staff, but this is a long-range process. It is suggested that a desirable attitude on the part of the principal, which is neither imposed upon nor concealed from the staff, may have desirable effects upon the operation of the promotion policy within the school.

A school which adopts, or makes progress toward, a continuous progress policy will not find smooth sailing. There will be criticism from all quarters because of the fact that the obsolete grade-standards philosophy is embedded firmly in our culture. The staff will be accused of lowering grade standards, to which the only answer is that in place of *minimum grade standards for all* it is substituting *maximum individual standards* for each child. It will be accused of soft, sugar-coated pedagogy, when as a matter of fact an education based upon a philosophy of continuous growth is far more difficult to operate than the usual subject-centered, grade-standards program with its artificial incentives based on fear and coercion. It will be accused of not preparing children to face failure in life. But failure in life doesn't occur by the year. It is something which can and does happen at any time, and at the time it happens the causes can be analyzed, and something done about it.

It can be seen, then, that this problem of promotion is far from a superficial one. Any realistic solution will involve extensive changes in almost all aspects of the instructional program of the school. It has not been usual to consider it in this light. Because promotion has been considered an administrative device, school staffs have spent much time attempting to refine it, with the result that they have failed to give attention to the fundamental changes needed to make such a device unnecessary. In years to come, it is likely that students of education will consider today's system of marking and promoting with the same tolerantly disapproving attitude that we hold toward the readin', writin', and hickory-stick education of yesteryear.

SUGGESTED READINGS

Adams, M. A., "Continuous Progress," *Baltimore Bulletin of Education,* vol. XXV, April-June 1948, pp. 258–264.

Barker, R. G., "Success and Failure in the Classroom," *Progressive Education,* vol. XIX, April 1942, pp. 221–224.

Caswell, H. L., and Foshay, A. W., *Education in the Elementary School,* 2nd ed., American Book Company, New York, 1942, ch. 13.

Elsbree, W. S., *Pupil Progress in the Elementary School,* Bureau of Publications, Teachers College, Columbia University, New York, 1943.

Moffitt, F. J., and LeBaron, W. A., *Pupil Progress in the Elementary Schools of New York State,* Bulletin no. 1297, University of the State of New York, Albany, N. Y., 1945.

Olson, W. C., *Child Development,* D. C. Heath & Company, Boston, 1949, pp. 363–368.

CHAPTER XI

EVALUATION OF PUPIL PROGRESS

Evaluation of pupil progress is one of the most difficult tasks confronting the school principal and the teaching staff. There are a number of reasons why this is true. Tradition has left an almost indelible imprint upon the thinking of members of the teaching profession, as well as upon the thinking of laymen, with respect to the nature and scope of pupil evaluation. With few exceptions evaluation is viewed narrowly and in terms of a school curriculum that has long since ceased to meet the demands of children. Related to this is the fact that education today is a complex matter and involves a number of goals and outcomes. A third consideration which perplexes educators is the difficulty of assessing the many intangible aspects of learning which defy exact measurement, especially in the realms of social behavior, emotional development, and esthetic tastes.

Evaluation, as most parents think of it, consists of giving pupils marks for the traditional subjects in the curriculum. In fact, parents commonly do not come into the picture as far as evaluation is concerned until the last phase of the appraisal process is reached. This often takes the form of signing a report card and, depending upon the nature of the report, interviewing the teacher or the school principal. Modern educators view evaluation more broadly than this. They consider evaluation to be any attempt to take stock of the school's success in achieving its objectives, whether the participants are staff members or pupils or both. Moreover, they are concerned with group evaluation as well as with the appraisal of the progress of individual pupils.

The conscientious teacher is primarily interested in pupils' progressing at a rate consistent with their ability. He is anxious that each individual pupil shall develop as a person, not that he shall merely forge ahead in traditional subject matter and skills at the expense, perhaps, of equally fundamental knowledges and skills in democratic living and social competence. Since good standardized tests have not been developed for some

"Suppose he doesn't get the best marks in his class. Do you get the highest salary in your office?"

of the more intangible areas of learning, the modern teacher has to resort to many ingenious methods to appraise pupil progress as a whole. The refinement commonly sought through grading or school marks is seldom achieved in these other measuring schemes. Marks are therefore only one form of evaluation, however important they may seem to parents.

Despite the fact that educators and parents view the problem of pupil evaluation quite differently, experience has shown that the wise principal does not turn a deaf ear to the requests of parents when introducing new appraisal procedures and policies. This does not mean that principals and teachers accept uncritically the point of view of laymen on matters that are largely professional, but it does mean that the approach to educational problems is best made by starting where most people are. The majority of parents are well acquainted with traditional marking arrangements. They know what examinations are like, and they have had papers read by teachers and returned to them with numerical or alphabetical grades on them. They have stood at the head or at the bottom of the class, or somewhere in between, and know the weight attached to such "standing." Because similar procedures to those just enumerated have been followed for over a century in public schools, parents are likely to place great value upon them and are usually suspicious of new schemes. The principal's job is to exercise leadership in introducing new and better methods of appraisal than have been employed in the past. Otherwise, the new arrangement is not likely to succeed. Needless to say, the reform should not be brought about by administrative fiat or edict; it must emerge gradually as a result of group thinking. The principal, however, must give thoughtful consideration to the problem at hand, if he is to fulfill his role as a leader. Some of the questions which will inevitably arise are related to school marks. Among these are the following:

1. What functions do marks, as commonly used in school systems, serve?
2. What marking systems are now used in elementary schools?
3. What do marks really mean?
4. How reliable are most marks?
5. What are the effects of traditional marking arrangements on the attitudes of pupils?
6. How can traditional marking systems be improved?

No one who is acquainted with the highly controversial nature of any of the above questions would claim to have the final answer to them. A belief in the efficacy of the grade-standard theory will undoubtedly color one's point of view on marking. Similarly, proponents of the theory of normal pupil progress have a characteristic viewpoint relating to marking schemes. A thoughtful and consistent position based on one's philosophy of education and child development is what every principal needs to work out. It would seem worth while, therefore, to study the questions listed above and try to reach some tentative answers to them. The following discussion attempts to present certain facts bearing on the questions raised and a point of view relating to school marking arrangements.

The Functions of Marks

Marks are claimed to serve several functions. First, it is argued that they provide administrators with information which enables them to decide whether or not a pupil should pass or fail, repeat the grade, or be promoted to a higher one. Marks are sometimes considered as a basis for a grade placement when pupils are transferred from one school to another. Often marks constitute one basis for determining the group to which a pupil is to be assigned within the grade. In other words, a pupil whose marks are consistently low might be placed in a "slow" group whereas a pupil with high marks would be assigned to a "fast" group. Occasionally marks are used as a means of judging how well the teacher is performing his job.

A second function which marks are employed to serve in the more traditional schools might well be labeled as a "motivating" function. Marks encourage and discourage scholastic efforts and motivate behavior. If the marking scheme were so devised that it motivated every child to put forth his best efforts, then this function would be so obviously desirable that it alone would justify the existence of the device in question. Unfortunately marks do not always evoke good behavior or arouse enthusiasm for hard scholastic work. On the contrary, there is good reason to believe that many pupils are discouraged because try as hard as they will, they are not intellectually able to compete with their fellow pupils and hence must always be satisfied with an inferior rating. Moreover, even those who are successful in their schoolwork are not necessarily motivated to strive for the right things. Their scholarship may be quite superficial but because of their brightness they still acquire high marks. They may be motivated to get the high mark but they are not interested in possessing the knowledge which is what the mark presumably implies. So the claim that marks motivate children must be examined with considerable care. It can also be argued that the instructional program must be pitifully weak if marks have to be used to motivate children to study and learn. A good educational program provides its own motivating power.

A third function which a marking system serves is to acquaint parents, the child, and even the teacher with the pupil's school success. There is no doubt about the fact that marks convey ideas to the three groups mentioned above regarding the relative success of pupils in school. They represent the school's estimate of the pupil's achievement. They do not, however, insure that the estimate is a good one, nor do they commonly provide much information which would help the pupil to improve his rate of achievement.

A fourth and final purpose of a marking system is to enable the pupil, the teacher, and the parents, working individually and collectively, to discover strengths and weaknesses in the pupil's educational development, and in the light of these facts, to organize his experiences and the resources of the school in such a way as to insure maximum progress on the part of the pupil concerned. This is without question the most important function of evaluation, of which school marks are but one aspect.

Present Marking Schemes

To fulfill one or more of these four functions, school administrators have set up a variety of marking systems, although they fall, for the most part, into five types.

The oldest and a rapidly vanishing marking arrangement is the percentage system. Pupils, according to this plan, are given percentage marks in all the regular subjects listed in the curriculum, such as 85 per cent in arithmetic, 92 per cent in social studies, and so on up and down the scale.

The practice of recording percentage marks is seriously questioned by present-day educators since it implies a refinement in grading which teachers, with available measuring instruments, simply cannot make. A cursory consideration of what is involved in attempting to distinguish between 101 different values on a percentage scale should lead one to the conclusion that it is ill suited for evaluation purposes in the elementary school. In the percentile system the values are all fixed from 0 to 100 and each unit is presumed to be equal in amount to every other unit so that the difference between the marks 64 and 65, for example, is deemed to be the same as the difference between 94 and 95, or the difference between 16 and 17. It has been repeatedly shown in studies of school marks that the actual difference between a score of 64 and 65 is far less than the difference between 94 and 95 and far greater than between 16 and 17.

The criticism growing out of studies of the percentage system as it is employed generally has finally led to the adoption of a less refined type of marking system in many schools. Recent statistics are not available showing the number of schools still using this percentage plan but the trend is clearly away from it.

Probably the most popular scheme of marking is a five-point scale with categories consisting of descriptive terms such as Excellent, Good, Fair, Poor, Failure, or the letter symbols A, B, C, D, and F. Under this scale, teachers do not have to make the fine distinctions inherent in the percentage plan. Moreover, the five-point scale makes it easier to defend a particular mark when questioned by parents than is the case when a specific numerical grade has been given.

An even less refined system is the two category arrangement whereby a pupil's work is labeled either as "satisfactory" or "unsatisfactory," or "pass" or "fail." Much less attention will be focused on marks by pupils and parents under this latter arrangement than under the first two schemes discussed above. Most pupils with only two classes of marks to worry about will be motivated by other considerations than marks and there is likely to be less artificiality in the learning situation than where five grades are assigned. While many school systems have introduced this plan into the primary grades, only a small percentage of schools thus far have extended it to the upper division of the elementary school.

Class rank is a fourth method which is not extensively used but which is employed enough to warrant mentioning. One finds this practice prevailing in many high schools chiefly because of the interest of college admissions committees in the scholastic standing of applicants. The elementary schools have thus far not been greatly influenced by this procedure, since there is no pressure from high schools to introduce this system. Ranking thirty-five pupils according to their relative achievement in eight or ten learning areas would be a huge task for one teacher and would serve no useful purpose in the elementary school.

Finally, check lists composed of several items are used fairly widely. They usually include items related to achievement in subject matter as well as those concerned with personal growth. Check lists are usually thought to be relatively easy for teachers to administer because once they are prepared they require little writing and no discretion is required on the part of the teacher as to the items to be considered. In the case of informal letters to parents, teachers have to decide for themselves which behavior characteristics they can most profitably discuss. Actually, of course, a good check list calls for a systematic appraisal of behavior traits for each member of the class and, when thoroughly handled, it is doubtful that it is a time saver.

There are other marking plans which do not fall in any of the foregoing categories, but they are not widely enough used to warrant discussion here.

Since parents are likely to favor the five-point scale or the percentage system, the principal will do well to examine carefully the pros and cons of these two plans. Some of the weaknesses of these arrangements are discussed in the pages which follow.

What Do Marks Mean?

If you put this question to a typical parent or to a teacher of the old school, you will probably get an answer that runs like this: Allowing for a few errors in judgment in grading papers and examinations, marks are on the whole a good measure of the achievement of pupils in their school work.

There is some evidence in one or more of the studies reported in the *Encyclopedia of Educational Research*[1] on "school marks" to support this answer. But if you make the question a little more specific and say:

Johnny got 88 in arithmetic last marking period. Just what does this mean? Does it mean the 88 represents Johnny's accomplishment in arithmetic or did the teacher take account of the fact that Johnny tried hard, his attitude was always good, he was co-operative and he never caused any trouble in class? In other words, what were the components that entered into the mark 88 per cent? Also one might ask this question, Does the 88 per cent in arithmetic mean that Johnny is equally skillful in (1) solving verbal problems, (2) achieving accurate results, (3) gaining command of number concepts? Or, to use an illustration in another subject, Mary gets a B in language arts. Can we assume from

---

[1] Walter S. Monroe, ed., *Encyclopedia of Educational Research,* rev. ed., The Macmillan Company, New York, 1950, pp. 711–715.

this that Mary stood at about the same point in (1) her grasp of vocabulary, (2) her oral expression, (3) her sentence structure, (4) her punctuation of sentences, (5) her knowledge and use of capitals? Or is this B which Mary got the average of her achievement in these five areas in which she has received some instruction?

To make what at first appears to be a simple question somewhat complex: Do these marks representing achievement mean the same thing to all teachers, or do some teachers take account of accuracy in their composites and others not. Is mastery a consideration, or ability to study independently? Were the B in language arts and the 88 in arithmetic based largely on the results of tests given at the close of the marking period, performance in daily recitations, or on scores earned in short tests given frequently throughout the semester or year? Since the relative weight given to these evaluation techniques varies widely from school to school and from teacher to teacher, it is difficult to know in the case of Johnny and Mary just what the 88 in arithmetic and the B in language arts really represent.

One basic fact must be considered in interpreting marks: no single symbol can be an intelligible index of pupil achievement unless the achievement represents a single outcome, or unless the achievement of several outcomes may be assumed to be identical. The likelihood of the achievement of several outcomes being identical is remote at best and the progress made in the various phases of English can scarcely be viewed as *progress* in a single outcome. Hence a B in language arts is likely to have no significant meaning for teacher, parent, or pupil. This conclusion holds equally true for all subjects.

The Reliability of Marks[2]

Not only will Johnny's and Mary's parents have difficulty in finding out what the respective marks of 88 in arithmetic and a B in language arts mean with respect to the progress of these pupils, but what is even more distressing, the parents cannot place much confidence in the reliability of the grades awarded. This does not arise out of the fact that Mary's and Johnny's teachers are unfair or lacking in integrity. They may be highly objective in their relationship with their pupils and as honest as the day is long, but still hand out marks which are not representative of the pupil's knowledge or progress. Marks are seldom vali-

[2] Monroe, *op. cit.,* p. 173.

dated in terms of educational objectives; both pupils mentioned above may know what is important in their respective fields and still get low marks, or vice versa. It is also a fact that most marks are not related in any way to standardized norms and are largely based on the subjective judgment of the teacher.

Experiments have shown that much of the unreliability of marks arises from the fact that teachers generally are neither skillful nor trained in giving and marking tests. This is important since a significant proportion of the mark commonly rests on test results. Starch and Elliott in a very early study of test scoring found that the scores assigned to a geometry paper by 116 teachers of mathematics ranged from 28 to 92 per cent. Other investigators have found that the difference in marking standards among teachers in distributing marks is often as great as one whole letter in a four letter system, or as large as 11 per cent in a percentage system.

While teachers generally are men and women of high integrity, they are human and are influenced by the personality of their pupils, by pupil conduct, and by the sex of the pupil. Such qualities as neatness, tidiness, and politeness often affect the marks of pupils. Interestingly enough, women teachers are more generous in assigning marks to girls than to boys and men teachers mark both boys and girls higher than do women teachers. And to increase the unreliability still further, teachers of different subjects have quite different standards. There is a tendency, for example, for teachers of mathematics, Latin, and other academic subjects to give lower marks than teachers in shop courses, home economics, physical education, music, and art. Similar differences in the subjects contained in the elementary school can logically be expected.

Johnny's and Mary's marks may be representative of their real achievement. But the chances are good that Johnny's 88 should be higher or lower and that Mary's B should be modified by a plus or minus if indeed the letter itself should not be changed to a C or an A.

Effects of Marking Practices on Pupils' Attitudes

The old school of thought with respect to marks emphasized "an eye for an eye and a tooth for a tooth" philosophy. Marks were often used for disciplinary purposes. If you earned a C or below you were denied certain privileges. If you were fortunate enough and, incidentally, bright enough to receive an A you enjoyed certain prestige, reserved for the favored few. Sometimes teachers, in an effort to stimulate the pupils' brain cells, administered corporal punishment to pupils whose scholarship was low. Ambitious parents who often hope to achieve through their offspring the goals which they themselves failed to reach prod their children unceasingly to strive for higher marks, and frequently with very bad results. There is a blind faith extant among adults that hard work alone on the part of pupils will bring outstanding success. This, of course, is a myth, for in school as in no other phase of life children of

"And what do you suppose my friends would say if I were to get an 'A' for good behavior?"

relatively low intellectual ability have to compete with the best brains in the community. Future laborers are competing with future doctors and lawyers. The race is unfair; the cards are stacked against the pupil of low or even moderate ability. But because of the ignorance of many parents and sometimes of school administrators and teachers, the old pattern of competitive marks persists.

There are several arguments which have been advanced against the traditional type of marking arrangement. Among these the following deserve careful consideration. First of all, many marking systems promote insincere scholarship in that the pupil's primary concern is for the mark and not for the knowledge or wisdom which it presumably symbolizes. The A or the Excellent comes to have "intrinsic" value in and of itself regardless of how little command the pupil may have over the subject matter or the skills taught. The mark is similar in nature to wages or rewards, and the motivation is false. Pupils who are governed by the traditional type of marking system are likely to attach little significance to knowledge and skill, and are likely not to look beyond the mark itself for its full implication.

Not only is the pupil likely to learn and retain less under the marking practices just discussed, but his teacher is also likely to be less efficient. For traditional marking devices tend to encourage poor teaching. Teachers can threaten their pupils with failure and thus frighten them into a state of attention without going to the trouble of making their teaching interesting and challenging. Many pupils are suffering from sheer boredom in the classrooms of the country. Part of this boredom is due to the fact that teachers who use marks as one means of controlling behavior do not have to expend as much time and effort in preparation for their daily teaching tasks as would be required otherwise. By wielding a big stick, they can command attention without all the hard work implied in devising ingenious methods of arousing interest in the subject at hand.

A fairly common principle of administration is that classroom supervisors should not be given responsibility for rating teachers. The theory behind this is that no barriers must be permitted to develop between supervisors and teachers—otherwise the former will lose their effectiveness. A parallel situation exists between teachers and pupils. Marks produce barriers and interfere with the friendly relationship which is essential for a sound learning situation. Pupils should not view the teacher as a judge, but rather as a friend and counselor. Few individuals will reveal their thoughts, their fears, or their weaknesses to persons whose function it is to grant them rewards or mete out punishments to them. One can never be certain how much the judge may be influenced by what he hears or sees. Pupils are reluctant to ask questions which reveal their ignorance or to seek advice which they think, perhaps, will be taken as evidence of their weakness. The result is that they do not get the helpful counsel they need. A safer plan for pupils under a typical marking scheme is to "cover up" their ignorance and fool the teacher if possible.

Marks do not necessarily create barriers between teachers and pupils. Some teachers are probably able to counteract this danger. But it is not often that teachers can establish good rapport with their pupils under a traditional marking arrangement. Marks commonly carry so much weight at home that pupils find it difficult to accept with equanimity grades of a denomination unacceptable to "father." Hence friction is likely to develop between pupil and teacher.

Probably the worst effects of marking are observable in the bad social attitudes which they produce in children. Many pupils develop "inferiority complexes" as a result of their failure to compete successfully in school for marks. A few get "superiority complexes." Neither of these states makes for happiness or for good social adjustment. While it may be true that a great deal of this world's work is done by individuals with inferiority complexes in their effort to compensate for their true feelings, nevertheless the school can scarcely justify encouraging young people to feel inferior. Children who are unsuccessful in their school work are likely to become discouraged and develop unpleasant associations with everything related to learning. Not only are feelings of inferiority painful in themselves but, what is equally important, they lead to maladjustments which interfere seriously with the social life of the individual. In extreme cases inferiority complexes lead to delinquency, alcoholism, and suicide. Administrators should certainly question any practice which produces mental and emotional states that threaten the whole future life of the pupil.

Superiority complexes are equally bad for the welfare of the pupil and the social group that has to endure him when he reaches adulthood. Pupils who continuously enjoy ratings superior to those of most of their fellow students are in danger of getting "swelled heads" and concluding that they are superior in all respects to their classmates, and later on in life, to their neighbors and associates. Most of us know a few intellectual snobs and some smug individuals but few of us really enjoy associating with them. They are ineffective in most leadership capacities and they seldom command the respect and affection which they would have enjoyed had their outlook been normal. It seems to be a general reaction of people everywhere to dislike individuals who feel superior and express such feelings in their everyday relationships. A reasonable amount of humility is an essential element of a great leader, and any school practice which breeds abnormal feelings of superiority is ill-designed to achieve the democratic purposes which the school ostensibly is established to serve. Since competitive marking systems tend to foster pride and selfish ambition, they are open to serious criticism, particularly in a public school.

A Broader Approach to Evaluation

The foregoing discussion has been focused largely on the weaknesses of traditional evaluation schemes. A school administrator should certainly be informed with regard to the issues involved in the controversy over school marks and know the limitations inherent in typical evaluation procedures. But a principal who stops here in his analysis of the problem will not be especially helpful to his teachers or to the parents represented in his school. He must discover what constructive steps need to be taken to improve the situation.

First of all, improvement in pupil evaluation can best be brought about through the concerted efforts of teachers, parents, pupils, and principal. There is implied here a faith in the democratic process and a willingness to be guided by the wisdom of the group. This at times will require both patience and vision. Experience has shown that a united attack on a major school problem of this character which capitalizes on the resources of all those who have a stake in the results is more likely to bear fruit than a decision reached by the principal working alone or with the counsel of a small group of staff members.

A second factor in developing a sound appraisal system relates to the formulation of goals and desirable outcomes. Goals should be defined to cover all aspects of pupil growth, including the physical, social, emotional, and esthetic as well as the intellectual phases of learning. These goals and outcomes should also be expressed in terms of specific behaviors rather than as vague generalities, and what is equally important they should be stated in terms of a child's immediate living rather than being projected into the distant future. Citizenship goals are an illustration of aims which are all too often remote rather than immediate in character. This condition probably accounts for the fact that many citizenship objectives are so infrequently achieved. Finally, goals should be attainable and within reach of the pupils for whom they are established.

Once the objectives have been clearly defined and arrived at cooperatively, some means must be devised for discovering to what degree they are being realized. There is no short answer to this problem. Evaluation involves the use of many devices, the recording of much data, and the expenditure of a great deal of staff time. Anecdotal records and cumulative folders are useful media in the process of assessing the changes observed in certain types of pupil growth and behavior. Teachers with supervisory help can learn how to detect and record evidences of growth and change; with guidance they can use the recorded data to great advantage in appraising their own teaching efficiency and in providing learning opportunities for children. Parents possess rich information on child behavior outside of school, which if known to teachers would aid greatly in the evaluation of pupil progress. Means must be developed for securing such information. Other adults who come in close contact with pupils outside of the classroom such as the playground director, the nurse, the school physician, could provide teachers with many evidences of pupil growth.

To collect pertinent data, however, on pupil behavior, one must be able to recognize evidence where one finds it and must be alert to situations where behavior traits can be best observed. The task of helping teachers improve their techniques of studying pupil growth rests chiefly with the principal.

Achievement tests can contribute greatly to the evaluation process if they are used wisely. Some educators have abandoned all achievement testing in the schools because of the abuses which have so commonly accompanied the testing programs. This is unfortunate since pupil progress toward worthy goals in several fields can be more reliably assessed by standardized achievement tests than by any other single device. The principal should be thoroughly familiar with the best tests available for measuring pupil progress in areas where standardized tests have been devised, and should give leadership to teachers in using these tests in diagnosing pupils' needs. Teachers should also be encouraged to improve their methods of preparing and giving informal classroom tests.

Evaluation Should Be Diagnostic

One fact which needs more emphasis than it has commonly received in the past is that pupil evaluation is a *diagnostic* process rather than a judicial one. Teacher and pupil together are trying to assess their individual and joint success in achieving common goals in order that they may enjoy still greater success in the future. There can be no other justification for an elaborate scheme of evaluation in the elementary school. The promotion of the child's best growth is the sole concern.

It seems obvious in light of the scope of evaluation that no single mark or descriptive word can possibly characterize the changes which have taken place in a large area of pupil experience. Hence, marks as commonly employed serve no useful purpose in a modern evaluation scheme. There is also reason for viewing evaluation as part and parcel of the teaching-learning situation and hence as a continuous process carried on over a long period of time.

It will not be easy to move from a traditional marking arrangement to an evaluation plan of the nature just discussed. Practical considerations will demand that the transition be made gradually, and some inconsistencies will inevitably accompany the shift. Certainly one can reduce the emphasis on competition and eliminate prizes and rewards for scholastic attainment. Overly refined attempts at evaluation in the form of the percentage system of marks, or the use of five or more letters, or single-word descriptive classifications, can also be set aside in favor of larger categories such as Satisfactory and Unsatisfactory. This change is less likely to alienate the believers in the traditional marking arrangement than the abolition of all marks at one single move. Leadership will eventually result in teachers, parents, and pupils viewing the evaluation procedure as an integral part of the educational process, and something wholly different from the marking schemes of yesteryear. For the acceptance of the implications underlying a modern program of pupil evaluation means a different way of looking at education and the school's task. Bringing about this change is a real challenge to educational leadership.

SUGGESTED READINGS

Buros, Oscar K., ed., *Third Mental Measurements Yearbook,* Rutgers University Press, New Brunswick, N. J., 1949.

Commission on Teacher Education, *Helping Teachers Understand Children,* American Council on Education, Washington, D. C., 1946.

Driscoll, Gertrude, *How to Study the Behavior of Children,* Bureau of Publications, Teachers College, Columbia University, New York, 1941.

McNally, Harold J., "Evaluation of What? For What?" *Educational Administration and Supervision,* vol. XXXV, January 1949, pp. 36–48.

National Society for the Study of Education, *The Measurement of Understanding,* Forty-fifth Yearbook, University of Chicago Press, Chicago, 1946, Part I.

New Jersey State Department of Education, *Self Evaluation in the Elementary School*, Elementary School Bulletin no. 1, Trenton, N. J., 1946.

Odell, C. W., "Marks and Marking Systems," in Monroe, Walter S., ed., *Encyclopedia of Educational Research*, rev. ed., The Macmillan Company, New York, 1950, pp. 711–715.

Strang, Ruth, *Reporting to Parents*, Bureau of Publications, Teachers College, Columbia University, New York, 1947, pp. 36–40.

CHAPTER XII

REPORTING PUPIL PROGRESS
TO PARENTS

There can be no doubt about the need for keeping parents informed regarding the progress of their children in school. In fact, parents are so concerned about their offspring's accomplishments that it would be difficult, if not impossible, for the school to ignore the matter of reporting. The chief means of communication in the past has been a report card bearing appropriate symbols written in by the teacher to indicate the pupil's standing in the various subjects of the curriculum. A wide variety of reporting forms have been and are now being used. The following are fairly representative:

1. Cards or small booklets are most often used. They list subjects and activities and contain blanks for recording letter symbols, such as A, B, C, D, and F (or numerical ratings) opposite each subject.

2. Forms similar to those described in number 1 above may be used, with descriptive words, such as excellent, very good, good, fair, and failing, instead of letter symbols or numerical ratings.

3. Another form is check lists varying in the number and character of the items included, with spaces provided for the teacher to record his judgment regarding the pupil's progress. Such descriptive phrases as the following commonly appear opposite the subject or achievement items included in this type of report form: "Does his best work," "Shows improvement," "Should do better."

4. Narrative or letter reports range from a small space provided on a specially prepared form to an informal letter report. In some instances the teacher is given no directions as to points to be emphasized in the

letter. In other cases, a list of suggestions is made available to the teacher so as to insure a somewhat more uniform and comprehensive coverage of pupil achievement. The District of Columbia report form (grades 3, 4, 5 and 6) contains a statement of what the school considers important by way of habits, attitudes, and appreciations, and provides space for four narrative reports annually. Typical of the items mentioned are the following: "Completes a task begun." "Observes safety rules." "Protects the health of others." "Listens while others are speaking." "Has a courteous and friendly manner."

5. Some school systems have combined the narrative report (number 4 above) with one of the preceding forms. They have made provision in their reporting forms for specific grades for each of the academic subjects and then, in addition, have left space for teacher comments. The latter arrangement is not uniform, and in practice, teacher reports range from short statements containing a few sentences to lengthy narrations covering several paragraphs. The Pupil Progress Report, Intermediate Grades, used in Manhasset, Long Island, schools is illustrative of this type of report form.

FIGURE 5. Report Form Used in Manhasset, New York, Public Schools

			Rating			Rating
				Mathematics	Vocal Music	
				English	Instrumental Music	
				Social Studies	Shop	
				Science	Home Economics	
				Art	Physical Education	

Manhasset Public Schools

NAME: ....

...................report covering the period from

.... to ....

ATTENDANCE:

COMMENTS:

Purpose of Reporting

The particular form of report card used may or may not reflect in any significant way the philosophy of the school. An informal report can conceivably be quite traditional in content, and its use in no way signifies that the teacher has a modern point of view. While it is true that the more traditional schools have tended to hold to percentage and letter-

SIDE GLANCES   **By Galbraith**

COPR. 1949 BY NEA SERVICE, INC. T. M. REG. U. S. PAT. OFF.

"When you read this report card, Dad, I'd like to explain that the teacher and I have very different ideologies!"

grade type reports and have emphasized achievement in the old line subjects, there is no certainty that informal reporting spells modern school practices, or vice versa. Administrators, teachers, pupils, and parents have commonly lost sight of the purposes to be achieved through reporting and, as a result, reporting policies and procedures have often been adopted that impede and obstruct the improvement of the school program.

A fairly common procedure employed by school administrators in revising their report cards is to collect forms used in comparable school districts and, after analyzing these and checking the content and design against existing cards, to develop a new set of report forms. It is true that from such a study, one may gain some useful information. The design of the card or booklet, the introductory statement, and the method of recording judgments may suggest improvements in general organization and format to those contemplating a change in existing arrangements. But this is not the place to begin. The first step in revising a scheme for reporting pupil progress might well be for the staff to discuss the fundamental question: What purpose does the school hope to achieve through reporting to parents?

The answer to this query may seem self-evident, but judging from the variety of replies to this question when put to administrators, teachers, and parents, too little thought has been given to it in the past. Some authors in listing the purposes of reporting have included the following: (1) stimulating teachers to become acquainted with pupils, (2) developing school support, and (3) keeping the public informed. It is possible that reporting to parents may sometimes accomplish one or more of these ends, but they are certainly incidental and secondary to the basic purpose of reporting pupil progress. The one major objective, or so it seems to the authors, which outweighs all others in reporting is *to provide the information necessary for a sound working relationship between the school and the home in the guidance of the child.*

It should be noted that there is no state law which compels schools to issue report cards to parents. Parents may put pressure on the school board, the superintendent of schools, and the principal to report pupil progress, and there may be no reasonable alternative but to comply. But this condition does not constitute the chief reason for keeping parents informed about their children's school life.

What Should Parents Be Told

Once the staff and parents agree on the basic function of reporting, then it becomes easier to develop devices to serve this purpose. A logical second question for the school staff to consider is "What specifically should the school tell parents about their children's achievement and behavior?" A general answer to this question is found in the foregoing statement of purpose, namely, provide information which promises to strengthen the relationship between home and school in their efforts to aid the child. A more detailed answer, however, can be developed by examining the several objectives of the school, assuming there is a set of well-defined purposes. A school that doesn't have clearly stated aims as a basis for its program is like a ship's captain without a compass, with no assurance of being headed in the right direction. Modern school objectives include pupil achievement and growth in areas beyond those included in the traditional subjects found in the typical school curriculum. They relate to knowledge and skill in healthful living; they concern achievement in the area of social competence and human relations; they have to do with the acquisition of esthetic tastes; they pertain to development in emotional adjustment and maturity; they relate to learning to think critically; and they bear on achievement in the art and skills of communication.

Parents, if they are to co-operate in guiding children's experiences, need information on children's progress in these latter areas as well as in the more traditional school activities. It is small wonder that most parents have assumed that the school's primary aim has been to teach pupils to read, write, and compute. Report cards have emphasized pupil gains in these subjects almost to the exclusion of all other areas of growth and development. What more natural result is to be expected than for parents to conclude that achievement in reading, writing, and arithmetic is the school's chief concern? Had the school consistently reported achievements in other important areas of school life as well, educational programs today might be more comprehensive. This in no way implies that progress in the three R's is not important nor that pupil achievement in the "fundamentals" should not be reported. It does suggest, however, that pupil progress in the other areas of experience delineated earlier should be given equal consideration in reporting.

Examining and clarifying aims, then, is indicated as an early step in appraising reporting practices. Once objectives are clearly understood, the next step in developing a reporting device is to decide how best to report pupil progress and needs in each of the broad areas included in the statement of objectives.

To accomplish this, it will be necessary to break down the major learning areas such as social competence, esthetic tastes, healthful living, or English expression, social studies, manual arts—whatever the curriculum organization suggests—into component behavior outcomes that are meaningful to both teachers and parents. This will not be an easy task, but it is necessary if parents are to co-operate with the school in a joint effort to help pupils achieve their greatest development in the fields specified.

The Essex Fells, New Jersey, public school report form "spells out" for each grade the objectives established in the various areas of the curriculum. To illustrate, in grade 4 under social studies the following four purposes are stated:[1]

1. To interpret various types of maps
2. To learn the effects of environment upon man's life activities
3. To gain understanding and appreciation of other peoples
4. To increase skill in planning and working out a problem together

Similarly in grade 1 the number-work objectives are set forth as follows:

1. To count to 100 by 1's, 5's and 10's, and write numbers in many situations
2. To begin discovery of addition and subtraction facts up to 9
3. To use numbers in daily life, by weighing, measuring, counting and buying

School systems will undoubtedly continue to pursue somewhat different objectives and will organize their learning programs into various patterns and designs. Some school systems will adhere to the more traditional categories in reporting to parents. But no matter what general objectives are established, there will be need for a considerable refinement of the broad areas into which the experiences of children can logically be classified. "English expression" connotes to most parents a general idea relating to communication but it does not always focus attention upon such specific purposes as are stated in the Essex Fells, New Jersey, report form for grade 5, namely:

1. To use good English in conversation or before a group
2. To write good simple English with correct use of capitals, sentence forms, paragraphs and punctuation
3. To express original ideas in plays, stories, and poems

The primary responsibility for clarifying learning areas and objectives rests with the school staff. It is essential, however, if the best results are to be secured that parents also share in the formulation of the school's aims and purposes. Schools are creations of the state; they belong to the people, and determining the content and nature of the curriculum is not

[1] Essex Fells Public School, Essex Fells, N. J. *Report for Grade 4* and *Report for Grade 1.*

by any means the *sole* prerogative of the teaching staff. Teachers, because of their training and experience, should play an important leadership role in deciding what should be taught. But parents have a big stake in the school program, and this fact should not be overlooked when school personnel set to work on establishing objectives and designing reporting devices.

How to Insure Helpful Communication

Once the objectives have been clarified and the curriculum areas broken down into meaningful parts, the next question to consider is how to insure helpful communication with parents relating to the achievement of their children. Here there is room for some differences of opinion. The check list which permits the teacher to record "satisfactory or normal growth," "exceptional progress," and "needs improvement" gives most parents a rather good picture of children's progress and identifies the areas most needing attention. But unless this type of reporting is accompanied by teacher comments at appropriate points, there is little opportunity afforded for discussing the cause of the poor achievement or the steps necessary to improve the situation.

One of the controversial issues in reporting relates to whether or not children's progress should be reported in terms of the achievement of the class group or in terms of the child's own abilities. Some authors[2] suggest that the report include both. Probably most parents should be advised from time to time of their children's relative progress, but it seems doubtful that this should be recorded on a report form. The report card is only one medium for informing parents about their children's achievement or potentialities. The danger in including a pupil's class standing in a formal report card is that this fact alone often overshadows all other information and creates a psychological block on the part of both parents and pupils.

Other Forms of Reporting

Telephone conversations, informal and prearranged conferences, and letters to parents on specific problems are other commonly used methods of acquainting parents with pupil growth and behavior. Several schools have found it practical to arrange for teacher-parent conferences where

[2] Ruth Strang, *Reporting to Parents,* Bureau of Publications, Teachers College, Columbia University, New York, 1947.

the pupil's progress and his needs are discussed. Such a plan has many advantages over a written communication. When the conference procedure is used, misinterpretation of the pupil's status can be reduced to a minimum. Allowances can be made for individual differences in parents, and children's interests can be safeguarded. Questions that arise in parents' minds as to specific helps and aids to child progress can be answered. Interviews with parents give teachers much greater appreciation and understanding of home background than traditional forms of communication. Face to face contacts can also strengthen the bond between home and school, and the interview procedure should supersede other reporting schemes in communities where it is feasible to use it. Unfortunately, in some industrial areas and in towns heavily populated with commuters it is more difficult to arrange conferences with parents, and the interview technique must be supplemented with other reporting devices.

Pupil Participation

Modern schools seek to involve the pupil in assessing his own efforts and potentialities as far as his maturity will permit. Recognition of this desirable procedure led some students of the problem to the conclusion that reports to parents should be prepared co-operatively by teacher and pupil. In Montclair, New Jersey, a report form entitled "My Growth Plan," was introduced in 1945 for use in grades 4, 5, and 6 and up to present writing has been used experimentally. This self-appraisal form was not intended to replace other forms of reporting but was designed to supplement the regular report of progress. A major purpose of "My Growth Plan" was to give the child the experience of clarifying his goals, evaluating his progress, and taking the initiative in planning next steps.[3] As it is illustrated on page 186, the form consists of a check list and provides an opportunity for pupils to record their progress and their needs as they understand them. While it is too early to appraise the results of this particular experiment, it seems certain that schools in the future will bring pupils into the evaluation process to the degree that such an arrangement is educationally profitable and feasible. It seems doubtful that self-appraisal schemes can be wisely substituted for the critical analysis of the teacher provided for in the better report forms.

[3] Montclair Public Schools, *Coordination of Home and School Through Use of Report of Pupil Progress and Pupil Growth Plan in the Elementary School,* Montclair, New Jersey, October 17, 1946, p. 1 (Mimeographed bulletin).

FIGURE 6. Pupil Self-Appraisal Form Used Experimentally in Montclair, New Jersey, Public Schools

MY GROWTH PLAN

While I, ... , expect to improve in many things, I am checking here those on which I plan to work hardest now.   I hope my teacher and my parents will make comments or suggestions which they think will help me in any of my work.

CLASS GOALS	√	MY NEXT STEPS	√	MY NEXT STEPS
MY HEALTH HABITS				
Keep myself neat and clean				
Sit and stand well				
MY RELATIONSHIP WITH OTHERS				
Work well with others				
Play well with others				
Accept guidance from persons of experience				
Show consideration for others				
MY WORK HABITS				
Listen carefully and follow directions				
Work well alone				
Complete and check my work				
MY SKILLS, KNOWLEDGE AND UNDERSTANDING				
LANGUAGE				
Speak so others understand me				
Write so others understand me				
Read with understanding				
Spell correctly				
Write neatly				
ARITHMETIC				
Compute accurately				
Reason in arithmetic problems				
PHYSICAL SKILLS				
Improve my skills in games				
UNDERSTANDING THE WORLD				
Use many different kinds of art materials				
Take part in music				
Read many different kinds of books				
Take part in the study of science				
Try to understand the people of all lands				

Much of the value of this GROWTH PLAN depends on conferences

The teacher will from time to time need to make his judgments and suggestions to parents independently of any appraisal which the pupil makes of his own needs and achievements.

Handbook for Parents

Reporting to parents is often viewed by principals and teachers as a specific communication from the school to the parents of a particular child about the latter's needs and progress. In many school systems no other written reports are sent to parents. There are, however, an increasing number of school systems that are extending their reporting media to include special bulletins and handbooks in which an attempt is made to interpret to parents the school program, administrative policies, and the general life of the school. This may be sent out from the central office to all parents of elementary school children, assuming a fairly high degree of uniformity among schools in matters to be reported, or such bulletins may be prepared and distributed by individual school units as circumstances warrant. The Battle Creek handbook entitled *You and Your School* contains an introductory message from the superintendent of schools expressing the hope that "this little booklet will answer some of the questions which you might have concerning the school life of your child."[4] Among the topics discussed are kindergarten entrance, school hours, school calendar, school clothing, absence policy, reporting procedures, carrying lunch to school, student council, safety patrol, trips, parent-teacher association, visiting teachers, school health service, the school farm, and the school camp. The booklet is well illustrated and interestingly written and it is easy to believe that it would make for better understanding and closer co-operation on the part of parents.

Many communities issue special bulletins to parents whose children are just entering school. The title "A Happy Year Ahead" appears on the Yonkers report for 1949 which is typical of several recent publications in this field. The information contained in these reports is especially valuable for parents unacquainted with the practices and procedures found in a modern school. Such an orientation provides a head start for children entering school and does much to create a sense of security on the part of parents.

[4] Elementary Schools of Battle Creek, *You and Your School—A Handbook for Parents,* Elementary Schools of Battle Creek, Battle Creek, Michigan, September 1949.

Trends in Reporting to Parents

As was emphasized earlier, reporting arrangements in public elementary schools vary widely and it is difficult to present an adequate description of current practices in a brief discussion of the topic. There are, however, certain identifiable trends which suggest what tomorrow's reporting procedures may resemble. These include:

1. A trend away from formal report cards to diagnostic letters and informal notes.

2. A shift from a rather limited report of scholastic progress to a more comprehensive report of the total development and growth of the child.

3. A trend (where printed report forms are used) toward stating the specific objectives to be attained in the various areas of the school program.

4. A trend in the direction of oral reporting through parent-teacher conferences.

5. Greater flexibility both with respect to time and manner of reporting. (Considerably more freedom in reporting is allowed individual school units and teachers than was formerly granted.)

6. A trend in the direction of soliciting the reactions of parents to the pupil's progress and to the teacher's report of pupil progress.

7. The preparation of special bulletins and handbooks for parents and other lay citizens to inform them about school policies and practices.

8. Some disposition as illustrated by the Montclair experiment to develop self-appraisal forms for pupil use in the upper grades of the elementary school.

Reporting policies and practices are closely interwoven with the total educational program, and their future cannot be separated. If the trend toward making the school curriculum more functional continues and a modern philosophy of pupil growth is accepted, then older forms of reporting will of necessity be replaced by arrangements more in harmony with the newer concepts of educational philosophy.

In giving leadership to teachers and parents in the improvement of school reporting, the administrator should keep in mind the following basic principles:

1. The chief purpose of reporting pupil progress to parents is to *pro-

vide the information necessary for a sound working relationship between the school and the home in the guidance of the child. Hence the reporting device or devices should be so fashioned as to contribute to this end.

2. *Parents should be kept informed about the growth and progress of their children in all aspects of the school curriculum.* This implies reporting evidences of change in the emotional, the physical, the social, and the esthetic phases of pupil growth as well as in the intellectual.

SIDE GLANCES   By Galbraith

COPR. 1950 BY NEA SERVICE, INC. T. M. REG. U. S. PAT. OFF.

"It could be a better report card, Dad, but let's not worry about it so much that we get ulcers!"

3. *Nothing should be included in an oral or written report to parents which seems likely to operate against the welfare of the child.* Principals need to raise this question continuously in relation to reporting. The knowledge possessed by teachers and principal regarding the child's home background and their awareness of the character and attitudes of the parents are the only safeguards that can be employed. It must not be forgotten that some parents are ignorant, neurotic, unreasonable, cruel, selfish, and that their children are unwanted. Reports should always be constructive.

4. *Pupil progress reports should be so written and constructed that parents understand well their role in guiding the child's development.* To accomplish this, the report should be diagnostic and indicate the relative seriousness of any behavior problem or growth factor requiring special attention of parents, suggesting how the latter can co-operate best in resolving the problem. Vague or general teacher comments are not likely to provide parents with the background they need in order to be helpful.

5. *Provision should be made for parent-teacher interviews, informal notes, telephone calls, and specially prepared bulletins and handbooks.* Reporting to parents should not be limited to letters or to the usual report forms. Too often reporting is viewed by principal and teachers to consist only of the report form which is sent periodically to the home. Both parents and teachers should be encouraged to examine the possibilities of improving the whole sphere of reporting.

6. *Reporting policies should be revised co-operatively by teachers, parents, and principal.* Many schools have made the mistake of revising their report forms without parent co-operation and the results have in some instances been disastrous.

SUGGESTED READINGS

D'Evelyn, K. E., *Individual Parent-Teacher Conferences,* Bureau of Publications, Teachers College, Columbia University, New York, 1945.

Driscoll, G., *How to Study the Behavior of Children,* Bureau of Publications, Teachers College, Columbia University, New York, 1941.

Elsbree, W. S., *Pupil Progress in the Elementary School,* Bureau of Publications, Teachers College, Columbia University, New York, 1943.

Irish, B., "What Is a Good Report Card?", *Educational Leadership,* vol. IV, April 1947, pp. 433–434.

McGaughy, J. R., *An Evaluation of the Elementary School,* The Bobbs-Merrill Company, Indianapolis, 1937, pp. 302–313.

Strang, Ruth, *Reporting to Parents,* Bureau of Publications, Teachers College, Columbia University, New York, 1947.

Traxler, Arthur E., *Techniques of Guidance,* Chapter XIII, "Reports to the Homes," Harper and Brothers, New York, 1945, pp. 235–283.

SCHOOL RECORDS

       The efficiency of a school is contingent to some degree upon the presence and use of appropriate records. Not only is it impractical for teachers and principal to keep all the important facts about pupil background and achievement fresh in their minds, but the mobility of staff personnel requires the establishment of a stable and systematic scheme if the welfare of pupils is to be safeguarded. Some records are required by the state as a part of the machinery essential for administering the compulsory attendance law, and in some commonwealths state aid to local districts is based on pupil enrollment and attendance data. Most states require the school to keep a permanent record card which contains attendance data and shows the work taken by pupils. There are also some records that are required by the administrators in the central office in their efforts to give an adequate accounting of stewardship. The principal, therefore, needs to be thoroughly familiar with existing requirements and alert to the needs for improving the records used in his own school.

Most record systems, if indeed they can logically be called systems, have not been developed as a result of a careful appraisal of needs and with consideration of the use to which they will be put. Too often the record scheme has grown up by a process of accretion. As a result, the making and keeping of school records often consumes a disproportionate amount of the time of teachers and contributes little to the efficiency of the school. One evidence of the need for some thoughtful consideration of this problem is the marked differences among school systems in the number and kinds of records used. One school with which the authors are acquainted has fourteen different record forms and another one boasts twice this number. The natural question arises: If 14 are sufficient, why use 28, and if 28 are necessary, how does the school with only 14 get along? The answer can be found only by giving thought to the role of records in administering the school and to their significance for the education of pupils.

Who Should Formulate Record Policies?

Like other administrative practices that affect every employee in the school, record policies should be formulated co-operatively by teachers and principal, and where they affect others (such as the custodian or parents) these persons also should have a share in determining the nature of the record forms adopted. In some instances the principal evolves a system of records with a minimum of assistance from others. More often, the central office has determined the record policy, and relatively little latitude has been given principals and teachers to depart from a city-wide system. Experience has shown that both the modes just mentioned of developing a record system have serious limitations. Representative teachers working with the principal should be made responsible for developing suitable pupil record forms and should, in the process, tap the wisdom of the whole staff of teachers in a school. Any other than this grass-roots approach overlooks the advantages that come from a group attack. Teachers will use what they themselves have developed and will be quick to see imperfections and eliminate them as experience warrants. The principal might well serve as co-ordinator of a committee whose job it is to revise the record system, and as a "resource" person he should make available such illustrative material and data as seem appropriate. But under no circumstances should he determine the policy single-handedly.

Relation of Records to School Objectives

Record arrangements should be viewed, like most other administrative policies, from the angle of their relationship to the attainment of the major objectives of the school. To the degree that they contribute to the achievement of the school's chief aims, to that degree they are good. With the possible exception of those records required by law, there is little reason for the existence of a record unless it promises to help children progress and learn.

A records committee, therefore, can wisely start with a statement of the school's objectives. From this point on, no single method of approaching the problem can lay claim to any certain superiority. In some cases, present records can be tested by asking to what extent, if any, each form is contributing to a major aim of the school. In this way superfluous forms can be eliminated, and the remaining records retained. The elimination of useless forms and those which have little value in the existing program is logically followed by a search for additional forms that hold promise of serving a useful purpose.

One Method of Improving a Record System

One approach which seems to the authors to be especially helpful in testing out the scope of the record system is for the record committee to take a hypothetical case of a child who is approaching the age of entrance and about to enter kindergarten, and to follow this child through a typical series of experiences from the time he is identified as a resident of the district, to his completion of the sixth grade, or his transfer to some other school. As each type of experience is considered, questions can logically be raised as to whether or not recording facts about the pupil, or the experience noted, will serve the interests of pupil and school. If so, what facts and in what form can they best be recorded?

The following is illustrative of the kind of analysis which might profitably be made in evaluating or devising pupil records: Fred Smith, whose parents moved into the district two years ago, enters kindergarten. If the school has conducted a summer roundup or a preschool clinic, considerable information about Fred will have been gathered before he appears at the building to begin his formal schooling, and the principal's office will have recorded certain essential facts about him. But in many instances Fred and his mother will arrive at school without any prior communication with the principal, and the matter of recording information about Fred will require some consideration on the part of a school official. In many schools this first step in pupil accounting is referred to as "registration," and the blank used in New Rochelle (see Figure 7, page 194) is typical of the better forms now used in elementary schools.

This type of registration form is made out in triplicate; one copy is retained in the school office, one copy is sent to the attendance office,

FIGURE 7. Registration Blank Used in New Rochelle, New York, Public Schools

					GRADE		
				M F			
LAST NAME		FIRST NAME	MIDDLE NAME	SEX	H.R. NO.		TELEPHONE
DATE ENTERED	SCHOOL		ADDRESS				

SCHOOL LAST ATTENDED BEFORE ENTERING THIS SCHOOL

	SCHOOL	CITY	STATE

	MONTH DAY YEAR	AUTHORITY FOR DATE OF BIRTH	HANDICAPS	ACTIVITIES
DATE OF BIRTH		☐ BIRTH CERT. ☐ OTHER LEGAL EVIDENCE	SIGHT	ORCHESTRA
PLACE OF BIRTH	CITY·	☐ BAPT. CERT.	HEARING	BAND
	STATE·	☐ PASSPORT	SPEECH	GLEE-CLUB

LANGUAGE SPOKEN IN HOME	DATE VERIFIED	SCHOOL	BY	ORTHOPEDIC	
☐ ENGLISH ☐ GERMAN					
☐ ITALIAN ☐	VACCINATION			NUMBER OF CHILDREN IN HOME	

NAME	RACE & COUNTRY OF BIRTH	OCCUPATION	RESIDENCE (RECORD ONLY WHEN DIFFERENT FROM STUDENT'S)
FATHER			
MOTHER (MAIDEN NAME)			
STEP-PARENT GUARDIAN			

REGISTRATION
TEACHER'S COPY
NEW ROCHELLE PUBLIC SCHOOLS

and one copy is given to Fred's teacher. While some additions to the items listed in the chart, or changes in headings, may be needed to fit local conditions, in the main the card contains the essential elements for enrolling Fred and identifying him as a member of the school community.

Record of Teachers' Interviews with Parents

Fred's registration having been completed, he goes to the kindergarten room and is there entrusted to the care of his teacher. His school career now really begins. Fred's teacher observes his behavior and forms tentative judgments regarding his personality traits, his mental, physical, social, and emotional maturity, and his interests. But to guide Fred's experiences wisely, the teacher needs more information than is included on the registration card just described. These additional data he hopes to secure through an interview with Fred's mother as soon as a convenient time can be arranged for it. Some parents will have been interviewed by teachers prior to entrance. This is advantageous but, unfortunately, it happens infrequently. Moreover, since there are several other children in the room Fred's teacher cannot rely solely upon his memory of what facts came out of the interview pertaining to Fred. He needs to record them for future reference. In some cases, when parents are willing, an actual sound recording of the whole interview between parent and teacher will be made and the discs filed for future reference. But many parents will be skeptical and fearful of sound recordings of such interviews and, with these parents, an interview form will have to suffice. This can either be filled out as the interview progresses or immediately following it. The specific nature of the form and the items included should be determined by what teachers and principal conclude to be essential for giving children the help they most need. Too frequently some vital fact bearing on a child's home background is learned by the teacher after months of bewilderment. The form used in Glencoe, Illinois, reproduced below, is illustrative of the type of information that can well be recorded.

> Record an answer to every question.
> Indicate negative replies by "no."
> Indicate "no response" by zero (O).

GLENCOE PUBLIC SCHOOLS

Teacher's Initial Interview with Parent

Please use as a supplement to the Enrollment Record. Ask the following questions of the parent or guardian directly and record their answers verbatim. It is not intended that advice shall be given in connection with the use of this blank. Original copy of blank is to be filed in the permanent record folder.

Name of Child _____ Sex _____ Birth Date _____
School _____ Grade _____ Teacher _____ Date_____

Relationship   Mother's
Informant _____ to Child _____ Maiden name _____
Language spoken in home: Dominant _____ Others _____

1. Has the child had previous school or play-class experience? Yes _____
No _____
Where _____ Date _____ How long _____
Where _____ Date _____ How long _____

2. Has there been anything unusual in the home conditions or the family situation which you think may have affected the child—such as: broken home, family deaths, unusual family illnesses, very frequent movings, etc.

3. Was the child's development unusual in any way? (i.e. walking, talking, able to make wants known, etc.)

4. For which hand does your child show preference?

Left _____ Right _____ Ambidextrous _____

If left-handed or ambidextrous, what is your attitude toward this?

5. List any of the following which your child has had; at what age, approximately?

Illnesses including contagious diseases	Age	Operations and Injuries	Age
_____	_____	_____	_____
_____	_____	_____	_____
_____	_____	_____	_____
_____	_____	_____	_____

Has the child had immunizations for the following?

	Yes	No		Yes	No
Diphtheria	____	____	Typhoid	____	____
Scarlet Fever	____	____	Whooping Cough	____	____
Small Pox	____	____	Tuberculosis Test	____	____

6. Are there any special conditions to be watched for in school at the present time?

	Yes	No		Yes	No
Elimination	____	____	Allergies	____	____
Hayfever	____	____	Others (specify)	____	____
Asthma	____	____		____	____
Sinus	____	____			

Is the child under treatment for those special conditions? Yes _____
No _____

7. Sleep and Rest Habits:

What is his usual bedtime? _____

Does he go to sleep promptly? _____

When does he usually arise? _____

Does child have a daytime nap or rest? _____

8. Does the child have any special defects or handicaps for which he will need special help now or in his later education?

Auditory _____ Visual _____ Others _____

Comments:

9. What is your estimate of your child's intelligence? Does he (or she) seem to you to be average, above average, or below average? Please be absolutely frank in your reply.

10. Does the child show any special interests? Yes _____ No _____
    (If "yes," specify)

11. Play activities: Are his usual playmates:
    Older _____ Younger _____ Same Age _____
    Same Sex _____ Opposite Sex _____
    Does he play happily with others? _____ Alone _____
    Comments:

    Does he listen to the radio? _____
    What programs _____
    Do you remember at what age your child started to listen to the radio?
    _____
    Do you remember what prompted him to begin listening to the radio?
    _____
    Do you consider the radio a problem? If so, specify.

    About how often does he attend movies?
        What type of movies? (Indiscriminately or carefully selected)

    Does he take music lessons?
    Does he take dancing lessons?

12. Does the child present any special problems at home? (The following suggestive list may be read to the parent; if problem has been either mild or serious, check whether in past or at present.

	Not Observed	Mild	Serious	Past	Present
Feeding					
Sleeping					
Enuresis (Wets self during day)					
(Wets self at night)					
Difficulty getting on with other children					
Sex (Handles sex organs)					
(Overly curious or conscious about sex)					
Teasing (Not coaxing)					
Fighting					
Cruelty (To other children)					
(To animals)					

	Not Observed	Mild	Serious	Past	Present
Deliberate destructiveness					
Jealousy					
Fears (specify)					
Temper outbursts					
Crying spells					
Whining					
Sulking					
Excessive day-dreaming (Withdraws into world of own thoughts when situation calls for other action.)					
Speech difficulties					
Thumb or finger sucking					
Nail biting					
Nose picking					
Other "nervous habits" (specify)					
Dishonesty (specify)					
Muscular co-ordination					
Difficult to manage (i.e. disobedience)					

Other problems may be listed below:

13. For what is he most often punished? \
How frequently? (approximately)   Daily _____ \
Weekly _____ Monthly _____ \
How effective is the punishment in preventing repetitions of the behavior for which he is punished?
14. Can your child: (a) Put on his wraps and galoshes? Yes _____ No _____ \
                         (b) Tie his own shoe laces?   Yes _____ No _____ \
                         (c) Take care of his toilet needs? Yes _____ No _____
15. What was child's attitude toward starting to school this year?

   What was child's first reaction after entering school this year?

   What is his present attitude toward coming to school?

16. Have you any specific ideas of what you hope your child will have gained by the end of his primary experience?

Anecdotal Reports

Fred's progress, his social behavior, and his needs as revealed through his everyday experiences at school will constitute the basis for future conferences with parents, and will help the teacher in guiding Fred's activities. His teacher will need to illustrate his statements about Fred's needs with concrete examples. To insure this, Fred's teacher might well have forms available upon which to record anecdotal statements bearing on his accomplishments and behavior. While an ordinary pad could conceivably be used for this purpose, a specially labeled form containing a blank for date, and space for interpretation and recommendations, will be less likely to be mislaid or lost, and can be kept in the teacher's desk where it will be readily accessible.

Fred's interests as manifested in his oral expressions, his attitude toward other pupils, toward his parents, and toward his teacher, are all of concern if the school program is to be most effectively directed toward his maximum growth and welfare. By noting specific examples from Fred's day-to-day behavior, the teacher will be better prepared for the interview with Fred's parents. What is of greatest importance, this chronological recording of pupil behavior will provide the teacher with invaluable information for use in guiding the learning and development of children. These anecdotal reports (or behavior journals as they are sometimes called) should be placed in Fred's cumulative personnel folder.

Health Record

Fred's health is a matter of concern to the school since it affects both his progress and his relationships with other pupils. Physicians have discovered through experience that recording information on their patients' health history leads to wiser counsel and treatment. If Fred's future welfare is to be adequately safeguarded, an early health examination and periodic reviews of his health must be made. Moreover, the physician's and nurse's observations need to be systematically recorded so that changes and improvements can be measured and studied. A good health record form is an excellent way to give teachers an understanding of one important *conditioner* of pupil progress and effort. Since Fred's behavior is related to his physical state, his teacher will need to make adjustments from time to time in line with the health data found on his

FIGURE 8. Health Record Used in Battle Creek, Michigan, Public Schools

Name..
(LAST)   (FIRST)   Sex................

Battle Creek Public Schools—Health Record
Date of birth..

		Disease	Date	Comments		Disease	Date	Comments
Communicable Diseases (List disease and date. Note effects.)	1				7			
	2				8			
	3				9			
	4				10			
	5				11			
	6				12			

		Type	Date	Comments		Type	Date	Comments
Prevent. Meas. Diphtheria, X-Ray, Whooping cough, Smallpox, T.B. tests. List type and date.	1				6			
	2				7			
	3				8			
	4				9			
	5				10			

	Date	Comments	Date	Comments
Physical Condition or Change. Teeth, eyes, ears, nose, throat, heart, handicaps.				

	Date	Doctor	Significant Findings and Treatment
Medical and Dental Examinations. (Please include pre-school health record if unusual.)			

Measures:

Year												
Height												
Weight												
Vision L												
Vision R												
Hearing L												
Hearing R												

Name:..

Battle Creek Public Schools—Health
Sex................   Date of birth..

TEACHER'S OBSERVATIONS OF PUPIL'S HEALTH STATUS

It is suggested that teacher's observations should include such things as undue restlessness, fatigue, thumbsucking, nail biting, excessive crying, tenseness, excessive use of lavatory, sleeping in class, very thin or very fat, very tall or very short, frequent colds, repeated absence for health reasons, operations, accidents.

Date:................	Date:................
...., Teacher	...., Teacher
Date:................	Date:................
...., Teacher	...., Teacher
Date:................	Date:................
...., Teacher	...., Teacher
Date:................	Date:................
...., Teacher	...., Teacher
Date:................	Date:................
...., Teacher	...., Teacher
Date:................	Date:................
...., Teacher	...., Teacher
Date:................	Date:................
...., Teacher	...., Teacher

200

card. However, doctors and nurses are not the only ones to detect physical disabilities. Teachers have a responsibilty here too. The Metropolitan Life Insurance Company has recently published a brief pamphlet entitled *What Teachers See*[1] which every teacher should read since it portrays most vividly the symptoms of some of the most common children's diseases and gives helpful information on what to look for.

Data on Fred's health then may be recorded on a special health form similar to the one on page 200 used in Battle Creek, Michigan.

Personnel Folders

The personnel folder constitutes an excellent device for getting to know Fred's potentialities and needs. Here should be filed most of the evidence and materials related to his problems and his achievements. A convenient arrangement is to put the personnel folder into a large envelope. Materials which should be filed in the personnel folder are:

1. A carbon copy of each report to his parents
2. The parents' reply to the report
3. Records of parental conferences
4. All confidential material
5. Any significant correspondence between parent and teacher, parent and administrator, from the psychiatrist, etc., which may have future use
6. Significant comments by doctor, nurse, special teachers, psychologists
7. Records of tests, behavior rating scales, "Guess Who" replies, and similar appraisal evidences
8. Specimens of handwriting, themes, art, etc.

The folder should be designed so as to serve as a permanent record form. The outside might well be filled out by the teacher when the child enters school, and the back page should be so arranged as to care for health information, achievement records, and other pertinent information.

In Passaic, New Jersey, a cumulative record form, similar to the personnel folder just mentioned, is the only form with which teachers have to be concerned except for the report to parents. It goes with the child

[1] Metropolitan Life Insurance Company, *What Teachers See,* New York, T 4669—(7–46).

from grade to grade and from school to school (within the city). In many schools, however, principals and teachers have felt the need for separate record forms (unlike the arrangement just described), either because they could be more conveniently filled out, or because they could be more effectively used.

As Fred progresses through the grades information is continually added to the data originally placed in his personnel folder, and the principal and teaching staff are thereby better equipped to counsel him because they know more about him.

At regular intervals the school will report to Fred's parents on his progress. The nature of modern reporting devices is discussed in Chapter XII; it will suffice here to point out that the report card or informal letter to the home bears a close relationship to other record forms and procedures. In fact, the report to parents is based largely on data gleaned from several of the record forms just described.

How to Report Accidents

It would not be unusual for Fred at some point in his elementary school experience to have a slight accident on the school grounds. If this should occur, certain factual data would need to be recorded, both to safeguard his interests and to protect the school and the staff against unjust criticism and possibly a charge of negligence. The requirements that a report be filled out immediately following an accident is a fairly common one and the better forms used include all the pertinent items. The report blank adopted in Seattle is an illustration of an accident form that is designed to increase pupil safety and also to record data bearing on the presence or absence of staff negligence. (See Figure 9.)

Transfer Record

Another possible contingency which needs to be anticipated relates to pupil transfer. Fred's parents may move to some other community during his elementary school career. If so, his new teacher and principal will profit greatly by having certain information about him from the school which he last attended. In order to furnish these data efficiently and at the same time retain a record in the school from which Fred is transferring, a form made out in triplicate is used in some school systems. While the specific items included on such a record form will vary somewhat depending upon the judgment of the committee or person

FIGURE 9. Accident Report Used by Seattle, Washington, Public Schools

SEATTLE SCHOOL DISTRICT No. 1

Report of Accident

This report is to be made in duplicate. Send both copies to the Superintendent's office. A copy should not be kept in the school file.

Name of person injured _____ Age _____

Date _____ Hour _____

Address _____ Phone _____

Name of school _____ Place of accident _____

Nature of injury _____

How did the accident happen? (Give full details) _____

Was accident caused by anyone other than the person injured? Give details and name of person responsible _____

How? _____ Time called _____

Was a doctor called? If so, give name of doctor _____

Address _____ Phone _____

Treatment _____

What was done with injured person? (Taken home, returned to class, etc.) _____

Were parents notified? _____

Who is blamed for the accident? _____

Was the accident avoidable? _____

Was the accident due to any paraphernalia used by the school? _____

What warning was given injured person, either just before the accident or by general instructions prior to the accident? _____

What was done by injured person, or others, to avoid accident? _____

Was the accident due to defects of or in any school property? _____

If due to defects of any kind, did person know of such defects? _____

Had these defects been reported to anyone? _____

If so, to whom were they reported? _____

When were they reported? _____

Any statement made by injured person? _____

Could injured person have prevented accident? _____

What are the characteristics of the injured person—careful or reckless? _____

Is the injured person easily amenable to discipline? _____

Names of witnesses: _____ Address: _____

_____

_____

(To be signed by the principal of the school)

FIGURE 10. Transfer Card Used in New Rochelle, New York, Public Schools

						M	F
LAST NAME			FIRST NAME	MIDDLE NAME		SEX	
NAME OF PARENT OR GUARDIAN			OCCUPATION OF PARENT OR GUARDIAN	MONTH	DAY	YEAR	
RESIDENCE BEFORE TRANSFER			NEW RESIDENCE OR PRIVATE SCHOOL	AGE WHEN TRANSFERRED		YRS.	MO.

GRADE	ROOM	HEALTH	CONDUCT	SCHOLARSHIP	DATE OF LAST ATTENDANCE	DATE OF TRANSFER

ATTENDANCE AND PUNCTUALITY

19	DAYS PRESENT	DAYS ABSENT	TIMES TARDY	19	DAYS PRESENT	DAYS ABSENT	TIMES TARDY
SEPTEMBER				FEBRUARY			
OCTOBER				MARCH			
NOVEMBER				APRIL			
DECEMBER				MAY			
JANUARY				JUNE			
SCHOOL			TEACHER		PRINCIPAL		

TRANSFER CARD	DEPARTMENT OF EDUCATION, NEW ROCHELLE, N. Y.
OFFICE COPY	FILL OUT FOR A PUPIL TRANSFERRING TO ANOTHER SCHOOL EITHER IN OR OUTSIDE OF CITY

designing the card, the one used in New Rochelle, New York, is illustrative.

The original record form illustrated above is salmon colored and is kept in the office; a second copy in white is sent to the attendance department for its files; and a grey third copy is sent to the new school.

It seems clear that the information included in the New Rochelle transfer card represents the minimum data needed to give Fred a start in his new environment. If this school is located in the same city or district as Fred's former school, then his personnel folder containing much detailed information on his achievement and interests should also be sent to the principal of the school to which he is transferring.

Permission to Take Trips

To safeguard Fred and the school it is also probable that a special form will be used which expressly records the parents' permission for Fred to go on scheduled field trips. While the primary object of this is to protect the school board and its employees against liability for accidents, it does serve as a means of advising parents of contemplated trips and calls their attention to whatever hazards to pupil safety may be involved. The following form used in Newark, New Jersey, while stressing the waiver feature does contain information of interest and worth

FIGURE 11. Trip Permission Form Used by Newark, New Jersey, Public Schools

---

BOARD OF EDUCATION   NEWARK, NEW JERSEY

Date...School

Trip to:...

Pupil:..

It is requested hereby that the above-mentioned pupil be permitted to take this trip, and in consideration of such permission it is agreed by the undersigned as follows: That neither the Board nor any of its employees assumes any responsibility in connection with the trip; that neither the Board nor any of its employees shall be liable to the undersigned or to the pupil for any claim arising out of the trip, such claims being hereby waived; and that the undersigned will indemnify and save harmless the Board and its employees from all liability for such claims as well as from claims of all other persons resulting from any act of the pupil during the trip. "Trip" includes the period between the time when the pupil leaves the school and returns home.

....
Parent

....
Parent

I waive all claims against the Board of Education and its employees for anything that occurs during the above mentioned trip.

Form 23A   ....
Pupil

---

to parents. (For a discussion of legal liability in connection with trips, see pages 30–31.)

Other Records

In facilitating Fred's journey through the school, a few other records than those discussed here will undoubtedly be employed. The state, for example, will require a systematic report on his attendance, and a special register for this purpose is often furnished to each teacher with directions for filling it out.

After this brief forecast of Fred's educational experiences, the records committee referred to earlier may still find a few needs for recording uncared for. If so, steps should be taken to fill in the gaps, and appropriate forms should be designed. The danger to be guarded against is the addition of pupil blanks which contribute but little to the major task of the school and add substantially to the work of teachers and principal. The test of usefulness should always be applied. Rarely, it would seem, can more than 15 different forms be justified. Bronxville, New York, provides elementary teachers with a handbook[2] in which the elementary

[2] Bronxville Public Schools, *Handbook for Teachers,* Bronxville Elementary Schools, compiled by Records Committee, 1940–41 (Mimeographed).

school records are enumerated and described. In this school system record forms have been kept to a minimum consistent with efficiency.

Housing Pupil Records

The development of suitable record forms is without question an important achievement. But the efficiency of the record system depends also upon certain other conditions. One of these relates to the *facilities provided teachers for housing records*. Every teacher should have a filing cabinet that can be locked, and it should be so located as to be reached easily from the teacher's desk chair. The practice of housing all the confidential records in the principal's office is inefficient since experience reveals that under those conditions teachers usually make relatively little use of them. Convenience and accessibility are important criteria to consider when filing arrangements are being planned. Moreover, teachers should be provided with manila folders, tabs, loose-leaf notebooks, carbon paper, and other materials that make for efficient record keeping and duplicating.

Clerical Assistance

There are few classroom teachers who do not feel that record keeping is an arduous task. Taking attendance in accordance with the law and filing reports are required by local school-board regulations, when accompanied by the systematic collection and recording of data inherent in any adequate scheme of pupil records, consumes many hours of the teacher's time. Any arrangement which gives promise of relieving the teacher of a part of the time now spent in record making and reporting, without sacrificing the pupils' interest, is certainly worthy of consideration. While no single formula can be expected to fit the needs of all elementary schools, the solution lies in furnishing teachers with some clerical assistance. An analysis of the record-keeping job would reveal many areas where a clerical worker could assist. Unfortunately, up to the present time most elementary schools have not been given adequate clerical help, and what little has been furnished has seldom relieved teachers of their everyday clerical duties. The time may come when, say, every ten teachers, or some other number, will be provided with a secretary. While this will present an administrative problem for the principal, it will serve both to lift teacher morale and to increase instructional efficiency.

From the foregoing discussion a few general principles can be deduced. First, it seems clear that *those who keep and use records should have an important voice, both in creating the forms on which information is to be recorded and in formulating the policies governing their use.*

Second, *record forms should be consistent with the objectives of the school and should provide for the recording of significant facts and experiences in the pupil's educational life.* A functional analysis, similar to the approach outlined earlier, is one practical way of reaching decisions as to the usefulness of record forms. Another good test that should be applied is to relate record forms to professed goals.

Third, it can safely be asserted that *the number of record forms should be kept as low as is consistent with educational demands.* This means that in most elementary schools, judging from the needs of pupils, not more than fifteen forms will be required. There is, of course, no magic in the number fifteen. Collecting and recording data are time-consuming tasks and add significantly to the teacher's load. The number, therefore, should be kept low.

A fourth principle relates to the use and administration of record forms. *Records should be so housed that they are readily accessible to those who need to use them most.* This principle, if accepted, would lead to considerable decentralization in filing arrangements.

Fifth, *records should be used to promote the welfare of pupils.* Many school systems have elaborate record systems, but the data collected are seldom used so as to serve the interests of pupils. Teachers need to learn how to make the best use of the data recorded and to interpret facts wisely. Some instruction and guidance can profitably be given teachers in the use and interpretation of pupil records.

SUGGESTED READINGS

Hamalainen, Arthur Emil, *An Appraisal of Anecdotal Records,* Bureau of Publications, Teachers College, Columbia University, New York, 1943.

Olley, Wendell C., *Cumulative Pupil Records,* Bureau of Publications, Teachers College, Columbia University, New York, 1943.

Strang, Ruth, *Every Teacher's Records,* Bureau of Publications, Teachers College, Columbia University, New York, 1941.

U. S. Office of Education, *Handbook of Cumulative Records,* Bulletin 1944, no. 5, U. S. Government Printing Office, Washington, D. C.

CHAPTER XIV

DISCIPLINE AS END AND AS MEANS

One of the most misunderstood and controversial areas in education is that which comprises the group of problems labeled as "discipline." Intelligent and well-meaning people charge that in modern schools the fundamental place of discipline has been forgotten, and that the "progressive" schools are the chief cause of the irresponsibility, lack of courtesy, immorality, and contempt of authority which these critics attribute to present-day youth. Such a charge is ridiculous, of course, but it serves to illustrate the misconceptions of modern education which exist in the minds of many people.

Far from having been forgotten, discipline is one of the greatest concerns of principals and classroom teachers, although conceptions of the nature and application of disciplinary principles have been changing in significant respects. Discipline is one of the most vexing problems of the beginning teacher; experienced teachers face it throughout their teaching careers; and it consumes appreciable portions of the principal's time in handling "disciplinary cases" which have become too much for the classroom teacher to handle alone.

Perhaps it will help, in considering this topic, to clarify what the term *discipline* means. Sheviakov and Redl, in their helpful little booklet, identify three distinctly different meanings for the term:

1. The degree of order maintained in the classroom. This is "discipline we *have*."
2. The means employed to establish, maintain or repair order in the classroom. This is "discipline we *use*."

3. The specific means we use to punish offenders. In this sense, discipline is a euphemism for punishment, and is, in effect, "discipline we *inflict*."[1]

To these, the authors would add one further meaning, which is implicit in the above volume. That is the concept of self-discipline, or self-control. This is the meaning employed when it is observed that, "George certainly is a well-disciplined individual." This might be termed "discipline we live."

There are, of course, other semantic variations in the meaning of the word, but the above will suffice. It will probably help in understanding the issues involved in the problem of school discipline if the meaning employed at any given point in the ensuing discussion is identified.

It may also be helpful to think of discipline in terms of levels. Socially desirable behavior may be achieved by several methods.

1. External compulsion may be used. Force and threat are the chief techniques of this approach (which is still too prevalent in the schools, wishful thinking to the contrary), and its appeal is to the emotion of fear.

2. Some teachers place great reliance upon the force of their own personalities, using their own approval as the motivation to good behavior on the part of the pupils. This might be termed the "paternalistic" approach.

3. Various types of rewards have been employed in attempts to motivate desirable behavior. Silver and gold stars, prizes, good conduct marks, and special privileges in the class all have been used for this purpose. This approach appeals to the desire of an individual for preferment, for personal recognition, or for personal gain. Note that it is an artificial motivation, and tends to develop the expectation of reward for correct behavior.

4. Social approval may be used as a motivation. In adult life custom frequently has greater force than law. Few individuals are willing to run counter to the customs and expectations of the group with which they must live. Many teachers and principals have used this fact to advantage by establishing school or class pride in acceptable behavior. The common code is developed co-operatively with the pupils, so that breaches

[1] G. V. Sheviakov and F. Redl, *Discipline for Today's Children and Youth,* Association for Supervision and Curriculum Development, Washington, D. C., 1944, pp. 21–22.

of it are met with strong disapproval from the rest of the group. Such an approach appeals to the child's need to belong, and is psychologically sound.

5. The highest level of behavior is that which is not enforced by external control. However, it has within it subtle nuances, and one may, perhaps, distinguish two types. First is the self-discipline which stems from "enlightened self-interest" and which is self-oriented, practical, and realistic. The individual disciplines his behavior because he conceives it to be to his own best interest to do so. Being honest because "honesty is the best policy" is illustrative of this meaning. There is a self-discipline, however, which is not primarily self-centered, but which is motivated by altruism and idealism. At this level, loyalties to such broad human principles as justice, rights of minorities, liberty, compassion for the underprivileged, and equality are the governing forces of behavior, in contrast to the petty personal motives which operate at the lower levels. This type of behavior usually comes relatively late in a person's development; some never achieve it to the point where it is characteristic of their behavior.

"It's his own idea—claims he saw it in a movie."

It is evident, then, that the problem of discipline is not a simple one, by any means, and that no easy prescriptions can be given. Certain basic considerations can be pointed out, however, which should be of help to the principal and teacher in working on the problem.

The Question of Discipline as End or as Means

Traditionally, discipline has been conceived as a means to learning. A quiet, orderly classroom has been an important objective of teachers and principals in the belief that this is the situation most conducive to learning. A classroom characterized by "pin-drop quiet" was considered the mark of a good teacher, and teachers were hired and fired largely on the basis of their ability as "disciplinarians." In teacher-training institutions, courses in "classroom management" taught the tricks of the trade in achieving a quiet and orderly classroom. How to forestall and detect noisemakers, spitball-throwers, whisperers, or pigtail-pullers, and the means of dealing with these wrongdoers was an earnest topic of study. Supervisors rated teachers largely on their ability to "maintain control" (usually meaning silence and lack of movement) in the classroom, and counseled teachers on how to conduct class so that one's back was to the pupils a minimum of the time, where to stand so as best to see what was going on, and to detect cheating and copying, and the best means of dealing with those who rebelled against the unnatural quiet and enforced passivity of the usual classroom.

A little reflection will indicate clearly the relationship of this concept of discipline to the educational philosophy which has prevailed in the public schools during most of the years since their inception. At the risk of some oversimplification, it can be pointed out that schools have been predominantly institutions in which teachers have tried to force children to achieve purposes which adults think they should achieve. Adults established a curriculum of subjects which, for one reason or another, they deemed important to be learned, and then demanded that children learn it. Only during the last few decades have educators questioned this curriculum, and they have come to realize that in all too many respects there is little relationship between the learnings required and the daily life and purposes of the children themselves.

Coupled with this learning program was a psychology of learning which authorities have since come to repudiate: the theory of faculty psychology and mental discipline. Believing the mind to be made up of such separate faculties as memory, will, reason, imagination, and attention, it was natural to believe that, like muscles, these faculties would be strengthened by exercise. It was natural, also, to conclude that exercise in unpleasant tasks was desirable for its disciplinary effect on will, attention, and perseverance. It seemed reasonable to assume that engaging in pleasurable activities had no such virtues.

Belief in these two theories (an adult-determined curriculum and the theory of mental discipline) makes understandable the theory of discipline which has been applied for so long. Discipline, then, is the device used to hold pupils to purposes which are not theirs, with which they do not agree, and which they but imperfectly understand. Since the curriculum experiences consist primarily in memorizing facts and practicing skills, a quiet, immobile classroom is deemed the most desirable and conducive learning atmosphere. Within such an orientation discipline is first, last, and always a means to an end—the end of developing seemly and conforming behavior, or the end of "learning" the required subject matter. Other influences which help account for the above point of view have been omitted deliberately: the role of the child in the early American home, the religious doctrine of original sin, the point of view that "children should be seen but not heard," and the like, because there is not the space to discuss them here, but they were complementary to the prevailing educational theory.

It will also be observed that this type of discipline was unequivocally authoritarian in its conception. The teacher was expected to rule his classroom with an iron hand, and usually did so; offenses against the classroom order were considered as offenses against his authority, and were punished as such. It would be pleasant to think that all this had been left behind, and completely replaced with a more effective and more pleasant kind of situation. It is all too true, however, that the above described type of discipline still is practiced in varying degree in a large number of American schools and classrooms.

It is encouraging to note that this type of disciplinary philosophy is becoming much less characteristic of modern schools. The findings of psychology and child study, a better understanding of the nature of learning, an extension of better-understood principles of democracy into educational theory and practice, and an increasing social orientation in the curriculum, have all caused many people to modify their conceptions of the nature, place, and function of discipline in education. Instead of being considered as nothing but a means to an end, discipline is coming to be considered as an end in itself.

The changing conception of the nature of discipline is closely bound up with changes in education and in our culture. Psychologists now maintain that education is not a matter of training the mind like a muscle, but that learning is a "progressive reconstruction of experience." In this process, the child selects from his environment those experiences which suit his purposes, and each experience is integrated into and changes the total child in a manner comparable to the change brought about in a chemical solution by the addition of a reagent. If this is the characteristic nature of learning (and the evidence is convincing) the importance of the purposes of the learner is very evident. No longer can education as an achievement of *adult* purposes by children be justi- fied. Since the child will select his *own* purposes, no matter what teach- ers do, *it becomes a psychological fallacy to believe that adult purposes can be imposed upon him.* Regardless of its palatability, therefore, the conclusion that learning must be built around the purposes of the learner is inescapable. This does not imply, of course, a willy-nilly learning pro- gram based on the whims and transient interests of the pupils. It is the role of the teacher to guide the development and satisfaction of pur- poses, and to help the children to grow in their ability to establish and work for the achievement of worth-while and constructive goals. A good expression of the modern point of view is that of McConnell:

> Learning experiences are meaningful when they are related to the indi- vidual's interests, when they are involved in his living, when they not only contribute to his purposes at the time but enable him to make more in- telligent adjustments in the future, when they involve discovery and problem-solving rather than formal drill or mere memorization, and when they result in satisfying social relationships. Teachers and pupils, working co-operatively, should set up goals which will make that kind of learning possible and necessary, and together plan the effective means of realizing these purposes.[2]

Under such a concept of learning, imposed purposes and discipline to hold children to those imposed purposes are just plain silly. Teachers may be able to exert physical control over children, but their minds can- not be commanded.

Furthermore, the growing concept of democratic theory rejects the

[2] A. I. Gates, A. T. Jersild, T. R. McConnell, and R. C. Challman, *Educational Psychology,* The Macmillan Company, New York, 1942, pp. 317–318.

practice of imposed, authoritarian discipline. Free men must be able to govern themselves, and will learn to do so only if given practice and guidance in the process. American schools must do what American schools have never done to any appreciable degree: they must educate for democracy in a practical, functional manner. It is now well known that one learns to do only in the doing, but for some reason it has been assumed that the learning of democratic living was an exception to that principle. Democratic living cannot be taught out of books, it cannot be achieved by exhortation, it cannot be demanded or imposed. It can be learned only by practicing its skills and techniques under able and sympathetic guidance. This end cannot be achieved with the usual concept of repressive discipline.

The concept of learning cited above emphasizes another fact worth noting. This is the fact that learning is not a memorizing, but a problem-solving process, and should be lifelike or "involved in living." Such learning cannot be expected to take place best when children are glued to their seats in enforced silence. The life of children is an active affair, and certainly quiet is unnatural to them. A learning program which ignores these facts is bound to be inefficient and unpleasant. Modern education allows for activity and "constructive noise" in the classroom, rather than imposing silence and immobility on growing children.

The goals of education, then, are changing. Instead of compelling rote learning of predetermined subject matter, schools are now concerned with developing children into self-disciplined individuals. In this sense, discipline—intelligently civilized behavior and constructive self-direction—is an *end, a goal* of education, perhaps the major goal. It becomes something that comes "from the inside out" in an individual. Its importance in this sense has been recognized through the ages, as evidenced in the Biblical observation that "he who ruleth himself is greater than he who taketh a city."

At this point it might be well to take a look at the meanings of "discipline" which have been employed. The discussion of the older concept and practice of discipline was talking mostly about "discipline we have" (classroom order), "discipline we use," and "discipline we inflict." In these senses, discipline is a means to an end, and in the usual school curriculum, that end has been the learning of the adult-determined curriculum. Nevertheless, it must also be fairly recognized that self-discipline was also an important goal in schools of the past. This emphasizes that changes have taken place in two respects: (1) in the conception of the meaning of self-discipline, and (2) in the conception of the "discipline we use" to develop self-discipline.

For this reason it is misleading to draw an easy comparison between the old and the new conceptions, and to say that the difference is that the old conceived of discipline as a means, whereas the new looks upon it as an end of education. Rather is it a matter of emphasis. The goal of self-discipline (when defined as "intelligently controlled behavior for socially constructive ends") is not a new goal, but has taken on a new and increasingly important significance in the modern world. It is coming to be realized that only as individuals grow toward increasing altruistic and world-minded self-direction can progress be made toward solution of the vexing human relations problems which beset us. In addition, new insight into the dynamics of learning and the meaning of democratic living has served to change ideas about the nature of "discipline we use." It is now being recognized that although some external and authoritative control over children's behavior is necessary, it should not be in the same degree or for the same purposes as has been customary. Child-development authorities point out that even in infancy more self-determination than used to be permitted is healthy and desirable. At early ages, however, children are considerably more in need of adult guidance than in later growth stages. The discipline employed in our classrooms should be designed to place upon the child more and more responsibility for his own choices, purposes, and behavior as he grows in the ability to shoulder such responsibility. Such "discipline," instead of being repressive and utilizing punishment and reprisal for missteps, will plan with the children the purposes to be achieved and through the social control of group approval and disapproval will teach the child to discharge creditably the responsibilities assigned to him by the group. Such a procedure is consistent with the principles of good learning, with democratic methods, and with the facts of child development.

Classroom control then becomes something for which all members of the class *feel* some responsibility because misbehavior jeopardizes the achievement of purposes *they* have planned. There is also a different conception of "classroom order." In place of the repressive silence once held to be so desirable, it is now recognized that children (or adults) engaging in worth-while and constructive activity will produce a certain amount of natural noise. The emphasis on co-operative as opposed to competitive learning requires discussion and studying together that was anathema under the individualistic, competitive learning program which has been characteristic of our schools.

The conclusion seems obvious that the maintenance of classroom discipline is a function of good teaching. It is the natural outgrowth of a well-conceived and functional learning situation in which the learners participate in formulating the purposes of their daily activities, and the regulations and conditions within which those purposes will be achieved. The *process* of the daily conduct of the class is in itself a learning experience under these conditions, and is as much a part of the curriculum as is any factual knowledge, and in many respects far more important. It is a type of classroom discipline which is truly educative in self-discipline, and which helps children to become increasingly able to shoulder their responsibilities as democratic citizens of a democratic state. It is no longer simply something which the teacher *maintains;* it is something she helps children *attain.*

Handling Individual Offenders

Under the very best of conditions, however, there will occur the case of the child who is a "disciplinary problem"; the handling of these cases is of concern to both the teacher and the principal. Before any steps are taken in the treatment of a "problem child," the school staff should make certain that they are not making a mountain out of a molehill, and that they have satisfied themselves that they are not the cause of the problem. For example, simple offenses against order in the classroom have frequently been emphasized out of all proportion to their importance. The teacher or principal must avoid taking such offenses personally.

A teacher *en rapport* with his pupils, who maintains a calm manner, achieves serenity that cannot be upset by the contumely of immature individuals. When he feels that he has been insulted by a pupil, he ceases to be a teacher and becomes a disturbed individual contesting with another disturbed individual.[3]

There are some individuals, however, whose offenses become so persistent, intensive, or abnormal that they cannot be ignored or easily dealt with. Under the old order, the "appropriate" punishment would have been inflicted, and repeated with increasing severity, perhaps ending

---

[3] M. J. Cohler, "A New Look at the Old Problem of Discipline," *School Review,* vol. LVI, October 1948, pp. 468–475.

with expulsion from school (an admission of defeat on the school's part, and an evasion of its responsibility).

It has been said that there are no such things as problem children; there are only children with problems. Children with problems will not be helped by punishment or expulsion from school; such children are in need of guidance. It must be realized that there is no such thing as a "lazy" child, or a "stubborn," "surly," "disobedient," "lying," or "dishonest" child. Children who are lazy under one set of conditions can be dynamos of energy when engaged in something important to them. The child who is disobedient to his teacher or mother may follow obediently the dictates of the leader of his gang. Laziness, disobedience, lying, stealing, and the like are means employed to adjust to problem situations which the child is unable to solve in a constructive manner. Punishment not only will not contribute to a solution of the problem; it is more likely to intensify it, as far as the child is concerned. What he is in need of is help and guidance, not punishment.[4] Take, for example, the case of Jack.

> Jack was in real trouble and he knew it. He didn't think the teacher knew about it yet, but the police had been told . . . The police were worried, too. Jack had been reported to them for some sex play with some younger boys. If the incident were repeated and they had taken no action in the first place, they would be open to severe criticism.
>
> Since the major responsibility of the police is to protect the community, in a case like this they may feel compelled to follow a course which they know is not the best as far as the individual is concerned. But at that time the police were in a position to make a compromise. They referred Jack to the Community Service for Children and asked for a report and recommendation.
>
> At first it appeared that the case worker from the community service who visited Jack's home could not accomplish much. The mother was frightened and defended her child blindly. She felt that the police had no right to mention the matter to anyone. She . . . threatened to get a lawyer and go to court herself. Interviews with Jack accomplished a great deal more. He, quite naturally, did not want to talk about what he had done, but he talked freely on other subjects and was willing to see the doctor (the organization's psychiatrist) and explain his side of the business which had been reported to the police.
>
> After a few interviews with the case worker Jack talked with the psychiatrist, who was able to assure the police that there was nothing to fear

[4] W. K. Estes, "An Experimental Study of Punishment," *Psychological Monographs,* vol. LVII, no. 3, 1944.

from the boy, and that no further action was needed. . . . The psychiatrist made Jack understand that he would be glad to see him any time he had anything he wanted to talk over. Jack acted on this invitation and had several interviews with "the doctor" on his own initiative. During these interviews the boy got the sex information he was seeking and, what was much more important, a self-confidence and a sense of companionship which his parents were failing to give him. . . ".

Had this episode led to court action, even if that had resulted in no more than a reprimand, the breach which separates the bewildered, suffering person from other people would have been widened. His problem would have become greater, not less. With a little help, Jack was able to orient himself to life around him, and to find his own acceptable place in it.[5]

The basic principles to be followed in such cases are well illustrated in the foregoing case. Since all behavior has causes, efforts should be aimed at identifying the causes of the child's problem behavior. The principal and teacher should not attempt this alone if there are specialists available. Nevertheless, they should not simply hand the case over to a specialist, but should participate by supplying whatever assistance they may be able to give. Parents, psychologists, psychiatrists, social workers, visiting teachers, the physician, guidance specialists, are all persons whose help should be solicited, if they are available.[6]

By using this kind of procedure, discipline can be made educative. In these cases, as in classroom procedures, the goal is the development of constructive and intelligently directed self-control in the achievement of worthy purposes.

Principles of a Constructive Policy of Discipline

Without attempting to be in any way exhaustive, it might be helpful to identify some important principles which the elementary school principal can apply in his school to the problem of discipline.

1. *Provide for a unifying philosophy of discipline on the part of the staff.* It is important, as in other respects in the school, that the staff come to some reasonable agreement in their point of view on this important matter. It is unlikely that such an agreement can be established in one staff meeting, or even in several. If the staff does not already have a com-

[5] U. S. Children's Bureau, *Helping Children in Trouble,* U. S. Government Printing Office, Washington, D. C., Publication 320, 1947, pp. 2–4.
[6] See chapter on Pupil Adjustment and Health Services on pp. 235–249.

mon point of view on discipline, the changes which are necessary to bring this about (which are changes in people) will take place but slowly. Discussions, with the help of outside specialists; study of individual problem cases in the school; study groups which use authoritative literature to assist their understanding—all are examples of activities which can help teachers understand better the problem with which they are dealing.

2. *Do not undermine the teacher's authority.* It is well for the principal to remember that all of us have shortcomings, and to be tolerant of those he sees in his teachers. In return, they are likely to be more tolerant of those they see in him. In this respect, it is never wise for a principal to upbraid a teacher in the presence of pupils, parents, or other teachers, or to take matters out of his hands obviously and peremptorily. Such action will only undermine the teacher's authority and lower his standing with pupils and parents. The teacher who is having difficulty in his classroom needs assistance, not censure. How he should be helped can be decided only by knowing the nature of his problem, and by knowing him. Some teachers can be helped directly; others resent such an approach, and the principal will have to use a more nondirective technique. It is likely, of course, that there will be those who will not be responsive to any kind of assistance the principal can devise. Even in such cases, it should be evident that censure can have no result but to worsen the human relationships in the situation.

3. *Encourage constructive teacher solution of disciplinary problems.* This principle is really part of the preceding one. In some schools the situation has been permitted to develop in which there is a constant stream of pupils being sent to the office by teachers for disciplinary attention by the principal. When this becomes the case, it is likely that teachers are abdicating a large part of their responsibility for the handling of such cases, and that the principal has not been encouraging or helping them to develop a better classroom situation. Furthermore, this practice tends to undermine the standing of the teacher in the eyes of pupils and parents.

It must also be recognized that the principal influences the nature of the "discipline situation" in classrooms through his own attitude toward what it should be. One psychologist has stated this clearly:

> Discipline in a school is a function of administration. The principal sets the pattern for the social relations in a school by his philosophy and interpretation of the meaning of education. . . . If the principal places great

emphasis on order, system, and quiet in the classroom, it is the unusual teacher who is able to achieve these standards by which he is to be evaluated without using methods that are in a degree repressive.[7]

4. *Do not handle extreme cases alone.* When it becomes evident that a child has a profound personality disturbance which is finding expression in marked misbehavior, the principal should seek qualified assistance. As a beginning, the principal can hold a conference with the child's teacher and parents to determine whether the child's problem is obvious and simple enough to solve without further trained assistance. If not, others who seem to offer hope of help should be called in to assist.

5. *Establish a referral procedure.* No matter how good the educational program may be, there are likely to be times when it is desirable to remove a pupil from the classroom for misbehavior. In such cases an established referral procedure should be set up. A referral slip, bearing the child's name, the teacher's name, the date, the time of the child's dismissal from the class, and a brief description of the nature of the offense, should be filled out in duplicate by the teacher, and the original taken to the office by the pupil. The principal should record the nature of the action taken so that a follow-up may be made. These data should be placed in a confidential file for the principal's ready reference.

6. *Use a follow-through report.* Any case which has been referred to the principal should be the subject of follow-through study. A record form can provide for data concerning action taken and the results observed. This will provide a continuing record which should help in the resolution of the child's problem.

7. *If punishment seems necessary, it should be corrective and therapeutic, rather than punitive.* There are times when it may seem desirable to impose some punishment for an offense. For example, damaged property may require physical labor to repair it, or may require that the offender pay for its replacement. In any event, punishment should not be administered in anger, or have any tinge of retaliatory action. The entire affair should be kept on an impersonal plane. Furthermore, punishment should never result in shaming the child before his peers, for such action is an offense against the pupil's personality, and is likely to result in resentment which will effectively prevent any good future influence of the

[7] P. M. Symonds, "Classroom Discipline," *Teachers College Record,* vol. LI, December 1949, pp. 153–154.

teacher or principal. Hence, corporal punishment, although legalized in some states is rarely, if ever, justified in school (see pages 41–42).

8. *As much as possible, the learning program in the school should be rooted in the problems of living of the learners and suited to their needs, interests, and abilities.* Whereas this may seem to be a principle of curriculum, it has direct bearing upon classroom discipline. If the life interest and needs of the pupils are made the core of the learning program, it is much more likely that the children will have learning purposes which are real, meaningful and zestful to them. Under such conditions problems of discipline are minimized.

9. *Co-operative teacher-pupil planning helps reduce problems of discipline.* This is closely allied to the foregoing principle. When the pupils have participated in the planning of the purposes and activities in school, they are likely to be impatient of any misbehavior which militates against the achievement of those purposes. Under such conditions, there will be little need to use force, threat, or other coercion to hold pupils to purposes which are not theirs, as in the traditional orientation.

It can be seen from these nine points, then, that discipline—like many other aspects of education—is somewhat Protean in nature. Its aspect changes with changes in educational and social theory, so that one's philosophy and practice of discipline depend upon the educational beliefs to which he subscribes. At least they should. It is this fact which lends emphasis to the importance of the principal and his staff clarifying basically what they believe the nature of good education to be. In a school that is administered well, the disciplinary practices will be consistent with the rest of the educational situation obtaining there.

It can be seen, also, that this business of discipline is a double-barrelled affair. It is at the same time both a means and an end, depending, of course, upon the aspect of discipline under discussion. In fact, it can be both end and means at the same time, for the discipline we have and use is but a means to the end of that self-discipline which we all agree is so desirable in a democratic state. Hence, the "discipline we use" should always be educative, and should be of a nature to encourage and release creativity, rather than being restrictive and confining. It should be co-operative and democratic rather than coercive and autocratic. Its objective always should be the development of constructive and intelligent self-control for the achievement of desirable objectives, permeated with respect for the personality of others and concern for the welfare of the group.

SUGGESTED READINGS

Association for Supervision and Curriculum Development, *Fostering Mental Health in Our Schools,* National Education Association, Washington, D. C., 1950, ch. XI.

Cohler, M. J., "A New Look at the Old Problem of Discipline," *School Review,* vol. LVI, October 1948.

Hockett, J. A., and Jacobsen, E. W., *Modern Practices in the Elementary School,* Ginn and Company, Boston, 1943, ch. VII.

Sheviakov, G. V., and Redl, F., *Discipline for Today's Children and Youth,* Association for Supervision and Curriculum Development, Washington, D. C., 1944.

Smith, Walter R., *Constructive School Discipline,* American Book Company, New York, 1936 (out of print).

Symonds, Percival M., "Classroom Discipline," *Teachers College Record,* vol. LI, December 1949, pp. 147–158.

Part IV ADMINISTERING SPECIAL SERVICES

The modern elementary school is much more than a place where children are taught subjects. Over the years it has assumed a number of other functions, all of them related, of course, to the central problem of helping children to be healthy, stable, functioning, informed citizens. To do this, many schools have added a number of "special services." In the section which follows, administrative aspects of a number of these special services are discussed.

The relationship of special services to the educational program has not always been adequately appreciated. In fact, common practice has been to conceive of them and operate them as activities quite unrelated to children's learning. There is a growing realization, however, that there are considerable learning opportunities for children in many of these services, and that all of them will be far more educationally effective if they are closely integrated with the work of the classroom teacher.

The administration of these services, therefore, is more than a job of securing qualified personnel and setting up efficient organization and economical operation. It is a job of professional leadership, seeing that their educational possibilities are realized as fully as possible, and that they are made as integral a part of the learning program of the school, and of the individual classrooms, as is feasible. Such a point of view is characteristic of modern administration of elementary schools.

CHAPTER XV

THE SCHOOL PRINCIPAL'S
RESPONSIBILITY FOR
SCHOOL ATTENDANCE

Most of the responsibilities which fall on the shoulders of the school principal are self-imposed. Within certain limits he has freedom to perform his major duties as he sees fit and at a time which suits his convenience. There are a few responsibilities and services, however, which are required by law and often the central office goes beyond the legal statute itself in prescribing how principals and the teachers shall proceed to carry out the state's mandate. This is the case with school attendance. In the compulsory education law the state lays down certain conditions which children and parents must meet. To insure the effectiveness of the law the state also requires periodic accounting from local school districts. While the school board and the superintendent are responsible for seeing to it that the law is observed locally, in reality the principals of the individual schools are the administrators who have the heaviest responsibility. Attendance officers, it is true, have enforcement powers and they do a lot of the detailed work related to school delinquency. But a good attendance program is dependent to a large degree for its success upon the efforts of the school principal. Moreover, the superintendent and the board of education will look to him for explanations of any violations of the law within his district and for the reliability of the information provided by teachers and others in his school. In some states the principal is legally responsible for reporting truancy.

Over and beyond the legal aspects just mentioned, compulsory school attendance is closely related to many other phases of school administration and supervision. In fact, the manner in which the attendance problem is approached often conditions the attitude of many children and parents toward the school.

When the social and educational implications are fully understood by the school principal and the philosophy of administering attendance is in accord with sound psychological principles, the bonds between home and school can usually be strengthened. In the past many school administrators have looked upon the absence problem as an isolated and independent one and have failed to see its relationships to either the home or the school environment.

Investigators have found that the amount of truancy and absenteeism in school systems is affected by policies relating to pupil progress and by the nature of the school offerings. The implications of these findings have led the more thoughtful administrators to take stock of their guidance provisions and to appraise their instructional programs critically. Students of the attendance problem emphasize the need for teachers to give thought to the mental health of their pupils. They also recommend that lock-step methods be abandoned and individual differences recognized. It is becoming increasingly apparent that the school should lead the way in bringing community resources to bear on the needs of pupils during their out-of-school hours. There are practical considerations too, that deserve mention. State aid to local school districts is commonly based on some measure of school attendance. Since schools are seldom, if ever, adequately financed, the loss of any money because of unnecessary pupil absence is serious. While this loss is unquestionably small in comparison to the economic loss arising from the failure of the pupil to use the educational opportunities intended for him, it cannot be treated lightly.

It requires no further cataloguing of relationships for the reader to appreciate how interwoven the attendance issue is with a wide variety of other school problems. The principal who sees these relationships clearly and helps to interpret them to the teaching staff, lay citizens, and pupils will be rendering a real service to public education.

Principals (especially those who are new to their posts) would do well to take stock of their knowledge relating to school attendance service and become well versed in this phase of their work. The following aspects of the attendance problem are especially important for the principal to consider:

1. The principal should know in detail the provisions of the state attendance law. He needs to know the compulsory age limits, the specific exemptions relating to work, to travel distance and to health, the scholarship bases for obtaining work certificates, and residence requirements in relationship to attendance.

2. He must know in detail the report forms required by the central office and by the state and should be thoroughly familiar with the attendance record-system used elsewhere in the school district (if there is more than one school).

3. He should make every effort to learn the causes of nonattendance in his own school and to understand their implications for the instructional program.

4. He should become acquainted with the services provided by other social agencies in the community, particularly as they relate to the problem of school attendance.

5. He should be thoroughly familiar with the procedures to be followed when cases are brought to court as a result of persistent violation of the law.

Knowledge relating to the foregoing items is primary and without it a school principal is unprepared for his job. A copy of the state school laws should be on the principal's desk (several of the states have issued special bulletins containing attendance provisions, the child labor law, and related regulations affecting child welfare), and perhaps what is more important, he should be thoroughly acquainted with the major legal provisions relating to attendance. This is not to suggest that knowledge of attendance regulations is so important that it deserves precedence over a command of the other phases of his administrative and supervisory work, but ignorance at this point will cause embarrassment and is sure to be discovered if and when attendance violations occur.

The positive side of school attendance service is, of course, the major concern of school administrators, not merely seeing to it that the law is enforced or that attendance records are properly kept. Preserving to each child his just and rightful opportunity for schooling and education—this is the real challenge in providing school attendance service. And it would be well for the principal to stress this objective with children and parents. The community goes to considerable expense to make available school opportunities for every child of compulsory school age. To insure the public that its objectives are being achieved and that all children capable of profiting from an education are receiving the benefits intended by the framers of the education law is the task of school administrators. Many school systems have set up machinery for keeping in touch with each child from birth to the upper age limit set by the school attendance law (sixteen or eighteen years). This is commonly done through a continuing school census consisting of a complete and accurate list of the children of a district, amended from day to day as information regarding changes is gathered. States generally provide registers to be used by teachers in recording enrollments and attendance information. These registers contain detailed instructions for teachers so that the principal's job of interpreting the attendance record system to his teachers is a fairly simple one. It is important, however, in the case of teachers new to the state, that the principal shall acquaint them with the procedures used, making certain that the teachers fully comprehend the method to be employed. Beyond this the principal should work out some systematic scheme for getting in touch with parents when children are reported absent, and for communicating with the attendance officer when cases require this latter individual's investigation. Much of the attendance work can be handled by the principal or his secretary over the phone. In relatively small schools, the eccentricities of both pupils and parents are likely to be well known to principals and teachers and the problem cases are easily identified. In highly industrialized communities, however, where the school population is fairly heterogeneous and schools are large, the problem of attendance is involved and consumes much more of the principal's as well as the attendance officer's time. Frequently a substantial proportion of the families in such communities have no telephones and can be reached only by mail or by a personal visit. In these situations a visiting teacher can render most helpful service.

The Causes of Irregular Attendance

Those most familiar with attendance matters have discovered that the problems of delinquency and nonattendance can be classified roughly as child problems and as school problems. To improve attendance service, then, the principal must, in some measure, be psychologist, educator, and sociologist. There is seldom a single cause for truancy. Usually there are two or three causes operating together and closely related, and often where the cause appears to lie in some weakness or abnormality of the child there is found at home some unhappy situation which partially accounts for the trouble. Moreover, where it seems clear that the school program needs adjusting in order that the delinquent pupil may enjoy and profit from his school experiences, it is usually important to give the pupil's parents a clearer understanding of school policies and practices. Otherwise, the revision in the school program is likely to be ineffective since it will be offset by negative home forces which in the life of most pupils are more powerful than the influence of the school.

The fact that repeated pupil absences are commonly caused by several factors rather than a single one complicates the problem for the school. There are, nevertheless, predominant causes of absence, which when known can become the basis for an attack on the problem. Among these the following have been commonly reported by investigators: personal illness, sickness in family, work at home, poverty, inclement weather, parental indifference, and miscellaneous reasons.[1]

The factors which operate in rural schools differ substantially both in amount and kind from those affecting attendance in city schools. Personal illness while one of the leading causes of pupil absence in both city and rural schools does not, according to some investigators, account for as large a proportion of the total absence in rural schools as it does in urban schools. Travel distance, on the other hand, ranks higher as a cause of absence in rural districts. Community attitude and type of teacher appear also to be factors in some schools.[2]

The chief value in examining the statistics relating to causes of pupil absence is to provide the principal with a basis for assessing his own situation. There is no substitute for a local analysis of nonattendance. The principal must know the causes of pupil absence if he is to make an intelligent attack upon the problem. If the illness factor appears to be abnormally large, then it is possible that the health division of the school system needs to get busy. If dislike of school work looms large in persistent cases of nonattendance, then some changes in the learning program might well be studied.

---

[1] W. S. Deffenbaugh and W. W. Keesecker, *Compulsory School Attendance Laws and Their Enforcement,* U. S. Office of Education, Bulletin 1935, no. 4, p. 4; *Absent From School Today,* Metropolitan Life Insurance Company, New York, 1949.

[2] G. H. Reavis, *Factors Controlling Attendance in Rural Schools,* Bureau of Publications, Teachers College, Columbia University, New York, 1920; Stephen C. Gribble, *Teacher Qualifications and School Attendance in New Mexico 1918–1946,* University of New Mexico Press, Albuquerque, N. M., 1948, p. 36.

Not only is it desirable to know the distribution of nonattendance factors in a school system, but it is even more important to know in the case of each individual absentee (where there is a history of absenteeism), the specific difficulty which seems to be the predominant cause of absence. To illustrate: Johnny is absent repeatedly on account of illness in the family. Which member of the family is ill? Is it likely that conditions will get better or worse? What role does Johnny play at home in relationship to the illness? Wherein lies the full explanation of Johnny's absence?

Fred is absent frequently and both he and his family report that he has work to do around home. What kind of work? Why does Fred have to help his father or mother? Is it financially necessary? Many similar questions need to be asked where other causes are reported.

When the principal has at his command as complete information as can be secured within the time limits set by his schedule of school duties, he should initiate some action to remedy the situation. Here the basic knowledge mentioned earlier will stand him in good stead. If he knows which departments and individuals within the school system are best qualified to assist him and what agencies in the community have facilities for correcting existing ills, he can make an effective attack upon the problem.

Sources of Help Within the School System

1. The work of the *school medical inspectors or school physicians* usually brings them in close contact with the health conditions of pupils. If the cause of absence is primarily one of ill-health, then constructive advice should be sought from the school medical inspector or the school physician.

2. *The school nurse* is in a good position to follow up the suggestions of the physician or medical inspector and can often treat children suffering from minor infections without excluding them from school. She can also go into the home and advise parents with respect to health matters with little disturbance to home or school. To the degree that the home situation can be remedied and the pupil's illness shortened, the nurse will be improving attendance and indirectly the educational background of the pupil.

3. Many school systems employ *visiting teachers, or school visitors,* whose primary job is to devote themselves to the needs of individual

children who are experiencing learning difficulties or whose conduct is baffling, erratic, or troublesome, or who show signs of neglect. This latter group often includes children who are irritable, worried, violent-tempered, repressed, abused or overworked, or a combination of the foregoing conditions.

Through her knowledge of child behavior as well as her understanding of adult psychology, she is in a favorable position to sense the child's basic trouble and bring about the changes that are essential for eliminating the difficulties. At least there is a better chance of improving home and school relationships and of insuring steadiness of school attendance when this service is available. Hence the principal should not overlook this source of help.

4. Most *attendance officers* in the past have been poorly trained for the constructive job of removing the causes of nonattendance. Even today there are some indications that the police conception of handling truancy has not been entirely eradicated. The principal, therefore, will need to take account of the background, the point of view, and the general wisdom of the existing attendance officer in deciding how far to rely upon him for assistance.

Because of the legal authority residing in the attendance officer, many homes do not welcome his presence. As one authority has aptly put it, "The rich families resent him and the poor fear him."[3] In some instances, of course, the attendance officer will be in a position to render outstanding help.

5. Fortunate is the school principal who is able to call upon such trained individuals as a *school psychologist, a psychiatrist,* and a *guidance specialist.* These employees have the background of knowledge and the technical skill that are essential for dealing thoroughly and scientifically with maladjusted children and abnormal parents. Sometimes their combined efforts are not sufficient to straighten out the difficulties, but the principal will have the consolation, at least, of knowing that the school has drawn upon its best resources.

6. The school truant often craves attention and, failing to achieve as much status as he needs in the classroom, he uses truancy as a means of satisfying this desire. When this appears to be the cause of the absenteeism, the co-operation of the *physical education instructor* should be

[3] George H. Chatfield and others, *Problems of School Attendance and Pupil Adjustment,* University of the State of New York, Albany, N. Y., 1932.

sought in an attempt to provide special opportunities for the pupil to earn recognition. If this step can be taken simultaneously with modifying the classroom program so as to meet the pupil's immediate needs there, the effort stands a good chance of succeeding.

Community Resources and the Attendance Problem

School systems have varying resources for dealing with underprivileged and maladjusted children. Even when all of the personnel just mentioned have put their shoulders to the wheel and attacked the problem of nonattendance, there will still be cases that defy their efforts. When poverty, health of the child or parents, broken homes, improper guardianship, or desertion is the cause of the difficulty, the help of agencies outside the school will need to be summoned before any permanent cure for many absence-ills can be devised.

The Denver, Colorado, public schools have issued a handbook of school and community resources entitled *Denver Serves Its Children.*[4] It was prepared by a committee of classroom teachers. This handbook is not only a most valuable guide to parents, but principals now have at their command an invaluable source to consult in attacking problems beyond the power of the school alone to solve. What help is available in Denver? Where is the service located? Who is eligible for the service? Is there a charge? These and other pertinent questions are all answered in the handbook. School districts generally would do well to prepare a bulletin of this type for the use of principals, teachers, and parents.

In every city school system, and most county and village systems, services which the school principal will find it desirable to utilize are provided either at public expense or supplied by private charity. The town health officials with their special authority in the home can often achieve results which the school physician and nurse are unable to secure, particularly where parents resist all normal efforts to improve their surroundings. The welfare commissioners are in a position to render financial assistance as are the appropriate officers in church and charitable organizations. Civic groups, such as the Rotary and Kiwanis, are always open to suggestions when some tangible need involving children is clearly expressed. These organizations often have education committees that can be approached directly, and in the past their aid has been

[4] Denver Public Schools, *Denver Serves Its Children,* 1948.

generously given in many communities. Where possible the principal, after conferring with the superintendent of schools, should present a specific recommendation to civic organizations based on a careful study of the help needed. The parent-teacher association is another socially minded group. Then there are county nurses, county child placement officers, specialists in child guidance clinics, and doctors in hospitals who are in a position to provide special services. Naturally, the principal will have to decide when to ask for assistance. Some community agencies may already be carrying as heavy a burden as they can efficiently handle, in which case their services may not be available to the school. Certainly, the school should exhaust its own resources first. On the other hand, overlapping of services should be avoided. The principal will need to get acquainted with the personnel responsible for policy making in the various organizations concerned and be in a favorable position to present the case for the children who most need help.

In a few instances state charity organizations and child labor committees may constitute good sources of help and a list of these agencies should be on file in the principal's office. The basic precept that should guide the school administrator is that no family situation that involves the welfare of a child in relation to his schooling should be neglected.

It will be clear from the number of agencies and services just mentioned that the task of insuring educational opportunities to all children of school age in a district is a big responsibility and requires a great deal of planning. Beyond the administrative and co-ordinating functions, there is the task of learning how to deal with children and adults successfully in the face of current living conditions. A thorough knowledge of mental hygiene is basic to a real appreciation of the meaning of much behavior. One must know that children who feel that they are unloved, unappreciated, or unjustly treated tend to lose some of their self-respect and, as a result, they turn away from those to whom they were formerly attached. As has been frequently pointed out, the behavior of a pupil often reflects his treatment at home or in school. Quarreling parents or stepparents may be the cause of estrangement, or undue preference of parents for a brother or sister, or the inability of the child to compete successfully with conditions or persons. It is also true that children who are exposed to ridicule by their classmates or reproaches by their teachers suffer humiliation and are in danger of becoming socially maladjusted and of losing their interest in school. Not infrequently pupils with marked physical deformities have great difficulty in adjusting to the school world around them. The creation of an atmosphere at school which will encourage these handicapped children to face their world with confidence is a challenge that should not be overlooked.

The ramifications of the attendance problem as indicated in the foregoing discussion are almost endless. More and more, experience has shown that the case method of approach involving as it does investigation, diagnosis, treatment, and follow-up, is the most hopeful means of bringing about fundamental changes in human behavior. Attendance work is an integral part of the educative process and as such it must be undertaken with a full realization of the psychological factors involved. Otherwise it will deal with the problem only superficially.

SUGGESTED READINGS

Chatfield, George H., and others, *Problems of School Attendance and Pupil Adjustment,* University of the State of New York, Albany, N. Y., 1932.

Citizens' Committee on Children of New York City, Inc., *Children Absent from School,* New York, 1949.

Deffenbaugh, Walter S., and Keesecker, Ward W., *Compulsory School Attendance Laws and Their Administration,* U. S. Office of Education Bulletin 1935, no. 4, U. S. Government Printing Office, Washington, D. C.

Hutchinson, John Harrison, *The Legal Basis of Public School Attendance in the United States,* The University of Chicago Libraries, 1941.

Metropolitan Life Insurance Company, *Absent from School Today,* New York, 1949.

New York City Board of Education, *The Prosecution of School Non-Attendants,* Bureau of Reference, Research and Statistics, New York, 1948 (Mimeographed).

U. S. Department of Labor, *Controlling Juvenile Delinquency—A Community Program,* Children's Bureau Publication 301, Washington, D. C., 1943.

CHAPTER XVI

PUPIL ADJUSTMENT AND

HEALTH SERVICES

The increasing emphasis upon individual differences among children has highlighted the problem of eliminating those differences which are undesirable, and capitalizing on those differences which are good. As a result of this, many school districts have added to their staffs various kinds of specialists to assist the schools in their efforts to meet the needs of children. These personnel include physicians, nurses, psychologists, psychiatrists, attendance officers, guidance specialists, remedial teachers, visiting teachers, and teachers of special subjects. With the addition of these workers has come the problem of how to administer their services so that best use can be made of their capabilities in the educational program.

The tendency, where these special services have been provided, has been for them to operate quite independently of the learning program in the classroom. Pupils are sent to the psychologist for testing, to the psychiatrist for study, to the nurse for checkup, to the doctor for treatment, but these services—valuable as they are—have not often been integrated with the work of the teacher himself.

More recently, however, there has been a trend toward a greater unification of special services. There are at least two factors which have contributed to this. First, the facts of organismic psychology and the philosophy of a more integrating approach to learning have emphasized the interrelationships which should exist in the learning program, and have motivated efforts to reduce the fragmentary nature of the usual school offering. Second, special workers employed in school systems have frequently been impressed by the extent to which their functions have overlapped. In dealing with educational, or social, or physical, or emotional maladjustment, they have repeatedly found themselves faced with a "which-came-first-the-chicken-or-the-egg" proposition, as they sought the cause of the difficulty. Realization of these interrelationships has resulted in administrative steps to co-ordinate the work of these specialists. In many schools considerable progress has been made in integrating their services with the work of the classroom teacher, so that a director of guidance is able to say, "The programs [of guidance] which have been established represent promising beginnings. They have avoided, for the most part, a mistake which has weakened many of the early guidance programs at the high school level, namely, a tendency to establish guidance as a highly specialized and separate department with only a slight relationship to the general school program and activities. Guidance as it is developing in progressive elementary schools is regarded as an integral part of the whole educational program."[1]

For this reason, the authors choose not to discuss the functions of each of the special adjustment services separately, but rather to look at them functionally, as they relate to a well-integrated program of pupil adjustment service. There are four major areas, in any one of which a child's need for special assistance may become evident: educational adjustment, social adjustment, physical adjustment, and emotional adjustment. In considering the effective administration of special services to meet these needs, there are four questions to be considered.

1. How may a child's need for adjustment be identified?
2. How may the causes of his maladjustment be diagnosed?
3. How can the services at the disposal of the school best be brought to bear on the problem of helping improve the child's adjustment?
4. How can these services be used to forestall pupil maladjustment?

Identifying Children in Need of Help

There are some children whom the teacher will easily identify as being in need of special assistance: habitual truants, extremely retarded readers, children with pronounced speech disorders, children with belligerently antisocial attitudes, children with markedly poor eyesight, and

[1] E. Kawin, in *Meeting Special Needs of the Individual Child,* Nineteenth Yearbook, Department of Elementary School Principals, National Education Association, Washington, D. C., 1940, p. 305.

the like. It has been repeatedly shown, however, that numbers of children definitely in need of assistance go unnoticed by the teacher. There are several reasons for this. First, large classes make it impossible for teachers to become well enough acquainted with individual children so that they can "spot" pupils with less obvious difficulties. Second, the teacher is more likely to notice children whose behavior disturbs the class situation than he is to become conscious of the needs of children whose shyness, daydreaming, and quietness may be more indicative of personal maladjustment than is the upsetting mischievousness of the disrupter of classroom order.[2] Third, and allied to the other two, is the fact that most teachers are inadequately prepared to recognize many of the symptoms of maladjustment for what they are. For these reasons, definite procedures must be set up for identifying children whose needs might otherwise go unnoticed.

Identifying retardation in basic skills. Difficulties in basic skills are more easily discovered by teachers than are those in other fields, since it is in this area that teachers are best prepared by their training. Nevertheless, the administrator can facilitate the efforts of the teacher in this respect. Perhaps the most efficient single method of identifying such difficulties is the administration of standardized tests. Tests for this purpose should be of the "survey" type (as opposed to the analytic or diagnostic test). They are usually termed "test batteries" since they consist of tests in more than one skill. Such tests as the Stanford Achievement Test,[3] the Metropolitan Achievement Test,[4] and the Iowa Every Pupil Tests of Basic Skills[5] are designed for this purpose. Examination of the test results will indicate those children who are markedly below the usual level of attainment for children of their age. It should be obvious that the least fruitful time at which to give these tests is at the end of the year, when there is little opportunity for putting the data they supply to some purpose other than determining promotion and nonpromotion of the pupils. Such tests are best given shortly after the opening of the school year, and teachers

[2] E. K. Wickman, *Teachers and Behavior Problems,* The Commonwealth Fund, New York, 1938.

[3] T. L. Kelley, G. M. Ruch, and L. M. Terman, *Stanford Achievement Test,* (revision of new Stanford Achievement Test, 3 levels), World Book Company, Yonkers, N. Y., 1940.

[4] G. H. Hildreth and others, *Metropolitan Achievement Test* (1947 edition, 5 levels), World Book Company, Yonkers, N. Y.

[5] H. F. Spitzer, *Iowa Every Pupil Tests of Basic Skills,* (new edition, elementary and advanced batteries), Houghton Mifflin Company, Boston, 1945.

should have the option of administering an equivalent form of the test to selected pupils during the course of the year, either to check the accuracy of scores they have reason to doubt on the first form given, or to determine the children's progress for purposes of further guidance and instruction.

It cannot be stressed too strongly that standardized tests, if the results are to mean anything, must be administered strictly in accordance with the instructions which accompany them. The directions given in the test manuals should be followed to the letter, and the time limits in particular should be observed to the second. In this respect, the school psychologist can be of assistance in making certain that teachers understand the importance of strict adherence to test directions.

Furthermore, a low score on the test is not *prima facie* evidence of retardation, and must be interpreted with caution. For example, a child whose reading skill is very poor will be handicapped on any other test which necessitates reading of any kind, such as arithmetic tests with written directions, tests of skill in punctuation, or group intelligence tests with verbal sections. In addition, low reading scores do not necessarily mean that the child's reading is far below expectation, for his score may be as high as one has reason to expect of a child of his level of verbal intelligence. For example, is a child retarded in reading if his chronological age is twelve years, and a standardized reading test shows him to be able to read only about as well as the usual ten-year-old? One cannot tell unless the pupil's mental age also is known. If his I.Q. is in the region of 80 to 85, then his mental age is about ten years, indicating that he is reading about as well as can be expected for a child of his ability. If his I.Q. is normal or above, on the other hand, then he is truly retarded in reading and is in need of some individual assistance. In these respects, the school psychologist or remedial specialist can be of great assistance to teachers in discovering those children who are truly in need of individual help.

The principal must be careful, however, not simply to thrust a testing program upon teachers, for under such circumstances it is likely to be looked upon as a chore, and its full possibilities not realized. Staff discussions of the problems of locating children in need of help and enlistment of the participation of the psychologist or remedial specialist (if these resource people are available in the system) should precede the testing. Through such discussions teachers will have their understanding

of the purposes of the tests increased, and are likely to contribute suggestions which will improve the program of administering them.

Identifying social and emotional maladjustment. When a socially or emotionally handicapped child's difficulty has progressed to the stage where
he is easily recognizable as such by the usual teacher, it is likely that
great difficulty will be met in attempting his readjustment. As in many
another respect, a stitch in time here may obviate the need of considerable mending at a later date. The difficulty falls in knowing where and
when to apply the saving stitch, and it is in this respect that special
workers again can be helpful.

All too frequently, however, the psychologist, psychiatrist, physician,
or remedial specialist have been called in only when a crisis has arisen,
at which time much damage has already been done. Certainly the rendering of assistance in critical cases is one of their functions, but it should
by no means be the only—or even the major—one. If the services of
these personnel are administered wisely, it is likely that they can do
much to help prevent many of the cases of maladjustment which develop
in our schools.

There are a number of tests on the market which purport to "measure"
personality. None of these has as yet been widely accepted by psychological authorities for the purpose of individual diagnosis.[6] However,
certain diagnostic methods—frequently called "sociometric technics"—
are being developed, such as the sociogram,[7] which reveal a great deal
about the reactions of pupils to one another. Sociograms are simply
graphic attempts to show significant personal interrelationships within
the group. They are usually constructed by plotting a chart of answers to
such a question as, "Who are your three best friends in this class?"
Figure 12 is an example of what the results might look like for a small
group. Such techniques will often indicate maladjustments that the teacher
did not suspect. A virtue of these methods is that there are usable ones
simple enough for one to learn easily without extensive training.

Finally, there is no instrument which can take the place of informed
observation. In order for the teacher to learn much from observation,

[6] Oscar K. Buros, ed., *Third Mental Measurements Yearbook,* Rutgers University
Press, New Brunswick, N. J., 1949, pp. 51–114, "Tests and Reviews: Character
and Personality."
[7] Horace Mann-Lincoln School of Experimentation, *How to Construct a Sociogram,*
Bureau of Publications, Teachers College, Columbia University, New York, 1947.

FIGURE 12. Sociogram for a Small Sixth Grade Group of Girls[8]

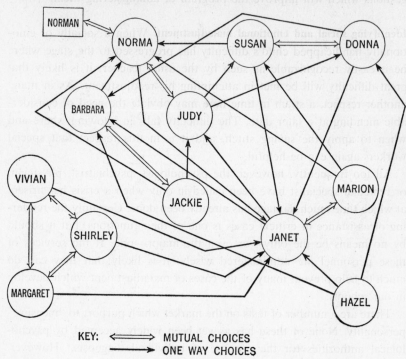

KEY: ⟺   MUTUAL CHOICES
          ⟶   ONE WAY CHOICES

however, she must know what to look for, and most teachers are not well prepared in this respect. The principal can render a service here by providing for staff conferences, with the psychologist and psychiatrist as consultants. Such conferences will be more fruitful if they arise from the recognized need of the teachers to know more about the evidences of maladjustment among the children. They might well start with a discussion of cases which are well known in the school, then move from there to discussions of the evidences of less obvious maladjustment. The objective of these conferences should not be the "solution" of the cases, but the growth of insight on the part of the teachers into the dynamics of children's behavior. A good example of how this was accomplished through the study of individual children is described at length in Prescott's *Helping Teachers Understand Children*.[9] This use of the specialized

[8] *Ibid.,* p. 19.
[9] Daniel Prescott, *Helping Teachers Understand Children,* American Council on Education, Washington, D. C., 1945.

resources of psychologists and psychiatrists will be much more fruitful in the long run than if they are used simply as the persons to whom problem cases are to be referred. In the latter case, their work takes on a cast of mystery and does little to enlarge the teacher's understanding of children's problems; in the procedures suggested above, the teacher has a chance to see what the psychologist and psychiatrist think and do about children with problems, and are therefore considerably better prepared to recognize signs of incipient problems in their classrooms.

Identifying physical difficulties. The identification of physical difficulties is important for at least two reasons. First, it is important to find those physical conditions which will be a handicap to the child who has them, so that something can be done to correct or alleviate the condition. Second, it is important to recognize quickly the symptoms of disease so that the child afflicted may get prompt treatment, and so that other children may be spared exposure to communicable diseases. The screening necessary to do this can be on at least three levels.

1. *Routine observation and checkup by the teacher.* A widespread and most desirable practice in elementary schools is the "daily checkup." When the children come in in the morning, the teacher, with his back to a window, examines them individually for: inflamed, watering, or otherwise unusual eye conditions; skin afflictions, such as impetigo or ivy poisoning; inflamed or spotted throat; stuffy or discharging nose; or any other signs of physical malfunctioning. If the teacher routinizes the procedure, this can be done in a relatively brief time. In addition to the daily checkup, the teacher will be observing other evidences of physical difficulties of pupils from day to day. Such things should be looked for as squinting, holding a book too near or too far from the eyes, listlessness, weight, evidences of poor hearing, toothaches, and the like. Through practice the teacher will become adept at "spotting" evidences of physical difficulty which are in need of attention. Upon the discovery of such evidences, he should immediately refer the case to the school nurse, if the school has one, otherwise to the person vested with excluding or referring authority.

2. *Examination by the school nurse.* If the school has a nurse, she should re-examine all children sent to her by the teachers. Her examination will be a more thorough and informed one, and she will make the

decision as to what should be done next. Another of her functions should be that of examining all children returning after absences on account of illness. They should carry an approval slip from her to be readmitted to their classrooms. The nurse should also conduct a periodic check on height and weight, to be recorded on the child's health record. Some schools do this monthly, while others do it but once a year (some not at all!). It would seem reasonable to conduct such a survey at least four times yearly. At this time, too, the nurse checks up on whether remedial work recommended by the school has been carried out.

3. *Thorough physical examination by a physician.* The most specialized level of identification of physical defects is, of course, that of the licensed physician. If the school has a physician retained by the school board, this duty will fall to him. If no such assistance is provided, the principal should seek it actively through his superintendent. In cases where the board of education has been unwilling or unable to provide such service, community organizations have been persuaded to fill the gap. The examination given by the physician should be fairly thorough, not cursory. Not less than ten or twelve minutes should be devoted to each child if the job is to be done right. The school should see that adequate assistance is provided to handle the routine which is attendant upon the examination: preparing the children for examination, taking care of such equipment as thermometers and tongue depressors, and recording data and filing records. This will permit the doctor to devote his entire attention to the examination with no waste of his time. It is also important that the examination be conducted in suitable quarters, which are reasonably private, well lighted and ventilated, and spacious. Where the school does not have a health room or suite, the principal will have to make arrangements suitable to the importance of this examination.

These examinations can be educative to parents and children alike, and it is good practice to have the parent present when the child is being examined. The physician can then explain on the spot whatever he may discover, and it will make an infinitely greater impression than will an impersonal form notice sent home with the child.

Diagnosing the Causes of Difficulties

Whereas the diagnosis of physical difficulties is primarily the job of the doctor, the uncovering of the causes of educational, social, or emotional aberrations is not so simple. Indeed, it has been discovered in recent years that even physical difficulties often have their causes in emotional disturbances. Frequently it becomes a matter, as was observed earlier, of being unable to determine whether the hen preceded the egg or vice versa. Is John's misbehavior in class the result of his poor achievement in reading and arithmetic, for example, or is the reverse the case? Or are both caused by a poor home situation? Or are they the result of a hyperthyroid condition? One cannot know until he has explored all these factors thoroughly.

Furthermore, it should be evident that examination of these different factors independently by the teacher, psychologist, visiting teacher, physician and remedial specialist is an unrealistic and nonfunctional approach to the problem. More and more, therefore, schoolmen are organizing the work of these specialists so that they work in concert. The most common arrangement which seems to be developing in this respect is the "case conference." This is a conference of those who are involved in trying to help the child: teacher, specialists, principal, parent, and sometimes the child himself. First, a conference is held to hear from teacher, parent, and principal the evidences of the child's maladjustment. From a discussion of these a plan of action is developed, so that each person in the conference knows his responsibility and the job of each of the others. After a period of data-gathering, the group can reconvene to consider what new insights have been uncovered in the understanding of this child's problems, and to determine what the implications are for future action with respect to the problem. In this manner, the diagnosis is a group consultation affair, and is likely to take into account many more of the significant factors of the case, and their interrelationships, than if the job were done by one person, or by several working separately.

In school systems where the above-mentioned specialized personnel are on the staff, this arrangement will not be difficult to bring about. In other systems, however, the schools should make an effort to secure the services of such specialists through the community, with the idea of eventually having the board of education retain them on a regular basis. Even so, it is possible that the pupil's family physician, for example, will not be the school's physician. In such a case, the school will have to try to have the physician attend the case conference without fee. Furthermore, there may be representatives of other community agencies which are concerned with the case, such as the public health nurse, the welfare worker, or the representative of the juvenile court. Usually these agencies will be most willing to co-operate in such a procedure, provided the school representatives do not make it appear as though they are arrogating to themselves responsibility for solving the problem. One should keep in mind that the schools are but one of a number of community agencies and, even though the school may act as the prime mover in getting a case conference procedure started, it should co-operate as but one of a number of influences upon the child. If a community co-ordinating council, or a council of welfare agencies is organized in that community, then the school should work with and through it.

Diagnosis, then, becomes a co-operative procedure, through which each participant gains greater insight into the child's problem because he sees it from a number of perspectives. Furthermore, the participants will develop new and deeper understanding of the dynamics of child behavior, and will become far less willing to jump to premature conclusions. They are also likely to be more able to interpret behavior symptoms which they see in the classroom. Instead of attributing John's failure in his studies to "lack of interest and application," the teacher will be led to wonder *why* that lack? Is it because of a physical condition? Insufficient sleep? Malnutrition? A learning program ill-adapted to John's needs, interests, and abilities? The "guidance viewpoint" will replace the judicial one, and study and diagnosis will replace premature snap judgment.

It can also be seen that this bears a very close relation to the previous section on identification of children with problems. The teacher and principal who participate in the co-operative study of the problems of a number of children will be far more sensitive to the symptoms of maladjustment in classroom and school, and far better able to interpret them intelligently. In addition, as we shall see in a moment, this also helps in the development of insightful and sympathetic adjustment procedures.

Pupil Adjustment Procedures

The plans for the adjustment program of pupils with serious difficulties should be developed co-operatively in the case conference. For less serious problems, or for children whose difficulty is relatively simple and obvious, the teacher and principal can develop a plan with the help of only the specialist who is needed. For example, if the problem seems obviously to be one of a child who needs more intensive assistance in reading fundamentals than the teacher is able to give, then the remedial specialist and the teacher should work together on the problem. The specialist will assist the teacher in providing classroom materials which are not above the child's reading level, and will suggest instructional procedures which the teacher can use to assist the pupil to improve his reading skill. In addition, the specialist may have the child meet with her periodically for specialized work. In scheduling such additional help certain precautions must be taken. First, it must be closely co-ordinated with the child's classroom work. Second, it should be carried on in a spot which is well lighted, cheerfully decorated, and clean. The authors have observed inexcusable situations in which such work was being attempted in dusty closets with a bare light bulb hanging down, no window, and very cramped quarters. It were better not to attempt such work than to carry it on under such conditions. Third, the child should not have such work scheduled in lieu of exciting activities he loves, such as recess, art, or physical education game time. Nor is it wise to keep him after school for such work unless he is very obviously eager to stay himself in order to get help. Finally, it should always be kept in mind that reading difficulty may have causes beyond the classroom, and that something may have to be done about these before the reading difficulty can be cleared up.

The same kinds of things can be said for other problems, of course. In any event, it cannot be stressed too strongly that it is the function of specialists to help not only children, but teachers as well. The remedial reading or speech specialist has the responsibility of helping the teachers to do a better job in reading and speech within the classroom. One specialist in speech suggests a threefold program to achieve this:

1. Teachers and parents of handicapped children should be given a short course in normal speech development and simple speech correction.

2. Teachers and parents must be given opportunity to observe the speech teacher as she diagnoses the child's difficulty and gives him remedial treatment. Together they should work out a program of speech hygiene for the child, and outline developmental procedure. The responsibility for carrying out this program must be placed upon the parents and the classroom teacher.

3. The speech teacher should act further as a consultant and should visit the child at least once a week. In the most serious cases she will work with the child herself, but active co-operation of those who are with him most is essential.[10]

[10] E. Miller, "Reorganizing the Speech Program in a City School System," Department of Elementary School Principals, *op. cit.,* Nineteenth Yearbook, p. 641.

In the program discussed in the above article, the teachers indicated that they got their greatest help from watching the speech teacher at work with children.

The teacher is the focal point. The point to be emphasized in this discussion is that the specialists should be engaged by a school system with the primary objective of assisting the teacher to do a better job with the children. This means, then, that their work will have to be closely co-ordinated with that of the teacher, so that he may gain the insights necessary to the doing of a better job with the group of children assigned to him. It is encouraging to note that many school systems are now recognizing this, and organizing their services with this as one of their important objectives.[11]

An illustration of the kind of outcome these co-operative procedures can have is found in the reaction of one teacher:

> The most intellectually stimulating experience in all my years of teaching has been my participation in these studies of the personality problems of children. This stimulation has been due primarily to the earnestness of all concerned, and to the variety of viewpoints represented by the teachers of all grades, . . . by the principal and supervisors of superior and poorly adjusted groups, by the school nurse and counselor, and by the psychologist from the department of research and guidance.[12]

The Prevention of Adjustment Problems

Whereas it is important to provide means of dealing with problems of pupil maladjustment, it would be even more ideal if such problems could be prevented. While the school cannot hope to eliminate all the factors which bring about these problems, there is much it can do about the conditions within the school which conduce to them.

Perhaps the most important area for such attention is the curriculum. Many of the problems of children in school either arise from, or are severely aggravated by, a learning program unsuited to their needs, interests, and abilities. It seems to follow naturally, therefore, that anything the school can do to vitalize and individualize its program of learning should result in fewer or less severe adjustment problems on the part of the pupils. In this respect the specialists on the staff can also be of

---

[11] Department of Elementary School Principals, *op. cit.*, Nineteenth Yearbook, pp. 567–588.
[12] *Ibid.*, p. 588.

assistance, and can act as resource consultants. Elsewhere the great desirability of co-operative endeavor in the matter of the development and modification of the learning program has been stressed, as has the degree to which specialist and teacher should work together in the adjustment of children with problems. The program of prevention will likewise gain if these staff members with special training are enlisted as part of the team in the development of the learning program for all children. Too frequently have we considered them as persons who are somehow outside the main stream of educational endeavor, and too often have they agreed that their function is so highly specialized that the specialist has little in common with teachers.[13] Through the joint participation of teacher and specialist, the findings of research and experience in psychology, remedial work, and other specialized fields will find an avenue into the classroom to become a part of the fabric of the teacher's daily work.

The program of prevention, then, has to be broadly conceived in terms of the all-around growth of pupils; it cannot be a single-shot affair of a guidance clinic only, or of a program of "adjustment classes." It must encompass the educational, social, emotional, and physical factors, and do so in a unifying, integrating manner. Such a program will have several requirements:

1. The teacher must seek an understanding of children in terms of what such understanding means in classroom teaching. This can be developed by the methods suggested above.

2. There should be a concerted program to identify early evidences of pupil maladjustment of any kind. This includes standardized testing, methods of detecting social and personality difficulties, informed observation, and a good system of cumulative records.

3. The staff should develop co-operatively a curriculum suited to the interests, needs, and abilities of *children living here and now.*

4. All the services that it is possible for the school to muster, which can be of help to the teacher in identifying and helping children with problems, should be provided. These services should be organized so that a co-operative approach to teachers' and pupils' problems is assured.

5. A program of health and physical education should be developed

---

[13] H. J. McNally, "Organizing School Curricula to Meet Individual Differences," *Journal of Consulting Psychology,* vol. VI, July-August 1942, pp. 200–204.

which will detect physical difficulties early, and will educate children and their parents in the conditions and measures which prevent physical malfunctioning and which promote good physical and mental health.

6. The principal should exercise unifying, democratic, and vigorous leadership.

The foregoing discussion may seem to imply that in order for a school to do anything about pupil maladjustment a whole battery of specialists is necessary. Not so. If it were, the outlook would be discouraging indeed for the many small schools and districts which do not have such specialized resources available. More important than specialists in the long run is the development of a true "guidance viewpoint" by the staff and parents, a viewpoint which recognizes that all behavior is caused, and that when the causes are discovered it is likely that we can do something about them. Teachers with such a viewpoint have been helping children with their problems for years in all kinds of schools. In these schools, teachers, principal, and parents can still work co-operatively in attempting to help pupils, and can call upon what resources there are in the community. There is likely to be at least a doctor, and perhaps a dentist, who can help.

Nevertheless, it has to be recognized that one can do a better job when one has more adequate tools. For this reason, small schools should do all they can to extend their resources of specialized help. In some areas, several school districts have banded together to purchase part-time service of these types. Such districts maintain their own individuality, but each contributes a part of the expense to pay the salary of a psychologist, for example. Such co-operative service holds promise for small districts in rural areas.

Summary

We can see, then, that specialized services are used best on a consultant basis, and that one objective of their use should be the improvement of the teacher's ability to handle problems in her own classroom, rather than to be an encouragement for her to shift the responsibility for such problems to someone else. The program has the four aspects of identification of problems, diagnosis of problems, treatment of problems, and a comprehensive effort to develop an over-all program of education which will go far in preventing pupil maladjustment by promoting better educational, social, emotional, and physical growth and adjustment. This, after all, is one of the major objectives of the school.

SUGGESTED READINGS

Association for Supervision and Curriculum Development, *Fostering Mental Health in Our Schools,* National Education Association, Washington, D. C., 1950.

Department of Elementary School Principals, *Appraising the Elementary School Program,* Sixteenth Yearbook, National Education Association, Washington, D. C., 1937.

————, *Meeting Special Needs of the Individual Child,* Nineteenth Yearbook, National Education Association, Washington, D. C., 1940.

Driscoll, Gertrude, *How to Study the Behavior of Children,* Bureau of Publications, Teachers College, Columbia University, New York, 1941.

Oberteuffer, Delbert, *School Health Education,* Harper and Brothers, New York, 1949, Part III.

Prescott, Daniel, *Helping Teachers Understand Children,* American Council on Education, Washington, D. C., 1945.

Wickman, E. K., *Children's Behavior and Teachers' Attitudes,* Commonwealth Fund, New York, 1928.

CHAPTER XVII

FOOD SERVICES

In any sound program of school organization the local principal is held directly responsible for the operation of the cafeteria. This implies on his part both a knowledge of what the elements of an adequate food service program are and a disposition to see that the educational benefits and possibilities of the cafeteria and related services are realized.

Although a great deal has been written about foods and food services, the elementary school principal need not be too discouraged about keeping abreast of the developments in this field because—despite some controversy among authorities over what comprises an optimum diet for people generally—there is considerable agreement as to the dietary needs of children. Moreover, there has been sufficient experience in this area to make it possible to know, in some measure at least, how successful the food service phase of the school program is.

One rather obvious test relates to nutrition. The recommended dietary allowances set up by the Nutritional Committee of the National Research Council may be used as one guide (see page 254 for recommended allowances). It is also possible to get a rough measure of adequacy by looking at the food budget itself. Expenditures for fruits and vegetables should be at least equal to that spent for meat, and approximately one third of the total food budget should go for milk. While these percentages may properly vary somewhat from school to school, they do reflect to a considerable degree how well the dietary aims are being achieved.

Practically all surveys of children's feeding show that too little milk is consumed, despite the wide publicity given to the importance of this item of food. Moreover, children require more fruits and vegetables than parents commonly provide at home. By studying daily statistics relating to the consumption of food, the principal can direct his efforts and those of his staff toward the achievement of a balanced diet for the children in his school.

An Integral Part of the Educational Program

The cafeteria program should by no means be thought of merely as a service feature of the school. It can be one of the most important of the teaching laboratories. Hence it is essential that food services be so organized that they are an integral part of the total educational program. The relationship of feeding to health education is obvious; the cafeteria program also provides an opportunity for education for citizenship, for growth in social effectiveness, for the lifting of esthetic tastes, for improvement in number skills, and for appreciation of economic principles. Teachers with imagination will utilize the cafeteria resources to great advantage in helping the child shape his total pattern of living.

To some degree pupils can become partners in the actual operation of the cafeteria and thereby learn to assume responsibility as well as acquire useful skills. So far as their maturity will permit, the co-operation of pupils should be enlisted. Work experiences in the food service area, if wisely planned and supervised, should enrich the school program significantly. Children in the upper elementary grades can be given some responsibility in supervising the lunch period. They can serve as hosts and hostesses and can help create and maintain a pleasant atmosphere in the cafeteria. Some schools have found it advantageous to set up a special committee composed of representative teachers and pupils to advise with the principal and the cafeteria supervisor or director on cafeteria matters. This committee can also assist in educating parents and the public generally with respect to the aims of the food service program. This may involve radio talks, publication of menus, and a variety of other activities relating to food services. The problem of educating parents regarding the relationship of diet to health, happiness, and scholastic attainment, represents one of the biggest tasks to be undertaken. "Spot" checks of children's lunches prepared at home but eaten at school have repeatedly revealed the abysmal ignorance of many parents with respect to dietary standards. One meal per day in the cafeteria, even if provided to all children, will not alone insure a balanced diet.[1] The co-operation of the home in giving attention to the total daily food consumption of children in relationship to their needs is essential if the best results are to be obtained.

Administering the Lunch Period

There seems to be little uniformity in practice with respect to the length of the school lunch period and the most efficient manner of supervising it. Some schools allow as little as twenty minutes for lunch and some as much as an hour. In some schools teachers are expected to eat with the children whereas in others they eat in a separate dining room. Where the latter practice obtains, a supervisor is commonly put in charge of the lunchroom activities.

No single formula can be safely laid down for scheduling and supervising the school lunch period. The physical facilities are related to both the time schedule and the supervision. Moreover, the philosophy underlying the lunchroom program is a determining factor in deciding what type of supervision is best. Those who feel that the school lunch offers a unique opportunity to teach manners and the social graces will be led to the conclusion that teachers should eat with the children. The proportion of children who go home for lunch is a consideration in deciding how much time to set aside for the lunch period. Presumably in communities where a substantial number of children go home for the midday meal a twenty-minute period is not sufficient; hence a longer lunch period is desirable.

Probably the best solution to the administrative problems relating to scheduling and supervising lunchroom activities can be reached through co-operative study and planning. Teachers, parents, and children all have an important stake in the policies adopted. Too little consideration has been given to the need of a rest period for teachers sometime during the school day, and unless some block of time can be set aside apart from the lunch period, it is somewhat shortsighted to insist that teachers eat regularly with the children. The fact that the lunch period offers additional opportunity for instruction is not the sole criterion to be applied. Teachers in the elementary school are under considerable tension and a failure to provide a break in the school day unquestionably results in

---

[1] A typical lunch will provide approximately one third of a child's daily requirements of calories, protein, minerals, and vitamins.

decreased efficiency on the part of many teachers. The advantages and disadvantages therefore, of assigning them lunchroom responsibilities should be carefully weighed. Parents sometimes assist during the lunch period. This may constitute the answer to the problem in some schools.

When the cafeteria facilities are adequate, it would seem desirable to allow a full hour for the lunch period and provide a program of activities following the meal which is conducive to relaxation and rest. Music, moving pictures when wisely selected, and games that require little exertion represent some of the approved after-lunch activities. The longer lunch period would permit those children who go home to have a more leisurely lunch with their parents.

Where the plant facilities do not permit all children to eat lunch at the same time and it is necessary to have several shifts, the time allowed may have to be substantially less than sixty minutes. These practical considerations will, of course, dictate policy. The principal should not be content, however, with compromise arrangements; he should make every effort to improve existing facilities even to the point of urging the central office to make substantial alterations in the building itself.

In-Service Program for Cafeteria Employees

Experience has shown that cafeteria employees are frequently not well prepared for their duties. They may be conscientious and industrious, but they often lack the necessary knowledge and skill required to do their work efficiently. Because of this it is desirable to establish training opportunities where the best procedures can be demonstrated and equipment problems thoroughly discussed. A two-day institute just prior to the opening of school is one means of introducing a program of instruction and improvement for food service employees. The various areas that might well be emphasized in such a training program include (1) food preparation with special reference to quantity recipes, (2) sanitary handling and storage of foods, supplies and equipment, (3) efficient work techniques both in food preparation and service, (4) elementary knowledge of nutrition, and (5) effects of methods of cooking on food nutrients.[2]

The principal's role in relation to the training of employees will vary depending upon the philosophy and organization of the central office

[2] *The Report of the Survey of the Public Schools of Montclair, New Jersey,* Institute of Field Studies, Teachers College, Columbia University, New York, 1948, p. 138.

staff. In some school systems, the principal may have little control over this phase of the program. Ideally, he should have the major responsibility for the supervision and improvement of all the employees in his school. In any event, he should become thoroughly informed on matters relating to food services.

Federal Subsidy

The school lunch program has been heavily subsidized in recent years by the Federal Government. This has made it possible in many communities to provide most children with a well balanced midday meal at very low cost.[3]

While there has been some reluctance on the part of a few administrators to apply for Federal aid in connection with their school lunch programs, superintendents and principals have generally favored this subsidy since it promises so much for child health and welfare. It is true that certain reports have to be made periodically and accounts have to be audited and some outside supervision provided. But to an efficient administrator these requirements constitute no serious barrier to the successful operation of a school lunch program. It would be well for the elementary school principal to familiarize himself with the details of the Federal program so he can fulfill his obligations to the central office and indirectly to the Federal Government, and at the same time be in a position to advise staff members and interested laymen regarding this program.

SUGGESTED READINGS

Association for Childhood Education, *Lunch at School*, Bulletin 1948.

Co-operating Committee on School Lunches, *A Yardstick for School Lunches*, Nutrition Education Series, Pamphlet no. 4, U. S. Office of Education, U. S. Government Printing Office, Washington, D. C.

Graff, Stelle W., *A Handbook for the Operation of School Lunch Programs*, Illinois Circular Series A, no. 34, August 1946.

---

[3] The much-discussed type A lunch consists of one half-pint of whole milk; two-ounce serving of protein in the form of meat, fish or cheese, or ½ cup (cooked measure) of dry peas, beans or soybeans, or 4 tablespoons of peanut butter; ¾ cup of raw, cooked or canned vegetable and/or fruit; one or more slices of bread made of whole grain or enriched flour; two teaspoons of butter, or margarine with added vitamin A.

Hemphill, James M., "Financial Advantages Under the School Lunch Program," *California Schools,* March 1949, pp. 68–71.

National Research Council, *Recommended Dietary Allowances,* Reprint and Circular Series, no. 122, rev., The Council, Washington, D. C., 1945.

Tansil, Blanche Allen, *Feeding Children at School,* unpublished Ed.D. project, Teachers College, Columbia University, New York, 1946.

"The School Lunchroom," *The School Executive,* vol. LXVIII, no. 11, July 1949, pp. 41–56.

U. S. Office of Education, *Making School Lunches Educational,* Nutrition Education Series, Pamphlet no. 2, U. S. Government Printing Office, Washington, D. C., 1944.

A LIBRARY THAT SERVES THE SCHOOL

The Changing Function of the Library

Prior to the present century, practically no elementary schools had functional libraries, as we now conceive them, for the simple reason that they had no need of them. In a school where the day is closely scheduled, where the curriculum is what is in the textbook, and where homework takes up an appreciable portion of a child's every afternoon or evening, what need is there for a library? It can be only an unjustifiable luxury, a silly educational faddish frill, a mad extravagance of "progressive education."

This picture has changed as educational thinking and curriculum practice have changed. Present educational theory and an increasing portion of practice emphasize problem-centered learning, in which numerous sources must be consulted, in which one cannot rely on the single textbook. In a study of modern communication, for example, children will be looking into technical books on radio, into books on smoke and flag signaling, into books discussing codes and their use, and into information on telegraph and telephone. Data will be sought on the United States Postal Service, on air travel and television, as well as on heliograph and flashing-light signaling methods. The pupils are likely to become interested in the messenger techniques of ancient times, the facts about carrier pigeons, the drum communication of African savages, or the Pony Express of American renown. In seeking the information they need, the pupils will utilize resources in the community, written inquiries to appropriate sources, museums, models, pictures, slide films, and other audio-visual aids, and—of course—many books. The poor old textbook of former days might touch lightly on some of the topics under study, but could not hope to satisfy the fully aroused curiosity of children. Even the usual type of supplementary textbooks will fail to do this. Not only does a modern program demand a much greater wealth of informational material than does the narrow "essentials" program of the past; it makes greater attempts to suit itself to the wide range of individual differences among the pupils, so that materials are needed which are varied not only with respect to content, but in level of difficulty as well. The only answer to the problem is the provision of a wide variety of books on a wide variety of topics. It is this need which has called the elementary school library into being.

It can be seen, then, that the elementary school library is relatively a newcomer on the educational scene. To date, its spread has been relatively slow; it has attained only a small portion of its ultimate growth, and is as yet far short of realizing its ultimate quality and possibilities. In spite of this, there is encouraging evidence that its growth is continuing

The Thrill That Comes Once in a Lifetime: BY H. T. WEBSTER

TOM SAWYER
HUCKLEBERRY FINN
TREASURE ISLAND
THE THREE MUSKETEERS
ROBINSON CRUSOE
20,000 LEAGUES UNDER THE SEA
THE ADVENTURES OF ROBIN HOOD
MEN OF IRON
THE ADVENTURES OF SHERLOCK HOLMES
THE JUNGLE BOOK
THE FLAMINGO FEATHER
KING ARTHUR AND HIS KNIGHTS
TWO YEARS BEFORE THE MAST
ONCE ABOARD THE LUGGER
LORNA DOONE
THE REDS OF THE MIDI
RABBLE IN ARMS
THE SEA WOLF
CUTLASS EMPIRE
CAPTAIN BLOOD
TYPEE
THE PROUD SHERIFF
THE ADVENTURES OF CAPTAIN HORN
WYATT EARP

THE BOY WITH A WEAKNESS
FOR ADVENTURE FINDS
A GOLD MINE

Copyright, 1950, New York Herald Tribune Inc.   2-11-

steadily. From its feeble beginnings the library has become recognized as a significant and vital part of the elementary school.

Although much progress has been made, a great deal needs yet to be done in this as in other aspects of education. Nevertheless, whatever is done should not be done simply to get a place on the bandwagon. The establishment, development, or improvement of library service in a school should be accomplished to satisfy a recognized need, and should be developed so as best to serve the expanding learning program of the school.

It is likely that little progress will be made without the leadership, or at least the co-operation, of the principal. As the school's professional leader, he should have little trouble in interesting the teachers in the establishment of library service in the school, for teachers interested in their job will be quick to see its advantages. Enlisting the co-operation of the superintendent and board of education may be more difficult, although many superintendents will welcome suggestions for school improvement. It seems obvious that unless leadership is exercised in the local school there is little chance of any appreciable effort being made to improve the library situation. If leadership *is* exercised, it is almost certain that something *can* be done, even if it is but a modest beginning.[1] There is vast room for improvement, and principals are in a strategic position to do something about it.

Extent of Elementary School Library Service

From the data which are available, it is difficult to give an adequate picture of the elementary school library situation today. Nevertheless, certain phases of it are fairly clear. Of the 232,174 elementary schools in the United States in 1935, about two in nine had some form of library service, about one in seven had classroom libraries only, and *less than one in ten* had centralized libraries in the school.[2] The Department of Elementary School Principals reported in 1948 that 62 per cent of schools with supervising principals had library rooms, and that 41 percent of schools with teaching principals had such facilities.[3] This does

[1] T. M. Hargrave, "P. T. A. Sponsors a School Library Project," *Wilson Bulletin,* vol. XXIII, October 1948, pp. 176–177, 179; Department of Elementary School Principals, *Elementary School Libraries,* Twelfth Yearbook, National Education Association, Washington, D. C., 1933, pp. 183–191.

[2] Bess Goodykoontz, *Elementary Education, 1930–1936,* U. S. Office of Education Bulletin 1937, no. 2, U. S. Government Printing Office, Washington, D. C., 1940, pp. 21–22.

[3] Department of Elementary School Principals, *The Elementary School Principalship —Today and Tomorrow,* Twenty-seventh Yearbook, National Education Association, Washington, D. C., 1948, p. 48.

not mean fully equipped libraries, of course; they range from converted storerooms and coal bins to beautiful walnut-paneled suites with all the trimmings. Of the supervising principals in whose schools there were library rooms, 35.4 per cent had a full- or part-time librarian, while but 18.9 per cent of the teaching principals had such personnel.[4] Apparently most elementary school libraries are being handled as an additional duty by the principal or one of his teachers. One very disturbing note in the picture is that only 13 per cent of supervising principals and 8 per cent of teaching principals indicated a librarian as one of their needs.[5] If a librarian is considered in his proper status as a teacher who works with every other teacher, with every child, and with the children's parents, helping the school to get the maximum from the tools at its command, his salary can be justified in schools enrolling as few as 175–200 pupils, and he will earn his salt. Some smaller school districts have co-operated so as to share among several schools the services and expense of a librarian, as well as of other school services. In rural schools of one and two rooms, the services of a full-time librarian cannot be justified, of course, but there is certainly greater need for the services of librarians than is indicated in the principals' expression of need cited above.

Nevertheless, these 1948 data indicate considerable progress over the 1935 figures, even though they are not strictly comparable in their classifications. It seems that today well over half our elementary schools have some form of library service, as compared with less than one-fourth a dozen years ago. This is considerable progress, but falls far short of being sufficient. Large numbers of schools are still without any form of library service, and the situation in many schools which have some library services is pitifully inadequate. From the authors' observations recently, it seems probable that only a tiny proportion of our elementary schools have library service which could be called reasonably satisfactory.

Types of Library Service

The preceding paragraphs indicate that there is great variety in the manner in which library service may be rendered in elementary schools, and this is very true. There is, of course, the school which has no such service at all. A cut above that is the school which has stored an assort-

[4] *Ibid.,* p. 62.
[5] *Ibid.,* p. 65.

ment of books, most of which are likely to be fiction, in what had been a storeroom, or a converted coal bin, or a large closet, or in a designated classroom, or in the principal's office. These books may be checked out by teachers, who may issue them in turn to the pupils.

In many schools teachers have built up "classroom libraries" or library corners. To call these libraries is a misnomer in the modern meaning of the term, for these are simply collections of books in a classroom, to be used by the children in that class. Such collections are built up by means of gifts of books, loans from the public library, books bought out of the teacher's own pocket, and sometimes by money provided by the board of education for the purpose. Teachers and pupils frequently prize these collections highly, despite their inadequacy, for often they represent considerable work, planning, and some sacrifice.

These two plans are characteristic of (though not confined to) schools in rural areas. Whereas there are exceptions, the books in these collections tend to be nondescript and inadequate. One librarian has described conditions as she found them in several western states:

> Frequently the same old books, ragged, torn, soiled, and unattractive, stand on the shelves for years. In most cases they are collections of worn-out texts, unattractive sets, cheap series, undesirable gifts, out-of-date and unsuited to the active needs of the pupils . . . Pupils never look at such books. Scores of children do not read anything but the textbook, and not infrequently there are no readable books in the homes or schools. At this time many texts in actual use are fifteen years out-of-date in subject matter. The text may be all right as far as it goes. At its best it is but one man's opinion out of many millions who may be just as authentic.[6]

In other schools, the entire book collection is placed in one classroom, and the teacher of that class is responsible for checking books in and out. Usually she sets up a schedule of times at which this may be done, and often pupil assistants from the upper grades are assigned to help her.

Large numbers of school systems have established relationships of various types with the public libraries.[7] These range from obtaining loans of "blocks" of books from the public library to the actual establishment of a branch of the public library in the school. In rural areas particularly this has been one solution for many schools, although there are adminis-

---

[6] Department of Elementary School Principals, *Elementary School Libraries,* Twelfth Yearbook, p. 367.

[7] *Ibid.,* ch. V.

trative problems involved in connection with the selection of books, the financing, differences in philosophy, and the difference in time schedules between the two institutions. Such an arrangement was institutionalized between the school and library authorities in Toledo, Ohio, in 1919, and it was provided that the library room in the school should be ". . . so placed in the school building as to be adaptable for use not only during but outside school hours, having both an entrance from the school corridor and a direct entrance from the street, and provided with adequate means of heating when the school is not in session."[8] Although relationships with public libraries are necessary to provide library service in many rural districts and have been used to advantage by some urban schools, this arrangement has not always worked out well.

Many rural areas which are unable to have extensive school libraries have supplemented their own meagre resources through "bookmobile" library service. A specially equipped truck visits each co-operating school, and carries a good selection of books. These are checked out or returned by the pupils at each visit of the bookmobile.[9]

In urban schools and in good-sized rural centralized schools, the central library in the school is more common. These libraries have one or more library rooms, a full- or part-time librarian, and large collections of books. It is not unusual to find schools with such libraries also operating "classroom libraries." These are usually reading corners in the classroom, stocked with books charged out from the school's central library for a period of time.

It is evident from this sketchy description of different types of libraries in existence that one cannot propose stated procedures for library administration which would be applicable to all situations. The following discussion, therefore, simply suggests some characteristics of good library service, and means of establishing or extending and improving library service in schools.

Characteristics of Good Library Service

There are a number of sources the administrator should consult to help him in the improvement of the library service in his school, some of the most pertinent of which are listed at the close of this chapter.

[8] *Ibid.*, quoted on p. 264.
[9] Ruth H. Wagner, "Bookward Ho!" *National Education Association Journal,* vol. XXXVIII, March 1949, p. 202.

Since there seems to be considerable agreement among investigators and writers on important aspects of library service, the authors present the following characteristics as a summarization.

1. *The centralized library is the best arrangement for a school library.* Under such an arrangement all the library materials are at the disposal of everybody in the school. Furthermore, there is the opportunity for the development of the "library habit" and for the teaching of library skills and attitudes, which is absent in the "classroom library" arrangement. The scope of the reading collection can be made much greater, and it gives children more opportunity to find materials suited to their interests and reading levels than do the limited classroom collections.

Nor is the contribution of the centralized library limited to the realm of library skills. It offers opportunity for developing abilities of independent work and responsibility. Pupil participation in the planning, building, and operation of a library has rich possibilities for social learnings, for building human relations skills and attitudes, for providing experience and insights in the satisfactions of good service well rendered. The use of the library by pupils offers learning opportunities in the areas of social responsibility and consideration for others. A school library which is well conceived and well operated, and whose possibilities are well understood by the teaching staff, can help a school attain its objectives in far greater measure than would otherwise be possible.

2. *The physical arrangements should, insofar as possible, comply with the minimum standards set up by authorities, and, if feasible, exceed them.* A few of the major provisions of such standards are:

a. The library room should be centrally located so as to be accessible to the largest number of pupils.

b. It should be located where expansion is possible. For example, a room placed between the principal's office and a stair well cannot easily be expanded, whereas one situated between two classrooms can be, provided more space becomes available in the school because of falling enrollments or building additions.

c. The room should be placed where it receives the maximum light.

d. It should be placed where there is a minimum of disconcerting noises.

e. It should be placed where there can be an entrance independent of the rest of the building, with suitable arrangements for heating, lighting, and sanitation.

3. *Space and equipment should be adequate.* There should be, at the minimum, space enough to seat the largest class in the school, plus about twenty more pupils, allowing for 25 square feet per reader. The library should comprise a large circulation and reading room, a small workroom, and a small conference room. Two regular size classrooms would provide for such an arrangement for a school of five hundred pupils. There should be adequate shelving, at least two sizes of tables and several sizes of chairs, a magazine rack or two, picture shelving, bulletin boards and display space, a circulation desk, card catalogues, a book truck, and a movable glass display case. The library should house much of the audio-visual material of the school, and space considerations for this should be included in the original planning. Other equipment can be added if desired. (See Suggested Readings at end of chapter for standards for shelf dimensions, amount of shelf space necessary, and other suggestions.)

4. *There should be a well-balanced book supply, in sufficient number and adequate variety.* The American Library Association recommends the following ratio of books to enrollment:[10]

SCHOOL ENROLLMENT	NUMBER TITLES	NUMBER VOLUMES
Up to 200	1,700	2,000
500	3,500	5,000
1,000	5,000	7,000
3,000	7,000	12,000
5,000	8,000	15,000

Where a library is already established, provisions must be made for adding new titles, and replacing lost, damaged, and outworn books. For this purpose, the American Library Association and National Education Association recommend a minimum figure of $2.00 per pupil,[11] an increase over their prewar and preinflation figure. Eaton, in the 1943 report of the Committee on the Library in General Education, recommended that, "according to standards set for modern school library practice, the library should spend on books at least $1.00 per pupil; $1.25 is better; $2.00 an ideal which . . . obviously permits a more

[10] Committee on Post-War Planning, *School Libraries for Today and Tomorrow, Functions and Standards,* American Library Association, Chicago, 1945, p. 21.
[11] Joint Committee of the American Library Association and the National Education Association, *The Price of Wisdom,* National Education Association, Washington, D. C., 1949 (pamphlet).

adequate collection."[12] In making recommendations for the city of New Rochelle, New York, in 1941, Jenney recommended $2.00.[13] Under present economic conditions, these prewar figures should be doubled. Actually, any "standard" of expenditure can be only a suggestion for those not approximating it, a "floor" for those with the financial resources to exceed it.

Care must also be taken to assure a balance between reference materials, information materials, and types of fiction. Subscriptions to magazines for children and teachers should also be provided for in the budget. The books should be arranged in some orderly fashion to facilitate the location of titles as they are called for. Since small libraries may grow into larger ones, the usual library should use a standard classification system, such as the Dewey decimal system. It is important that all books in the school which are the property of the school be catalogued in the central library, even if they remain "permanently" in some teacher's classroom, for only in this way can it be known where they are or if they are in the school at all.[14]

5. *Book selection and ordering should be done according to approved practice, utilizing expert resources where they are available, and enlisting pupil and teacher participation.* It is most important that the selection of books for the library be done carefully to assure that the book collection will include only books of good quality, of usefulness to the school program, and of durability. The participation of teachers is valuable, for they will know best the books needed to serve the learning program in their classrooms. In addition some specialized assistance is needed in the person of one who sees the over-all school picture, and who is more expert in the area of children's books. If the school has a regular librarian, she will be that person; otherwise the librarian of the public library may be enlisted, or some teacher who has specialized in children's books at all levels of the elementary school. In some larger schools a committee has been given the responsibility of co-ordinating the work of selecting the titles, the chairman of which is usually the

[12] A. T. Eaton, "Book Selection for the School Library," in *The Library in General Education,* Forty-second Yearbook of the National Society for the Study of Education, University of Chicago Press, Chicago, 1943, ch. X.

[13] Orlo K. Jenney, *A Plan to Improve the Functional Services of Libraries in the Public Elementary Schools of New Rochelle, New York,* unpublished Ed.D. project, Teachers College, Columbia University, New York, 1941, p. 115.

[14] Committee on Post-War Planning, *op. cit.,* ch. IV; Phyllis R. Fenner, *The Library in the Elementary School,* Hinds, Hayden and Eldredge, New York, 1945, ch. V.

librarian. Through this committee the suggestions of all the teachers are solicited. Numbers of schools have enlisted the help of pupils in the selection of library books with considerable success. Pupils can participate directly in selection as part of the selection committee, or they may contribute their suggestions through their teachers, who relay them to the selection committee. In some schools, classroom committees formulate the list to be requested by that class. Children are the best judges of what they like, and their suggestions have proved helpful to teachers and librarians, not only in the immediate matter of the book order, but in gaining insight into the nature of children's reading tastes as well.[15] There are numbers of sources to render assistance in book selection. Such lists as: the *Children's Catalog,* published by the H. W. Wilson Company of New York; Nora Beust's *Five Hundred Books for Children,* available through the U. S. Office of Education; the *Handbook for Teacher Librarians* of the American Library Association; *The Booklist,* a monthly publication of the American Library Association; and Mary G. Davis' reviews of children's books in the *Saturday Review of Literature,* all have been used widely by schools in selecting their library books.[16] Such current sources as the New York *Times* and New York *Herald Tribune* book review sections will likewise be found helpful.

It will also be of invaluable assistance if an annual inventory is taken of the books in the library, and the balance of books of different types looked at critically. At this time it will be helpful to review critically the requests for materials, which the library has been unable to answer, or to answer but poorly during the year. (A record of such requests should be kept.) Modern library theory considers this more important than conformance with some arbitrarily recommended proportion of fiction, nonfiction, and reference materials. Such an inventory helps, too, in the job of clearing out "dead wood" from the library collection, which otherwise might remain on the shelves gathering dust, serving no purpose.

Practice in the ordering of library books varies from school to school. Books bought for libraries are usually of the type known as "trade books," and are subject to considerably larger discounts than books of

[15] Department of Elementary School Principals, *op. cit.,* Twelfth Yearbook, "The Pupils Build a Library," and "A Library Organized and Managed by Parents," pp. 183–191.
[16] An extensive listing of such sources will be found in Department of Elementary School Principals, *op. cit.,* Twelfth Yearbook, ch. X.

the "textbook" type, regardless of the quantity in which they are ordered. Consequently, it is about as economical to order library books monthly as annually, and introduces far more flexibility into the picture. Books can be ordered as the need for them becomes evident, a fact which will enhance interest in the library. Pupils or teachers who request a book, and find it in the library within a few days or weeks, are likely to have a much higher opinion of the library than if they have to wait until next year for their requests to be filled. Such practice entails a little more work, but it pays off.

Except where book orders from a school system run to thousands of dollars, it will be more economical to purchase through book jobbers who will handle the entire order, even though the books have different publishers. Jobbers' discounts on trade books vary, but usually are 20–25 per cent on trade editions, and may run as high as 33–35 per cent. Douglas lists a number of such jobbers in her helpful handbook.[17]

6. *The library should be so administered as to become an integral part of the entire school program.* It has been said that the library should be "the living room of the school." The library should be so inextricably a part of the school's program that the teaching staff considers it absolutely indispensable. It is inexcusable for a fine library to be built into a school, only to remain closed for large portions of the day. Such practice is sheer waste of tax money and of one of the potentially most valuable learning resources within the school. It was noted earlier that the changing elementary school program has enhanced the importance of the elementary school library, and has made of it a virtual necessity. Fortunate is that school in which the library was developed to meet recognized needs growing out of that changing program! Good administration can make it serve those needs well.

Care must be taken in scheduling. If at all possible, the library should be open during the entire school day, and before and after school; and individual children should have access to it during all that time. It will be used by entire classes for book review programs, for story hours, and for purposeful practice in the use of varied library materials. Such activities should be handled so that conflicts are avoided. Opportunities should be provided for children simply to "browse" around to find books they would like to read, and to get help in finding materials bear-

[17] Mary P. Douglas, *Teacher Librarian's Handbook,* 2nd ed., American Library Association, Chicago, 1949, pp. 94–95.

ing on class problems and on hobbies and interests of their own.[18] Children should also be able to come individually or in small groups from their classrooms to find materials bearing on topics and problems they are studying. Modern schools tend to have pupils use the library in small groups rather than have classes go *en masse*. Such practice makes it possible for the librarian to give much more effective and functional guidance.

For these conditions to obtain, it is necessary that someone be in the library at all times during the school day to assist the children. In one school one of the authors was in recently, for example, he found children dissatisfied because the best time they had for browsing was at lunchtime, and since the librarian also ate lunch at that hour, the library was locked up! Any teaching staff and principal can devise a way to get around that problem.

Some schools resort to the use of parent and pupil assistants. This can be helpful if it is well and carefully handled. Parents who participate cannot do so on a haphazard basis, and should realize that they are under the jurisdiction of the principal while in the school. Pupil assistants have been used with varying success. In schools expecting too high a standard of performance of such assistants, the pupils and the school have had an unsatisfactory experience. Fenner says, "It must be remembered that having children work is often more trouble than is saved by the work they do, and *it is not for the benefit of the librarian, but for the benefit of the child that he is allowed to help*. Superintendents who think that the work done by children saves the librarian time, and that therefore she does not need other help, should be set right."[19] Miss Fenner should know, being herself a highly successful elementary school librarian.

7. *The school library should be in charge of a person trained adequately both in teaching and in library service.* In libraries of schools enrolling less than 200 pupils, a teacher-librarian with some training in library service, or a part-time professional librarian, should be placed in charge. For schools enrolling between 200 and 500, a full-time librarian should be engaged. Another full-time trained librarian should be added for every additional 500 pupils or major fraction thereof.[20]

[18] Department of Elementary School Principals, *op. cit.*, Twelfth Yearbook, ch. VI, "Integrating the School Library and the Classroom."

[19] P. R. Fenner, *op. cit.*, p. 22.

[20] Committee on Post-War Planning, *op. cit.*, p. 17.

There has been little agreement as to what constitutes adequate training for a school librarian. A committee of the American Library Association recommends that teacher-librarians should have completed 12–18 semester hours of work in library science, and that the full-time school librarian should have taken a regularly organized college program in library science, comprising from 30–36 semester hours.[21] Whatever her formal training, she should be a person who can work well with teachers, and whose major objective will be to see that the books get *off* the shelves, rather than jealously keeping *her* books on the shelves.

It may be that the reader will say to himself, "This is all very well, but we just can't have most of these conditions in my school." True, possibly, at the moment, but the above characteristics are proposed simply as goals to be striven for, stars to which library wagons may be hitched. It is not likely that there is any school which cannot make some progress in the direction of the standards now considered desirable in school libraries.

That raises the parallel question of what can be done. School situations vary so widely that about all the authors can do is to repeat the old platitude, which is nevertheless very sound, of "Start where you are." This implies *knowing* where you are, which in turn points to some assessment of your situation. In numbers of schools, the parent-teacher association has been the starting point, and it is a matter of record that these organizations have been very helpful in establishing and improving school libraries. It would seem best to have a committee of staff and parents survey the present situation, and determine present needs. Then steps can be taken to meet those needs. The co-operation of the local and state libraries will be found easy to obtain, for their personnel are usually eager to help and are waiting only to be asked. The resources of the state department of education can be tapped, and they are often considerable. In numbers of states, the state will supplement local efforts with funds, *but the local effort must first be evident.* Assistance can also be solicited from the American Library Association and from the Library Service Division of the U. S. Office of Education in Washington. It is easy to see that lack of sources of help is not an excuse for doing nothing about school libraries.

The best plan for the school can then be decided upon. If space is

[21] *Ibid.,* p. 18.

absolutely impossible to find within the school for housing a central collection, then the classroom collection plan will have to do for the present. If space is available, even if it seems far from meeting the standards suggested above, it is best to make a start, for the space situation may improve at a later date. Many schools have had considerable success with makeshift arrangements, with the satisfaction that comes from making something out of almost nothing.[22] It is clear that nothing will be accomplished just by hoping; only purposeful, planned, and vigorous co-operative effort will bring results. In answer to the question of how to begin, we can only quote Arnold Bennett's, "Dear sir, you simply begin!"

In conclusion, it can be said that the basic essential of good library administration is that point of view which considers the library as an effective tool to make a valuable portion of the school's resources readily available for the use of teachers and pupils in the interests of better teaching and learning. Its administration is but the employment of any and all procedures designed to do this in the best possible way, within the limits of prudence, economy, and feasibility. All the evidence points to great need for the development and improvement of libraries in elementary schools. In this respect elementary school principals have an opportunity to write their names large in the book of those who have led in the improvement of elementary education in our country.

SUGGESTED READINGS

American Library Association, *A Handbook for Teacher Librarians,* The Association, Chicago, 1931.

————, *Planning the School Library Quarters,* The Association, Chicago, 1950.

Committee on Post-War Planning, *School Libraries for Today and Tomorrow, Functions and Standards,* American Library Association, Chicago, 1945.

Department of Elementary School Principals, *Elementary School Libraries,* Twelfth Yearbook, National Education Association, Washington, D. C., 1933.

---

[22] American Library Association, *Handbook for Teacher Librarians,* The Association, Chicago, 1931, "Making Over an Old Classroom into a Library," pp. 44–49; Department of Elementary School Principals, *op. cit.,* Twelfth Yearbook. (Many of the articles in this yearbook are descriptions of how schools made the best of what they had for school library purposes.)

Douglas, Mary P., *Planning and Equipping the School Library*, State Department of Public Instruction, Raleigh, N. C., 1946.

————, *Teacher Librarians' Handbook*, 2nd ed., American Library Association, Chicago, 1949.

Fenner, Phyllis R., *The Library in the Elementary School*, Hinds, Hayden and Eldredge, New York, 1945 (pamphlet).

National Society for the Study of Education, *The Library in General Education*, Forty-second Yearbook, Part II, University of Chicago Press, Chicago, 1943.

Oberholtzer, Kenneth E., "Administrators Consider Problems of the School Library," *American Library Association Bulletin*, vol. XLVI, January 1950, pp. 18–20.

Otto, Henry B., *Elementary School Organization and Administration*, 2nd ed., D. Appleton-Century Company, New York, 1944, ch. X.

CHAPTER XIX

THE PROGRAM OF AUDIO-VISUAL INSTRUCTION

Audio-visual methods of teaching are by far the oldest means of instruction in the world, and for many purposes are still the most effective. Before man could talk or write, his learning took place through direct experiencing. The development of a written language of abstract symbols, however, has enabled him to extend his experience into areas where it is impossible for most of us to experience directly. Unfortunately, our schools have tended to use the abstractions of language as substitutes for direct experience in learning, instead of as an extension and elaboration of that experience. Instead of using direct experience as the starting place, many educators have advocated using direct experience primarily as an extension and elaboration of the abstractions we have in books—a clear case of interchanging cart and horse!

More recently, however, educators have been regaining perspective and realizing anew that experience itself is the primary stuff of learning. The result is that they are now seeking to utilize the firsthand experiences of children as the heart of the learning program, and are using books to extend that experience instead of starting with books and relating experience to them, which has been the common practice. For those concepts for which actual experience is not possible, the most closely allied substitutes are being used in the form of audio-visual instructional materials. These provide the sensory experiences necessary to give meaning to the abstractions of written language, for what meaning can such an abstract symbol as *dog* have until a child has had the kind of experience necessary to associate a wagging tail and a bark with such a combination of inert symbols as d-o-g?

Concurrent with this growing emphasis on learning through more direct experience has been the rapid development of such mechanical audio-visual methods of communication as the motion picture, filmstrip, radio, recordings of various types, and television. These can augment firsthand experience in a most meaningful manner (indeed, they are often but once removed from it); hence they are powerful aids to the teacher and have made for themselves a firm place in the roster of instructional materials. It follows, then, that the elementary school principal should do all he can to provide these materials for teachers' use and to organize and administer their use so that they may be used to maximum advantage.

Scope of the Program

The spectacular development of motion pictures and radio in recent years, and the use of motion pictures in the training programs of the armed forces, has caused them to overshadow other audio-visual equipment and means of instruction in the minds of people generally. In fact, to many people audio-visual materials *means* motion pictures, plus filmstrip, slides, and television, perhaps. However, there are methods and materials of audio-visual instruction which existed long before Edison, DeForest, or Marconi made their epochal discoveries, some of which are far more effective for many learning purposes than film and radio. The following list, for example, indicates what one authority considers the most commonly used (when they *are* used!) types of audio-visual instructional materials.[1]

I. Repetitive Materials
   A. Blackboards
   B. Bulletin boards
   C. Duplicating devices
II. Pictorial and Graphical Representations
   A. Photographs
   B. Textbook illustrations
   C. Prints and etchings
   D. Cutouts
   E. Post cards
F. Newspaper clippings
G. Drawings and sketches
H. Charts, graphs, and tables
I. Cartoons
J. Pictorial statistics
K. Posters
L. Maps and globes
M. Diagrams and schematics
III. Projected Still Pictures
   A. Stereographs (unprojected)
   B. Lantern slides

[1] James S. Kinder, *Audio-Visual Materials and Techniques,* American Book Company, New York, 1950, pp. 7–8.

C. Filmstrips
D. Opaque projections
E. Positive transparencies
F. Micro-slide projections
G. Tachistoscopes
IV. Projected Motion Pictures
A. Silent motion pictures
B. Sound-on-film motion pictures
V. Auditory Materials
A. Phonograph records
B. Electrical transcriptions
C. Radio broadcasts
1. Amplitude modulation
2. Frequency modulation
D. Centralized sound systems
VI. Audio-visual Aids in Combination
A. Sound motion pictures
B. Television
C. Sound filmstrips

VII. The School Journey
VIII. The Museum
IX. Representations and Relief Displays
A. Models
B. Objects
C. Specimens, collections, samples
D. Relics
E. Dioramas
F. Sand tables, miniature sets, floor representations
G. Mock-ups
H. Miniatures, dolls, etc.
X. Dramatizations
XI. Demonstrations
XII. Miscellaneous
A. Flash cards
B. Albums
C. Illustrated booklets, scrap books

The principal will realize, then, that the audio-visual program of instruction will have to be broadly conceived, to include all the above aids to effective learning. The use and effectiveness of all of them can be improved by well-planned administration, and some of them necessitate careful organization.

It is frequently pointed out that schools in small rural districts are in no position to purchase the necessary materials and equipment. In some places this difficulty has been overcome by developing a central co-operative audio-visual service to serve a number of districts. In states with county superintendents, his office is the logical co-ordinating agency. Through such a service, sound motion picture projectors, films, and filmstrips can be provided on a scheduled basis for small one- or two-room schools which could not alone afford such service.

Provision of audio-visual materials of instruction will, of course, involve additional expense; the only sound way to finance the program is to include its expenses in the regular school budget. However, because of the general inclination of the public to regard such a program as an "extra," as sugar-coated education, and as an educational luxury, it is often not possible to obtain budget appropriations for it at the start. Schools have raised the necessary funds through parents' organizations, through the philanthropy of interested individuals, and by means of funds raised at school entertainments. Once the equipment has been obtained, continuous efforts should be made to get regular budgetary appropriations for the continuance of the program.

Administering the Program

It is to be noted that the success of efforts to improve use of audio-visual methods of instruction will not be assured simply by getting teachers "steamed up" about multisensory methods of teaching. Unless the program which is developed is well administered, it is likely that teachers will lose their interest and enthusiasm. One helpful source states that the "4 R's of a school's audio-visual education program are . . . to make sure that the:

RIGHT MATERIALS AND EQUIPMENT get to the
RIGHT PLACE at the
RIGHT TIME, and see that they are used in the
RIGHT WAY!"[2]

When faculty discussions have developed an intelligent sense of need on the part of the staff, the "Right materials" question likely to arise is, "What material and equipment should we try to obtain first?" This is a critical step, for initial expenditures for machines and related equipment may run to sizable sums. Manufacturers of various makes of equipment will be happy to demonstrate their products in the school, and perhaps even leave them for a brief tryout period. Not only must the excellence of the equipment itself be considered; its suitability to a given school situation should be taken into account. It is desirable to have the entire staff participate in the evaluations and decisions in buying this equipment.

The co-ordinator. Once the equipment has been purchased, plans should be laid for the organization and administration of the program. Experience has shown that responsibility for the program should be vested in one person. In very small schools the principal will assume the entire responsibility for co-ordinating the activity, but in larger schools this responsibility has usually been carried by one of the teachers. In school systems which employ a person to administer audio-visual instructional

---

[2] Audio-Visual Education Association of California, *Setting up Your Audio-Visual Education Program: A Handbook for Principals,* Stanford University Press, Stanford, Calif., 1949, p. 4.

materials on a system-wide basis, it is still necessary to provide for co-ordination at the local school level. As there is considerable work entailed in this where the program is at all adequate, it is desirable to free the co-ordinator from regular teaching duties for a part of the time each week. This has been done variously by having the job handled by a primary grades teacher whose classes are usually dismissed a half hour to an hour before those of the upper grades, by providing a substitute, or by doubling up arrangements within the school.

The duties of such a co-ordinator will vary with the size and needs of the school. One listing which is suggestive is as follows: "(1) to assist teachers in the selection and utilization of audio-visual material; (2) to see that equipment is always in proper working condition; (3) to train student and teacher projectionists; (4) to schedule equipment and materials; (5) to plan previews of new materials; and (6) to maintain a liaison with the central Audio-Visual Department."[3] Kinder lists seventeen responsibilities of the co-ordinator, dividing them into administrative, supervisory, and technical categories.[4] It should be obvious that the person who is to discharge these responsibilities should have the requisite characteristics; desirably, he should have an understanding and knowledge of the nature of the educational program throughout the school. He should be a person convinced of the value of audio-visual instruction, eager to see its use extended, be well acquainted with the major types of equipment, and educated in the best techniques and procedures of audio-visual education. Finally, and as important as any of the rest, he should possess those personal qualities which will enable him to work constructively and harmoniously with the teachers, with the viewpoint that his responsibility is akin to that of the expediter in industry; he is there to help teachers, including himself, in their efforts to do a better job, not to impose any methods upon them. This latter qualification is a prerequisite; the others can be learned readily by a person with such an outlook.

Selecting materials. As in the selection of other learning materials, the selection of audio-visual materials should be a co-operative venture, in which teachers have ample opportunity to indicate their needs, express their wishes, make evaluations, and cast their vote for or against mate-

[3] Department of Elementary School Principals, *The Principal and Audio-Visual Education,* National Education Association, Washington, D. C., 1948, p. 16.

[4] Kinder, *op. cit.,* pp. 542–543.

rials examined. The co-ordinator should lead the teachers in the planning of a selection procedure which will satisfy these conditions. To assist in this process, all schools should have access to the printed sources which can be of invaluable help; trying to select audio-visual materials without these sources is like trying to pick out a good place to eat along an unfamiliar highway, for there is now a tremendous quantity and variety of such materials available.

Dale lists sources of teaching materials, film catalogues, and film sources including: (1) references on utilization, (2) basic sources of audio-visual materials, (3) radio program listings, (4) phonograph records and transcriptions, (5) keeping currently informed, and (6) film catalogues and film sources.[5] McKown and Roberts devote an entire chapter to an extensive listing of sources of materials and equipment, including information on such diverse items as projectors, charts, film cabinets, maps, illustrative materials on industrial products, audio-visual periodicals, and the like.[6] Weinman recently prepared an extensive bibliography of such materials for elementary schools.[7] Such publications as the following are invaluable to the point of being essential in a school using educational films and filmstrips:

> *Educational Film Guide*, H. W. Wilson Co., New York (Published annually, with monthly supplement).
>
> *Filmstrip Guide*, H. W. Wilson Co., New York.
>
> Vera M. Falconer, *Filmstrips*, McGraw-Hill Book Company, Inc., New York, 1948.
>
> *Educators' Guide to Free Films*, Educators Progress Service, Randolph, Wis. (Published annually).
>
> *Blue Book of 16-mm. Films*. Educational Screen, Inc., Chicago (Published annually).
>
> Library of Congress, Motion Picture Division, *Guide to United States Government Motion Pictures*, Superintendent of Documents, Washington, D. C., 1947.

Administering projected materials. In selecting for purchase such commercial projected materials as films, filmstrips, and slides, it is important

---

[5] Edgar Dale, *Audio-Visual Methods in Teaching*, Dryden Press, New York, 1946, pp. 310–313 and 474–475.

[6] H. C. McKown and A. B. Roberts, *Audio-Visual Aids to Instruction*, 2nd ed., McGraw-Hill Book Company, Inc., 1949, p. 14.

[7] Constance Weinman, *Bibliography on Audio-Visual Instructional Materials*, Bureau of Publications, Teachers College, Columbia University, New York, 1950.

to establish routine previewing procedures. Some systems make a practice of first renting films, and seeing them in use before buying. However, commercial distributors will co-operate with schools or systems having regular previewing procedures, and will provide requested films for such viewing. It is important that the films be viewed and appraised by several people, and that some criteria and rating procedures be established to systematize the evaluations.

Teachers will understand criteria far better and will apply them with infinitely greater insight if they have had a part in the development of them. Simple, straightforward criteria are preferable and facilitate appraisal.

FIGURE 13. Film Preview Form Used in Rochester, New York, Public Schools[8]

Preview and Evaluation of Motion Pictures for Use in Primary Grades
May 21, 22, 23, 1946

From the films to be previewed we want to select the very best—in terms of their probable usefulness in primary grade instruction. Those pictures that are rated highest by the previewing committee will be acquired by the Board of Education.

RATING—Indicate your over-all judgment of the film as

X—an excellent film, closely related to teaching needs, and one that will be continually useful

G—a good film, one that might be used, but generally supplementary in nature

P—a poor film, one that would have little or no value in teaching

Will you also please indicate the specific grade level for which the film is best suited?

REMEMBER, WE ARE NOT EVALUATING MOTION PICTURES AS MOTION PICTURES, BUT AS MATERIALS FOR ACHIEVING CURRICULUM OBJECTIVES.

FILM TITLE   GRADE LEVEL   RATING

A group of several criteria might be mimeographed on an evaluation form, on which the selection committee could record their evaluations. An example is presented in Figure 14, page 278. Kinder lists a number

[8] Paul C. Reed, "Selecting Films to Meet Curriculum Objectives," *Educational Screen,* vol. XXV, June 1946, p. 304.

FIGURE 14. Film Appraisal Record

Film Title:..

Producer:...Price..........

Age (or grade) level.............Evaluator..........

Directions: Indicate your appraisal of this film by placing an X in either column 1 (highly satisfactory), column 2 (satisfactory), or column 3 (unsatisfactory).

	1	2	3
1. Is the subject-matter of the film closely related to the classroom learning program?			
2. Will the film be understood easily by children of the age group for which it is intended?			
3. Is it a good technical job: Factually authentic; clearly and interestingly presented; well acted; clear and sharp; to the point and clear in purpose; up-to-date?			
4. Does it treat the subject adequately?			

Place a check in the appropriate box below:

☐ I am enthusiastic about this film; we'll use it a great deal. Let's buy it!

☐ This is a good film, and is likely to be used frequently.

☐ We would probably use this film occasionally, but its purchase is not urgent.

☐ I cannot recommend this film for our use.

Date_____

of appraisal forms which illustrate the variety possible. He includes forms of the Educational Film Library Association, Inc., of New York, several suggested in an American Council on Education publication, and one drawn up by himself.[9]

In small schools, the entire staff might constitute the selection committee, whereas in large schools it will be found more economical to have a representative selection committee. Numbers of schools include pupils in the reviewing procedure to ascertain their reactions, since they —after all—are the real consumers!

Housing the equipment. Where should audio-visual equipment be kept? There is now a strong trend to place the materials and equipment in the central library, in those schools which have one. In any event, it should be placed in an accessible spot, where the danger of damage and deterioration will be at a minimum, and where it will not be in the way. Films should be kept in a cool spot where the rays of the sun will not fall on them, for heat will tend to make the film brittle. Suitable shelving, drawer space, and boxes should be provided for slides and filmstrips and should be suitably labeled to facilitate easy location.

Operators. Modern visual equipment is simple to operate, and its operation can be learned easily by teachers. However, the teaching should be done individually or in small groups, for each teacher will learn only by operating the equipment himself under supervision. The program of in-service training should be well planned, with regularly scheduled times set aside for instruction in machine operation.

In many schools, pupil operators have been used very successfully, leaving the teacher entirely free to devote her attention to teaching. Experience has shown that fifth- and sixth-grade pupils can become quite skillful in projector operation, provided they are given adequate training.

Distribution. Distribution procedures will vary, of course, with the nature of the school's organization of audio-visual service. In school systems with an audio-visual center, the local school co-ordinator will serve as the channel for the requisitioning, distribution, and return of films. After his procedure is organized, much of the work is clerical and can be handled by the school secretary, if the school has one. In any event,

[9] Kinder, *op. cit.,* pp. 583–588.

a regular requisition form should be provided, on which the teacher makes her request with all the necessary information. White suggests a 3 x 5 card, as shown in the following illustration.[10]

FIGURE 15. Film Request Card

Teacher . . . . Date . . . .

No. . . . . Title . . . .

Reels . . . . Price . . . . Date of Use . . . .

Source . . . .
. . . .

Date   Confirmed
Ordered . . . .   to be used on . . . .

Teacher's opinion of film . . . .

In large school systems, it will be necessary to request films considerably in advance. The ideal situation, of course, is to be able to get the film the day it is ordered, but this is seldom possible except in schools which have their own film library right in the building. Some forms, suggestive of the kinds which can be used in the distribution and control of audio-visual aids, are listed in Kinder's recent book.[11] These include requisition forms, renewal slips, overdue notices, receipts, rating forms and the like, appropriate for use in larger schools and school districts.

Where shall projected materials be shown? Because projected materials need a darkened room for best visibility, there has been considerable discussion over whether they should be shown in a special room, or whether they can be used right in the classroom. Each school will have to make its own decision, of course, but it seems obvious that the most natural situation is to have the film in the classroom, and this is the arrangement recommended by authorities.[12] However, if the classroom cannot be darkened sufficiently, it is but a minor disturbance to have to go to another room. It is generally agreed that the auditorium is *not* a

[10] Department of Elementary School Principals, *The Principal and Audio-Visual Education,* p. 36.
[11] Kinder, *op. cit.,* pp. 597–603.
[12] Helen H. Seaton, *A Measure for Audio-Visual Programs in Schools,* American Council on Education Studies, Series II, no. 8, The Council, Washington, D. C., 1944, p. 35.

good place for showing instructional films, although entertainment films, of course, are shown there to best advantage. Numbers of schools have outfitted one room as an audio-visual room, and have then proceeded to prepare one additional classroom each year, until all classrooms were equipped with darkening and electrical facilities. It should be pointed out that one need not be so particular about darkening a room as was the case formerly, for the newer screens, and projection machines using 750–1000 watt bulbs, provide good visibility without complete darkness of the room. Opaque projectors, however, which project a reflected image, still need a darkened room.

Administering Other Audio-Visual Materials

The materials and equipment involved in providing projected instructional media tend to usurp more administrative attention than do other audio-visual materials of instruction. In fact, some of these other materials, such as graphs, charts, and posters, need little in the way of administrative arrangements other than provision of the materials to make them. The use and effectiveness of others, however, can be enhanced by well-conceived administrative arrangements.

It should also be noted that considerable improvement can be made in audio-visual methods of instruction without the purchase of projectors, films, and filmstrips. Few schools, if any, are realizing the full possibilities of such audio-visual media as pictures, charts, graphs, maps, stereoscopes, models, school museums, and field trips. By taking thought, the principal and his staff can, without excessive exertion or expense, provide more of such instructional materials, and set up administrative procedures to facilitate their effective use in classrooms.

The following are a few suggestions for administering specific phases of the program of audio-visual instruction which—after all—is an inseparable part of the teaching-learning program of the school as a whole. More detailed suggestions for specific techniques will be found in the Suggested Readings at the close of this chapter.

Pictures. A profusion of pictures is available in the *National Geographic Magazine, Life* magazine, and in many other publications. A good picture collection can be built up over the years, and can be housed in such a manner as to be easily and quickly available for use. While individual classroom collections are useful, many schools have found that housing the picture collection in the school library, or in some other central place, makes it widely available to all teachers in the school. With each teacher contributing a number of good pictures each year, the collection can be built up at a good pace. The librarian (when there is one) should be responsible for caring for the collection and for culling out pictures in poor condition.

It has usually been recommended that flat pictures be mounted on stiff backing and filed in a vertical file under a subject-heading system or by Dewey decimal classification. Careful mounting of pictures is time consuming, however, and one is reluctant to discard nicely mounted pictures even when their usefulness is apparently outlived. For these reasons, some schools have used envelope mounts. These consist of stiff backing with a transparent plastic front, and are open at one end. Pictures are slipped in the open end and are thus temporarily mounted. After use they can again be filed, and in their unmounted form they take up considerably less space. This was the system used by the late Horace Mann-Lincoln School of Teachers College, Columbia University. Pictures certain to see long and frequent use may, of course, merit careful permanent mounting. They might even be sprayed with transparent plastic, so that they can be wiped off with a damp cloth.

Maps. Although they have not always been used most effectively, maps have long been respected instructional materials. The principal should make arrangements with his staff to see that the maps in the school are used widely and to best advantage. Teachers should be discouraged from considering particular maps as their own property, and should realize the value and economy of having maps and globes circulate from room to room as they are needed. Care should be taken to see that maps are kept up-to-date. A student of one of the authors recently stated that in her school they are still using political maps which antedate World War I! Such a situation is inexcusable. Only up-to-date maps can teach correct concepts. Furthermore, in this day and age, no school should be without air-age projections of the azimuthal type, since the old Mercator and conical projections present distorted or untrue pictures of air routes.

Models. From time immemorial, models and such related materials as specimens, objects, and mock-ups have been used as effective instructional materials. As in the case of pictures and maps, good administration can assure that teaching and learning media of this nature can be made readily available to teachers. Collections of historical objects, objects typical of peoples of other lands, working models, and the like can be stored and catalogued so as to be located and used easily.

The school museum. A place where collections and models might well be kept is the school museum. Children love to collect things, and there is little excuse for a school not to have a museum, for the expense is negligible. The administrator has the responsibility of working with the staff to organize such a museum if one does not exist in the school, and to find space to house its collections and exhibits. The most natural method of "stocking" it is to preserve the appropriate materials collected or made in the course of the regular instructional program. Insect, mineral, botanical, and other collections can be properly mounted and labeled, and models, exhibits, and dioramas which the different classes produce can be placed there. Care should be taken to avoid letting the museum become simply a cluttered aggregation of unused objects. The collection should be properly mounted and labeled, and attractively arranged. Descriptive material should be developed, and one teacher should be given the responsibility specifically to oversee its care and development.

The "instructional materials center." A promising and relatively new idea worth the principal's attention is the instructional materials center. This is a center in which all instructional materials are housed and administered. In Cleveland, Ohio, the Educational Museum for the school system serves this function. Films, slides, photographs, pictures, exhibits, and charts are available from there for circulation, and film and slide projectors are furnished for loan.[13] In Santa Barbara, California, a central instructional materials office includes a system library, a textbook collection, and all types of audio-visual material and equipment. In a recent survey of the schools of Montclair, New Jersey, it was recommended that:

> The audio-visual department be housed in a single central location, with adequate space for a library, a receiving and shipping room, a workroom, photographic darkrooms, a preview and conference room with a seating

[13] Dale, *op. cit.*, pp. 176–178.

capacity of 30 to 40, and a private office for the director. These rooms should be adequately equipped with needed facilities such as dark shades, electrical outlets, and running water. The library and receiving and shipping room should be on the ground level. This department should also be located near the offices of the director of curriculum and guidance.[14]

There is no reason why a similar plan on a less ambitious scale is not feasible within larger individual schools. In this manner, textbooks, library materials, and audio-visual instructional materials of all types for school-wide use could all be administered by one person, or team of persons, and even housed in the same suite of rooms. The authors know of no school using such a plan; it remains for an enterprising principal to test how satisfactory it would be in practice.

Field trips. Within the school, and easily accessible to the members of the school are many teaching and learning resources. In most schools these resources are inadequately used. In other schools, frequent trips outside the classroom vitalize the learning program by taking children to see what they have been discussing.

A field trip can be taken to the school's boiler room or carpenter shop, to the neighborhood grocery store or fire house, or may extend so far afield as to necessitate bus or automobile transportation. In any event, there are a number of ways in which such trips can be encouraged, and much of the responsibility for this rests on the principal's shoulders.[15]

First, it is important that the school staff understand the reasons for such trips, and how to make the most of them educationally. This is primarily a job of in-service education. Second, the community should understand why a small crowd of school-age children is swarming all over the fire house or water works during school hours. This is a job of school-community relations, a topic discussed in another section of this book.

Third, the principal is responsible for seeing that proper routines are established for such trips: application for permission to take one, notification of parents, and obtaining of their permission, arrangements with those to be visited, and transportation arrangements. The staff should understand clearly the safety measures to be observed.

[14] *The Report of the Survey of the Public Schools of Montclair, New Jersey,* Institute of Field Studies, Teachers College, Columbia University, New York, 1948, p. 711.
[15] See the discussion of the legal aspects of the school's liability in field trips, on pages 30–31.

Fourth, consideration should be given to financing problems. Definite provision should be made in the budget for the expense of hiring buses, if school buses are not available, or for other transportation expense.

Fifth, the provision of systematic information to help teachers on such trips is highly desirable. Dale[16] proposes that teachers file a list each year of trips they have taken, the officials who should be consulted, and other helpful comments on the trip for the guidance of other teachers. He further suggests that the staff might work out a more formal check list to guide the teacher in her comments. Such comments, based on the following list, will be invaluable to other teachers taking the trip later.

1. Name, address, and phone number of organization to be visited
2. Visiting days and hours
3. Suggested transportation
4. Time required
5. Name of person in charge
6. Admission fee, if any
7. Nature of guide service
8. Eating facilities
9. Specific details about getting into plant
10. Age of children permitted
11. Grade level for particular excursions
12. Nature of printed material available from the company
13. Evaluation of excursion for intended purposes[17]

Radio, television, and recordings. Relatively new on the educational scene are several media of communication which have intriguing possibilities for education. As yet, these media—radio, television, and records and recordings—have had relatively little use in public education; nevertheless, their use is growing rapidly. A large proportion of our schools make use of standard disk recordings, and their number has grown steadily. A number of school systems now have their own radio broadcasting stations, and many school classrooms are now equipped to receive radio programs. For example, Kinder reports that during a single month in Pittsburgh, the KDKA School of the Air programs were heard by 848 classes and 28,120 teachers and pupils.[18] It seems unquestionable that use of these educational resources will grow considerably in the near future. Enterprising principals and their staffs who realize the vast edu-

[16] Dale, *op. cit.*, pp. 141–143.

[17] *Ibid.*, p. 142.

[18] Kinder, *op. cit.*, p. 435.

cational possibilities will utilize these visual and auditory aids in modernizing and vitalizing the educational programs of their schools.

As with other audio-visual media, there are numerous administrative problems involved in making effective use of radio and television. There are the problems of finance, of equipment selection and purchase, of program evaluation and scheduling, and of in-service growth of the staff in developing and making use of the program.

The principles underlying the approach to these problems are much the same as those applying to other instructional media. Certainly the money for the program should be included in the regular budget, as in the case of other instructional aids, such as textbooks, maps, globes, and motion picture equipment. The development of the program should be a co-operative affair, involving in the planning the staff, interested parents, pupils, any persons in the community who can give specialized assistance, and, of course, the principal.

These means of communication and education should be thought of not only as means of supplying material to listen to and look at; much educational value can be derived from the pupils doing broadcasting of their own. The following types of broadcasting activities are listed by Kinder as being appropriate for students: (1) announcements, (2) newscasts, (3) musical programs, (4) drama, (5) talks or reports, (6) interviews, (7) panels, round tables, forums, (8) junior town meeting or town hall programs, (9) quiz programs, and (10) variety programs.[19]

Recorders and recordings, including disks, tape, wire and film sound recordings and recorders, constitute another educational medium of great possibilities. A large proportion of our schools have been using disk recordings for years to assist in their programs of music appreciation. A modern program goes much beyond that, to include:

1. The radio receiving set
2. The record and transcription player
3. The recording machine or recorder
4. The public address (PA) system
5. The central sound system (complete)[20]

Discussion of the possibilities and use of all of the foregoing is beyond the scope of this volume. The reader is referred to Part Three of

[19] *Ibid.,* pp. 450–452.
[20] *Ibid.,* pp. 505–506.

J. S. Kinder's recent book, which includes the most comprehensive discussion of radio, television, records and recording, and facsimile recording for educational purposes, known to the authors at this moment.[21]

Certainly these are educational tools with which the principal and his staff should be familiar. If we are to pretend to have a modern program, we cannot ignore these powerful instruments of communication, entertainment, and education. They have now become common household items. We cannot let them remain rarities in our schools.

Initiating Improvements in the Audio-Visual Program

As in other instructional matters, an improvement of the use of audio-visual materials will come only with a broadening of the understanding by the teachers of the techniques and use of these helps to learning. This would seem to imply some discussion and study of the matter by the staff. Many well-equipped programs have failed simply because this common sense principle was not observed. An increased understanding, on the part of the staff, of the principles underlying audio-visual methods of instruction will not only increase use of the mechanical equipment; it will vitalize the entire learning program.

Interest in the topic may arise in a number of ways impossible to predict, but it seems safe to say that the principal can find ways to be the initiator. In one school, the starting point was a gift of money for which the staff had to decide the best use.[22] In another school, it may be that a teacher who has been at summer session in a college has taken a course in audio-visual methods of instruction (perhaps at the suggestion of the principal!). His new knowledge and enthusiasm may be the lever the principal can use to get things started. The principal can use audio-visual media in staff meetings, and perhaps start a discussion of how their use might be improved and extended in the classrooms. There are any number of possibilities. The point to be made is that here, as in other aspects of the learning program, change must take place first in the attitudes and thinking of the teachers if it is to have any appreciable effect upon what happens in the classroom. For this reason, teachers should recognize a need for a more adequate audio-visual program before any extensive expenditures for equipment are made. That such a need is not widely recognized is reflected in the results of a recent study of audio-

[21] *Ibid.*

[22] Department of Elementary School Principals, *The Principal and Audio-Visual Education,* pp. 15–17.

visual education in American cities, which indicated "that in the typical school system about 15 per cent of the elementary teachers use films frequently as contrasted with 37 per cent who never use them.[23] In many a school the expensive movie projector donated by the P.T.A. is like the weird vase received from Aunt Agatha as a wedding gift: it is taken from the closet and used now and then to keep the donors happy, but for the most part it sits out of sight gathering dust because nobody knows what to do with it. In a well-conceived and well-administered program the equipment will be used constantly.

Consequently, the principal should give thought to the nature of the in-service education program which can help teachers to branch out from a "talk and read" routine of "teaching" to teaching methods rich in multisensory methods and materials. This should not simply be an effort to convince teachers that they need "audio-visual aids"; it should be centered upon how all teaching and learning in the school can be improved. The desirable outcome is sharpened and deepened insight into the fact that the usual read—listen—recite teaching pattern is inefficient instruction, and that use of a wide variety of experiences and multisensory instructional materials is not only more effective but much more interesting to teacher and pupil alike. What is more, it is not truly difficult, though it certainly takes more planning and time than the familiar and interest-killing routines of the usual verbal approach.

In an interesting discussion of the in-service growth program in audio-visual methods of instruction, Dr. Bernardis insists "that this growth is a continuous process which must be integrated into the total educational program.[24] He lists the following as factors of a successful program: "(a) fit the program to the needs of the teacher, (b) proceed slowly, (c) provide for group planning, (d) provide for effective leadership, (e) keep size of group small (meaning teacher study groups), (f) provide for adequate time, and (g) provide adequate facilities, materials, and equipment."[25] These principles are consistent with those underlying a successful program of general teacher growth in service. (See Part VII.)

---

[23] National Education Association, *Audio-Visual Education in City-School Systems,* Research Bulletin, vol. XXIV, December 1946, pp. 147 and 149.

[24] National Society for the Study of Education, *Audio-Visual Materials of Instruction,* Forty-eighth Yearbook, Part I, University of Chicago Press, Chicago, 1949, p. 123.

[25] *Ibid.,* pp. 123–124.

Evaluating the Program

The chief objective of the audio-visual program is, of course, better learning and growing on the part of the children. In the vast majority of schools, however, it is not possible to evaluate the effectiveness of the audio-visual program in these terms. Moreover, it is unnecessary to do so, as we already have convincing evidence that the use of audio-visual methods increases the effectiveness of instruction. The local school, then, will direct its attention more feasibly to the question of whether the program is meeting certain operational criteria. Dale, for example, suggests these "Questions for Evaluating Your Program."[26]

1. Is a particular individual or committee made responsible for the program?
2. Have steps been taken to assure adequate and continuous financial support through the Board of Education?
3. Are the projectors, screens, models and other equipment of good quality and in good working order?
4. Have materials been selected which relate directly to the objectives of your school and community?
5. Has an in-service training program been developed to help teachers use the materials?
6. Have the materials been properly cataloged and stored?
7. Is provision made for regular inspection, care and upkeep of materials?
8. Is it easy for the teacher to get the materials when she needs them?
9. Is there regular evaluation of your program and materials of instruction?
10. Have you kept the public informed as to what you are doing?

While these criteria, proposed by a specialist, may be good, it should be noted that there is considerable value in having the teachers themselves develop the criteria by which the program is to be evaluated. They should have access, of course, to professional literature, but considerably more insight into the meaning of the criteria will be developed if they are products of the co-operative thinking of the staff.

Whatever form the evaluation takes, it should be definitely provided for. In many respects it should be a continuous process which includes such periodic activities as inventory of materials, with an eye to weeding out "dead wood," and looking at the over-all balance of materials.

[26] Dale, *op. cit.*, p. 487.

Summary

The audio-visual program is similar to many other aspects of the program of the school in that the attitude and actions of the principal will have a considerable influence upon its nature, extensiveness, and success. Even though he may delegate much of his responsibility for the program to a co-ordinator or committee, it is still necessary that he be well informed about the program, and about audio-visual methods and materials in general. He should be acquainted with latest thinking on the topic, with the available equipment and its cost, and with the best administrative practice and experience in the field. Fully as important as these, he should know what constitutes good instructional use of such materials, so that he may help his staff to make the most of the audio-visual resources at their disposal. Even where projection machines and film are not provided, there is a wealth of material available to appeal to the eyes and ears of the pupils in the learning program. Although the problems of administering films are greater, and tend, therefore, to usurp a disproportionate amount of discussions of audio-visual media, it remains true that the mainstay of good classroom instruction will continue for some time to be effective use of pictures, models, maps, globes, demonstrations, dramatizations, the blackboard, posters, recordings, and the like.

For this reason, it is obvious that a good "program" of audio-visual instruction is simply part of a good learning program in general. If this is true, then the best way to insure effective use of audio-visual equipment is to make improvement in this respect a part of the general program of curriculum improvement, instructional improvement, and growth of teachers in service. In such an orientation, the program of audio-visual instruction will assume its proper place in the over-all perspective of the instructional program of the school.

It must also be recognized by the reader that this discussion does not pretend to exhaustiveness—nor even to adequacy—in the treatment of this topic. Such references as those of Kinder, Dale, and of McKown and Roberts, frequently alluded to throughout this chapter, should be on the shelf of the school's professional library, along with other source materials on the problem. McKown and Roberts suggest a minimum list of books on the topic,[27] in addition to which the school should

[27] McKown and Roberts, *op. cit.,* pp. 551–552.

have appropriate catalogues and periodicals dealing with the topic.
The recent developments in the field of audio-visual materials have
provided us with powerful means to improve learning in our schools. The
elementary school principal is in a position, therefore, to contribute significantly to the improvement of education by: (1) sensitizing his staff
to the value of audio-visual methods, (2) helping them attain skill in
the application of audio-visual methods in their classrooms, (3) providing the best audio-visual equipment possible for the school and community to provide, and (4) so administering the equipment and materials that they are easy for teachers to obtain and use. The principal who
does these things does much to assure a successful learning program in
his school.

SUGGESTED READINGS

Audio-Visual Education Association of California, *Setting Up Your Audio-
visual Education Program: A Handbook for Principals,* Stanford University Press, Stanford, Calif., 1949.

Avid of Indiana, *Handbook for the Audio-Visual Program,* Indiana University, Bloomington, Ind., 1948.

Dale, Edgar, *Audio-Visual Methods in Teaching,* Dryden Press, Inc., New
York, 1946.

Department of Elementary School Principals, *The Principal and Audio-
Visual Education,* National Education Association, Washington, D. C.,
1948.

Kinder, James, *Audio-Visual Materials and Techniques,* American Book
Company, New York, 1950.

Library of Congress, *Guide to United States Government Motion Pictures,*
Superintendent of Documents, Washington, D. C. (Periodic).

McKown, H. C., and Roberts, A. B., *Audio-Visual Aids to Instruction,*
McGraw-Hill Book Company, Inc., New York, 1949.

National Education Association, *Audio-Visual Education in City-School Systems,* Research Bulletin, vol. XXIV, December 1946.

National Society for the Study of Education, *Audio-Visual Materials of Instruction,* Forty-eighth Yearbook, Part I, University of Chicago Press,
Chicago, 1949.

Seaton, Helen H., *A Measure for Audio-Visual Programs in Schools,* American Council on Education, Washington, D. C., 1944.

Sub-Committee on Audio-Visual Study, "Better Teaching Through Audio-Visual Materials," *North Central Association Quarterly,* vol. XXIII, October 1948, pp. 196–226.

The Audio-Visual Way, State Department of Education, Division of Instruction, Tallahassee, Florida, Bulletin no. 22B, January 1948.

Weinman, Constance, *Bibliography on Audio-Visual Instructional Materials,* Bureau of Publications, Teachers College, Columbia University, New York, 1950.

CHAPTER XX

TRANSPORTATION

Some principals have no responsibility for school bus transportation since the pupils come from homes that are located within easy walking distances of the school. Each year, however, an increasing number of pupils throughout the United States are being carried to school at public expense, and elementary school principals in areas where school consolidation has recently been effected and in the more sparsely settled parts of the country need to be informed on matters relating to school transportation. Nor is the administration of this service as simple as it may appear on first consideration. There are legal regulations to be enforced; there are state board of education rules to be observed; there are problems of safety to be resolved; and there are educational and health implications of bus travel to be weighed. Parents have a right to expect that those responsible for the guardianship of their children will take all the steps that are necessary to ensure their safety and well-being. To do less is to be guilty of gross negligence. The principal, while by no means solely responsible for school transportation, plays an important role in its administration. He is nearer to the children and their parents than any other single official of the school system. He supervises the education of the children in his district, and it is to his care that children are entrusted when they are enrolled. Hence from the time pupils leave home in the morning until they arrive home in the afternoon, the principal has a responsibility for their welfare.

Students of the problem have stressed four criteria that should be applied in evaluating pupil transportation. These are (1) safety, (2) economy, (3) adequacy, and (4) efficiency. As both an administrator and educator, the principal must be concerned with all four.

Safety is partly a matter of education and partly a matter of the condition of the school buses provided to transport children. The educational task, however, is more difficult to resolve than the matter of improving school bus standards. Young children are reckless. They are often oblivious to danger and rush across the road without looking. They are careless in other ways. They assume that the school bus will always be operated skilfully. Pupils further take for granted that red lights and other signs are always working properly and that motorists universally observe them. Experience has taught most adults that these last mentioned dangers are seldom if ever fully eradicated, and children must be made alert to them, if they are to travel safely. This can be done without lessening the fun that comes from a group experience such as riding to school in a bus with one's schoolmates. An important task of the principal is to encourage the inculcation of habits of safety in children.

To achieve this, some imagination must be exercised by those who teach safety. Handing children written rules or suggestions is probably the least effective way of educating children to be careful, unless perhaps it is by telling them the rules orally. From the time they are old enough to stand on their feet they are being admonished to "be careful," and before they reach kindergarten many of them have developed a thoroughly skeptical if not indifferent attitude toward their parents' warnings. Anne Hoppock in an interesting and helpful article entitled, "If Your Children Travel By Bus" points out a most pertinent fact, namely, *"When children are transported, bus travel becomes a necessary part of the curriculum."*[1]

Somehow or other, pupils must be made to see and understand what is involved in safety; and equally important for their welfare, they must themselves want to be safe and want their fellow bus travelers to be safe also when riding to and from school. In other words, learning to be good bus travelers is not something separate and apart from their education. It is a vital part of it.

The modern school accepts the responsibility for making the curriculum interesting and functional. Young children in the primary grades enjoy dramatizing safety practices. In one school Miss Hoppock reports that a group of primary children pretended to be bus riders; they chose

[1] *School Health Education,* vol. XXII, no. 2, November-December 1948, New Jersey Tuberculosis League, Inc., Newark, N. J., p. 6. Italics ours.

a driver and operators of other vehicles, and marked out a highway on the floor. Children played walking to the bus stop, waiting to cross the road until the bus and the traffic had stopped, and acted out other phases of bus travel. The pupils raised questions afterwards and in so participating they were in a favorable position to learn some very important safety lessons.[2]

Slides and moving pictures provide still other media for educating children about safety problems.

In the upper grades it is possible to give children a share in educating one another with respect to the elements involved in safe transportation. A project in which children are encouraged to take a major responsibility in making safety education work will enlist their co-operation and interest, and the learning results will be astonishingly great. A group discussion at the beginning of the school year led by the bus driver or drivers on how to travel safely to and from school is certain to have fruitful results. Later in the year another conference might well be held at which time teachers, bus driver, and children could review the chief problems arising during the months just preceding.

It is possible through various forms of pictorial representation, some commercially made and others made by children and teacher, to portray vividly the dangers encountered when bus rules and precautions are not observed and when motorists are careless. By focusing attention on the behavior appropriate for persons riding in buses, a pattern of safe conduct can be instilled in children. Unquestionably no single medium will suffice in resolving this educational program. A combination of several approaches seems more likely to achieve the results desired.

The *education of bus drivers,* while not a responsibility of the principal, is a matter of concern to him, and he must be constantly alert for opportunities to encourage the kind of training befitting a person entrusted with the community's most precious possessions. Ignorance, carelessness, and irresponsibility should not be tolerated in bus drivers. The most enlightened programs of bus driver training, wherever used, should be called to the attention of the superintendent of schools; and an effort should be made to give the local drivers similar training.

Research has shown that bus drivers are often responsible for accidents. One student[3] of the problem, in reporting the findings of an ex-

[2] *Ibid.,* p. 6.
[3] Sergeant Conover of New Jersey State Police.

perimental study, listed the following major causes of school bus accidents:[4]

1. Bus drivers' lack of driving experience.
2. Speeding.
3. Careless driving.
4. Bus drivers' lack of co-ordination.
5. Unwillingness to assume responsibility.
6. Physical lack, such as poor eyesight.
7. After-effects of drinking.
8. Hurry to complete route.
9. Ignorance of the law.
10. Difficulty in controlling children.
11. Assuming that the school bus has the right of way.

The same investigation reported the following five unsafe things which bus drivers do:[5]

1. Sometimes they hurry children off the bus.
2. They have children start for the door before the bus stops.
3. They leave the door open in hot weather.
4. They drive off before the children have crossed the road.
5. They stop the bus so that children step out in the gutter.

Even if children were educated to fulfill their responsibilities as bus travelers and bus drivers were well trained, there would still be a big task remaining of educating motorists to drive carefully and observe the rules when approaching and passing school buses and when driving by bus stations where children are congregating. At the present time in several states where school bus laws are either inadequate or poorly enforced, motorists are unacquainted with the major provisions of the school bus law.[6] Cars speed by while the bus is loading or unloading, and they do not stop when children are crossing in front of the bus.

This problem of educating motorists is obviously beyond the power of the elementary school principal alone to resolve. But he can make a significant start by working with the car owners in his own district. In one school, reported by Hoppock, where grownups appeared to be uninformed with respect to the school bus law, the older students decided to undertake the job of interpreting the major provisions of the law to the public. They invited the county superintendent of schools to inform

[4] Taken from *High Points of Conference on School Transportation,* Trenton Teachers College, June 24, 1948, Form C-203, p. 1.
[5] *Ibid.,* p. 1.
[6] In New Jersey, according to a sampling of 2700 motorists in 1948, only 2 per cent knew the school bus law.

them about the law. They interviewed the bus drivers and got *their* opinions as to the need for more strict observance of the law. They checked for several days to note whether the violations were by local residents or by out-of-state motorists. Then they prepared a brief, mimeographed it, and distributed it to the residents in the district explaining in a courteous manner the purpose of their drive. Similar efforts, if carried out throughout a state, would achieve substantial results. Naturally other media should be used to supplement such undertakings. Newspaper articles, radio broadcasts, and the strategic location of road signs giving speed regulations can be employed to good advantage in reducing the hazards of school bus travel.

As for the criterion of "economy," the principal can only suggest to the superintendent areas in which justified savings can be effected. This may involve rerouting buses, adjustment of existing schedules, or an analysis of the relative economy of school-owned buses as opposed to contract arrangements. If the principal is well informed on matters pertaining to pupil transportation, his knowledge is likely to be sought when transportation policies are being considered. In making proposals for improvement, he should be careful to keep within the province assigned him as an elementary principal. In other words, he should not assume responsibilities which belong to the superintendent of schools or some other administrative official in the central office. Fortunately, one need not violate any principle of ethics in assisting in making school bus transportaton as economical as circumstances permit.

The adequacy of school bus service relates to the proportion of school children living beyond a fixed mileage from the school for whom transportation is provided. States differ widely in their provisions of compulsory education laws regarding exemptions of pupils living at a distance from a public school. Some states have set three miles as the outer perimeter and unless pupils who live beyond this radius are transported at public expense, they are exempt from the compulsory provisions of the attendance law. Since public schools are established for the purpose of furthering the cause of democracy, it is obvious that pupils in sparsely populated areas cannot be allowed to remain ignorant if this major objective of public education is to be achieved. Many pupils, if they are to receive schooling, have to be transported. One rough measure of the adequacy of bus service, therefore, is the degree to which present arrangements reach children who fall in the area beyond the state specified limits of one, two, or three miles, or whatever mileage the law designates.[7]

A more refined measure will take account not merely of whether or not transportation is provided but what quality of transportation is furnished. Are there enough seats, considering the number of pupils to be carried? The following illustration of this standard is taken from the New Jersey State Board of Education rules and regulations governing pupil transportation:

> No standees shall be allowed. In determining the maximum seating capacity of a bus, 15 inches of seat length shall be allowed for each high school pupil, and 13 inches for each grade pupil . . . No contracts (exclusive of renewals) shall be made for the transportation in any bus of more than 50 high school pupils, or 55 pupils where grade pupils are to be carried except by specific approval of the county superintendent of schools.[8]

Later on in this same bulletin, there is another rule to the effect that "seats shall be spaced at not less than 26 inches," and "the depth of seats shall be at least 14 inches."[9]

The construction and equipping of school buses is no longer in the experimental stage.[10] Enough data have been assembled to demonstrate the wisdom of including many features in school bus construction and excluding others that unfortunately are still in evidence in various parts of the country.

Principals need to be alert to the progress achieved in standardizing school buses as well as to the principles governing the administration and operation of school bus transportation. The task of interpreting to parents and taxpayers the importance of meeting high standards of safety and comfort in pupil transportation will rest largely in the hands of school principals.

"Efficiency" is another criterion which can properly be applied in evaluating pupil transportation. This factor involves such practical mat-

---

[7] According to a recent bulletin of the Research Division of the National Education Association, 16 states have laws making it mandatory for school boards to furnish transportation under certain circumstances. The variation in distance between home and school for which transportation in these states was required extended from five-eighths of a mile to three miles. (*The Legal Status of the Public School Pupil*, Research Bulletin, vol. XXVI, no. 1, February 1948, p. 17.)

[8] State of New Jersey, Department of Education, *Pupil Transportation Rules Adopted June 4, 1948*, The Department, Trenton, N. J., 1948, p. 15.

[9] *Ibid.*, p. 17.

[10] Standards of safety for school bus equipment and operation have been established in many states.

ters as laying out bus routes, in relation to time and safety; scheduling; location of loading stations; utilization of buses during school day for trips and excursions; supervision of children on buses; drivers' reports, accident reports, and principal's reports to the central office. The school principal will share in the foregoing tasks although he may have relatively little control over several of the items mentioned. But he must be informed on the general efficiency of the services provided. Authorities in the field of school bus transportation recommend that the principal file a periodic (once a week) report with the superintendent of schools, containing data for each school bus used in transporting children, the total number of miles traveled, changes in bus schedule, and comments on the nature of the services rendered.

Behavior on the Bus

Some of the most difficult problems growing out of school bus transportation concern behavior while the pupils are traveling to and from school. In fact, a study of behavior problems in rural schools showed that such problems occurred more frequently in school buses than any other spot, with the one exception of the playground. Pushing, scuffling, nudging, and arguments over favored seats are the types of misbehavior most likely to occur. Shouting at passengers in passing cars or pedestrians, and extending hands and arms out of windows were also reported as troublesome. Moreover, boys tend to misbehave on buses more often than girls, and behavior problems are more likely to occur on the home trip than on the trip to school. Special bus trips to museums are also more productive of misbehavior than regular trips.

It is important for the principal to know these facts for his own school group so they can be taken account of in revising schedules and in providing supervision. Most important of all, data of this character can well constitute the basis for a program of education on "How to be a good bus passenger." Children can learn early the importance of respecting the rights of others, of being a good citizen on a bus as well as in the classroom.

The behavior problem for the most part grows out of the inactivity of bus travel. Sitting quietly for an hour or more without anything to do is a poor pastime for an alert and energetic child. What is needed is a good program of activities that can be carried on in a bus. Group singing is one illustration of a useful and pleasant experience that can be carried on while children are sitting still in a bus. Simple games which can be played by the children sitting in their seats could also be utilized.

As a foundation for individual guidance, the bus behavior of pupils has unusual possibilities. The bus driver's reports to the principal should contain as much information on behavior as time and the driver's own knowledge will permit.

The role of the principal in many school systems is that of an intermediary in bus transportation. He is between the superintendent of schools and the bus driver. The former, as the executive officer of the board of education, is responsible for the administration of the service. He must delegate some of it to those on the "firing" line. He cannot be on hand every day to see whether or not the over-all plan is actually working out. Moreover, if he insists on exercising close supervision or on making every decision personally, he will have little time left for his other duties. The principal is almost certain, therefore, to find that resolving transportation problems is part of his daily assignment. He will need to apply constantly the criteria of safety, economy, adequacy, and efficiency to the service as he observes it. And what is perhaps of even greater significance, he must make bus transportation an inherent part of the curriculum of the school. If this latter is done successfully, the problem of pupil safety will have been greatly diminished, and pupils will have learned to conduct themselves in a manner that promises most for the comfort and satisfaction of the group as a whole.

SUGGESTED READINGS

Butterworth, Julian F., and Ruegegger, Virgil, *Administering Pupil Transportation*, Educational Publishers, Inc., St. Louis, 1941.

National Council of Chief State School Officers and National Commission on Safety Education, *School Bus Standards*, National Education Association, Washington, D. C., 1946.

National Education Association, *The Legal Status of the Public School Pupil*, Research Bulletin, vol. XXVI, no. 1, February 1948, pp. 16–18.

Noble, M. C. S., Jr., *Pupil Transportation in the United States*, International Textbook Company, Scranton, Pa., 1940.

State of Alabama, Department of Education, *Administrator's Handbook on School Transportation*, Montgomery, Ala., Bulletin no. 4, 1950.

State of New Jersey, Department of Education, *Pupil Transportation Rules Adopted June 4, 1948*, Trenton, N. J.

Part V

MANAGEMENT OF THE SCHOOL BUILDING, SUPPLIES, AND EQUIPMENT

Several decades ago the educational administrator was considered to be, above all else, the manager of his school or system, an "educational efficiency expert." Whereas the viewpoint of educational leaders has broadened considerably beyond that, it must be recognized that management is still one of the important functions of the elementary school principal, and is likely to remain so indefinitely. Because of the fact that the specifics of management vary widely according to the size and nature of the school to be administered, it is impossible to present any blueprint of management procedure for a principal to follow. Even if such were possible, it is without the scope of this volume.

Nevertheless, there are a number of generalizations which seem to the authors to be important in this area of administering the business affairs of the school. It is the belief of the authors that all too little attention has been given to the relationship of office, plant, and supplies management to the educational program of the school; in the pages of this section they attempt to indicate that relationship. Furthermore, if this relationship is to be a functional and successful one, the teachers should have a far greater part than is usually the case in the making of many of the decisions which have ordinarily been considered the prerogative of the principal in his capacity of business manager of the school. It is hoped that the discussion which follows may help indicate how this may be achieved.

CHAPTER XXI

ADMINISTERING THE SCHOOL OFFICE

In recent years an increasing amount of attention has been focused on the role of the school office in the program of the school. As a matter of fact, the office in the elementary school is largely a creature of the present century, for prior to 1900 few elementary schools had facilities which could properly be called an office. True, some buildings in the latter part of the last century had a space designated in the plans as an office, but almost universally it was little more than the size of a closet. The expanding conception of the function of the principal began to be reflected in better office facilities in the second decade of this century. The idea spread rapidly, so that in 1928 there were 98 per cent of a group of 614 supervising principals questioned who stated that they had offices in their buildings. Of these, 67 per cent had but one room, about 27 per cent had two rooms, and not quite 5 per cent had more than two rooms in the office suite.[1] Yet, even today, few discussions of school plant or of administration give any appreciable space to the school office.

As in the case of other aspects of the school, the function and importance of the school office must be seen in relation to the school's philosophy and program. In situations in which the important aspects of program and policy are determined outside the school, where the learning program is narrowly conceived so as not to require the services of auxiliary personnel, where professional leadership on the part of the principal is neither expected nor encouraged, and where the principal's

[1] Department of Elementary School Principals, *The Elementary School Principalship*, Seventh Yearbook, National Education Association, Washington, D. C., 1928, pp. 267–268.

responsibilities are conceived to be mostly clerical, office facilities in the modern sense are largely waste space. In the school of today, however, the closet-like offices to be found in the buildings of a half century and more ago are grossly inadequate.

The office in the modern school is in many ways the nerve center of the school. It is the place in which the records of teachers, pupils, materials, and equipment are centered, to which reports are sent, where visitors are received, where telephone calls are directed, from which supplies are administered, where the principal does his desk work, where the teachers have space to work on instructional materials, where mail is delivered and received for the school, where important matters of school policy and emergency are referred. The school office is in large measure the public relations office of the school, a service center for teachers, a "home base" for the principal, the center of business activities; in short (as Micawber would say), it is the co-ordinating center for the entire school.

The expanding nature of the modern school program enlarges the importance of the office. Even in a school with a relatively restricted and narrow concept of education the above-mentioned functions would endow the office with considerable importance. In the modern school an adequately functioning office is all but indispensable.

FUNCTIONS SERVED BY THE OFFICE

Throughout this volume the increasing complexity of the elementary school principal's responsibility has been pointed out. This has considerable implication for the nature of the office, since—as has been mentioned—it serves as a "home base" for the principal. The need for secretarial help, which will be discussed later in this section, points to the need for secretarial working space. If the principal is to have a spot where he can work and hold conferences in relative privacy, then it follows that the office should contain at least two rooms. In his own work room, the principal can then more efficiently do his desk work free from interruptions, maintain his own private library of professional books, keep files of his personal work, and in general have a place to himself. In addition, he will have a place where he can see a teacher, a pupil, or a parent in relative privacy, a condition which is conducive to satisfying conferences.

Service Center for Staff

Whereas the office was once thought of as "the principal's room," it is now more properly conceived as "the school office." This reflects the expanding conception of its purposes and functions, and the fact that it is now considered as a service center for the entire school. It is thought of, for example, as a professional center for the teachers. In it are their mail boxes, and perhaps the teachers' professional library. There is a growing trend toward providing workroom facilities for stencil cutting and duplicating of instructional materials, and a room which can be used for staff conferences or for socializing and relaxing. All these functions and services tend to have a unifying effect upon staff relationships and on the school as a whole.

Center for School Services

Recent years have witnessed an expansion of the service personnel provided for schools. Nurses, dentists, physicians, remedial specialists, school psychologists, speech correctionists, and guidance workers are being added in increasing numbers to the staffs of better-financed schools and systems. At first these specialists were assigned to whatever quarters could be found for them, with the result that they were scattered through-out the school building. Principals soon found that this was not an efficient arrangement, and the trend now is to provide space for many

FIGURE 16. Administrative Suite in a Small Elementary School, Grades 1–8[2]

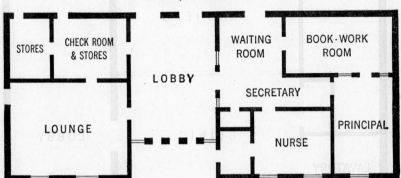

[2] F. W. Cyr and H. H. Linn, *Planning Rural Community School Buildings,* Bureau of Publications, Teachers College, Columbia University, New York, 1949, p. 37.

of these services within, or adjacent to, the suite of administrative offices. This has been particularly true of the health services. Figure 16 illustrates the application of this in an office suite plan for a small rural elementary school. It will also be noted that the storeroom for books and supplies is easily accessible to the secretary, saving the time wasted in many schools where the secretary must run down to the basement, or to a closet on another floor, in order to get books or supplies for herself or for the teachers. It is true, of course, that in very small schools these types of office layouts will be neither feasible nor necessary. Nevertheless, even in the one-teacher school, the provision of a small workroom which the teacher can call her own will facilitate the efficient discharge of the teacher's responsibilities. Figure 17 is the plan of the administrative suite for a six-teacher school with a teaching principal.

Public Relations Medium

In addition to being the administrative and co-ordinating center for the professional activities of the school, the school office is inescapably a medium of school public relations. In many cases, the office is the only

FIGURE 17. Office Plan for a Six-Teacher Rural School with Teaching Principal[3]

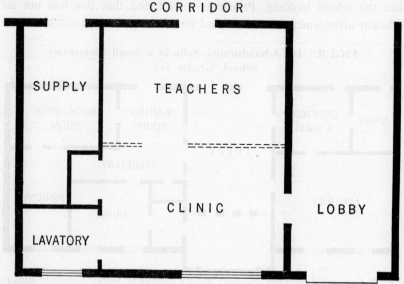

[3] *Ibid.,* p. 39.

major part of the interior of the school which is seen by a visitor. It is the first point of contact for parents, visitors, other school officials, reporters, and business agents. The appearance and atmosphere of the school office are likely, therefore, to color the visitor's impression of the rest of the school. The manner of handling telephone calls and the communications which emanate from the office will also have considerable influence upon the impression the school makes on the public.

IMPROVING OFFICE ORGANIZATION AND SERVICE

It is clear, then, that the school office is serving increasingly numerous and important purposes, but it is a fact that the great majority of school offices are not yet organized to serve those purposes as well as they might. By taking thought, most principals and their staffs could appreciably improve the service which the office should render to the school. In order to do so, it will be profitable for the principal to provide for the co-operative appraisal of the functioning of the office by his instructional and service staff. Many suggestions and ideas which would not occur to any one person alone will emerge from group discussions by those who have relationships with the school office. The parents and pupils should not be neglected when soliciting opinion, for they see the office in a different way than do the professional personnel of the school, and are directly affected by its functioning.

There are a number of aspects of the office which should receive attention. The advantages and limitations of the office layout should be critically appraised, and the adequacy of the equipment considered. The work load, responsibilities and functioning of the secretary, the efficiency of the principal in relation to office arrangements and time use, and the teachers' relationships to and responsibilities for the functioning of the office all should come in for their share of scrutiny. On the basis of such careful and co-operative appraisal, plans should be formulated for the improvement of the situation where such improvement is feasible.

Office Layout

If the office is to be a service and co-ordinating center for the school, it seems logical to assume that it should be centrally located. In many schools, the logic of this does not seem to have been apparent to the planners and architects. A statement made by the editorial committee of the Seventh Yearbook of the Department of Elementary School Principals back in 1928 is still very pertinent in all too many cases: "One is struck by the failure of architects to observe minimum essentials as to the arrangement and location of offices. Some offices were found in the basement, while others were on the third floor. This condition has been due to a failure of those in authority to realize the importance of the office, and to consider its placement with the same care bestowed upon classrooms. After the classrooms have been located, the principal's office shares with the supply rooms, storage rooms, and janitors' closets in utilizing vacant spaces."[4] Plans for most schools now being built appear to be recognizing the necessity for locating the school office centrally and accessibly. There are many older schools, however, in which—as attested by the above quotation—the office is not desirably located. Numbers of schools in which this has been true have managed to remedy the situation by converting a centrally located classroom into an office suite. Such a classroom can be partitioned to provide an office for the principal, a reception room and secretarial work space, a health clinic, and a small room for supplies or books.

In many schools it will not be possible to include the health clinic, a storage room, a teachers' work and conference room, a reception and waiting room, secretarial work space, and the principal's private office all within the same suite of rooms. Some schools have placed the teachers' room and the health clinic directly across the hallway from the principal's office, so that all are easily accessible. Anything, therefore, which the staff and principal can do to concentrate these service facilities in a central and accessible place will make possible greater efficiency in the administration of the school.

Office Equipment

One very effective method of improving office efficiency is to provide labor- and time-saving equipment in it. Certainly, in this day of science, technology, and efficiency we should expect our schools to exemplify the uses to which modern equipment can be put. In this respect, surveys of office equipment in elementary school offices, made by the Department of Elementary School Principals in 1928 and in 1948, are revealing. A comparison of the data of these surveys is presented in Table 1.

[4] Department of Elementary Principals, *op. cit.,* Seventh Yearbook, p. 271.

**TABLE 1. Equipment in Elementary School Principals'
Offices in 1928 and in 1948[5]**

ITEM OF EQUIPMENT	SUPERVISING PRINCIPALS 1928	SUPERVISING PRINCIPALS 1948	TEACHING PRINCIPALS* 1948
City Telephone	95%	98%	87%
Central Sound System		16	8
Building Telephone	34	26	8
Bulletin Board	67	85	71
Filing Case (Letters)	74	85	57
Typewriter	56	92	69
Duplicator	80	86	70
Safe	7	22	14
Bookcase	86	82	67
Automatic Clock	34	66	32
Adding Machine (or equivalent)	5	34	10

Teaching principals' equipment provisions were not studied in the 1928 survey.

An inspection of these data indicates that whereas some progress has been made in almost every category illustrated, the situation is still far from being satisfactory. Some principals are still without a city telephone, an instrument which one almost considers indispensable in the modern school. The number who are without such important and helpful pieces of equipment as computing machines, bookcases, duplicators, and the like is really disgraceful. It will also be noted that the teaching principalship today is in about the same position in these respects as was the supervising principalship in 1928. In twenty years some progress has been made, but certainly not enough.

Although there seems to be no documentation available for the statement, it seems likely that principals have not realized the extent to which such equipment can contribute to their efficiency and to their effectiveness in their jobs. It is logical to assume that if a principal and his staff, with perhaps some pupils and some laymen in the community (possibly including a person familiar with good office practice and management in business), were to sit down and give serious study to the improvement of the efficiency and attractiveness of the school office, a considerable number of improvements could be made. It would then be realized how much time can be saved by certain items of equipment, and how much better a job can be done. It is hard to see how the principal

[5] Adapted from Department of Elementary School Principals, *ibid.*, p. 270, and Department of Elementary School Principals, *The Elementary-School Principalship —Today and Tomorrow,* Twenty-seventh Yearbook, National Education Association, Washington, D. C., 1948, p. 51.

can do an effective job, for example, without a file case in which to file materials systematically, without a telephone, without a bulletin board, or without a bookcase. Nor does it seem that it should take much effort to secure these items. The cost of telephone service is very little; bulletin boards can be constructed and put up for next to nothing; a bookcase can be put together from scrap lumber and does not require much skill with saw, hammer, sandpaper, nails, and paint; a file case can be constructed in a high school woodworking shop, or obtained inexpensively at second hand. Some of the other items cost somewhat more, but a principal who has a good conception of how they can help the school—not just him alone—do a better job should be able to convince his board of education, his superintendent, or his parent-teacher association of the wisdom of providing them.

Furthermore, there are items not listed in these surveys which will make of the office a pleasanter place, hence a place in which better and more work is likely to be done. Acousticized ceilings should become standard in school offices, as in other parts of school buildings. Newer methods and types of illumination not only can improve the attractiveness of the office, but improve the quality of work done there and reduce eye fatigue. The principal's day could be made much more efficient by a machine to record dictation, so that correspondence and memoranda could be dictated at any time and be transcribed by the secretary at her convenience. As simple an item as a buzzer between the desk of the principal and the secretary will save innumerable steps. In the large city schools, electrical machines for classifying and sorting data would save tremendous amounts of time. The so-called "visible file" or "visible record" can be helpful in making personnel and pupil data readily available in a moment or two. A triple-tiered desk file, with "In," "Out," and "Pending" divisions, or "Immediate," "Deferred," and "File" sections, will promote efficiency in the handling of the paperwork which otherwise accumulates in discouraging piles on the principal's desk.

In addition, attention can be given to the interior decoration aspects of the office. There is no good reason why the school office should be, as it so often is, drab, dingy, painted in yellow and mustard tones, with unattractive olive-green equipment, a dark, scarred, and chipped desk, and uncomfortable and unsightly chairs. A bit of imaginative planning, enlisting, perhaps, an art teacher or a person in the community with skill in interior decoration, can work wonders with the usual unattractive office quarters. Attractive colors can be used on the walls and in bookcases; desktops can be refinished in serviceable and attractive composition or inlaid linoleum; the newer steel-grey files can be obtained, or old ones repainted in pleasing and unobtrusive colors; bright and simple draperies can soften otherwise hard lines; and bulletin boards can be painted in soft, pleasant colors with a water-base paint. In the more modern offices of business and industry, the massive oak and walnut desks are giving way to light and functional modern designs in light, cheerful tones, desks which provide ample work space, but eliminate the useless drawers that so often serve only to accumulate material which should be in the filing cabinet (where it can be quickly and easily located), or in the wastebasket. In too many cases, desk drawers serve only the purpose that is served by the rug for the untidy housekeeper: they are simply a facility for hiding that which one does not know how to dispose of otherwise.

One group working under the chairmanship of Dr. W. Paul Allen, principal of the Fox Meadow School in Scarsdale, New York, strikes a note that has been strangely silent in published discussions of the school office. They say:

> When designing [the general office space] of the school office, let's not forget the children. In all too many schools the primary child stands on his toes, and even then all the secretary can see over the top of the counter is a stray lock of hair. The chairs in the waiting room are for grownups, and lying on the high table are adult magazines.[6]

In his own inner office, Principal Allen provides a corner with some child-sized chairs and a low table where he can sit down with children informally. He also recommends shelves and a bulletin board for small displays of children's work. These are concrete expressions of the much-used phrase, "consideration for children's personalities."

Whereas some of these suggestions may seem unrealistic to many principals in view of their present situations, there are others for whom none of these is unrealistic at all. It also seems likely that in any office there are real possibilities for improving the situation if only some time and thought will be devoted to the problem. Industrial research has proven conclusively that such improvements as those mentioned above result in marked improvement in output and performance. This applies

[6] W. Paul Allen, chairman, *Planning An Elementary School,* Board of Education, Scarsdale, New York, 1949, p. 40.

as much to esthetic improvements as to labor-saving devices, for the greatest single factor in the efficiency of workers is morale. Refuge should not be taken in the excuse that the board or the superintendent will not approve budgetary appropriations for improvements. First of all, nothing will be lost by proposing such expenditures and finding out whether or not they will be denied (not asking for the moon all at once, of course). Second, many of these improvements can be made without increasing the budget if they are done co-operatively by teachers, pupils, parents, and the principal.

Time and the Principal

Another item in which analysis may prove helpful in bringing about improvement is the principal's use of time. The most recent study of the number of daily working hours of the principal[7] agrees in its findings with most other studies which have been made: the average principal spends about nine hours at school each school day, and a little time on Saturday. By far the greater amount of this time is spent in administrative and supervisory duties (see Table 2). Whereas these data reflect some increase over 1928 conditions in the time devoted to supervision, and some diminution in the time taken up by clerical duties,[8] it is evident from Table 3 that principals wish these differences were even greater.

In the modern concept of the elementary school principal's job, the provision of professional leadership is looked upon as his foremost re-

TABLE 2. Percentages of Principals' Time Given to Major Functions in 1928 and 1948[9]

GROUP OF DUTIES	SUPERVISING PRINCIPALS 1928	1948	TEACHING PRINCIPALS 1928	1948
Administration	30.2%	29.3%	9.9%	10.4%
Supervision	33.8	38.9	10.0	12.4
Clerical	18.3	15.1	9.5	10.7
Teaching	4.3	2.3	64.4	59.5
Other Duties	13.4	14.4	6.2	7.0
	100.0%	100.0%	100.0%	100.0%

Note: In 1928 "pupil personnel" was included under "supervision"; "community activities" were put under "other duties." These adjustments have been made in the 1948 percentages.

[7] Department of Elementary School Principals, *op. cit.,* Twenty-seventh Yearbook, p. 85.
[8] *Ibid.,* p. 89.
[9] *Ibid.,* p. 89.

TABLE 3. Percentages of Principals' Time Given to Major Functions under Actual and Ideal Conditions[10]

GROUP OF DUTIES	SUPERVISING PRINCIPALS		TEACHING PRINCIPALS	
	ACTUAL	IDEAL	ACTUAL	IDEAL
Administration	29.3%	24.2%	10.4%	18.5%
Supervision	24.1	37.3	6.8	24.4
Pupil Personnel	14.8	17.3	5.6	14.6
Clerical	15.1	3.5	10.7	5.5
Teaching	2.3	2.6	59.5	22.8
Community	9.3	11.0	4.5	9.5
Miscellaneous	5.1	4.1	2.5	4.7
	100.0%	100.0%	100.0%	100.0%

sponsibility. This is particularly true in the case of the supervising principal, who has been relieved of all or most of his teaching responsibilities expressly for the purpose of enabling him to devote more of his time to the improvement of the school's program. If the principal is not careful to give considered thought to planning time for the exercise of this function, he is likely to find it consumed with minor and relatively unimportant activities. Careful time planning can help the principal to achieve his objectives in an efficient manner, and to avoid the frittering away of precious time which results from lack of planning. Such planning will help avoid the conscious or subconscious neglect of those duties and responsibilities which are nevertheless necessary to the adequate performance of the principal's task.

The planning of the principal's time cannot be done without reference to the time of others with whom the principal works or has close association. For this reason the teachers, secretary, and custodian should have some share in planning the principal's weekly and daily schedule. By this it is not meant that all these persons will sit around the principal's desk and tell him what should be done and when. In a meeting with the teachers, for example, the principal can determine with them the best time at which to schedule staff meetings, the time which it is most desirable to keep free for teachers to come in to see him in his office, and the time and manner of handling other matters relating to teachers. With his secretary he can settle upon the best times for scheduling the various facets of the office routine. With the custodian he can decide the best time for periodic conferences about the school plant, and the times and manner of plant inspection. With these mat-

[10] *Ibid.*, p. 90.

ters decided, the principal can then draw up a schedule which can truly be said to have been co-operatively developed.

The experience of principals has indicated that there are numerous ways of making more effective use of their time. It is to be emphasized that this problem cannot be considered apart from other aspects of the school's operation and program; the principal's time use will be affected by the secretarial assistance he is provided, by his conception and practice of supervision, by the way supplies are administered, by his relationships with his teachers, by the conception and practice of discipline in the school, and the like. This emphasizes that there are a number of aspects of the problem to which co-operative action can contribute. The following are a few of the techniques many principals have found helpful in improving time utilization.

1. *Planning and using a schedule.* The use of a written daily and weekly schedule will save far more time than that which is necessary to make it. Care must be taken, however, to guard against letting the schedule become so rigid that desirable deviations cannot easily be made from it. Each day can be divided into hour-long blocks of time, and each hour assigned appropriate duties. The avoidance of too "tight" scheduling and of scheduling in too great detail will allow for flexibility without wrecking the schedule. Examples of weekly schedules appear in the Ninth Yearbook of the Department of Elementary School Principals and in Kyte.[11]

The most successful principals have found that it is highly desirable to schedule a definite time for office hours, at which time parents and teachers will know that the principal will be in the office, and can be seen without an appointment. Usually these hours are scheduled at the beginning of the school day, right after lunch, and at the close of the day. It is helpful to plan to arrive at school about an hour before the "teaching day" begins. This gives the principal a bit of time to organize for the day's work, to confer with the custodian, to meet with parents, teachers, and pupils who wish to see him, and to attend to other necessary matters which can be taken care of at that time. With these details disposed of, the principal can then turn his attention to his other professional duties with less chance of interruption. He can give the greater part of

[11] Department of Elementary School Principals, *The Principal and Administration,* Ninth Yearbook, National Education Association, Washington, D. C., 1930, p. 200; G. C. Kyte, *The Principal at Work,* Ginn and Company, Boston, 1941, pp. 88–89.

the day to observing pupil activities, taking a teacher's class so that she may attend to some school responsibility, helping in the preparations for an all-school affair, meeting with community groups, and the like.

It is also desirable to set aside a definite time in which attention is given to severe disciplinary problems. In numbers of schools, the principals spend far too many hours in the "handling" of "problem" children. First of all, as we have pointed out elsewhere in this volume, teachers should be encouraged to handle the behavior problems of children within their classrooms. If the staff will agree to the desirability of this, they may also agree to the undesirability of sending pupils to the office when the principal has no information other than the child's word about what happened in the class. A form can be developed, stating the name of teacher and pupil, date, and the nature of the offense. It is very likely that this procedure alone will diminish the number of pupils sent to the principal's office. Setting a definite time for dealing with cases which have been too much for a teacher also permits the teacher to see the principal and talk over the case before the principal sees the pupil. Principals have found that such a procedure saves much time.

2. *Using the bulletin board.* The bulletin board can be a useful and time-saving piece of equipment. On it the principal can post his schedule so that teachers may know when they can and when they cannot see him, and so that they can know when to invite him to their classrooms. In addition, most of the routine notices which many principals announce in staff meetings, or send around to classes by messenger, can be posted on the bulletin board at a saving of time to both principal and teachers. Some schools have drawn up a form with the names of all staff members mimeographed on it, and a space at the top or bottom for a message. The notice is typed on the form and posted on the bulletin board. The teachers simply place their initials by their names to indicate that they have read it. Teachers are responsible for looking over the bulletin board at the opening and at the close of the school day.

3. *Time-saving equipment.* Much time can be saved by the use of time-saving equipment, such as we mentioned in the discussion of office equipment earlier in the chapter. A buzzer in the principal's office and at the secretary's desk will save much unnecessary walking back and forth. A dictaphone will enable the principal to take care of his correspondence at his convenience, and the secretary to type it at hers. A mechanical computer will speed up the various jobs of school accounting which have

to be done. An interclass telephone system can save much time and many steps, although the principal has to guard against unnecessarily interrupting teachers in their classroom work. Many schools have installed a public address system throughout the school, so that the principal can communicate with any class at will, and can "pipe" radio broadcasts to all or part of the building. Whereas this can be helpful, most teachers dislike it, feeling that it provides too great a temptation for the principal to "snoop" on them by tuning in on their rooms without the knowledge of the teacher. Visible files and regular storage files can render data readily accessible. A good-sized memorandum calendar will help keep track of daily engagements. Large schools might consider using the type of electrical recording, classifying, and sorting equipment which is manufactured by any of several business machine corporations, equipment which can do in a few minutes that which manual methods would require hours to complete. The principal who will analyze the work he does from day to day can decide upon the equipment which would help him do it more expeditiously.

4. *Teachers' handbook.* Another device which can save time is a teachers' handbook which contains explanations of the school's routines. Such a book can be planned co-operatively by the staff, and will obviate much of the question-asking which is otherwise likely to consume much time. It also serves as an aid in inducting new teachers, and as a continuing orientation for the others.

5. *Establishment of routines.* One of the greatest timesavers of all is the routinizing of the numerous activities which can be so handled. The administration of supplies, the handling of notices, pupil accounting, the school milk program, and the like can take inordinate amounts of the principal's time unless he regularizes the methods of handling them. The use of well-planned record forms will assist considerably in this respect.[12] (See Chapter XIII for a discussion of school records.) Definite times should be agreed upon by the staff for the ordering and delivering of supplies, for the submission of attendance records, for the handling of discipline cases, and the like, and these times should be adhered to in reasonable fashion. There are times, of course, when common sense will dictate departure from routine, for the routines are for the purpose of serving, not ruling, the school.

---

[12] E. D. Bennett, "Standard Record Forms Conserve the Principal's Time," in *The Principal and Administration, op. cit.,* pp. 207–212.

More important than any of these expedients in the efficient use of the principal's time is, of course, the attitude of the principal himself. Some principals just do not want to be "efficient" in the sense in which we are using the term in this discussion. They loudly proclaim their disgust with "mechanical administration," and claim that their creative abilities and those of their staffs cannot blossom under routines. It is to be pointed out here that routine, creativity, and democracy are in no way incompatible. They all bear a close relationship to self-discipline, and few will quarrel with the desirability of that. It seems evident to the authors that if staff and principal will plan together for the employment of routine where they deem it desirable, democracy is being observed. Further, it seems only the part of common sense to routinize those chores which do not demand "creative ability," and thus release far more time for the exercise of professional leadership and creativity.

It is possible that in the case of many principals this latter situation is not desired. Those who are insecure, who do not wish to talk with parents, who are doubtful of their ability to help teachers, are likely to take refuge in filling their days with penny-counting, form-sorting, tabulating, and other routine busy-work as an escape from more important responsibilities.

The School Secretary

The elementary school principalship has come a long way from the time when it was conceived as a sort of glorified clerkship. The current concept of professional leadership as the chief function of the principal requires not only that he be relieved of teaching responsibilities; assistance must be provided him to take care of the minor routine and administrative duties which would otherwise usurp a disproportionate part of his time. For this reason, the school secretary is becoming an established position in our elementary schools. In a study of 1413 supervising principals in 1947–48, it was found that 47 per cent had one or more full-time secretaries or clerks, an increase of 18 per cent over the 1927–28 figures.[13] Whereas this increase is encouraging, it is to be noted that 35 per cent of elementary school supervising principals have no clerical assistance whatever.[14] To perform his duties adequately, it is safe to say

---

[13] Department of Elementary School Principals, *op. cit.,* Twenty-seventh Yearbook, p. 57.
[14] *Ibid.*

it is imperative that today's principal have clerical assistance. That principals are conscious of the importance of the secretary, and wish the assistance of such a worker is evident. In the survey referred to above, the "school clerk" was by far the type of assistance most frequently requested by principals.[15]

There are no universally accepted standards for a proper secretary-pupil ratio, and practice varies widely in this respect. In a study of thirty western cities, Smallenburg found a range in elementary schools from one clerk per 311 pupils in one district, to one clerk per 1557 in another, with the median at 510 pupils. Among his conclusions he states that: "Many factors could be taken into consideration as a basis for determining the amount of clerical assistance to be granted. From a practical standpoint, however, enrollment and type of school constitute a satisfactory basis." He recommends the following:[16]

SCHOOL ENROLLMENT	ELEMENTARY CLERKS	TOTAL CLERICAL TIME
Less than 400 pupils	One half-time	½
401 to 800	One full-time	1
801 to 1200	One full-time and one half-time	1½

It is reasonable to assume that a contemporary community school operating a modern activity program will need more secretarial help than the usual type of school, and that the above secretary-pupil ratio would therefore be too conservative.

That the secretary is an important and necessary person is indicated by the many duties she performs in schools. McClure identified a list of 92 different duties reported with varying degrees of frequency by school secretaries back in 1930.[17] It seems likely that today the list would be even longer. A briefer illustration of the types of duties performed by school clerks and secretaries is given in Table 4.

Functions of the school secretary. It is obvious that the job of the secretary will vary with the size of the school. A little less obvious, perhaps, is that it will vary also with the philosophy of the school. The modern school,

[15] *Ibid.*, p. 65.

[16] H. Smallenburg, "Assignment of Clerical Assistance in Elementary and Secondary Schools," *School Board Journal,* vol. CX, February 1945, pp. 37–38.

[17] W. McClure, "The Duties of Elementary School Clerks in Seattle," in Department of Elementary School Principals, *op. cit.,* Ninth Yearbook, pp. 250–257.

**TABLE 4. Most Important Duties Performed by Clerical Help,
Reported by 294 Supervising Principals**[18]

CLERICAL DUTY	FREQUENCY OF MENTION
1. Supplies, books, and stockroom	149
2. Reports	146
3. Telephone	105
4. Typing and stenographic work	77
5. Records	65
6. Attendance	59
7. Correspondence	56
8. Mimeographing	47
9. General office and clerical work	40
10. Filing	36
11. Banking	33
12. Messenger	31
13. Enrollment	27
14. Milk program	24
15. Receive callers and parents	17
16. Library work	16
17. Bells	10
18. Cafeteria	10
19. First aid treatment	9
20. Summaries and tabulations	8

for example, with its informal program, will require more duplicated materials, will have a wider variety of supplies, and will entail fuller pupil records than will a less contemporary curriculum. Furthermore, the community of the school will also influence the secretary's function, certain duties and relationships being more prevalent in a greatly underprivileged area than in a well-to-do residential district.

1. *Clerical and stenographic service to teachers and principal.* In many ways the secretary is the extension of the arm of the principal. By typing his letters, filing his correspondence and professional materials, keeping his schedule, making appointments, and performing minor and routine administrative duties, she enables him to concentrate on his chief function, that of bringing to bear his professional ability, training, and experience on the improvement of the learning program of the school. In like manner, she assists the teachers by performing clerical duties for them, such as typing important letters, cutting stencils and duplicating materials for instructional purposes, handling mail, and the like. In these respects, she is trained to do the job better than the principal and teachers; she is a valuable addition to the staff for her clerical skill alone.

[18] G. C. Kyte, *op. cit.,* p. 449, adapted from Department of Elementary School Principals, *op. cit.,* Seventh Yearbook, p. 260.

2. *Receptionist.* There are other duties she performs, however, which are of importance equal to those of a clerical nature. She can be one of the key persons in the public relations program of the school. We have indicated the importance of the office in the public relations of the school; the secretary can make or break it in this respect. The manner in which she answers the telephone, for example, is of great importance. A large portion of the school's public has its only contact with the school over the telephone, and the secretary's voice is the first "school voice" they hear. A courteous greeting of, "Good morning! This is the Washington School, Miss Gordon speaking," will have positive public relations values far superior to an abrupt, "Hullo?"

Not only is the secretary's voice the first one likely to be heard on the phone; she is very often the first and sometimes the only person to be seen by a visitor to the school. In this respect she should be equally pleasant and courteous to all. Hollingshead has recently documented clearly the fact of class stratification in the community and school of an American town, and has shown that the "lower" classes are consistently discriminated against by school personnel.[19] Whereas this condition may be common "American" practice, it certainly is not consistent with American democratic ideals of equality and respect for personality. School personnel, including the secretary, should not be a party to the perpetuation of class, racial, or religious discrimination. In practice, this means that the secretary (and other school staff) will greet all parents in an equally courteous manner, whether they be named Wichtowski, O'Toole, Steinberg, Chen, Martin, Velasquez, or Smythe-Vincent, and will treat all with equal courtesy. The fact that first impressions mean so much, and are often so lasting, magnifies the importance of this principle.

3. *Handling routine and minor administrative duties.* There are many other matters which the secretary can lift from the principal's load. The many minor administrative duties which would otherwise "clutter" a principal's day can be handled as well by her. She can check invoices upon the receipt of supplies, see to their storage, and later to their distribution to teachers. She can keep the records of textbooks issued to teachers, and compile the book orders for the succeeding year. In her hands can be placed most of the responsibility for pupil accounting, including records of attendance, and care for the files of cumulative rec-

---

[19] A. B. Hollingshead, *Elmtown's Youth,* John Wiley & Sons, Inc., New York, 1949, p. 29.

ords. The school bells, the handling of the milk program, the Red Cross Fund, and other similar responsibilities can very well be handled by the secretary under the supervision of the principal. Such delegation must be done with care, however, so as to avoid having the secretary overrate her importance. In some schools she has come to think that it is she who "runs" the school, and she issues peremptory ultimatums to teachers and pupils. The secretary should be helped to understand that she, like the principal, is there to serve the teachers in their efforts to conduct a good learning program, that schools have been known to get along without secretaries and principals but not without teachers and pupils.

In this respect, it is also important to delineate clearly the duties of teachers and secretary to avoid misunderstandings. It should be well understood who is to do such things as cut stencils, type teachers' letters to parents, file pupil records, compile age-grade reports, check registers, correct standardized tests, and the like. This might seem almost axiomatic, but there are numbers of schools in which an inadequate understanding of these responsibilities has resulted in animosities and poor morale.

Selection and in-service training. Practices in the selection of school clerks and secretaries vary widely. There are instances in which almost any personable individual willing to accept the job at the salary offered has been hired. In other cases, high school graduation and some typing ability have been the prerequisites. Some school systems require specific stenographic training beyond the high school, particularly the larger city systems. The trend is definitely toward the systematizing of selection procedures, and the codification of requirements. Louise Henderson, supervisor of secretarial services in Philadelphia, Pennsylvania, states that the following five steps are employed in the selection of secretaries in her city:

1. Candidates submit a transcript of their school record.
2. Take an examination which will test their skill in stenography and typing.
3. Take an intelligence test which involves situations which they will have to face on the job.
4. Come before a committee for a personality rating.
5. Pass a physical examination.[20]

[20] L. H. Henderson, "The Important Role of the School Secretary," *School Management,* vol. 16, January 1947, pp. 4–6.

Standards of preparation for the school secretary are as yet in the formative stage, although efforts are being made to establish such standards and to award certificates attesting to their attainment. Klonower suggests that the program of preparation should be three-pronged:

1. *General education,* to help assure a broad, common background necessary to all-around development.
2. *Technical education* in the specialized skills of secretarial work.
3. *Laboratory experience* of an internship or apprenticeship nature.[21]

Hoyer suggests three classifications of secretaries, the middle and highest classes having as prerequisites 24 and 60 hours of work of college level, respectively.[22]

One must be realistic, of course, in this respect. A school system which pays its school secretary $1500.00 annually certainly can't demand much of her in the way of preparation. Nevertheless, the position of the secretary is so important that the person engaged should be prepared to discharge her duties well. Certainly she should be reasonably competent in the skills of secretarial work: typing, taking and transcribing dictation, filing. Since she is an important element in the public relations program, she should present a neat and clean appearance, and should give evidence of possessing a pleasant personality and the ability to work well with others.

Once on the job, a certain amount of in-service training will be necessary, for the work of the school secretary differs from that of those in other enterprises. Some of the large school systems have a supervisor of secretarial services, whose function it is to improve that service in the schools. In smaller systems, however, and in large measure even in the large ones, the chief responsibility for helping the secretary do a better job rests with the building principal. Much can be accomplished by discussing the demands of the job with the secretary, and formulating with her the procedures to be used. It will also be helpful to solicit suggestions from teachers. If it seems that the secretary will be remaining in the school for some time, it will be profitable for the board of education to send her to take further training. Such experiences as those provided in summer workshops, which have been held at some colleges (including

[21] H. Klonower, "Education and Certification of the Public School Secretaries," *Roads to the Future, Twenty-eighth Annual Schoolmen's Week Proceedings,* University of Pennsylvania, 1941, pp. 74–77.
[22] L. P. Hoyer, "Is a System of Classification of School Secretaries Desirable?", *ibid.,* pp. 78–80.

the University of Pittsburgh; the University of Pennsylvania; Teachers College, Columbia University; Kent College, Ohio; and Purdue University), have proven extremely valuable to the secretaries who attended.

Conditions of employment. Since the secretary is an important member of the school staff, it would seem that she should be paid adequately and have other satisfactory conditions of employment. The figures for 1948–49, however, indicate that as a group, school secretaries are paid inadequately indeed. The average (arithmetic mean) salaries for "clerks in principals' offices" are given in Table 5 for each of six classes of cities.

TABLE 5. Salaries Paid Clerical Employees in Principals' Offices in 1948–49[23]

Cities over 500,000 population	$2,576.00
Cities of 100,000–500,000 population	2,015.00
Cities of　30,000–100,000　　"	1,978.00
Cities of　10,000– 30,000　　"	1,860.00
Cities of　5,000– 10,000　　"	1,784.00
Cities of　2,500– 5,000　　"	1,693.00

It seems to the authors that for well-qualified secretaries these salaries should be considerably higher, at least high enough to compete with industry and business for good secretarial talent.

There are factors other than salary in a secretary's working conditions which affect her morale. The secretary, no less than the teachers, should have the reasonable security which is provided by tenure and retirement privileges. Hospitalization and group insurance plans should be available to her, as to other school employees, as well as sick benefits and sabbatical-leave provisions. Whereas none of these provisions is present in many school systems, a modern school should either provide them or be considering how it can do so. Certainly our schools should be as up-to-date in these respects as business and industrial enterprises, which have found that these measures improve the morale, efficiency, and productivity of their workers in a manner to justify fully the expense involved.

In general, then, it is evident that the school secretary can contribute greatly to the educational enterprise. School secretarial service to the school can be improved by an intelligent program of recruitment and

[23] Adapted from National Education Association, *Salaries and Salary Schedules of City-School Employees, 1948–49,* Research Bulletin, vol. XXVII, April 1949.

selection, good working conditions, an in-service training program, steps to develop understanding of the secretary's function by the principal, teachers, secretary, and school patrons, and by the provision of the office equipment conducive to efficient work.

PRINCIPLES OF OFFICE ADMINISTRATION FOR ELEMENTARY SCHOOLS

From the above discussion we can derive a number of principles which perhaps will serve to summarize and sharpen the major emphases intended. It is the opinion of the authors that observance of them will result in greatly increased service to the school by the office, and in consequent improvement of the entire school's operation.

1. *All administrative functions of the school should be centered in the school office.* In this way, greater co-ordination can be effected and school efficiency be promoted. Although this would seem to be a common sense principle, it is surprising to see the frequency with which it is not observed.

2. *Every elementary school should have a school office or its equivalent.* Even in a "one-room" school, there should be a space to give the teacher privacy for working and conferring with pupils, parents, school officials, and other school visitors.

3. *The office should be centrally located and easily accessible to visitors and staff alike.* In general, this means that it will be near the main entrance and on the ground floor.

4. *In schools employing a secretary, the office suite should consist of three or more rooms.* There should be at least a "public space" occupied in part by the secretary, the principal's inner office, and the health clinic. In addition, there should be a storage and book room, a private toilet and washbasin, a workroom for teachers, a teacher's social room (large enough for staff meetings), and a small room to be used for individual psychological examinations, for group meetings with small groups of parents, and for private telephoning by teachers.

5. *The school office should be attractively decorated* in soft colors, with colorful pictures (not the usual drab brown reproductions of ancient ruins!), matching drapes, and plants. Neatness and orderliness will add to its attractiveness. Certainly this is not much to ask, nor hard to

achieve, and its morale effect is well worth the small amount of planning, time, and money necessary.

6. *Office routines and procedures should be established, utilizing staff co-operative planning where such planning can help.* The time and labor-saving features of this have been discussed. It is to be emphasized, however, that these routines should not be permitted to smother desirable activities which necessitate breaking the routine temporarily, or establishing a new procedure. Routines should stand the test of *serving* an ever-improving school program.

7. *There should be a clear delineation of the responsibilities, and the limits of responsibility, of the school secretary.* Numbers of school systems have developed a handbook for secretaries, stating specifically what the secretarial duties are. In addition, the principal should discuss the function of the secretary with her and with the teachers, clarifying it so that the teachers will not make undue demands on the secretary, and the secretary will not refuse duties properly hers nor assume responsibilities not rightfully hers.

8. *The principal should plan his time with care, and incorporate his plan in a written schedule posted for all to see.* This will help avoid wasting time, and will help others to know when they can see the principal for conferences. The schedule, while it should be reasonably adhered to, should be flexible enough to allow departures from it when desirable.

9. *The secretary should be carefully selected and trained, and given desirable working conditions.* A good secretary can make the office a pleasant spot and a real service agency, which will influence for good the entire school program. A poor secretary, on the other hand, can wreck school morale, slow up its work, and inhibit progress. Careful selection, in-service training and supervision, and good working conditions will help assure capable handling of secretarial duties.

Like many other aspects of our schools, the school office is just beginning to come into its own. In the past it has been largely an afterthought, but modern planning and administration are giving it its rightful place as the nerve center of the school. New schools planned by foresighted administrators are providing for functional, centrally located office suites which are attractive and comfortable. It remains for principals to realize to the fullest the service possibilities of the school office in the schools of today and tomorrow.

SUGGESTED READINGS

Department of Elementary School Principals, *The Elementary School Principal,* Seventh Yearbook, National Education Association, Washington, D. C., 1928.

————, *The Principal and Administration,* Ninth Yearbook, National Education Association, Washington, D. C., 1930, chs. IV and VI.

————, *The Elementary School Principal—Today and Tomorrow,* Twenty-seventh Yearbook, National Education Association, Washington, D. C., 1948.

Henderson, L. H., "The Important Role of the School Secretary," *School Management,* vol. XVI, January 1947, pp. 4–6.

Klonower, H., "Education and Certification of Public School Secretaries," *Roads to the Future, Twenty-eighth Annual Schoolmen's Week Proceedings,* University of Pennsylvania, 1941, pp. 74–77.

Kyte, George C., *The Principal at Work,* Ginn and Company, Boston, 1941, chs. V, IX, and XXVI.

National Education Association, *Salaries and Salary Schedules of City School Employees, 1948–49,* Research Bulletin, vol. XXVII, April 1949.

Reavis, W. C., and others, *The Elementary School, Its Organization and Administration,* University of Chicago Press, Chicago, 1938, ch. V.

Smallenburg, H., "Assignment of Clerical Assistance in Elementary and Secondary Schools," *School Board Journal,* vol. CX, February 1945, pp. 37–38.

CHAPTER XXII

ADMINISTERING INSTRUCTIONAL
SUPPLIES AND TEXTBOOKS

INSTRUCTIONAL SUPPLIES

The administration of instructional supplies is one of the important functions of the elementary school principal. He should handle this responsibility in such manner that the needed supplies are provided in adequate amounts at the time when they are needed, in conformity with educational requirements of the teacher and his pupils. Furthermore, he should establish machinery for accomplishing this so that he does not consume unreasonable amounts of time in the process.

It is interesting to note that there is little systematic information available specifically relating to this problem at the elementary school level. There are probably at least two reasons for this. First, larger school systems maintain a central administrative office with a superintendent of schools and, perhaps, a business manager or purchasing agent. These officials are responsible for preparing the school system's budget, and have commonly had most of the responsibility for determining the nature and quantity of supplies to be obtained, and for their actual purchase. There is now a strong trend toward giving the local school staffs considerably more part in deciding the type and quantities of supplies to be provided. Most of the books and studies on the topic, however, discuss the problem on a system-wide basis. Second, the training of elementary school principals has not commonly included instruction in supply management. However, because the methods of selecting, storing, distributing, and controlling supplies and equipment—and the equipment itself —are so closely related to the nature and functioning of the instructional program, it seems desirable to consider how the principal can handle supply management so as to improve the general teaching-learning program within the school.

Relationship of Supplies and Equipment
to the Educational Program

The kinds of supplies and equipment provided in a school and the manner in which they are administered can have a considerable influence upon the program of teaching and learning. It is obvious that poor and insufficient instructional supplies will severely hamper the efforts of a teacher. Somewhat less obvious is the fact that poor administration of them can vitiate the usefulness of even the most excellent instructional supplies.

As has been pointed out elsewhere, current trends in education are placing great emphasis on flexibility in the educational program, a trend which is having a considerable effect on the nature of the instructional materials used. In our older grade-standard theories and practices, we assumed that children should be seen and not heard, that the chief reason children were in school was to store up knowledge and to perfect number and communication skills, that the chief method of accomplishing this was to have children memorize facts and drill on the skills assiduously, and that the condition most conducive to these ends was pin-drop quiet and bodily immobility. We assumed further that all the children in a given grade should master the materials of that grade level, and that they could all, therefore, study the same materials at the same time, in the same way and in the same sequence. Whereas some separate provision was frequently made for the children of obviously extreme learning ability (high or low), it was generally true that the above assumptions were expressed in practice. Such a learning program places a premium upon furniture which will tend to keep children in one place —the traditional fixed desk fastened securely to the floor. Since all children were to learn the same things, uniform sets of textbooks were the logical learning medium. The other materials of the instructional program were also relatively easy to specify, and to supply uniformly, making the job of administering them relatively easy.

This situation has changed radically in many schools over the past few decades. Instead of the emphasis being placed on storing up knowledge and mastering skills for future use through a uniform curriculum, it is now placed on learning in relation to the problems and needs of children, where skills are learned because children have need of them to live satisfyingly, where knowledge is sought because children need it in order to solve real problems of living they have identified, and where learning is a function of *doing,* of activity. A program such as this finds fixed desks inhibiting, impeding, frustrating. Uniform sets of texts simply clutter up space, and are of little use. A wide variety of materials is necessary, to be available as *needed,* a stipulation not always easy to satisfy. Supplies should be made available not only when they are needed, but should be of the quantity and type necessary to the activity for which they are needed.

This illustrates the fact that supplies and equipment, and the manner of their administration, bear a strong relationship to the educational philosophy and program operating in a given school system. Since systems vary widely in these respects, it is obviously impossible to specify any "best" procedure or plan of administering these items. The job becomes progressively more difficult as we move toward a more contemporary and flexible learning program, but the job can be done efficiently, effectively, and democratically if we do not bind ourselves by the patterns of the past.

Principal's Responsibilities in Relation to the System-wide Organization and Procedures for Business Management

Before discussing the remaining problems, it may be well to consider in general terms the principal's responsibility for them. From the data available from studies on the topic it is evident that the nature of this responsibility varies from system to system, being influenced by a number of factors, including the size of the system and the philosophy of supply management held by central-office officials. Studies of supply management in school systems indicate that the principal's responsibility for the various functions ranges from full responsibility to no responsibility at all. In some school systems, for example, the principal is the agent who does the actual purchasing of educational supplies, although in the overwhelming majority of cases this function is exercised by some other official.[1] In the determination of the amount of supplies for each school, on the other hand, principals carried all or part of the responsi-

---

[1] R. W. Hibbert, chairman, *Selection, Purchase, Storage, and Distribution of Supplies,* National Association of Public School Business Officials, Bulletin no. 1, Trenton, N. J., 1932, p. 11.

bility in about half of the systems studied.[2] In one of the earliest studies of the problem, Taylor found that in sixteen cities of from 15,000 to 100,000 population principals in fourteen of them were responsible for the preparation of the annual supply requisition for their schools.[3] The principal's responsibility seems to vary similarly in the other functions of supply management.

In practice, the central office of the superintendent has determined the budgetary allotment for the school's supplies, has done the purchasing, and has requested the distribution to the schools. Where a standardized list of materials has been maintained, with specifications, the central office has maintained it, and has been responsible for its periodic revision. In very small school systems, the principal is likely to share these responsibilities with the board of education, but in systems of more than one or two schools, the principal rarely has been responsible for these operations.

The chief functions of the principal in supply administration will be in assuming responsibility for helping his staff to compile a list of their needs and to prepare an annual estimate of his school's needs for the ensuing year, receiving supplies, storing them and distributing them to teachers, keeping accurate records of their receipt and consumption, and making an annual inventory at the end of the year. Furthermore, he is responsible for the care and use of the material goods within his school, to see that waste and abuse are avoided.

Preparation of the annual estimate. In general, there are two methods of preparing the annual estimate (or annual requisition). In those systems in which the supply list and the allotment per pupil have been standardized, the principal simply orders from the standardized list in terms of his building's allowance. In systems in which the supply list has not been standardized, the teachers and principal usually work together to prepare a list of their needs for the coming year.

In systems where a standard list is maintained, the principal should work co-operatively with his staff to arrive at an estimate of the following year's needs. This will be based upon an inventory of present supplies, and a consideration of how well the previous year's allotment met

[2] *Ibid.*, p. 16.
[3] R. B. Taylor, *Principles of Supply Management*, Teachers College Contributions to Education no. 228, Bureau of Publications, Teachers College, Columbia University, New York, 1926, p. 16.

the school's needs. When the teachers have indicated their opinions and needs, it is a relatively simple process for the principal to order from the standardized list and to indicate necessary deviations from the provisions of that list.

In schools where a standardized list has not been developed, the principal can provide for a kind of standardization within his own school by the maintenance of adequate records. If this is done carefully, an allotment figure per pupil for each item can be arrived at, thus eliminating the guesswork in determining amounts to be requisitioned. For example, if the school has records showing that over the past five years 12.06 pencils were used per pupil per year, the amount of uncertainty involved in determining the quantity of pencils to be ordered for next year is considerably reduced. It should not be difficult to enlist the teachers in the standardization project, for it is easy to see that it reduces the work of the teacher in the long run.

Such standardization is relatively simple to effect. Each teacher should keep a record of the amount of each supply item consumed in his class during the year. This is easily done by checking the total amount issued during the year against the amount on hand at the end of the year. The amount consumed is divided by the average daily attendance (A.D.A.) figure to determine the average amount consumed per pupil. If this is done over a period of years a reliable per pupil allotment figure will be available to assist in making up the supply requisition. For example, if the average pupil consumption of pencils in grade five has been 12.06 yearly, and the estimated A.D.A. for the ensuing year in that grade is 60 pupils, the estimated requisition of pencils will be 724 pencils.

Since in most schools the annual budget is prepared in the spring and adopted by April or May, estimates of needs for the following year must be made in January or February. The timetable for this varies with school systems. Usually, however, the principal will be asked to prepare his estimate of supply needs in January or early February. This is done by entering on an appropriate form a description of the item, the amount which was delivered for the year, the probable surplus or probable shortage for the year, and a statement of changes in needs for the next year. If a perpetual inventory (which we shall discuss later in this section) is maintained, the making of this estimate is a relatively simple job.

While it is both necessary and desirable to prepare yearly estimates in advance, such estimates should be considered only as the approximations they are. If schools or individual teachers find that they need supplies not included in their advance estimates, it should be possible to obtain them without difficulty and without being made to feel that they are at fault, or that the provision of the needed supplies is a tremendous favor. Unfortunately, there are situations where those in charge of supply administration have allowed the system to become so rigid as partially to defeat its purpose, and teachers who make requests in addition to their annual estimates are treated as naughty children. Those in the business office must realize that in a modern functional program of learning, needs cannot be as accurately foretold as in the regimented education which is so well suited to the autocratic police state. A *reasonable* rather than a *rigid* economy should be the goal.

It is most important that the teachers participate in the formulation of supply estimates. While it is true that the job of teachers is teaching, it is they who use the supplies in their classrooms, and for that reason it is they who are best prepared to say what the needs for instructional supplies are. At the outset of this discussion it was observed that there is a close relationship between the instructional program and the supplies used in it. Administrative officials must take care to prevent the machinery of supply management from becoming so rigid, standardized, and impersonal that it exercises a restricting influence on the learning program. One must remember always that the function of administration, whether it is of supplies, plant, curriculum or what not, is to serve the teacher in his efforts to improve the job he does in the classroom. The authors have seen systems in which business management had been permitted to get to the point where it ruled rather than served the teacher.

Storing and distributing supplies. Studies which have been made indicate great variation among school systems in their storage and distribution practices. Most larger school systems use central storage buildings, from which deliveries are made to the individual schools as supplies are requisitioned. Other systems have deliveries of supplies made directly to the school by the vendor. In systems with central storage facilities, frequency of deliveries to local schools varies from deliveries as needed to delivery but once a semester or year. It is evident that the principal's responsibilities for storage and distribution in his school will vary with the supply storage policy of the systems.

Depending on the amount of supplies to be accommodated, therefore, the principal should provide storage facilities within his building. Items should be stored in such a manner that they are readily identifiable, readily located when needed, easily accessible, and protected from damage and pilfering. Most schools provide for a central storage room, fitted with bins and shelving suited to the nature of the materials to be stored there.

Linn suggests the following "rules" to be observed in storing supplies:

1. Supplies should be available when needed.
2. Older stock should be used up so that it will not deteriorate or become obsolete.
3. Stock should be arranged so that time is not wasted in searching for items wanted.
4. Stock should be arranged so that a minimum of time and effort is required for storing and distributing supplies.
5. Accurate records must be kept to show amounts of supplies received and distributed, and where distributed.
6. The stock should be protected against theft and fire.
7. There should be some definite individual responsible for releasing the stock. Individual employees should not be given freedom to help themselves as they please.
8. Individual employees should not be given knowledge of the amounts of supplies in storage. Some individuals become careless and wasteful when they see a considerable stock of supplies on hand.
9. A periodic inspection of storage rooms should be made by some responsible authority.
10. A periodic inspection of supply cabinets in classrooms should be made by some responsible authority.
11. Individuals should not be permitted to hoard supplies in classrooms.
12. An inventory of supplies should be taken annually.
13. A perpetual inventory should be kept of all supplies, by items.[4]

In storing supplies in storage bins or classroom cabinets, new stock should be placed on the rear of the shelves, old stock at the front, otherwise the old stock will deteriorate and become unfit for use. As suggested in numbers 9 and 10 above, a periodic checkup by the principal will help insure that supplies are stored in a functional manner.

[4] Henry H. Linn, *Practical School Economies,* Bureau of Publications, Teachers College, Columbia University, New York, 1934, pp. 90–91.

The distribution of supplies should be the responsibility of one person. Practice varies with respect to who this person is. The principal, the school secretary, the custodian, or a teacher may be the responsible agent. Since the function is essentially a clerical one, it is unwise for the principal to let it consume his time or that of teachers. Where the school is supplied with secretarial help the secretary would be the logical person to discharge this function.

In forming a distribution policy a nice balance must be struck between efficiency and flexibility. In some schools the teacher requisitions supplies at the end of each month for a month in advance, and is not permitted to draw supplies at any other time. In other schools each teacher draws supplies when she wishes. It would seem best to make an arrangement whereby teachers requisition supplies periodically, trying to anticipate their needs for a period of time, but to permit teachers to draw supplies which they find urgently necessary between times. A committee, comprising the principal, teachers, and the person responsible for issuing supplies, can probably arrive at a satisfactory arrangement.

Supply Records and Accounting

The key to a good system of administering supplies is an adequate system of supply records. Records should be kept of the types and amounts of materials received, the amounts distributed to the various teachers, and the amounts consumed in the course of the year. Only in this way can an accurate basis be provided for estimating the school's needs from year to year.

Linn emphasizes the values of the school inventory in the handling of supplies, noting that it has moral as well as economic and efficiency effects.[5] Daum also mentions this.[6]

Taking inventory. Many, though by no means all, school systems make a regular practice of taking a periodic inventory of supplies and equipment. It seems highly desirable that this should be done annually for various reasons. Such an inventory makes available a ready record of the location and amount of equipment and supplies, and may avoid unnecessary purchase of duplicate articles. It will also provide a basis for

[5] Linn, *op. cit.*, p. 33.
[6] Henry F. Daum, *A Plan for the Inventory of School Furniture and Equipment Useful in General Administration,* unpublished Ed.D. project, Teachers College, Columbia University, New York, 1949, p. 13.

determining the insurance needs of the school, serve as a record to help determine material lost through disaster or theft, and assist in budget-making. In addition, the periodic inventory will help to identify outworn, obsolete, and defective materials which should be replaced or simply disposed of.

The principal and his staff play an important part in planning and taking the inventory. Daum found that principals were mentioned most often, with superintendents second and teachers third, in a list of those participating in planning inventory procedures.[7] He found that in 78.6 per cent of the school systems the principal was reported to have direct supervision over the actual inventory process, and the persons who actually take the inventory were primarily the teachers, custodians, clerks, and department heads.[8] Apparently, the teachers make the count of supplies in their rooms; the custodians will take inventory of their work spaces and storage rooms; and clerks will take inventory of the school offices. Other spaces should be checked to make certain no equipment is overlooked. Daum suggests that in taking the inventory a distinction be made among furniture, equipment, and supplies.[9]

Most schools take inventory annually, and that would seem to be the most desirable interval. Apparently the great majority take the inventory at the end of the school year.[10] When taken at this time, it will help check up on what has happened to equipment during the year past, and will provide a basis for readjustments during the ensuing year. Daum recommends taking it prior to budget time so that the results may be

[7] *Ibid.*, p. 55.

[8] *Ibid.*, pp. 72–74.

[9] *Ibid.*, pp. 169–171. He recommends the principles of the Committee on Uniform Accounting of the Public Schools Business Officials Association of the State of California, as presented in their *Handbook of Instruction for the Classification of School Expenditures,* Bulletin no. 4, California State Department of Education, Sacramento, May 1939, pp. 30–31. "Supplies" are defined as follows:
1. Articles destroyed or consumed actively or constructively when used.
   Examples: Paper, pencils, cleaning materials, nails, etc.
2. Articles of relatively short service life, requiring frequent replacement.
   Examples: Brooms, chamois, rubber stamps, etc.
3. Fragile articles frequently broken, and small articles frequently replaced with ordinary usage.
   Examples: Test tubes, thumb tacks, keys, scissors.
4. Articles which are not readily classifiable under any one of the preceding three classifications, and which normally would be classified as equipment, but which usually cost less than $5.00 and are frequently lost, broken, or worn out in normal use and replaced, should be classified as supplies.
   Examples: Small shop tools, small office appliances, home economics dishes, small utensils, small items for the science laboratory.

[10] *Ibid.*, p. 43.

available for budget-making purposes.[11] If the school maintains a perpetual inventory this would be unnecessary. Those in the local situation will have to weigh all factors, and make their own decision.

In making the inventory, use of appropriate forms can save time and facilitate the purposes to be served. There are many kinds of forms used, ranging from blank sheets of paper to complicated tabular sheets. Illustrated in Figure 18 is page 1 of the form designed by Daum for Abington Township, Pennsylvania, which has a number of advantages. The items to be included are already listed when the teacher receives the form, thus saving time. The items are listed in the same sequence on all teachers' sheets, making them comparable and easy to total. The listing tends to guard against items being overlooked by the teacher, and tends to standardize the specifications of items listed. Some systems like to have some indication of the value of each item, a provision not present on the form illustrated.

When the teacher has completed filling out such a form, one copy should be placed in her own file, and the other two submitted to the principal. He, in turn, should file one of the two copies from each teacher, and send the remaining copy to the responsible official in the central administrative office.

Some school systems maintain a perpetual inventory in addition to, or in place of, the annual inventory. Daum found such inventories, in their true form, to be used in but 13.6 per cent of the 285 school systems he studied.[12] Such an inventory system makes record of every loss, withdrawal, or addition at the time it occurs, so that one can tell at a glance what is on hand.

Whereas the perpetual inventory is more characteristic of very large schools, it has real advantages for any but the smallest schools wherein the amount of supplies is so small that it is easy to keep track of without such records. Such an inventory can be kept on a form which gives a description of the item, the date received, the amount received, and the total amount on hand. Additional columns provide for the amounts distributed to each grade, such amounts to be subtracted from the "on hand" figure as they are distributed, as one does in maintaining a running balance in a checkbook. In this manner, there is always available an indication of the amount on hand at the moment and the amount

[11] *Ibid.*, p. 166.
[12] *Ibid.*, p. 141.

FIGURE 18. Inventory Form Used in Abington Township, Pennsylvania, Public Schools[13]

INVENTORY FORM I

SCHOOL DISTRICT OF ABINGTON TOWNSHIP

GENERAL CLASSROOM FURNITURE AND EQUIPMENT

School _____ Room _____ Grade _____ Date _____

Inventory taken by _____

Directions: Inventory all items of furniture and equipment. Do not include supplies. (See list 1 for classification of items.) Show the total of each item on hand, indicating how many are in good condition, fair condition, and poor condition. (See Bulletin #1 for complete instructions on listing items.) If an item does not appear in the list, enter it in the blank spaces provided at the end of the form.

Prepare three copies of the form. Keep the third copy as your permanent record and return the first two to the principal.

1	2	3	4	5	6	7
Total on Hand	Number			Item	Size & Features (If not listed under 5.)	Leave Blank
	Good	Fair	Poor			
				Aquariums, L W H		
				Blocks, Patty Hill sets		
				Bookcases—Sectional	No. of sections	
				Bookcases—Unit	No. of shelves	
				Chairs—Bentwood		
				Chairs—Folding, wood		
				Chairs—Folding, metal		
				Chairs—Miscellaneous	Seat ht.	
				Chairs, Pupil 12"		
				" " 14"		
				" " 16"		
				" " 18"		
				Chairs, Teachers	Straight Back	
				Chairs, Swivel		
				Clocks, Elec. plug-in		
				Clocks, hand wound		
				Ditto machines		
				Desks, Office, Double Ped.		
				Desks, Pupil, Fixed #1	(Count desk and seat	
				" " " #2	as one unit)	
				" " " #3		
				" " " #4		
				Desks, pupil Moulthrop	12" seat ht.	
				" " "	14" seat ht.	
				" " "	16" seat ht.	
				" " "	18" seat ht.	
				Desks, Univ. A		
				" " B		
				" " C		

[13] Henry F. Daum, *A Plan for the Inventory of School Furniture and Equipment Useful in General Administration,* unpublished Ed.D. project, Teachers College, Columbia University, New York, 1949, p. 13.

consumed that year to date. This serves to simplify the drawing up of the annual estimate of needs in January, and provides a check on the amounts of each item used by each teacher. Examples of such forms are given by Taylor[14] and Jackman.[15] It is suggested that this form be kept in the supply room, perhaps on the inside of the door, and that the person responsible for supplies distribution make on it the appropriate entries as the items are drawn.

A teacher's requisition form should also be provided, whereon the teacher can indicate in writing the quantities of each item he needs. The form should provide space for noting the name of the teacher, the date of the requisition, the room and the grade, a description of the item needed with its number, the quantity needed, and the quantity on hand. There should be space for the principal's approving signature, and for the teacher's signature when the articles are received. When distribution has been made, the form should be filed in the principal's office.

After studying practice in a number of city school systems, Ramseyer also suggests forms to be used to facilitate the operation of the annual and perpetual inventory of equipment. These forms can be adapted for use in smaller schools.[16] A copy of the inventory should be filed in the principal's office, and additional copies filed with the appropriate central office official, or as required.

The petty cash fund. The development of an enriched and problem-centered program of learning in our schools is calling for a considerably greater variety of supplies, and frequently makes it difficult to predict in advance a number of items for which need may arise in a classroom in the course of a year. That it is desirable to maintain flexibility in supplying needed materials was mentioned earlier. To provide for contingencies, many schools and systems are setting up petty cash funds to be used for the purpose of supplying such emergent needs. In many systems it has been impossible to get such funds provided in the regularly constituted budget, but numbers of enterprising principals have not permitted that to stand in the way. In co-operation with their parent organizations, they have managed to realize income from plays, benefits,

[14] R. B. Taylor, *op. cit.,* p. 76.
[15] W. C. Jackman, "A Plan for Distributing Instructional Supplies in Small Schools," *American School Board Journal,* vol. LXXXIII, July 1931, p. 44.
[16] L. L. Ramseyer, *The School Inventory,* National Association of Public School Business Officials, Bulletin no. 4, 1933, pp. 24–34.

"fairs," and the like. These funds have been allotted to teachers as a sort of "mad money" to be used for the purchase of items not included in the standardized list of supplies, for which unforeseen need may arise in the learning program.

While the provision of such a fund used to be considered as a generous and desirable gesture, it has come to be looked upon as virtually a necessity in modern schools. The authors have heard teachers attest to the values of such a fund to their learning programs, values all out of proportion to the small additional sum of money. Such a fund for each teacher is a strong positive morale factor as well. Such practice lends much-needed flexibility to supply management, and encourages teachers to be creative in their classrooms, unhampered by lack of needed materials.

Summary

It is evident that the administration of supplies is an important function. Good administration of them can contribute significantly to the excellence of the school's program, to the morale of the teachers, and to the economy of the school's operation. It is by no means suggested that the foregoing is the "last word" in this process; on the contrary, we know all too little what is best practice in supplies administration in the elementary school. While the administration of supplies and equipment for school systems has had considerable study, there are very few references in the literature to the problem as it is faced by the elementary school principal. Nevertheless, certain suggestions seem to be evident. One of these is that the principal should not himself spend large amounts of time on supplies management. By careful planning with his staff, these duties can be delegated so that their demands are not great on the principal. Second, an adequate system of records is a must. Such records should be kept to their simplest minimum, but should be adequate to account for supplies and equipment satisfactorily. Third, the administration of supplies must always be viewed in its proper perspective: as a service to teachers, not as a chore for them or as a checkup on their honesty or extravagance. In line with this, as much flexibility as is consistent with efficiency should be maintained in the process. Finally, it is likely that these conditions will be met if the administrator enlists teachers in the planning of the selection, distribution, use, and control of supplies, soliciting their thinking as to how the process can be made to serve them better and still remain reasonably simple. Under these conditions it is likely that teachers will be able to get supplies they need, when they need them, and in adequate amounts, the ultimate goal of good supplies administration.

TEXTBOOK SELECTION AND CONTROL

One of the most important, most influential, and certainly most ubiquitous elements in American public education has been, and still is, the textbook.[17] In many schools the textbook has constituted the course of study for the "major" subjects, and teachers have felt obliged, almost to the point of emotional compulsion, to "cover" the textbook in the course of the semester or year. It is true that in recent years there have become evident trends which tend to lessen the importance of the textbook as the substance of the curriculum. Some educators are advocating practices which repudiate the textbook, in its usual sense, as an item for instructional use. In spite of these factors, however, it is likely that the textbook will continue for some time to come to be a most—if not the most—important item among the materials of instruction.

It is to be noted, also, that the question is not only an academic one; it is an economic one as well. The textbook industry in the United States is now one of multimillion-dollar proportions, and various factors now operating make it likely that the industry will expand in the near future. Even though textbooks are a relatively small part of total expenditures, they constitute a sizable item in school budgets, running well into thousands and tens of thousands of dollars in city school systems.

For these reasons the problem of textbook selection and control in schools assumes considerable importance. The principal should consider carefully how books may be chosen so as best to insure high quality, economy, and community endorsement of the materials used.

The Textbook and the Educational Program

It is readily evident that there is a close relationship between the nature of the educational program and textbook use. The type and manner of use of books varies markedly with different types of educational pro-

---

[17] National Society for the Study of Education, *The Textbook in American Education,* Thirtieth Yearbook, Part II, Public School Publishing Company, Bloomington, Ill., 1931, pp. 1–26.

grams. For example, the textbook was the mainstay of the usual subject curriculum, and frequently constituted the course of study. The subject matter for history (and almost every other subject) was determined by what was in the textbook, although some teachers supplemented the text with other references. The usual policy in this type of curriculum was to supply every child in the grade with the same textbook in each of the several subjects (or to require him to buy or rent those texts). In such situations, the chief task of selection was that of selecting *the* text to be used in each grade for each subject. Unfortunately, such a program and practice are not museum specimens; they are in operation in many of our schools today.[18]

The encouraging aspect of the matter, however, is that there is a definite trend away from letting the textbook dominate the learning program. Although almost all our schools are still subject-centered schools, many of them are a far cry from the institutions of memoriter learning against which modern education has reacted strongly. With the shift in emphasis from fact-learning to problem-solving, reliance on the single textbook began its decline. Under a problem-solving plan of learning, it is necessary to rely upon more than one book. In fact, study of a problem in social studies may necessitate consulting books which are not "social studies" books at all in the usual sense, but books in arts or crafts, anthropology, archaeology, vital statistics, health, and the like.

Some few schools are carrying the problem approach to learning even farther. For example, instead of limiting themselves to problems in the area of social studies usually found at a given grade level (such as, "Old World Backgrounds of American History," or "Peoples of Other Lands") they are identifying problems for study in the everyday living of the pupils. This does not mean that no content will be studied, of course. If one of the problems happens to be that of intercultural relations in the community, it is likely that the pupils will study the nature and problems of peoples of other lands (and of varied groups within our own country) more eagerly and meaningfully than ever before.

Such a program poses knotty problems in the matter of selection of books to be used in the learning program. It is obvious that the class will be unable to rely on a single text. How, then, shall the books to be

[18] L. J. Brueckner, *The Changing Elementary School,* Inor Publishing Company, New York, 1939, p. 140; A. J. Penn, *Current Practices in the Evaluation and Selection of Textbooks in the Elementary School,* unpublished Ed.D. project, Teachers College, Columbia University, New York, 1948, ch. III.

used be selected? How can we know which books to select when we do not know what the learning program for the year will be?

The problem is further complicated by the implications of the recent emphasis on individual differences. With children in a given grade varying from five to ten years in their reading levels (the usual condition) it is obvious that a single fifth-grade text will not suffice; nor is it sufficient to provide varied materials in subject matter, but all on a single level for each grade. Furthermore, it should also be obvious that any attempt to keep materials in a given grade uniform as to either content or level of difficulty, or both, will gravely handicap the efforts of the teacher to develop a learning program suited to the widely varied needs and abilities of the children.

For these reasons it can be seen that the policies adopted and followed in the selection of textbooks will inevitably have a strong influence upon the type and excellence of the learning program operating in the classrooms of the school. It is a considerable challenge, therefore, for the principal and his staff to develop policy and practice of textbook selection and use which will be likely to encourage a good and ever improving teaching-learning program.

The Problem of Selection

The principal is seldom, if ever, completely free to devise his own method of textbook selection. In many areas, certain aspects of the problem are prescribed by law.[19] One of the most important provisions in this respect is the one designating the selecting authority. Penn found four state determined patterns of selection, as follows:[20]

1. State or county adopts a single list of textbooks, allowing the local districts no option.

2. State or county adopts a multiple list of textbooks from which the local districts may choose. Individual schools may not adopt books not on this list.

3. The local school district, independent of any other agency, selects and adopts its own textbooks.

4. County superintendent determines method of selection for the

[19] W. L. Coffey, "Legislative Agencies for Textbook Selection," in *The Textbook in American Education,* Thirtieth Yearbook of the National Society for the Study of Education, Part II, Public School Publishing Company, Bloomington, Ill., 1931; Penn, *op. cit.,* ch. VI, and appendix A.

[20] A. J. Penn, *op. cit.,* pp. 17–18 and 107.

county. This was true in but one state, Maryland, and the counties vary in the methods used.

The National Society for the Study of Education, in 1931, recommended strongly against the state adoption technique.[21] While the breakdowns of Penn and Coffey are not made in such a manner as to be comparable, a brief study of their data seems to indicate that this recommendation has had little effect as yet on practice over the nation. It is interesting to note that these methods of selection, when plotted on a map of the United States, show a definite regional pattern.[22] The northern states tend to use the local district option method, while the state and county adoption with no local option is more characteristic of the southern states. State and county multiple list procedures seem to be more or less between these two, regionally as well as in practice.

Within the local districts of each of these plans there is even further variation. In the states permitting local option, for example, some of the local boards of education prescribe the books to be used in all the schools in the district; others set up a multiple list from which the schools may choose; while still others permit each school to decide upon the books it wants.

It will be seen, therefore, that in some systems the principal is given almost no responsibility for textbook selection. In other districts, however, the picture is quite different. Where local districts are permitted to do their own selecting, Penn found the principal to be the most frequently mentioned participant in the process. In all respects except the determination of the budgetary allotment for textbooks, the principal's effective responsibility for textbook selection exceeds that of any other person. It is interesting to note that in most situations this responsibility is shared with others (teachers, supervisors, superintendent), and that only rarely does the principal have sole responsibility for any aspect of the selection process.[23]

Modern theories of education and administration have direct bearing on this problem. If, as we are now maintaining, the educational program should be directed to helping children to grow best in the environment in which they live, and to change the environment for the better in the process, then the teacher must carry considerable responsi-

[21] Coffey, *op. cit.,* p. 306.
[22] Penn, *op. cit.,* p. 107.
[23] *Ibid.,* ch. IV.

bility for the formulation and direction of the learning program for his group of children. While broad guidelines of the curriculum should be developed by the community and the school's professional staff, the specifics of problems to be dealt with in the classrooms are rightly the province of the teacher.

If this is true, it follows that the teacher should have major responsibility for selecting the materials of instruction to serve the learning program in his class. This is not to say that the teacher should be given free rein to stock his room with any and all materials he wishes to gather together. For one thing, he must work under a budget limitation. For another, the principal and superintendent are even more responsible to the community for the educational program than is the teacher. These considerations would seem to point to a procedure in which teachers, supervisors, administrators, and perhaps laymen and pupils, co-operate in groups and as individuals in the selection of the book materials of instruction. Certainly the teacher, who is the person using the materials with pupils in the classroom, will have valuable insights concerning the faults and excellences of different textbooks, even under the most rigid curriculum.

Examination copies. In order to make comparisons of books for selection purposes, it is necessary to have examination copies. There is a great variety of practice in the manner in which these are obtained and handled. In this respect, the most sensible plan seems to be one which collects sample copies in a central collection available for examination by those participating in the selection process. This puts competing books in one place, and saves the publisher from having to send numbers of duplicate samples to several people in the same school system. Whipple found a wide variety of practices in use in locating new materials for consideration. "They include the following: interviewing publishers' representatives, sending notices to publishers, examining publishers' announcements of books, purchasing examination copies, borrowing copies from publishers for exhibits, visiting bookstores, visiting publishers' exhibits, . . . asking public librarians to suggest titles or lend books for review, . . . and asking other staff members to recommend titles."[24]

[24] G. Whipple, *Procedures Used in Selecting Textbooks,* University of Chicago Press, Chicago, 1936, p. 49.

Criteria for evaluating textbooks. Numbers of school systems have developed written criteria which are used in the evaluation of textbooks. Since evaluation implies the use of some criteria, it would seem wise to specify them in writing so that they may be applied more objectively and uniformly. These criteria are frequently expressed in the form of a score card, which assigns values to each item. A number of such score cards are illustrated in the literature.[25] Such score cards should be developed by committees of teachers and other staff personnel.

There are several cautions to be observed in the use of score cards. First, they should not be looked upon as taking the place of the "subjective" appraisal of their suitability for the educational program. They are merely supplementary devices, and should not be permitted to dominate selection. Furthermore, the total scores on such instruments should be interpreted with caution. It is possible, for example, for a book to obtain a relatively high score by being excellent in all respects except vocabulary difficulty, and thus be entirely too difficult for the children for whom it is intended, while another book might be considerably better in this respect, yet score lower because it was not so high-ranking in numbers of less important items.

Use varied means of selection. The status of selection procedures is in a chaotic state, with wide variation in practice among school systems. This is to be expected because of the diversity in the legal provisions for selection and the differences in the curriculum, to say nothing about the dissimilarities in philosophy of school administration. Schools and school systems can profit from successful practices used in numbers of other school districts.

1. Establish a central collection of examination copies. Publishers are usually happy to supply sample copies for such collections.

2. Set up system-wide and local-school textbook committees, with teacher representatives from all grade levels. These committees should be responsible for receiving recommendations from teachers, for interviewing publishers' representatives, for establishing criteria of selection,

[25] J. A. Clement, *Manual for Analyzing and Selecting Textbooks,* Garrard Press, Champaign, Ill., 1942; National Society for the Study of Education, *The Textbook in American Education,* Thirtieth Yearbook, Part II, Public School Publishing Company, Bloomington, Ill., 1931, ch. VIII; I. R. Waterman, "A Plan of Textbook Evaluation," in Sixteenth Yearbook, Department of Elementary School Principals, Washington, D. C., 1937, pp. 547–557.

and for improving the methods of textbook selection in the school or school system.

3. Develop (through the above committee) written criteria to help objectify the selection process.

4. Carry on the evaluation procedure as a continuous process throughout the year, rather than as a hastily organized affair immediately prior to book-ordering time.

5. Develop methods to screen out quickly the more obviously undesirable books, so that attention can be concentrated on evaluation of the better ones.

6. Enlist wide teacher participation in the selection process. Examination of copies should not be restricted to the selection committee. This committee is only the means of co-ordinating the selection activities of the school or system. Teachers who are to use the books should have opportunity to examine and criticize them. Some schools place "pilot" sets in one or two classrooms for tryout before making decisions.

7. The personnel of selection committees should not change too frequently. Membership should be for relatively long periods of time (at least a year, preferably two or more), and should be staggered so that the majority are always experienced in textbook selection.

8. The selection process should be closely related to the program of curriculum development and improvement. After all, the textbooks are there for the purpose of serving the learning program, and should be selected with the needs and conditions of that program in mind. A book that may be judged excellent for one school's program may be utterly unsuited to that of another.

Providing for individual differences. One of the obstacles to the development of more functional and effective teaching has been that teachers have not had materials in their classrooms which are suited to the variability of the pupils. In a few schools the principal and staff have done more than wring their hands and lament this situation. Enlisting the help of librarians and publishers, lists of books in each of the subjects have been compiled, ranging widely in reading difficulty. Using these lists as a basis for selection, and with the co-operation of administrators who understood the importance of supplying materials of different difficulty levels for each class, schools can make materials available to teachers which will help them tremendously in individualizing and vitalizing their instruction. This procedure is particularly valuable in a problem-centered curriculum, but is also applicable to a subject-oriented learning program.

The materials so gathered may not be used to best advantage if placed in the classrooms. A better plan would be to have a large part of them centrally located in the school, to be made available to each teacher as he needs them, for they will be usable for different problems of study in different class groups. In order for such materials to be used in this way, it is important that they be carefully catalogued. Topical lists, with page references, can be made available to the teachers. The compiling of such topical lists, with approximate grade levels of difficulty indicated, is not an easy job, but it is a most interesting one. The task can be divided by topics, and committees can be formed around each topic, insuring a spread of the labor and the wide participation which develops understanding of the purpose and pride in the result.

Textbook Accounting

As in the case of other instructional supplies, careful accounts must be kept if the administration of textbooks is to be efficient and economical. As books are received, record should be made of the author, title, quantity received, and date of receipt. The principal should keep a master record of textbooks, similar to the perpetual inventory of supplies. This record should note the title and quantity on hand, and should provide for entering the number issued to teachers, and the number lost, destroyed, or so damaged as to be unfit for use. As books are received and recorded, they should be placed in a bookroom provided with proper shelving. Each book should be numbered, and stamped with school identification.

In issuing books to teachers, the principal should have them sign a form indicating the title and number issued, with provision for noting the number returned at the close of the year. The teacher, in turn, should keep a record of the books issued to pupils (if the school operates under a free textbook or textbook rental system). This record should include the name of the child, the number of the book, and its condition at issue and on return. Facsimiles of forms suitable for the above purposes appear in Jacobson, Reavis and Lodston's text.[26]

[26] P. B. Jacobson, W. C. Reavis, and J. D. Lodston, *Duties of School Principals*, 2nd ed., Prentice-Hall, Inc., New York, 1950, pp. 634–636.

At the close of the year, all textbooks should be returned to the central storeroom, and an inventory of them made. This is part of the annual inventory of all school supplies. By following these simple procedures, adequate control can be maintained over the numerous textbooks within the school.

SUGGESTED READINGS

Hibbert, R. W., chairman, *Selection, Purchase, Storage, and Distribution of Supplies,* National Association of Public School Business Officials, Bulletin no. 1, Trenton, N. J., 1932.

Jacobson, Paul B., Reavis, William C., and Lodston, J. D., *Duties of School Principals,* 2nd ed., Prentice-Hall, Inc., New York, 1950, ch. 20.

Linn, Henry H., *Practical School Economies,* Bureau of Publications, Teachers College, Columbia University, New York, 1934.

National Society for the Study of Education, *The Textbook in American Education,* Thirtieth Yearbook, Part II, Public School Publishing Company, Bloomington, Ill., 1931.

Ramseyer, L. L., *The School Inventory,* National Association of Public School Business Officials, Bulletin no. 4, Trenton, N. J., 1933.

Reavis, William C., Pierce, Paul R., and Stullken, Edward H., *The Elementary School: Its Organization and Administration,* rev. ed., University of Chicago Press, Chicago, 1938, ch. XVII.

Reeder, Ward G., *The Fundamentals of Public School Administration,* rev. ed., The Macmillan Company, New York, 1941, chs. XVI and XXVI.

CHAPTER XXIII

ADMINISTERING THE SCHOOL PLANT

Many elementary principals will probably not have an opportunity to participate in the planning of a new school building. They may share in the expansion and renovation of an old building, but because new construction entails considerable cost and because the shells of most school buildings erected during this century are still structurally sound, there is a reluctance on the part of boards of education to abandon completely any school building which meets the elementary requirements of space and safety. It will be the privilege, however, of some principals to be on the ground when a new building is being constructed. In the latter event opportunity should be provided the principal and the members of his staff to participate in preparing the plans. In fact, there is a growing tendency for school boards to include representatives of many different groups in the planning of a new school building. Superintendent, members of the board of education, principals, teachers, custodians, pupils, parents, architect, and technical specialists all have a contribution to make in determining space requirements and needed school facilities.

As the responsible head of the local school unit, the principal has a unique leadership role to play in the organization and work of planning committees. While no single pattern has been devised for developing school building plans, experiments[1] similar to the one reported by Seagers for a New York State suburban community suggest that the prin-

[1] Paul W. Seagers, *Community Participation in School Building Planning,* unpublished Ed.D. project, Teachers College, Columbia University, 1950.

349

cipal must provide considerable direction and guidance if groups are to work together harmoniously and effectively.

Among the specific steps which can logically be taken are (1) the clarification of the school's philosophy and the determination of the type of educational program for which a building is being planned, (2) the appointment of committees to investigate special needs related to the proposed plant such as library, audio-visual arrangements, shops, gymnasium and play facilities, multiple purpose rooms, kindergarten, and storage and space provisions for custodian, (3) the arrangement of trips to selected school systems for firsthand study of the characteristics of modern buildings, and (4) the presentation of slides and pictures portraying special features of selected modern elementary school buildings.

The above is by no means an exhaustive list of the steps to be inaugurated by the principal in planning a new building, but is illustrative of the many tasks that confront the administrator and the staff if a thorough analysis is to be made of community needs in planning a new school. The elementary principal, in deciding what his own responsibilities are, will have to be sensitive to the roles played by the superintendent of schools, the architect, and the board of education. Certainly the principal should be given a major assignment in helping the local community interpret its school needs. In creating committees the principal will need to proceed cautiously and democratically. He should seek the advice of the superintendent of schools, the officers of the parent-teacher association, and members of the advisory council if one exists. The school principal can logically be expected to advise the various working committees with respect to their duties and the scope of their activities; he will need to inform them of any legal requirements that have to be met and should counsel them with regard to the nature of their reports to the administration. He may find it advisable to request that a written record of committee discussions and actions be kept. The coordination of committee activities will necessitate considerable planning and work.

In order to fulfill the responsibilities just outlined, an elementary school principal needs to be informed in the area of school plant management. This can be achieved in a number of ways. One can learn a lot about modern school buildings from books and current periodicals. The Twenty-seventh Yearbook of the American Association of School

Administrators entitled *American School Buildings* contains a mine of information. Various architectural journals such as *Progressive Architecture, Architectural Record,* and *Architectural Forum* contain modern plans and illustrate trends in design. Moreover, excellent articles appear currently in such school administration journals as *School Executive, American School Board Journal, Nation's Schools,* and *School Management.* Principals who wish to extend their knowledge still further might profitably examine *The American School and University,* a yearbook on school plant planning, equipment, operation and maintenance. Principals in rural areas can profitably consult a recent publication sponsored by the National Council of Chief State School Officers entitled *Planning Rural Community School Buildings.*[2] A second means of acquiring essential information on school plant planning is through workshops, conferences, and university courses dealing with school building problems. The principal who is well informed on matters relating to the school plant will be a great resource to those participating in the planning of a new school building.

Additions to Existing School Buildings

As was indicated earlier, not every principal will be so fortunate as to have a new building planned and constructed during his administration. The old structure may *have to do* for many years to come. But it often happens that additions are contemplated even when money is scarce and the public is opposed to undertaking major school building projects. The principal at some time in his career is almost certain to be confronted with the necessity for helping to plan some school building extension. The nature and extent of the alterations will determine how much time and energy will need to be given to a study of needs. Certainly teachers, pupils, and parents should be consulted with respect to any major changes and their ideas weighed and considered. Whatever data are needed in order to insure sound recommendations should be collected. Often it is possible to make improvements at relatively small cost over and beyond the tentative proposals of the board of education. No opportunity should be lost to call the attention of the administration to this fact. Some of the steps suggested earlier for planning a new building are equally appropriate when major alterations are contemplated.

[2] Frank Cyr and Henry Linn, *Planning Rural Community School Buildings,* Bureau of Publications, Teachers College, Columbia University, New York, 1949.

Rehabilitation

Apart from making an addition to a building, which happens infrequently, school systems often set aside funds in the school budget for rehabilitation. It may require several years to bring about the desired reforms. The latter will be expedited if a systematic approach is made, based on a careful appraisal of needs. By surveying the building and listing in detail the specific improvements needed, a principal with the aid of the custodian and his teaching staff can render a great service to the community. This may involve painting and decorating classrooms and corridors, providing new lighting fixtures, refinishing classroom floors, installing new radiation, removing wood wainscot, acousticizing certain rooms, providing new toilet stalls, supplying new chalkboards, and a host of other changes in the direction of modernization.

Buildings which appear old and dingy on the outside can, if wisely planned, be made attractive and pleasing to the eye on the inside. Moreover, it is possible to schedule rehabilitation work so that it is relatively economical in those school systems which have their own maintenance crews.

Improving the Esthetic Qualities of the Classroom

There is a noticeable trend toward painting classrooms the color which individual teachers prefer, or at least to give teachers a choice among several different colors. Observers have reported that pupils and teachers show more alertness and enthusiasm when colors and light schemes are properly balanced. While individual tastes vary widely with respect to color, there are some principles long recognized by artists and interior decorators which should be adhered to. There are, for example, some known psychological responses to color which ought not to be ignored such as the fact that red and orange are warm and energizing colors, whereas blue and green are cool and soothing. Attention also should be given to color in relation to the intensity of light, to atmospheric conditions, and to the furniture and equipment used in the classroom. The light-reflecting values of various colors should be considered when a classroom or corridor is being painted. Ceilings should be painted white because an 80 per cent reflection factor is needed to give pupils sufficient light. If a sidewall reflection factor of 60 per cent is to be obtained, then those colors commonly known as the pastel tints must be used. Similar considerations to those mentioned above enter into the painting of furniture and equipment. When opportunity arises the old grays and browns should be replaced by new bleached-straw or light honey color.

Authorities have pointed out that color can be used to promote safety by marking various types of hazards with distinctive colors, and that color can contribute to efficiency by using it to codify and identify tools, switches, valves, pipes, playground equipment, and the like.

Selecting Furniture and Equipment

The principal must be a jack of all trades or so it seems, for not only must he have a good knowledge of school plant management but he must also be well informed about furniture and equipment. While the literature in this field is still rather meager, principles are gradually being developed to guide administrators in selecting furniture and equipment.

One important factor which enters into the decision as to which type of classroom furniture is to be purchased is the philosophy of education held by those making the choice. A conservative administrator will lean toward fixed desks, chairs, and other furnishings, whereas the progressive principal or superintendent will look with favor on furniture which permits considerable flexibility in arrangement. The latter point of view stems from a belief that the whole child comes to school and not just his intellect. If this assumption is granted, it is important to consider the pupil's surroundings and activities and the effect of those on his interests and his growth. Sitting in a chair all day is an unnatural pattern of behavior for children; in fact, adults as well as children, not infrequently become hostile and rebellious when compelled to sit in one position for long periods of time. Psychologists tell us that the whole organism learns, not just the brain. It follows then that principals and teachers should consider the classroom environmental factors that relate to the emotional, the physical, and the social phases of a pupil's life, as well as those designed primarily to stimulate his mental powers.

The first generalization that can be reached is *that school furniture and equipment should be in harmony with the pupil's interests, his maturity, and his needs*. This suggests among other things adherence to the doctrine of individual differences and calls for movable furniture including chairs, tables, bookcases, shelves for blocks, easels, screens, cabinets, work benches, and bulletin boards.

When furniture and equipment can easily be moved around to suit the needs of the children it is possible to provide a rich and varied program of activities. Free floor space is limited to a single area when the furniture is fixed, but once the building is furnished with movable equipment any area in the classroom can be freed and used to suit most any purpose the group has in mind. Anyone acquainted with a modern program of education knows that certain floor spaces are better suited for dramatic play than others, that a project requiring use of a work bench may be carried on with less disturbance to those engaged in other activities if the bench can be moved to a distant corner, and that greater flexibility in room arrangement makes teaching easier.

A second principle relating to the selection of furniture is that it *should be the right size for the pupils it is designed to serve.* This means that some of it must be mechanically adjustable, and that various sizes of chairs and tables are provided in each classroom so that account can be taken of individual differences in size of pupils. Some school authorities recommend chairs of three different heights per room in grades 1 through 6.[3]

Not only should furniture be adjusted to the size of the pupils but it should be easily moved about by the pupils themselves. Regrouping should not be a chore for the teacher. Chairs and tables that are light in weight and easily carried or pushed around are now on the market and are preferable to heavier types of furniture. Some manufacturers are experimenting with metal tubing, aluminum, and plastic in order to provide the lightness and attractiveness not easily obtained when the more traditional materials are used.

A third rule to observe in choosing classroom furniture is to emphasize *variety.* Tables of different sizes and shapes make a room more interesting and, if wisely chosen, more adaptable for classroom use than where one single size and shape is selected. The choice need not be confined to round or square tables. Oblong, hexagonal, and oval shapes are equally useful and add to the esthetic appearance of the room. Thought should be given to the need for sloping surfaces as well as flat surfaces when purchasing desks. The adjustable feature will permit various arrangements with respect to slope not possible with the more traditional desks.[4]

[3] A. B. Shaw, "A List of Equipment for Classrooms in a Modern Elementary School," *American School and University,* 1948–49, pp. 283–287.
[4] Teachers should be given instruction in adjusting desks; otherwise pupils will be just as handicapped as with the traditional type of seating.

It is obvious that all classrooms should not be furnished exactly alike. The kindergarten room will need special equipment to care for the needs of very young children. Cots, rugs, or mats for use during rest periods should be provided and some thought given to their storage; provision for small construction projects should be made in primary rooms. The latter may consist of a built-in hardwood bench or a folding bench or a hardwood top placed on two saw horses. A work sink, low and large enough for sailing boats as well as for washing paint pots and for watering flowers, is especially needed in the kindergarten room.

The equipment needed in other classrooms will depend somewhat upon the general building layout and the degree to which it is efficient to share special equipment with other groups. Exhibit cases, garden tools, insect and animal cages, pianos, aquaria, planetaria, terraria, platforms, sewing machines, voice recorders, and many other items of equipment can usually be made to serve the needs of children in more than one room if sufficient planning is done well in advance of use.

When the time arrives for the selection of the specific furniture and equipment items, the detailed knowledge possessed by the principal and his staff will count enormously. It is important to know that tentative standards have been developed to insure health and comfort, and that intensive research has been carried on with regard to chair and desk heights, seat depths, spacing, lighting, and a number of other matters bearing on school equipment.[5]

Where furniture and equipment needs are great the principal will be wise to consult books and periodicals dealing with the subject and make special inquiries of seating companies. The exhibits commonly held in connection with the meetings of the American Association of School Administrators afford a wonderful opportunity to see and examine school equipment; also, university schools of education are giving thought to the problem of classroom furniture and not infrequently some member of the university staff is well versed in this field and can offer wise counsel to the principal. The responsibility for choosing the right furniture, while shared with many others including teachers and superintendent of schools, is one which rests heavily on the shoulders of the principal. Since

[5] Darell Boyd Harmon, *The Co-ordinated Classroom,* American Seating Company, Syracuse, 1949; Harry Eastman Bennet, *A Study of School Posture and Seating,* and *The Height of Kindergarten Chairs,* American Seating Company, Syracuse, 1925; Paul W. Seagers, "How About Your Furniture?", *Journal of the National Education Association,* December 1949, pp. 676–677.

children will be affected very directly by his efforts, he cannot afford to treat the problem lightly.

Housekeeping Responsibilities

The old maxim "As is the teacher so is the school" may be basically sound; but it overlooks the fact that children learn from their environment and that the condition of a building, as well as the qualifications of teachers who make up the staff, leaves its imprint upon the habits and tastes of pupils. Classrooms that are ill kept, improperly lighted, poorly ventilated, drably painted, and disorderly arranged create pupil reactions that are not conducive to efficient learning. A principal, therefore, cannot afford to overlook his responsibility to supervise the housekeeping duties of teachers, custodian, and pupils. To do this efficiently he needs to possess some practical knowledge pertaining to toilet room facilities, floors and cleaning materials, chalkboard surfaces, illumination, sanitation, playground surfaces, heating and ventilating, and several other phases of plant management.

An intelligent and well-informed custodian can be of great assistance in keeping the building in good order. But this employee because of his limited training qualifications cannot appreciate the full educational significance of housekeeping activities. The principal has to be in a position to appraise the condition of the building at all times. To do this he has to know what's right and what's wrong about the building and the way it is being operated and maintained.

It would require a textbook (see page 366) devoted solely to housekeeping duties to answer the scores of questions about operation and maintenance which will arise in the course of a principal's career or even in a small segment of it. This discussion is limited to a few of the major items every principal has to consider in supervising the daily use of the school plant.

Attention to Sanitary Conditions

From the standpoint of health as well as the esthetic needs of children, the matter of sanitation deserves first consideration. Lack of care and improper care are the chief causes of bad sanitary conditions in schools. It is not uncommon to find unsanitary conditions in school toilet rooms. The latter should be free of all strong odors, including those which are produced by the use of chemical deodorants and disinfectants. A pupil should not be subjected to unpleasant smells or sights when he goes to a toilet room. Proper construction, ventilation, sunlight, and frequent cleaning are the only means of correcting bad toilet room conditions and insuring proper esthetic and health standards.

The principal himself should know and, if necessary, should advise the central office of the fact that all fixtures, floors, and walls in toilet rooms should be constructed of material that has a smooth, nonabsorbing finish. Tile floors and walls are vastly superior to concrete for toilet rooms since the latter material is permeable and is more difficult to keep clean. If the central administration cannot supply a new tile floor at once, an intermediate step may be substituted. A concrete floor can be improved by painting it with a floor enamel. Moreover, penetrating seals are temporarily effective when applied to terrazzo and concrete.

Another factor in improving sanitary conditions in toilet rooms relates to the supplies furnished the custodian for cleaning. Suitable brushes (several of which are now on the market) for washing toilet bowls and other plumbing fixtures when furnished the custodian will encourage regular cleaning. The custodian's task in keeping toilet rooms sanitary should be made as pleasant as the nature of the assignment will permit. Given the right equipment, the job becomes less objectionable than otherwise.

Provisions for Hand Drying

Cleanliness is a trait which schools generally profess to include among their curricular aims. Unfortunately school systems often fail to provide the environmental conditions which encourage children to practice cleanliness consistently in their everyday habits. Many toilet rooms have wash bowls but no towels for drying hands. This leaves children with the alternatives of omitting washing their hands altogether, drying them with toilet paper, or using their handkerchiefs. The latter practice leads children to do a superficial job of washing and at best results in the child's returning to the classroom with a soiled handkerchief in his pocket.

Administrators sometimes argue that it is impractical to provide children with paper towels because they are so destructive and wasteful. They sometimes tear them up, throw them on the floor, or litter up the corridors with them. This makes extra work for the custodian. While there can be no denying that this situation obtains in some schools, it does not follow that all hand-wiping facilities should be removed from toilet rooms. Children sometimes destroy textbooks but this doesn't result in the abandonment of all instructional materials. Rather it suggests some improvement in supervision and in the general morale of the school.

Schools have experimented with at least three types of hand-drying arrangements: cloth towels, air dryers, and paper towels. Cloth towels are not practical in large schools; the cloth roller towel is insanitary and the individual cloth towels are expensive both from the standpoint of laundering and original cost. Air dryers tend to slow up traffic somewhat where large numbers of children are involved. They are, however, reasonably economical to operate once they are installed and they have the advantage of being completely sanitary.

Paper towels are unquestionably the most popular form of hand-drying provision. They are available in rolls and in individual cabinets. Until some better provision is discovered principals are justified in recommending good quality-paper towels for use in toilet rooms. They should be placed in a container and not left on window sills. Needless to say, the containers should be filled regularly.

Inspection Tours Necessary

There is no substitution for frequent inspections by the principal of conditions in the toilet rooms and for regular conferences with the custodian as to problems encountered in keeping standards high. During inspections, the principal should note such details as whether or not there is liquid soap, toilet paper, paper towels, and should observe the general condition of toilet bowls and urinals.

Usually it is desirable for the custodian to follow a carefully planned schedule of activities geared to the program established by pupils. He should arrange to visit toilet rooms after school is dismissed, taking care to refill the containers installed to hold toilet paper, liquid soap, and paper towels, and making sure that all toilets are flushed and are working properly. Pupils have a right to expect that toilet rooms will be clean, attractive, and fairly odorless. The fact that some children may come from homes where relatively low standards prevail and who, because of their ignorance and bad habits, may add to the custodian's task of keeping toilet rooms sanitary in no way excuses the school from maintaining high standards of cleanliness. The slow but inescapable influence of the school environment upon the everyday habits and appreciations of children will make itself felt as the years roll by. This is what education is designed to achieve—to lift sights and appreciations to higher levels, to raise standards—in short, to improve the living habits of those whom it touches.

The principal and the school custodian cannot accomplish all that is desirable through inspection and cleaning. The co-operation of teachers and pupils is necessary if good housekeeping habits are to be instilled in children. In the case of toilet room care, pupils should be taught to flush toilet stools and to avoid leaving waste paper on the floor. If waste containers are available near wash bowls and emptied before they are overflowing, there will be less of a tendency for pupils to throw used towels on the floor. But there will still be need for instruction. Pupil committees (one for boys and one for girls) serving for limited periods of time, perhaps for two weeks, could further good housekeeping objectives by participating in the management of toilet rooms. Suggestions for improvements and some responsibility for reporting on conditions (towels, soap, toilet paper, and general cleanliness) would focus attention of pupils generally on a problem of concern to every pupil citizen in the school.

Adequate Storage, a Factor in Good Housekeeping

From an educational standpoint, the matter of storage has received far too little consideration both in the literature dealing with schoolhouse construction and in the plans of school architects. It also bears directly on housekeeping efficiency. The teachers and the custodian are the ones who appreciate this fact most of all. As was stressed earlier, kindergarten and first-grade teachers have such obvious needs for storage of blocks, easels, paints, and other materials commonly used in the primary grades that it seems strange that so many rooms designed to house small children are so poorly provided with storage facilities. This is a problem that is fairly easily resolved, once it is recognized as a matter of importance. A carpenter can usually build the cases required for supplies, books, clippings, and illustrative materials so that these teaching aids can be easily located and preserved in usable form. He can also build cases to house globes, maps, charts, and building blocks, and make special drawers or letter files. If these storage needs are anticipated before the building has been erected, then it is desirable to provide for them in the architect's plans. This will make it possible to safeguard esthetic standards which conceivably will have to be satisfied if alterations of considerable magnitude are required after the building has been constructed.

It is difficult to keep a classroom neat and orderly when storage facilities are lacking.

Apart from classroom needs, consideration should be given to storage requirements generally. Keeping a building clean, attractive, and safe requires tools, equipment, and cleaning materials. Unless some thought is given to storage space and design, improper and inadequate provision will be made. There should be a closet with a service rack on each floor and a fireproof storeroom for oil, gasoline, and other inflammable materials, in addition to space for tools and equipment. The custodian should have a comfortable place to attend to his record-keeping activities and as headquarters. In planning storage rooms and determining their location and the space needs, the custodian should be asked to contribute ideas.

Arrangement and Care of Classrooms

Children and teachers spend a large segment of their lives in school. This fact alone should serve to focus attention on the physical conditions which obtain in classrooms. While the teacher frequently exercises direct control over the arrangement of the classroom, he needs the assistance and the support of the principal and the custodian in making it as habitable and as conducive to learning as possible.

One of the first things a visitor notices when he enters a classroom is the condition of the window shades. If they are cracked and stringy, they detract from the appearance of the room. The teacher and the principal should urge the central office to supply translucent fabric shades that are hung so the light may be admitted at any part of the window. If these shades are suspended so that one half of the shade pulls up and the other half pulls down, the teacher can adjust them so as to control the amount of light. There are many advantages in installing Venetian blinds, especially in the South where ventilation constitutes a problem. From an esthetic standpoint Venetian blinds are superior to shades. Because of the higher initial cost of Venetian blinds, however, the translucent fabric shade is more commonly used in school buildings.

It is important that classrooms get a maximum amount of sunlight. Since it is not always desirable to admit the direct rays of the sun while children are reading at their desks, an effort should be made at the close of school and early in the morning to adjust shades so the sunlight penetrates to every possible corner of the room. A regular routine of adjusting shades is the only sure way of insuring enough sunlight.

Many teachers are unconscious of light needs. They become so absorbed in the topics being discussed that they fail to sense how dark it is in various parts of the room. In some instances they ignore the shades and turn on the electric lights. The principal should observe these conditions and set about correcting them in the interests of conserving children's eyes, and in some cases, where artificial illumination is used, the taxpayer's money.

Chalkboards

A second item of classroom equipment which requires considerable attention on the part of both principal and custodian is the chalkboard. The type of educational program which a school undertakes to provide has much to do with the chalkboard space needed in classrooms. The modern school requires less space than the traditional one since all children are not expected to be doing problems at the board at the same time. It is not necessary to have chalkboards on all sides of the room. They absorb light and take up space which can be more profitably used for other purposes. A chalkboard sixteen feet wide stretching across the front of the room is quite adequate. Other wall space should be reserved for tack boards, bulletin boards, and display cases. Light-colored glass and composition chalkboards are becoming fairly popular and it is probable that they will supersede older types of chalkboards. Natural slate comes only in black and is relatively expensive. The standard chalkboard width is 36 inches for elementary classrooms and the height of the chalk rail from the floor varies from 28 inches for first- and second-grade children to 32 inches for fifth- and sixth-grade rooms. A fairly safe rule to follow when installing chalk trays is to add one inch to the standard established for the grade below, starting with 28 inches for grade one. Where several grades share a room, the board should be set for average height.

The principal of the school may inherit chalkboards that are poor in quality and badly distributed. His wisest course in this case will be to outline the steps that need to be taken to correct the mistakes made originally, get an estimate of the cost of such a program, and recommend to the superintendent the changes desired, outlining the work to be done and the specific materials needed.

Sometimes the trouble confronting teachers and children is not the quality of the chalkboard, although this is undoubtedly important. It is rather with the crayons used and the method employed in cleaning the board. A good crayon is one with a 95 per cent chalk content. Such a crayon has many advantages. It will prolong the life of the board, will prevent eyestrain, will wear longer than cheaper brands, and will create less dust.

Chalkboard erasers are frequently so full of dust that they smear the board rather than clean it. Erasers should be cleaned daily and dust trays should be used so that the erasers do not lie in the dust. Chalkboards should also be cleaned regularly with a turkish towel or some other soft cloth.

Where the principal and his staff are permitted to choose, cork bulletin boards should be selected ahead of other types. Soft fibre boards are acceptable substitutes if cork is not available or appears too expensive. Some schools rely upon burlap covering. This type of display device collects dust and is more difficult to keep clean than cork or fibre boards. Where burlap is used it should be cemented to a soft composition backing.

Floor Care

Keeping classroom floors in condition constitutes another problem in housekeeping which in all too many instances is poorly resolved. It is not uncommon to find dark, unattractive floors in classrooms, due to the accumulations of heavy oil and dust. There is perhaps no single method of cleaning floors that is clearly superior to all others. But one can say with reasonable assurance that penetrating seals are now available which when used on wood floors make the cleaning job both easier and more effective. After applying the seal, the floors can be maintained by frequent sweeping with a dust mop or an appropriate floor brush treated with a small amount of wax or seal. On wood floors, wax, unless it has been preceded by a seal treatment, has a tendency to peel and wear off in traffic lanes. Where floors are badly worn and where seal is not practical to use, a floor-oil treatment may be the only satisfactory answer. While this problem may rest on the shoulders of some central-office employee in many school systems, the principal will still need to keep abreast of developments in the floor-cleaning area and be sure the custodian is taking full advantage of the improved materials and methods. Otherwise, classroom floors may remain less attractive than they need to be.

Classroom furniture should be dusted thoroughly every day so that pupils' clothing will not get soiled and as a protection against the spread of bacteria and germs. It also adds to the esthetic appearance of a room to have it free of dust. While it may be difficult for the custodian working alone to maintain the high standard of cleanliness implied above, every effort should be made to keep classrooms "spic and span." Children can help in the process. A pride equal to that commonly felt by sailors in the appearance of their ship should be achieved by the school personnel.

Decorating the Classroom

Sometimes the appearance of a room can only be improved by the application of paint. In fact, some authorities say that classrooms should be painted every three to five years. As mentioned before, the colors used in classrooms and corridors have an influence on the general atmosphere of a school building. They may energize, they may soothe, they may irritate. Discriminating adults do not restrict the rooms in their homes to a single color. Why should the school? It costs only a little more to provide teachers and pupils with a fairly wide variety of color choices and it gives a school building life and vitality which the traditional buff does not provide.

Teachers have it within their power to make classrooms attractive or drab depending upon their own sensitivity to the esthetic quality of the furnishings, the pictures, and decorations. Plants and flowers add to the homelike atmosphere of a room and should be selected with the aid of the children. Pictures, if chosen with discrimination, will improve the general appearance of a room. While the principal must not insist that the members of his staff accept his choices of furnishings, he nevertheless has a responsibility for seeing to it that the esthetic quality of the building is kept high. Hence he must encourage the wisest possible selections.

Attention to Heating and Ventilation

Temperature is an important factor in maintaining pupil and teacher efficiency. Not only do poorly ventilated rooms make pupils listless, but they often lead to respiratory troubles. Teachers need to be urged to look at the thermometer frequently and to maintain, as far as they control the matter, a proper temperature for health and comfort. This is usually acknowledged to be around 70 degrees. In controlling temperature the teacher should make certain that pupils are not subjected to drafts. Where mechanical ventilation is employed, it is desirable to check conditions periodically to be sure that the ventilating system is working properly. The principal should make certain that teacher and custodian co-operate effectively in keeping classrooms properly heated and ventilated. Where each employee understands his responsibilities and sees the importance of carrying them out efficiently, there is little trouble in keeping pupils comfortable.

Heating units are sometimes quite complicated and require some technical knowledge to operate. Usually these units are installed in large high schools where high pressure boilers are used and are not commonly found in elementary school buildings. While the principal cannot be expected to know everything about the mechanical phases of the school plant, he should not be totally ignorant of them. He should know how to operate every piece of equipment in his school and know when it is in order and out of order. This does not imply that he should know how to repair equipment nor that he should spend his time operating it. But as head of the plant in which hundreds of boys and girls are housed, he must possess the knowledge necessary to protect them. If custodians fail to show up for work, he must be able to fill the gap or instruct others how to do so. In short, the principal must be building conscious and well informed on its operation and maintenance.

Playground Care

Recreational activities in the modern school play an important role in the educational development of children. It is not enough simply to provide space. The grounds must be properly surfaced, and thought given to the various games and activities in which children are encouraged to participate. Usually the principal will be bound by the space the board of education has already provided, and, except as parents and the school may influence the "powers that be" to extend existing boundaries, improvements will have to be confined to surfaces and equipment already available. Playground surfaces are often ill suited to the games and activities of children, particularly since children usually go directly from playground to classroom. Sometimes cinders are used on playgrounds. They are injurious to floor finishes and often result in injuries to children. Poorly drained land is also unsatisfactory. Play surfaces should be clean regardless of weather conditions. Authorities are now generally agreed that turf or "black top" is the most satisfactory playground surface. Unfortunately, turf can be maintained only when the number of pupils per playground acre is relatively limited. Small school sites require some other type of play surface. "Black top" which is composed of bituminous emulsified asphalt is probably the best "all weather" playground surface.

Adequate walks leading from the street to the school building and around the building will aid in keeping the classrooms and corridors free of mud and dirt. Footscrapers and mats should be provided and children instructed to use them. Not only will these make housekeeping easier for the custodian, but they provide an opportunity to instill habits in children which will have value throughout life.

Keeping the grounds as attractive as conditions permit should be a co-operative project involving pupils, teachers, principal, and custodian. It can be made a matter of considerable pride and satisfaction, if wisely engineered. Pupils should be encouraged to contribute ideas and to participate in the care and improvement of school grounds. In this way they will develop a sense of responsibility for community property and will learn how to do many of the tasks which are inherent in caring for yards and grounds.

As was indicated earlier in this discussion, the task of supervising the operation and maintenance of a school plant requires wide knowledge and experience. Only a few of the major areas have been touched upon in the preceding pages in an effort to give the reader some appreciation of the relationship of this work to the total job of the school principal. To achieve the objectives of the school it is necessary to have the building operated efficiently. Pupils must not only be comfortable and safe but their physical environment should serve to elevate their appreciations and their tastes. Hence the efficiency with which the plant is cared for becomes a matter of considerable importance to the principal and his staff.

SUGGESTED READINGS

American Association of School Administrators, *American School Buildings,* Twenty-seventh Yearbook, Washington, D. C., 1949.

American Council on Education, Committee on School Plant Research, *Specification for Chair Desks,* Studies Series VII School Plant Research no. 2, The Council, Washington, D. C., 1942.

Betzner, Jean, *School Housing Needs of Young Children,* Association for Childhood Education, Washington, D. C., 1939.

Birren, Faber, "Functional Color in the Schoolroom," *Magazine of Art,* vol. XLII, April 1949, pp. 136–138.

Bursch, Charles Wesley, and Reed, John Lyon, *You Want to Build a School,* Reinhold Publishing Corporation, New York, 1947.

Childhood Education, *Better School Homes for Children,* Reprint Service Bulletin, compiled from 1945–46 issues.

Engelhardt, N. L., and Engelhardt, N. L., Jr., *Planning the Community School,* American Book Company, New York, 1940.

Letson, John Walter, *Better School Planning for Alabama,* Bulletin 1950 no. 3, State Board of Education, Montgomery, Ala., 1950.

Linn, Henry H., Helm, Leslie C., and Grabarkiewicz, K. P., *The School Custodian's Housekeeping Handbook,* Bureau of Publications, Teachers College, Columbia University, New York, 1948.

Mitchell, Mary Alice, "Classrooms Need Movable Equipment," *The School Executive,* vol. LXIX, November 1949, no. 3, pp. 61–63.

National Council on School House Construction, Central Standards Committee, *Guide for Planning School Plants,* The Council, Nashville, Tenn., 1948.

Seagers, Paul, "How About Your Furniture," *Journal of the National Education Association,* Washington, D. C., December 1949.

Shaw, Archibald B., "A List of Equipment for Classrooms in a Modern Elementary School," *American School and University,* 1948–49, American School Publishing Corporation, New York, pp. 283–288.

Wiley, Will E., and Wiley, John H., "New Developments in Elementary School Seating," *American School and University,* 1947–48, American School Publishing Corporation, New York, pp. 184–187.

Part VI INTEGRATING SCHOOL
AND COMMUNITY LIFE

Until relatively recently the topic of school-community relationships has received little attention in educational literature. This is only a reflection of the fact that little functional relationship between school and community has existed, or has been thought necessary in the vast majority of schools. The typical American school has been isolated (one might even say insulated!) from its community.

In recent years, however, a noticeable change has been taking place in the attitude of educators toward the relationships which should exist between the school and community it serves. Olsen found, for example, that the number of articles in the educational literature which deal with community study and participation increased from 37 in the period 1930–33 to 402 during 1938–41, an increase of 986 per cent.[1] There is an increasing demand by schoolmen for information on how to improve school-community relations, a fact reflected in the demand for courses, books, and other information about the topic.

A recent study of the elementary school principalship yielded data which are illustrative of the trend.[2] It was found that the "average" supervising principal spends between three and four hours weekly in community activities outside school hours. A similar study made twenty years ago indicated that the typical supervising prin-

[1] Edward G. Olsen and others, *School and Community,* Prentice-Hall, Inc., New York, 1945, pp. 14–15.
[2] Department of Elementary School Principals, *The Elementary School Principalship—Today and Tomorrow,* Twenty-seventh Yearbook, National Education Association, Washington, D. C., 1948, ch. IX.

cipal then spent slightly under two hours weekly in such activities.[3]
*The 1948 study also concluded that ". . . it is clear that principals
today are more likely to belong to lay organizations than the groups
reporting in 1928. . . . Although comparisons with the 1928
study are limited by the data available, it appears that the proportion of supervising principals engaging in community activities has
multiplied at least tenfold."*[4]

These seem to be tangible evidences of progress in the direction
of closer school-community ties. However, the Yearbook Committee
goes on to say, "We do know that at least half of the principals are
definitely engaged in constructive community activities. The Committee finds that the other 50 per cent did not show much evidence
of community interest and participation."[5]

In view of this trend toward closer association between the
school and the citizens it serves, it seems important to examine the
reasons for it, the purposes such relationships should serve, the
essentials of good school-community relationships, and the role and
responsibility of the principal in improving the interrelationships between school and community.

[3] Department of Elementary School Principals, *The Elementary School Principalship,* Seventh Yearbook, National Education Association, Washington, D. C., 1928,
p. 250–251.
[4] Department of Elementary School Principals, *op. cit.,* Twenty-seventh Yearbook,
pp. 129, 130.
[5] *Ibid.,* p. 131.

CHAPTER XXIV

CLOSER SCHOOL-COMMUNITY
RELATIONS—FOR WHAT?

In the quest for an explanation of the current concern with school-community relations, there are at least three important factors which can be identified. The first is the change which has taken, and is taking place in the nature of the goals and methods of our schools. Second is the increasing importance being attached to the need for public support of public schools. Third is the evolving and expanding meaning of democracy.

Closely related to these factors are the purposes of such relationships. Should schoolmen concentrate on *telling* the public how good the schools are? Is the chief purpose of "public relations" to *inform* the people of what schools are doing and trying to do? Is the objective the *greater use of community resources?* Should the school aim to *improve community conditions?* These are questions frequently raised, and therefore merit discussion here.

REASONS FOR CLOSER SCHOOL-COMMUNITY TIES

The Developing Character of the American School

Naturally, the objectives of school-community relations are closely tied in with the objectives of American education in general. These objectives have undergone gradual modification with the years. Our earliest schools were established primarily as "book-learning" schools, a pattern which persists today. Their major purpose was to teach reading, writing, and arithmetic, and for them to do that job, little relationship between school and community was necessary.

In the first two decades of the current century, American educational philosophy and psychology, under the leadership of such men as John Dewey and Edward Thorndike, began to take on distinctive characteristics. Philosophers of the "Dewey school" pointed out the non-functional character of much of the learning program in our schools, and argued cogently for an education more consistent with the nature of learning and the realities of present-day life. Results of the standardized tests developed by the psychologists highlighted the facts of individual differences. Other venturesome men, stimulated by these ideas, worked experimentally to develop better educational methods.

Out of the resulting educational ferment grew the movement which came to be known as "progressive education," which advocated shifting the emphasis from a book-centered type of education to a learning program which would be *child centered*. While these child-centered schools did not demand any real integration of school and community, they did *utilize* the community to a much greater extent than did the former academic schools. Very few thoroughgoing "child-centered" schools were actually established, but the movement did have some effect on schools generally; more attention came to be given to individual differences and needs than had been the case before, and many teachers reached out more into the community for learning experiences and materials.

A number of educators were dissatisfied with the concept of the child-centered school, however, feeling that it placed too much emphasis on the needs and interests of the individual, and too little on the demands of the culture and on functional social relationships. In its formulation of purposes in 1938, the Educational Policies Commission listed four groups of purposes, only one of which was concerned primarily with the individual. Their four major groups were:

1. The Objectives of Self-Realization
2. The Objectives of Human Relationship
3. The Objectives of Economic Efficiency
4. The Objectives of Civic Responsibility[1]

Educators thus have steadily broadened the definition of the curriculum to include all the experiences the child has within the jurisdic-

[1] Educational Policies Commission, *Policies for Education in American Democracy,* National Education Association, Washington, D. C., 1946, p. 189.

tion of the school. They also stress the fact that learning and growing is an uninterrupted, continuous process; it takes place everywhere, all of the time. Consequently, much more attention must be given to the relationship between the in-school and out-of-school influences on the child's development, and home and school will have to work more closely together if the best educational results are to be achieved.

Because of these emphases, more and more attention has been given to the relationships which should exist between the child's in-school and out-of-school life. There has been a growing conviction that much more of the stuff of the educational program must be found where most of the child's living and learning takes place: in his home, neighborhood, and community. Thus there is developing the concept of the "life-centered school," and in its logical extension, the "community school." Although bona-fide "community schools" are very rare at present,[2] many other schools are modifying their practice to relate the school program more closely to the life of the community, to serve the community, to enlist the community in service to the school and in planning school policy and program, and to exercise leadership in the co-operative improvement of the quality of community living.

Hence, it can be seen that the changes which have been taking place in educational thinking and practice are one factor contributing to the trend toward closer school-community ties.

Need for Public Support of Public Schools

The second group of factors which have impressed upon schoolmen the need for closer integration of school and community center around the very practical problem of school support. This has always been a matter of concern, of course, but has been brought sharply to the attention of many administrators in recent years because of several developments.

Throughout the depression years of the thirties and the following war years, school construction was almost at a standstill. Aside from a brief flurry of building from 1938 to 1941, relatively few new school buildings were erected. During the war almost none went up. In addition, the war

[2] See: Elsie R. Clapp, *Community Schools in Action,* Viking Press, New York, 1940; Samuel Everett, ed., *The Community School,* D. Appleton–Century Company, New York, 1938; L. S. Tireman and M. Watson, *A Community School in a Spanish-speaking Village,* University of New Mexico Press, Albuquerque, N. M., 1948.

and postwar years brought tremendous increases in the birth rate. The result, which had been foreseen but about which little had been done, was widespread overcrowding and acutely inadequate school facilities.[3] To make matters worse, construction costs had risen to be more than double the prewar figures. Authoritative sources estimated that it would take from 10 to 12 billions of dollars for the decade 1948–1958 simply to cover rockbottom building needs—a billion or more a year.

Another factor in the situation has been the necessity for "raising" teachers' salaries to keep pace with the rising cost of living. Although these raises did not keep pace with the skyrocketing living-costs index, they *looked* large to the taxpaying public, many members of which balked at the increases in taxes made necessary to meet education's enlarged payroll and to pay for the bond issues necessary to construct new school buildings.

In many communities, also, it was found that the citizens neither understood nor sympathized fully with the objectives and methods of the schools. This has been particularly true in relatively recent years during which the experimentation of venturesome educational authorities, the practices developed in "lighthouse schools," and the impact of new and evolving ideas resulted in numerous innovations in the operation of many American schools. A public which had been given almost no opportunity to gain any real understanding of the reasons for these changes was naturally confused and frequently suspicious of the new-fangled "fads" and procedures which often seemed so different from what they had experienced as pupils in school. Recognizing this, many administrators have been seeking procedures by which to help the public understand what the schools are trying to do, and to enlist the support of the community in efforts to provide improved education.

Expanding Concepts of Democracy

In any discussion of the reasons for changes in the character of the schools of our country, and of the movement toward greater school-community integration, there is one factor which cannot be overlooked. That factor is the subtle changes which are taking place in the working concept of democracy. From its earlier connotations of political and governmental forms, it has been enlarged to mean a way of life, under-

[3] National Education Association, *School Housing Needs in City School Systems, 1947–48,* Research Bulletin, vol. XXVI, December 1948.

lying which are a number of basic principles. Whereas there is no universal consensus on all of these principles, there is at least one on which spokesmen in the United States seem to agree: that every individual should have a part in making the decisions and regulations by which he shall live.

This principle is by no means new, but its application has until recently been primarily political in nature. There is a growing belief that the precept should apply to all areas of life and in all institutions, although public school personnel, particularly the administrative agents, have not yet generally realized its implications in practice. One of these implications is that those to whom the schools belong should have the opportunity to influence school policy. This principle has been affirmed by leading educational authorities, and is explicitly stated in a widely acclaimed publication of the Educational Policies Commission. They state as the fifth of twelve "Hallmarks of Democratic Education" the following:

> Democratic education guarantees to all the members of its community the right to share in determining the purposes and policies of education.[4]

The framers of our federal government recognized this principle by avoiding any type of federal control over education, leaving all jurisdiction of this most important institution to the states. Most of the states, in turn, have delegated much of their authority to the local boards of education. It is probable that the vast majority of Americans (including teachers, administrators, and boards of education) do not realize how unique this practice is among nations. At this writing, in fact, the authors know of no other nation in which control of education is similarly decentralized.

It is easily seen, then, that in their organization our schools are close to the people. In actual practice, however, the people usually have little part in deciding the policies or practices of their schools. Many administrators and boards of education have neither provided for nor welcomed public participation. Numbers have gone so far as to block the formation of parent-teacher associations because they did not wish "outsiders" meddling in the school program. In many cases, the boards of education themselves have not truly represented the people of the community.

[4] Educational Policies Commission, *Learning the Ways of Democracy,* National Education Association, Washington, D. C., 1940, p. 36.

Fortunately, schoolmen of vision and board members of dedication have been attempting in recent years to realize in practice the democratic principle of public participation in policy-making. For example, a group of school superintendents, constituting "the Committee of 14, Subcommittee of the Committee on Lay Understanding of the Metropolitan School Study Council," listed as one of their "Principles Underlying Public Participation":

> Public participation in educational planning finds positive justification because a democracy demands full participation of everyone concerned. Democracy opposes separation of government from the people.[5]

This is indicative of the trend of the thinking of leaders of American public education. It serves to reflect the influence in education of the expanding definition of democracy, and its realization in practice.

These, then, are three of the major reasons for the current concern with the "problem" of school-community relations: the changing nature of education, the critical need for public support, and the expanding concept of democracy. These reasons bear a close relationship to the purposes which should be served by the schools' programs of so-called public relations. The second part of this chapter is a discussion of such purposes.

PURPOSES OF SCHOOL-COMMUNITY RELATIONSHIPS

In order that a program of school-community relations may be well planned and intelligently conceived, it is necessary that those who are involved have a clear understanding of the purposes of such a program. Otherwise such relationships tend to be random, haphazard, incidental, and relatively ineffective.

There have been a number of concepts of the purposes of community or public relations in the schools. There have been (and are) those who think of them as a means of "selling the schools to the public" to gain financial support (a concept we shall discuss later in this section). Others have thought of it simply as a program of informing the public about school affairs and policies. Still others have considered them as a means of enriching the school's learning program. Some have developed such

[5] Committee of 14, *Public Action For Powerful Schools,* Metropolitan School Study Council, Teachers College, Columbia University, New York, 1949, p. 8.

relationships for the purpose of learning more about the pupils' living environment outside school, so as to suit the learning program better to the children's needs. Still others have been interested in closer community ties so as to develop closer co-operation between the home and the school in the education of the pupils. Recently there has been a group of educators who envisage a wider social responsibility for the school, and see such relationships as having the function of improving community living. Doubtless the reader can think of other more or less commendable purposes for which relationships between school and community have been employed, but the above serve to illustrate the wide-ranging nature of such purposes.

These purposes, upon thoughtful examination, seem to relate themselves to three major goals.

1. To improve the quality of children's learning and growing.

2. To raise community goals and improve the quality of community living.

3. To develop understanding, enthusiasm and support for the community's program of public education.

It is to be emphasized that at one time or another each of these purposes will assume pre-eminence, and *at that time* be the most important purpose to be served. In the long-range program, however, all three purposes must be emphasized to attain the "balanced and adequate program" spoken of by the Educational Policies Commission, in *Education for All American Children*.[6]

Improving the Quality of the Program of Children's Learning and Growing

Elsewhere in this volume the changes that have taken place concerning the concept of what a desirable program of education should be have been discussed. The developing concept appears to be that education should be neither "book centered" nor "child centered," but should be "life centered." Such an education has a number of implications relating to the community.

First, it requires that the staff of the school know well those con-

---

[6] Educational Policies Commission, *Education for All American Children,* National Education Association, Washington, D. C., 1948, p. 279.

ditions surrounding the lives of the children which are important to the educational program. What kind of a community is it in which the children are living and learning? What kinds of problems are they meeting daily in their living? What kinds of ethnic groups and intercultural problems are there in the community? What are the occupations and economic situations of their families? What are the recreational opportunities and limitations for children? What are their parents' attitudes about child raising and education? What is the pattern of the educational level of parents and other community members? What kinds of activities make demands on the time of the children outside school hours, and how much time do these activities require? These and other similar questions need to be answered if the program of learning and growing in the school is to be intelligently related to the learning and growing boys and girls are doing outside school.

Second, the school staff should become familiar with the resources in the community which may be utilized to enrich and supplement the school program. Looking upon the community as a laboratory for learning, it is necessary to know what the facilities of that laboratory are. Points of historical interest, industries and businesses which can be studied, governmental agencies, civic institutions, geographical characteristics, natural resources, flora and fauna, conditions affecting health, social problems of housing, of zoning, of streets, of water supply and of conservation, and transportation and traffic conditions are all examples of community factors which are grist to the mill of a life-centered learning program.

Third, the school should be cognizant of institutions, organizations, and agencies with which the school can co-operate in the interests of children's learning, growing, and welfare. Churches, Boy and Girl Scout organizations, public health agencies, welfare agencies, service clubs, the police, civic organizations, the education committees of labor unions, and the chamber of commerce are examples of such resources. Almost invariably these organizations and agencies are most willing to co-operate with the schools in giving attention to the welfare of children.

Fourth, schoolmen should be alert to those community resources which can be enlisted in the planning of an improved education. Citizens of the community are always interested in the kind of education their children are receiving. They constitute a vast reservoir of intelligence which can assist professional educators in educational planning. Some school systems have set up procedures to tap this reservoir systematically, and where this has been done under able leadership, remarkable results have been achieved. Participation by citizens in the planning of the policies and program of their schools is not only consistent with the principle of democratic participation mentioned earlier, but is also effective in improving the school program and in developing community understanding and support of the schools which are, after all, theirs.

Raising Community Goals and Improving the Quality of Community Living

Numbers of educators are now proposing that the schools have a function in helping the adult members of the community to recognize and meet community problems intelligently and informedly. This point of view was well stated in the Twenty-fourth Yearbook of the National Department of Elementary School Principals.

> In a democratic society the school should be a positive agent of social change. A school worthy of the support of a community owes it to that community to be a school of social action . . . It is a service institution, devoted to improving the quality of life lived by all the people of the community.[7]

An excellent example of improvement in the quality of living, from the economic standpoint, is provided by some experimental work underwritten by the Sloan Foundation, with Professor Harold Clark of Teachers College, Columbia University, as consultant. In three different states, these experiments have demonstrated clearly how an educational program which enlists adults as participants, and which is intelligently adapted to meet specific community needs, can markedly improve the food, shelter, and clothing aspects of living.[8]

In Mount Pleasant, Michigan, parents, teachers, children and other citizens planned together to establish indoor recreational facilities for teen-agers.[9] Numbers of other communities, through co-operative plan-

[7] Department of Elementary School Principals, *Community Living in the Elementary School,* Twenty-fourth Yearbook, National Education Association, Washington, D. C., 1945, pp. 12, 13.

[8] Clara M. Olson and Norman D. Fletcher, *Learn and Live,* Alfred P. Sloan Foundation, New York, 1946. See also W. K. McCharen, *Improving the Quality of Living,* Division of Surveys and Field Services, George Peabody College for Teachers, Nashville, Tenn., 1947.

[9] Association For Supervision and Curriculum Development, *Group Planning in Education,* National Education Association, Washington, D. C., 1945, pp. 82–85.

ning in which the school has taken the initiative, have similarly improved their recreational facilities and programs.

The city of Springfield, Massachusetts, has attracted attention because of its citizenship program. This program was developed through considerable co-operative planning, and co-ordination of the schools with community organizations and agencies.[10] One report of this program concludes with the following significant statement:

> On the practical side, they [the schools] are so tied in with youth-serving and other social agencies that when something of great concern is before the public the schools are considered a part of it as a matter of course. The wonder is that when one school system really goes "all out" in spearheading the attack on local problems, it should become famous, particularly in a country where all schools should be doing just that.[11]

The schools themselves are one aspect of community life for which community goals can be raised by means of co-operative study and planning. Mort and his associates have discovered, in their investigations into adaptability of schools, that one of the community conditions most closely correlated with good schools is public understanding of what education *could* do and *should* do. Note that this is different than simply knowing what the schools *are* doing; it is a matter of vision, of goals, a sensitivity to educational and community needs and possibilities. This type of educational vision on the part of the public seldom comes about simply by happenstance. It is something the schoolmen can do much about by inviting citizens of the community to work side-by-side with them in identifying and attacking school and community problems, and developing educational policy.

It is to be emphasized, therefore, that unless schools do contribute significantly to the betterment of community living, unless they serve to raise community goals, unless they lead in exemplifying democratic leadership, followership and co-operative planning, unless the community considers its schools as agents of community improvement, then the schools fail of their purpose in the American Democracy. They are but empty showcases, going through the motions of a polite, innocuous, ineffective process which is contributing little to the improvement and enrichment of life. Such a concept presents a great and exciting challenge

---

[10] Leonard Power, "Evaluating a Community Program of Education for Citizenship," in Department of Elementary School Principals, *Community Living in the Elementary School,* Twenty-fourth Yearbook, Washington, D. C., 1945, pp. 66–71.
[11] *Ibid.,* p. 71.

to the principal, who is so greatly the determiner of the educational program developed in his school.

Developing Understanding, Enthusiasm and Support for the Community's Program of Public Education

In order that tax-supported schools may be maintained it is necessary that the taxpayers be convinced that public schools are a good investment. Furthermore, it is also necessary that the general public support school improvements which necessitate increased expenditures. Such support is one of the goals of any program of school-community relations.

There have been (and are) different opinions as to the best method of gaining this support. Many educators have thought of community relations (or "public relations," as these men usually term them) as a program of "selling the schools to the public." The chief objective of such a plan is to convince the community that what is operating in the schools is as good as, or better than, programs operating elsewhere. Such a selling program is usually conceived in advertising terms; newspapers, speeches to influential groups, and school pageantry are dominant instruments. Whereas these methods frequently have been successful in achieving immediate objectives (such as plant improvements or additions, additional materials, or avoidance of budget cuts), alone they have seldom achieved basic understanding of and enthusiasm for modern educational methods and objectives.

The failure of the selling approach to achieve this latter objective has reasons which should be obvious to one familiar with the nature of the learning process. The understanding of school policies and methods which is necessary to engender support requires *learning* on the part of the community and staff. Educators should know that the least effective means of learning is simply to be told, however lucidly. Learning takes place most effectively by identifying, confronting, and solving problems, not by being told the answers. The selling approach places primary emphasis on telling, and fails to emphasize co-operative efforts at making gains in community understanding.

Furthermore, there is a danger in the selling approach which should not be overlooked; it may hinder improvement of the community's schools by engendering complacency. It is probable that many mediocre schools have been "sold" to their communities quite successfully. In such situations the community is likely to be satisfied with the schools as they are, and quite understandably resist and question efforts to bring about needed improvements. The goal of a community relations program in the schools is not, or should not be, to secure satisfaction with the status quo of the school program; rather, it is to develop intelligent support for efforts to bring about an ever-improving program, a program which is constantly striving to find better ways of educating children.

Nevertheless, while publicity techniques alone are not the answer to an enlightened program of school-community relations, such techniques need not be banished from efforts to develop public understanding and support of public education. Such methods can be a valuable part of the school-community relations program, as long as they are seen in their proper perspective and are outgrowths of and adjuncts to the broader program.[12]

SUGGESTED READINGS

See pages 394–395.

[12] Department of Elementary School Principals, *The Public and the Elementary School,* Twenty-eighth Yearbook, National Education Association, Washington, D. C., 1949, ch. VI; American Association of School Administrators, *Public Relations for America's Schools,* Twenty-eighth Yearbook, National Education Association, Washington, D. C., 1950, ch. XII.

CHAPTER XXV

PRINCIPLES OF GOOD SCHOOL-COMMUNITY RELATIONS

Now that some of the important reasons for closer school-community ties have been examined, and purposes they should serve have been proposed, some of the important guiding principles governing such relationships can be considered. The following nine principles could very likely be condensed into fewer, broader and more general ones, and could undoubtedly be increased to a larger number which would be more specific. Nothing but space would be gained by condensing them; the specifics can be covered in our discussion of each principle in turn.[1]

Know What You Believe

The elementary school principal should take steps with his staff to develop a unified outlook and philosophy of education. Internal dissension within the faculty arising from widely divergent and conflicting educational points of view, or inability of the principal or staff members to explain to laymen why they employ certain educational procedures rather than others, certainly does little to generate confidence in the school and its staff. On the other hand, when parents or other laymen discuss educational policy or method with teachers of different grades and find them holding similar points of view, and able to tell why they use certain educational procedures rather than some others, respect for and con-

[1] American Association of School Administrators, *Public Relations for America's Schools,* Twenty-eighth Yearbook, National Education Association, Washington, D. C., 1949. This reference has a somewhat different discussion of "Principles of School Public Relations," in its first chapter.

fidence in the profession is stimulated. The attitude of the community is much more likely to be, "They know what they are about." Methods of developing such a unified staff point of view are discussed on pages 412–426.

Operate a Good and Friendly School

One of the most effective means of achieving community co-operation and support is to operate an obviously good learning program, to administer the school well, and to maintain an atmosphere of warmth and friendliness. One top-level elementary school principal known to the authors is fond of saying, "I keep reminding the teachers in our school that they send home twenty-four to thirty little newspapers each day—their pupils. It is largely from them that our parents form their opinion of the school, and believe me, from those kiddies they can spot our strengths and weaknesses pretty well." A school where children are happy, and are learning those things which help them to live better does not have a difficult time in enlisting the sympathy and support of its community. Furthermore, a school that is friendly and welcoming to visitors from the community gains a good will that is forfeited by a school which is aloof, suspicious, and resentful of any visit or inquiry.

Know Your Community

It was pointed out earlier that a modern life-centered curriculum requires that the staff be familiar with the nature of the community: its characteristics, its problems, its resources. This is also a prime essential of good school-community relations.

The community survey. There are a number of means of getting to know the community. The community survey, for example, has been used extensively by schools to compile information about the community. However, some misunderstanding about the nature of the community survey has frightened many schools from attempting one. A number of authorities have discussed the school survey as though there were no other type than the comprehensive, exhaustive survey which gathers information on all aspects of community life and conditions. As a matter of fact, it is probable that few schools need to, or are able to, make such a survey. The exhaustive community survey is properly the province of the sociologist. What the school *should* do is to study those aspects of the community which clearly can yield information or identify problems which contribute to the better functioning of the learning program, the welfare of the children, or the improvement of community living. Several examples may help to illustrate this point.

In Des Moines, Iowa, the teaching staff became aware of the fact that community resources were being used on a rather haphazard basis, largely because the teachers were not familiar enough with them. Discussion of the problem led to organization for study, and to the enlistment of community members to help in the project. A survey of community resources for the learning program was made and the results embodied in a *Handbook of Community Resources.*[2] The sixth-grade class of the Edison School in Hayden, Colorado, made a survey of community history. The children and members of the community participated enthusiastically in what was apparently an exciting and rewarding learning experience for them all. The summary of outcomes stated:

1. The curiosity of the pupils in the people, places, events, and future of their own community was so aroused that many of them will continue to study and be interested in the welfare of their community.

2. *The study was instrumental in bringing about a close co-operation of the home, the school, and the community.*

3. A better understanding of the term "history" resulted.

4. Experience was gained in gathering information that is not arranged in lessons or chapters in some book of reference.[3]

This is truly an example of a life-centered type of learning.

In the city of Topaz, one of the War Relocation Authority's projects in central Utah, the teachers and administration faced the problem of familiarizing the school children with their new and unique community. Numbers of surveys of aspects of the community were carried out throughout the grades. A second-grade group studied the water supply. Other groups studied the food supply, transportation, communication, and other areas of community life until the children eventually knew their community. It is interesting that here, too, it was found that closer school and community ties were developed, and that "the school and its students became significant and important to the community at large."[4] It is to be noted that in these examples only one aspect of the community was "surveyed" at a time. Only that information pertinent to the

[2] Department of Elementary School Principals, *Community Living in the Elementary School,* Twenty-fourth Yearbook, National Education Association, Washington, D. C., 1945, pp. 33–38.

[3] *Ibid.,* pp. 45–47. Italics ours.

[4] *Ibid.,* pp. 54–57.

problem at hand was sought. One of the finest discussions of the nature, purposes and process of surveys is that of Mason.[5]

Documentary materials. Olsen points out that much can be learned about the community through the medium of documentary materials. Such sources as encyclopedias, biographical dictionaries, municipal yearbooks, The World Almanac, publications of the United States Government Printing Office, the United States Census,[6] additional information from the Bureau of the Census, reports of local studies by scientific, business, political and civic organizations all can be helpful in supplying information about the community.[7]

Membership in Community Organizations. It is important that the principal and staff know the community not only "from the outside" but from the "inside" as well. For this reason, it is desirable for them to be real community members in every sense of the word. Membership in community organizations helps to effect this. Service clubs, veterans' organizations, fraternal orders, business and professional organizations, cultural groups, churches, youth-serving organizations, and civic improvement bodies are all examples of the kinds of organizations in which membership is desirable and profitable in terms of better school-community relationships. Obviously, it is better to belong to but a few of such organizations and be effectively active in them than to be a "joiner" of many and unable, by limitations of time and energy, to contribute much to any one. One must also take care in choosing organizations to join to avoid giving reason for charges of prejudice or partisanship with respect to school affairs. This is not to say that the administrator and teacher should not take a stand on political issues. It is simply that one should be careful to avoid petty factionalism with respect to educational policies in the community.

Visit Pupils' Homes. One of the most effective means of developing community support is to maintain close contact with the homes of the pupils.

[5] In Edward G. Olsen and others, *School and Community,* Prentice-Hall, Inc., New York, 1945, p. 172. Chapter 3 by Lois Clark and 9 by Eldon Mason are excellent discourses on the problem. See also, Part II of *How to Know and How to Use Your Community,* Department of Elementary School Principals, Washington, D. C., 1942.

[6] Frank W. Hubbard, "How the Principal May Use the 1940 Census," in *How to Know and How to Use Your Community,* pp. 37–41.

[7] Olsen, *op. cit.* Chapter 4 by Brunner and Mendelsohn is an extended discussion of types and uses of documentary materials.

Naturally, the parents are those who are most interested in the schools. From eighteen to twenty hours daily of the child's life during the school year is spent in home and school. Contacts with homes of the children should therefore be frequent and systematic. The authors are reminded of a cartoon appearing in a newspaper some years ago. In the principal's office are the principal, a youngster, and another male adult; the youngster is saying, "And this, Mr. Smith, is my father, who unfortunately has never been invited here to learn of the many times I have behaved perfectly." Humorous, yes, but a telling comment on most schools in which home contacts are made only when the school has something unpleasant to discuss. Numbers of schools now make it standard procedure for teachers to schedule at least two personal interviews with one or both parents of every child in her class. Some others provide for at least one visit by the teacher to the home of each pupil during the year. One method of facilitating this is to release teachers a part of one school day each week or month. It is an imposition on teachers to expect them to make such visits in the evenings entirely on their own time. Such visits can take the place of formal reports to parents, for what better report can one make than when talking to a parent?

These latter considerations, however, are correlative to the problem under discussion, that of getting to know the community. In discussions with parents the teacher and principal can obtain insights into community living conditions such as could be obtained in no other way. This is particularly true when the interviews take place in the pupils' homes. The information thus gathered should be most valuable in suiting the educational program to the children's needs, lives and problems, and in planning educational projects for the improvement of community life.

Serve Your Community

It has been pointed out that the school is a service agency in the community. Yet many schools have served their communities little beyond taking care of the children five hours a day, five days weekly, and teaching them the three R's plus some other rather unrelated knowledge. The ways in which the school can serve its community range from those which are relatively obvious, simple, and easy, to those which are more complex, and which require considerable planning and activity.

Among the most obvious means of serving the community is that of making the facilities of the school plant available for community projects and activities. In fact, it has been puzzling to many that communities will invest large sums of money on that community institution which is the school, and then permit school authorities to deny them its use outside the thirty-odd hours weekly during which school is in session. Why should a school plant with meeting rooms, library, shops, gymnasium, auditorium, playground, and perhaps other facilities, lie idle afternoons, evenings, week ends, and all summer? What a flagrant waste of an investment of tens or hundreds of thousands of dollars! Communities which have utilized their school buildings for community recreational, cultural, educational, and civic purposes value their school much more because of that fact. The school tends to be considered an integral part of the community, not simply that institution where the children are kept under control for five hours a day.

A second type of community service which is common among community-conscious schools is that of participating in such community projects as the Community Chest drive, the Red Cross campaign, clean-up campaigns, safety campaigns, civic beautification projects, patriotic celebrations, and the like.

These are some of the service possibilities which are relatively obvious and simple. Some schools, however, have gone beyond these relatively trite (but nevertheless effective) forms of community service. They have made constructive studies of intercultural relations in the community, of housing conditions, of health hazards, of recreational needs, of conditions fostering juvenile delinquency, and have handled their results in such fashion as to bring about civic action on their recommendations to rectify undesirable conditions they uncovered.[8] In *Learning the Ways of Democracy,* four levels of student participation in community activities are identified.[9]

1. Firsthand study of community conditions and problems by means of excursions, field trips, and informative surveys. This may involve no action by the students beyond the recognition of the facts discovered. (Note that this is simply a level of participation, not of service. The activities which it would properly include are those discussed above under "Know Your Community.")

[8] See Part IV, "Meeting New Community Needs," in Department of Elementary School Principals, *op. cit.,* Twenty-fourth Yearbook.
[9] Educational Policies Commission, *Learning the Ways of Democracy,* National Education Association, Washington, D. C., p. 327.

2. Participation of school youth in community activities which are under the direction of adults . . . These involve action by the students, but the action is determined by others.

3. Activities in which school youth help to plan and execute, sharing responsibility with adults.

4. Activities which students initiate, plan, and carry out, taking advantage of the counsel of adults, but nevertheless bearing the responsibilities themselves.

Accompanying this analysis in the above publication, there are numerous and absorbing accounts of service projects carried out by youth in communities of all types, and representing all four of these levels. Morris Mitchell, of the Macedonia Co-operative Community, Georgia, presents an interesting discussion of service projects,[10] and in another pamphlet, lists 167 "thumbnail" examples of youth service to the community.[11] This is a most suggestive listing, including not only examples of the more usual types of projects, but such interesting ventures as the development of co-operatives, fire prevention demonstrations, pest extermination, mosquito control, smoke nuisance control, and the building of a new school. In Detroit, Michigan, pupils attacked the problem of getting out the vote, bringing about significant increases in the number of voters in the districts embraced by their schools.[12] Such projects as these make the school a vital force in the community. They improve the "public relations" of the school, serve as real and life-centered content for the school curriculum, and contribute to the improved quality of community living, thus serving all three of the goals of school-community relations which we proposed earlier.

School staffs should not rush blindly into projects for the sake of doing projects, however. Nor can projects be sporadic and spasmodic, tacked on as the tail, so to speak, to the kite of the usual book-centered, academic program. They must be an integral part of the school's learning program, and be given continuous emphasis throughout the school and school year. They should be an outgrowth of the development of

---

[10] Olsen, *op. cit.,* ch. 12.

[11] Morris R. Mitchell and others, *Youth Has a Part to Play,* American Education Fellowship Service Center Pamphlet, Hinds, Hayden & Eldredge, Inc., New York, 1942.

[12] "Little Vote-Getters," reported from *American Heritage,* December 1948, in *Education Digest,* vol. XIV, February 1949, p. 16.

educational beliefs on the part of the staff that children's learning takes place best when children are identifying, studying, and doing something about actual problems of living. Naturally, such a philosophy and program will not spring into being full-blown. Small beginnings will have to be made, and certainly some service projects are better than none. Such projects should not be considered as "tricks of the trade," or monotony-relieving diversions, but should be the expression of a developing philosophy of education on the part of the administration, staff and community.

Encourage Your Community to Serve the School

Community relations must be a "two-way street." We are all aware of the principle that one of the best ways to make a friend is to permit him to perform some service for you. Applied to the community, this principle has several advantages. First, as implied above, it tends to form closer school-community bonds. Citizens who contribute time, effort, talent, and materials to the school then have a personal stake in that school. In a very real sense it becomes *their* school, and they support it loyally. Second, the arm of the educator is extended, bringing into the school specialized services and assistance that the staff alone could not supply. Third, it enriches and improves the learning program of the children, and increases their understanding of and respect for the abilities and services of community members.

There are many ways in which the community may serve the school. Here, again, however, these services cannot be left to chance, but must be definitely planned for and encouraged. Principals who have parent-teacher organizations in their schools know, for example, that the organization will be little more than a desultory social affair unless the school staff and P.T.A. officers take positive steps to encourage concern with school problems. One school made a survey of the specialized abilities and talents of community members, and has them catalogued in a file. New information is continuously sought to keep the file up-to-date. When the school needs assistance in music, dance, construction, certain aspects of science, costuming, customs and articles of other lands, hobbies, etc., it simply consults its file and requests community members who have the abilities or backgrounds needed to help out. They get an enthusiastic response. People like to have their special talents and abilities recognized and made use of. One principal who translated this into action stated,

"If the eighty-three parents who are on the staff . . . were to neglect their duties, the school library would not be open, ten hobby groups would not meet, milk would not be sold during the noon hour, the noon-hour recreation room would be closed, and the visual education and school publicity services would be seriously disrupted. For these parents do not 'assist'; they are 'in charge' of these activities, being subject only to the supervision of the principal, as are other staff members."[13] Such participation obviously serves to break down the traditional isolation of the schools and enriches the learning program immeasurably.

One group of schools in the Metropolitan School Study Council of New York gathered the facts on the large amount of parent participation in their school programs. Impressed with the common success of their schools in this respect, they wrote a description of the different ways in which that participation was enlisted and administered, with suggestions for others who might wish to try the same thing, and intriguingly named it, *Fifty Teachers to a Classroom*.[14]

Provide for Broad Participation of the Community in the Study of School-Community Problems

It can be gathered from the above discussion that co-operative school-community action is perhaps the most effective means of eliminating the stubborn barrier between them. When school and community work together on problems of common concern, a sense of the essential kinship and oneness which should exist between them is fostered. There are many opportunities for the school and the citizens of the school community to plan together for improved educational facilities, broadened facilities for recreation, improvement of the financial status of the teaching staff, elimination of safety hazards for children, problems of district reorganization, and the like. Likewise, the school can participate with the community on such community problems as community health, housing, intercultural relations, library, increasing the number of voters, adult education, and the care of very young children. Far more opportunities of these kinds exist than have been capitalized upon by the schools in general, although some pioneer schools have blazed trails in this area.

In Newton, Massachusetts, parents who were critical of the school

[13] "Eighty-Three Parents Are on Our Staff," in Department of Elementary School Principals, *op. cit.*, Twenty-fourth Yearbook, p. 120.
[14] Committee on Human Resources of the Metropolitan School Study Council, *Fifty Teachers to a Classroom*, The Macmillan Company, New York, 1950.

system were included in joint committees of parents and teachers to study school problems. As a result, they worked constructively on those problems instead of spending their energies in destructive criticism, and became strong supporters of the schools.[15]

In the Bronx Park area of New York City, a project has been initiated under the aegis of the Metropolitan School Study Council of Teachers College, Columbia University, which is enlisting broad citizen participation in the study of school problems. Dr. Paul Mort, originator of the project, believes such local citizen-teacher co-operative study of schools is one way to keep the schools of otherwise "impersonal" big-city school systems close to the people and sensitive to local pupils' needs.

When co-operative ventures of such sorts are undertaken, both pupils and adults gain new insights into the possibilities of democratic co-operative action, and school and community become one. There is then no need of "bridges" to span the moat which usually isolates the school; the moat ceases to exist, and the school becomes what it should be, an integral and functional part of community life.

Establish Working Relationships with Other Organized Community Groups Interested in Children's Welfare and Community Betterment

In every community there are organized groups seeking many of the same objectives as the schools. Unless their efforts are co-ordinated, there tends to be much waste effort and duplication of function. Most schools have established contact with some of these groups, but it is safe to say that few schools have realized the full possibilities of co-ordinated planning and effort with these institutions and agencies. One issue of the Bulletin of the Department of Elementary School Principals contains a number of accounts of the working together of the school with such "auxiliary agencies" as the Boy and Girl Scouts, the Junior Red Cross, the health department and the parent-teacher association.[16] Close functional relationships with each of these agencies and institutions should be standard practice.

Going a step farther, however, some communities have formed "co-ordinating councils" which serve to integrate and systematize the work of these agencies in working upon community problems. It behooves the

[15] J. B. Everett, "Parents—Potential School Leaders," *Educational Leadership,* vol. VII, October 1949, pp. 11–12.
[16] *The National Elementary Principal,* Bulletin of the Department of Elementary School Principals, vol. XXVII, April 1948.

school, as the institution whose influence and function in the community is most pervasive, to ally itself with such a co-ordinating organization. In doing so it is but taking its rightful part as one of the important community-serving agencies.

Keep Your Community Informed About the School

Schoolmen are currently much concerned about the problem of "public relations." Publications of several national educational organizations, including the Department of Elementary School Principals, have been devoted to phases of the problem,[17] and articles and books on school public relations and publicity have increased appreciably in recent years. It will be recognized that our discussion to this point has been dealing precisely with that topic. Schools which have achieved close community integration have found that little attention had to be given separately to "public relations." In these schools the problem of public relations is placed in a broad setting, and all aspects of the school program have public relations significance. Publicity techniques become a part, and only a part, of the entire plan for informing the public and securing better public understanding and support for the schools.

Nevertheless, we must not make the mistake of assuming that information and publicity about the schools will take care of itself, and we should not look down our noses at use of legitimate methods of "beating our own drum" about the successes and problems of our schools. It is an obligation of the principal and staff to make certain that all segments of the community and the broader public are kept aware of the school's goals, procedures, and achievements. To accomplish this, schools employ a number of procedures usually termed "publicity" or "public relations" techniques. Since an extended discussion of these techniques is beyond the scope of this volume, the reader is referred to the excellent discussions to be found elsewhere.[18]

[17] American Association of School Administrators, *Public Relations for America's Schools,* Twenty-eighth Yearbook, National Education Association, Washington, D. C., 1950; Association for Supervision and Curriculum Development, *Building Public Confidence in the Schools,* National Education Association, Washington, D. C., 1949; Department of Elementary School Principals, *The Public and the Elementary School,* Twenty-eighth Yearbook, National Education Association, Washington, D. C., 1949.

[18] American Association of School Administrators, *op. cit.,* Twenty-eighth Yearbook, ch. XII; Department of Elementary School Principals, *op. cit.,* Twenty-eighth Yearbook, ch. VI; Benjamin Fine, *Educational Publicity,* Harper and Brothers, New York, 1943; Gunnar Horn, *Public School Publicity,* Inor Publishing Company, New York, 1948.

The staff and administration should seek to make themselves as competent as possible in the methods of each of these media. News reporting and radio script-writing, for example, while not particularly difficult for school purposes, do not "come naturally." There are published sources which offer much help, however, and these should be diligently consulted. If the responsibility for different phases of the program is delegated to various staff members, they can include courses on the problem in summer session work, or during the year if a university is nearby. Members in the community with specialized competencies in these areas can be enlisted in the program, and might actually "take charge," under the principal's supervision, of some parts of the program. A fact to give us pause is that unless certain of these media are well handled, the effect may be the opposite of that intended. A poorly planned and executed radio program, for example, is likely to have negative public relations results.

Observe the Principles of Democratic Group Process

Our ninth and final principle has to do with the human relations aspects of the public relations program. If they are not well handled, they can vitiate the effectiveness of the entire program of school-community relations; for, after all, the program is essentially a program of relations among people. Professional members of the school staff should be functionally conversant with the methods of group discussion, of group leadership, of parliamentary procedure, and of group work on problems. If care is taken to observe democratic principles including, above all, consideration and respect for the opinions, rights, abilities, and feelings of others, it is more than likely that fine relationships between school and community will result.

SUMMARY: THE COMMUNITY SCHOOL

It can be seen, then, that one's beliefs concerning the source and nature of learning experiences has a determining influence upon one's point of view as to the relationship which should exist between school and community. The current trend of thought on the part of many leading educational thinkers and in our "lighthouse" school systems appears to be in the direction of rooting the educational program more and more firmly in the everyday living problems of the pupils, problems which they face as they try to fit themselves into community life as acceptable citizens and integrated individuals. There is also a strong trend toward wider participation on the part of teachers, pupils, parents, and other community members in the formulation of the policies and program of the school, a trend which is consistent with democratic principles.

Such a point of view certainly implies positive, pleasant, and co-operative association of school and community. In addition, current problems of public school financing and of progressing educational theory and practice actually demand that the public understand and willingly support the changes which are necessary to provide all children equally with the best educational facilities and program we are capable of providing. American schools are by law and in fact the people's schools. Yet they have, in many cases, become dangerously far removed from the people. Unless this situation is corrected, our system of free public schools may find itself being supplanted by some other less effective and less democratic institution.

The thesis of the foregoing pages is that desirable community relations are a natural outgrowth of a life-centered educational program. Such relations cannot be developed simply by talking about them, by "selling the schools to the public," by publicity alone. The key to such relations is the co-operative working together of community and school on common problems and projects. Carried to its logical conclusion, this point of view results in what has come to be termed "the community school." In a school of this type, the "public relations" program is not a thing apart; good public relations result naturally from the school's daily functioning in and with the community.[19]

It is unrealistic, of course, to expect the usual American school suddenly to become a community school. That is not the way it happens. However, a school which studies the life needs of its pupils, informs itself about the conditions within which the children live and grow twenty-four hours a day, and tries to develop a program that will help the children to live and grow better in that environment cannot help becoming more and more of a community school. When it tries to improve the community conditions themselves, then it becomes a community school in fact.

[19] S. E. Torsten Lund, *The School-Centered Community*, Anti-Defamation League of B'nai B'rith, New York, 1949.

It should be noted that this emphasis on making the immediate living problems of the pupils the starting point for learning does not mean that the schools should be provincial, that they should not look outside the borders of the community. Most of the common living problems of children and of communities are duplicated in one form or another in other communities, in this country and throughout the world. In fact, clues to the solution of these problems are usually to be found in the ways people in other communities and in other times went about solving these problems.

Thus, the study of their personal and community problems will, under the leadership of understanding teachers and principals, lead the children out into the study and understanding of the living of other people of other lands and of other times. In so doing, it will help the pupils and the community better to gain perspective and see the time and place setting of their own problems, so as to be able more intelligently to do something about them. A school which helps its pupils and its community to do this is operating a practical, down-to-earth, effective and psychologically and democratically sound program, and is moving away from the politely theoretical character of the bookish academic program which has characterized American schools since their inception.

Will elementary principals accept this challenge? On their answer depends in great measure the nature of our educational development for the future, for principals are largely the determiners of the nature of their schools. On the nature of our educational development may well depend the future of American democracy. If principals can lead in the development of the kind of school-community relations which stem from community participation in the development of a truly functional education, a tremendous contribution will have been made to the preservation and extension of our American way of life.

SUGGESTED READINGS

American Association of School Administrators, *Public Relations for America's Schools,* National Education Association, Washington, D. C., 1950.

Association for Supervision and Curriculum Development, *Building Public Confidence in the Schools,* National Education Association, Washington, D. C., 1949.

Clapp, Elsie R., *Community Schools in Action,* Viking Press, New York, 1940.

Committee of 14, *Public Action for Powerful Schools,* Metropolitan School Study Council, Bureau of Publications, Teachers College, Columbia University, New York, 1949.

Department of Elementary School Principals, *How to Know and How to Use Your Community,* National Education Association, Washington, D. C., 1942.

————, *Community Living in the Elementary School,* Twenty-fourth Yearbook, National Education Association, Washington, D. C., 1945.

————, *The Public and the Elementary School,* Twenty-eighth Yearbook, National Education Association, Washington, D. C., 1949.

Everett, Samuel, *The Community School,* D. Appleton–Century Company, New York, 1938.

Fine, Benjamin, *Educational Publicity,* Harper and Brothers, New York, 1943.

Horn, Gunnar, *Public School Publicity,* Inor Publishing Company, New York, 1948.

Lund, S. E. Torsten, *The School-Centered Community,* Anti-Defamation League of B'nai B'rith, New York, 1949.

Olsen, Edward G., and others, *School and Community,* Prentice-Hall, Inc., New York, 1945.

————, *School and Community Programs,* Prentice-Hall, Inc., New York, 1949.

Clapp, Elsie R., Community Schools in Action, Viking Press, New York, 1939.

Committee of 15, Public Action for Powerful Schools, Mercer Cottage School Study Council, Bureau of Publications, Teachers College, Columbia University, New York, 1949.

Department of Elementary School Principals, What to Know and How to Use Your Community, National Education Association, Washington, D. C., 1942.

———, Community Living in the Elementary School, Twenty-fourth Yearbook, National Education Association, Washington, D. C., 1945.

———, The Public and the Elementary School, Twenty-eighth Yearbook, National Education Association, Washington, D. C., 1949.

Everett, Samuel, The Community School, D. Appleton-Century Company, New York, 1938.

Frost, Benjamin, Educational Publicity, Harper and Brothers, New York, 1947.

Hunt, Gunnar, Public School Publicity, Inor Publishing Company, New York, 1948.

Lund, S. E. Torsten, The School-Centered Community, Anti-Defamation League of B'nai Brith, New York, 1949.

Olsen, Edward G., and others, School and Community, Prentice-Hall, Inc., New York, 1945.

———, School and Community Program, Prentice-Hall, Inc., New York, 1939.

Part VII
INSTRUCTIONAL IMPROVEMENT AND TEACHER GROWTH IN SERVICE

A slight noise from the doorway caught her attention. She saw the burnished knob turn and watched the door swing open slowly and silently on its well-oiled hinges. Her heart leaped in her breast as she recognized him. Softly he stepped into the room and, careful to make no disturbance, made his way noiselessly along the left wall. He chose his vantage-point carefully, and from it his eyes seemed to miss no detail. She watched him tensely, trying to pull her scattered thoughts together, but was shaken anew as his hand went to his pocket and withdrew the black, flat object he habitually carried there. With a great effort of will she tore her eyes from him . . .

An episode from a mystery thriller? No; simply a description of a principal making a routine supervisory visit in the manner recommended by some authorities a decade and a half ago or more. Even today it is characteristic of practice in many schools.

The fundamental changes which are taking place in the culture and in education, however, have influenced the common conception of supervision considerably. The situation depicted above is becoming less typical as less formal and more effective means are evolved for the improvement of education. These changes, like many others in education, have been the cause of considerable confusion and misunderstanding. If one does not employ the older supervisory practices, what does one do? Some have suggested that the position of "supervisor" be abolished and that the classroom visit be elimi-

nated as a supervisory technique. Should the classroom visit and the supervisory conference be discarded? What about the demonstration lesson? How are teachers to be evaluated? What is to be done about weak teachers?

To answer these questions satisfactorily, and to come to some consistent and reasonable conclusions, it is necessary to understand the relationship between the kind of education desired and the methods which will be effective in developing it, for, like all other educational practices, supervision is a function of the learning program.

At the outset of this discussion, it will be well to make clear that this is not an attempt to cover all aspects of the tremendous problem of instructional improvement and teacher growth in service. Volumes have been written on the topic. Within the limited space available an attempt will be made to clarify the "modern" concept in its relation to the elementary school principal in his own school. System-wide supervisory activities and problems and their administration are outside the scope of this discussion.

CHAPTER XXVI

THE CHANGING DIRECTION
OF SUPERVISION

The changes which have taken (and are taking) place in instructional supervision can be divided, theoretically, into three aspects: (1) changes in purpose, (2) changes in scope, and (3) changes in nature. Each of these is so much a part of the others that it is difficult to separate them, even for purposes of discussion. In their totality, however, they are outgrowths of the changes in the purpose, scope, and nature of education itself, and of cultural developments and influences which are the reason for the modifications that have taken place in educational thought and practice.

Types of Supervision

As a result, there have been a number of types of educational supervision in the American schools, each of them reflecting certain purposes, certain points of view concerning the nature of teaching and education, and certain points of view of what democracy in education implies in practice. An excellent statement of types of supervision is made by Barr, Burton and Brueckner.[1] They identify four types: laissez-faire, coercive, training and guidance, and democratic leadership. Whereas it is not possible to draw sharp chronological lines between these four types in time, they seem to have developed roughly in that order. It is important to note, however, that none of them is an extinct museum piece as yet; all four types are still to be found in American schools.

[1] A. S. Barr, W. H. Burton, and L. J. Brueckner, *Supervision*, D. Appleton–Century Company, 2nd ed., New York, 1947, pp. 6–15.

Laissez-faire supervision. The laissez-faire type of supervision is actually not constructive supervision at all. Its clearest expression was in the early inspectorial supervisory methods, in which the teacher and his pupils were observed, but nothing was done to help him to improve the job he was doing. Frequently the first intimation he had of what the inspecting officer thought of the teacher's work was the fact that the latter's teaching contract was or was not renewed for the next year. The chief function or purpose of this type of "supervision" (if we can dignify this practice by that name) is to rate the teacher or to appraise his effectiveness for one reason or another.

Although this type of supervision once was characteristic of an earlier period in American education, it has by no means disappeared from the scene. Like economic laissez-faire, many have mistaken it for democracy. Many are the principals who take pride in their "democratic" attitude toward their teachers. "I let them do as they like," they say. "They may teach what they wish in the way they wish. All I ask is that their classes measure up on the national norms. Yessir, no autocratic dictation to our teachers here. We're democratic!"

As the reader is very well aware, this is not democracy, but spinelessness, and an evasion of the principal's responsibility as a professional leader. Whereas there undoubtedly are teachers who want to be let alone —professionally, at least—most teachers welcome some help in the job they are trying to do. This is particularly true of inexperienced new teachers, for whom their first teaching job is frequently a sharp break with their previous life, and for whom the assumption of complete responsibility for teaching a class without constant supervision is an unprecedented and frightening experience. The principal who follows a "hands off" policy in supervision will not gain the respect of his teachers for his professional leadership, for he will be exerting none, and he will be evading his responsibility for the improvement of his school's learning program.

Coercive supervision. This concept is closely bound up with the curriculum and instructional philosophy which came to permeate almost all our schools, and even now is by no means dispelled. As public education was extended to all, the subject curriculum and the graded school came to be the distinguishing features of its pattern. Two of the assumptions basic to this pattern are that out of all the knowledge available, there is a certain well-defined body which it is desirable for all pupils to learn; and second, that it is possible and desirable to establish an annual time-table, applicable to practically all children, for the learning of it. It should be clear that this is an authoritarian concept, which attributes to some authority the omniscience necessary to make these truly momentous decisions. For those of such mind, it is easy to assume also that there are known best methods of teaching this graded subject curriculum, and that certain authorities, in the persons of principals, supervisors, and superintendents, know what these best methods are. Persons possessed of such a philosophy find it easy also to believe that the most effective means of getting teachers to the point where they teach the prescribed subject matter on schedule, and in the manner which the supervisor thinks to be the most effective, is to use coercive methods.

In this type of supervision, teachers are visited by the principal for an observation period. Following the observation of the lesson, there is a conference between the teacher and the principal, in which the teacher is commended for those respects in which his lesson coincides with what the principal "knows" is good teaching, and then has pointed out to him his errors of omission and commission. Follow-up visits are made to check on whether he modifies his teaching in conformance with the dictates of the principal. Before the enactment of tenure laws, it was easier to enforce the principal's mandates; such enforcement is still possible in the case of teachers not yet on tenure, or in those states and districts in which salary increments are awarded on the basis of merit ratings.

It should be needless to point out the reasons why such a type of supervision is undesirable. It has been observed several times elsewhere in this volume that the assumptions which underlie this approach are fallacious. It is ridiculous to entertain the idea that some "authority" or group of "authorities" should be able to decide those things which children whom they do not know should learn. The idea that there is any one best way of teaching is also now being rejected, and there is overwhelming evidence that coercion is ineffective in achieving anything but superficial observance of the dictated behavior. Such supervision is also most inconsistent with democratic principles. It does not respect the personalities of those whom it affects, and fails to include them (the teachers) in the making of the decisions most vital to their work in the classroom; its conception is authoritarian throughout. Furthermore, it violates the principles of good mental hygiene, being excellently designed to produce feelings of inadequacy and insecurity, frustrations, fears, and repressed antagonisms. It is destructive of good human relationships and is certain to cause the teacher to hide those weaknesses in which she is most in need of help.

This analysis of coercive supervision puts it, quite unintentionally, in a somewhat diabolical light. It is to be noted, however, that those who employed it did so (and still do) with the best of intentions. Their ultimate objective was that of all of us: to improve the quality of education carried on in our schools. For the most part, such persons are quite unaware that they are acting in an autocratic fashion, or that the assumptions under which they are operating are false. In fact, it is likely that most of them have given little thought to the social and philosophic assumptions governing their practice. Consequently, it is unfair to depict them (as has sometimes been done) as ogres, villains, stuffed shirts, and pompous executives. Like all of us, they were (and are) educators doing their jobs in the manner they believed best. This in no manner justifies the process, however, anymore than our own good intentions will serve to justify our errors in the eyes of future generations of educators.

Supervision as training and guidance. The early decades of this century saw significant changes in educational theory and practice. Numbers of the factors mentioned earlier in this discussion, and elsewhere in this book, combined to change teaching from being a rote memorizing process to a process that sought to stimulate children's interests and to enlist their active participation in the learning process. It was increasingly recognized that education should be the process of guiding growth. The emphasis was still, as yet, on the learning of subjects; growth was still conceived primarily in terms of bookish learning and academic skills and generalizations. Teachers and supervisors were learning, however, how inefficient coercion is as a teaching technique, and realizing the importance of the learner's voluntary co-operation in the learning process.

The same forces which brought about this change left their imprint on the nature of instructional supervision. Instead of trying to force teachers to follow prescribed methods, emphasis was placed upon the teaching of teachers. By this time, new teachers were entering classrooms with an appreciable amount of preservice preparation in normal schools; supervision assumed the task of continuing that training on the job. A new assumption was implicit: that teachers were themselves interested in doing a better job. Supervision now became the process of teaching them how to do it. This point of view, which is now the prevailing one, is well expressed in the following statement:

> The purpose of supervision, broadly stated, is the improvement of instruction through the direction, guidance and training of teachers. The implication of this view is that instruction may be improved and that the efficiency of teachers may be increased . . . The importance of the situation in the elementary school warrants the appointment of a principal to render constructive assistance in training the teachers in service and in organizing and directing the instruction in his school.[2]

Whereas the change in emphasis is important, a moment's thought will indicate that many of the old assumptions are still there. It is still assumed that there is a known best method of teaching. It is still assumed that, somehow, the principal "has the word," that he is the one who knows best how to teach. It is still assumed that it is the teacher's duty to "improve" in the pattern approved by her "superiors." Many authorities observe that this type of instructional supervision now dominates the educational scene. In many places the belief prevails that the best teacher (or one of the best teachers) is the logical person to fill the job left vacant by the principal who is leaving. For this reason schools frequently (though not invariably) lose a top-level classroom teacher without gaining a good principal, for a good teacher does not necessarily have the attributes necessary to a good administrator; the reverse, of course, is also true. Under the older, more limited conception of supervision as the teaching of teachers, however, it is logical to select the person who knows best how to do the job of teaching, and to put him in a position where he can teach others how to do it.

Supervision as democratic professional leadership. The sharpening and enrichment of the functional meaning of democracy, which have already been mentioned, recent contributions of psychological research to our knowledge of the learning process, current emphasis on the practical importance of good human relationships, and a developing understanding of the "dynamics" and processes of group work all have contributed to the formulation of a philosophy of supervision which is now emerg-

[2] W. R. Reavis, P. R. Pierce, and E. H. Stullken, *The Elementary School: Its Organization and Administration,* rev. ed., University of Chicago Press, Chicago, 1938, p. 293.

ing. It is difficult to present a brief characterization of this newer point of view and way of working which will be very meaningful to a reader, but salient points of difference between this and the older types will be pointed out, and important characteristics of professional leadership in the improvement of the learning program will be identified.

It was observed earlier that the differences between the older and the newer types of supervision could be separated into three categories: purpose, scope, and nature. These will be separated, for purposes of discussion, despite the fact that they are inseparably related in operation.

Purpose. Whereas it is true that under both orientations the ultimate purpose of supervision is the improvement of the learning program, certain immediate purposes can be differentiated for the contrast we wish to make. Under the philosophy which is now obsolescent (though still prevalent), it was believed that the best way to improve the learning program was to improve the teachers. Supervision was therefore focused on the teacher, and its immediate purpose was to teach him how to teach better. The approach was direct, and assumed that the principal had knowledge and ability sufficiently superior to that of the teachers to qualify him to do that job.

The purpose of modern supervision is subtly different from this. Instead of focusing its attention directly on the teacher, it concerns itself with the *improvement of the total teaching-learning situation.* While the concept of supervision as "the training of teachers in service" found considerable justification in the fact that teachers were at that time lamentably undertrained, such a situation no longer exists in such degree. Today's teachers are less in need of training in service, more in need of able leadership to foster their growth as teachers and to co-ordinate their efforts to operate a good school. The purpose of modern supervision, therefore, is to supply the leadership which will help the staff to improve the instructional situation, and in doing that, to grow professionally themselves. Instead of showing or telling teachers how better to do their jobs, the supervisor or principal works with them in the study and analysis of the total teaching-learning situation in efforts to find out how to improve that situation. Under these conditions, one authority has noted that "the improvement of teachers is not so much a supervisory function in which teachers participate as it is a teacher function in which supervisors participate."[3]

[3] Barr, Burton, and Brueckner, *op. cit.,* p. 10.

A concise definition of supervision was formulated by Elliott in 1914, and has been much quoted since: "Supervisory control is concerned with *what* should be taught; *when* it should be taught; *to whom, by whom, how,* and *to what purpose.*"[4] That definition is still valid in many respects, but there is one significant change necessary to make it currently acceptable; that is the deletion of the word *control.* Under the older conception the what, when, to whom, by whom, how and the purpose were all decided in the higher administrative levels, after which *control* of the teachers was exercised by the supervisor to assure that they carried out those decisions. Under the modern conception, the school instructional staff, including the principal and others with supervisory responsibility, together and in groups study the factors in the learning situation, and *together* decide upon the what, when, how and why. The principal's responsibility is to *release and co-ordinate,* not to control, the creative abilities of the teachers.

It can be seen then, that there has been a significant shift in the purpose of supervision, a shift which has occurred because of the change in viewpoint concerning the scope and nature of the process. Instead of imposing upon teachers "better" methods of teaching, the principal works with the teachers in groups and as individuals to help them *and himself* to discover how the total teaching-learning situation might be improved. Instead of striving for the blind adoption of techniques, he works for basic understanding of workable principles and generalizations which teachers can translate into effective practices adapted to the needs of the situation.

Scope. It should be evident by now that the scope of modern supervision is considerably broader than under the older philosophy. Usually the scope of the supervisor's job has been largely limited to the activities of classroom visits, individual teacher conferences, recommending books and other instructional materials, teacher rating, and "study groups," in which the supervisor usually taught the teachers some aspect of the teaching job.

Now, however, the principal and teachers are to be concerned with the *total teaching-learning situation.* What does this mean? Certainly it includes the teachers, the classroom, and the pupils. It also includes the curriculum, the materials of instruction, *and the administrative factors*

---

[4] E. C. Elliott, *City School Supervision,* World Book Company, Yonkers, N. Y., 1914, p. 12.

involved. Such administrative factors as scheduling, school and curriculum organization, policies of pupil progress, methods of pupil evaluation and of reporting to parents, allocation of funds for materials and equipment, the manner of selecting and administering those materials and equipment, and others all affect the teaching-learning situation, and are subject to study and appraisal by the teachers and principal, and in some respects by the pupils and their parents.

Furthermore, the evolving point of view holds that the curriculum should be life-centered. In that case, the nature and needs of the learners, and factors in their community and family life are rightly part of that teaching-learning situation. It is evident, therefore, that the scope of supervision has broadened considerably, and that all the factors which affect the learning and growing of the pupils are defensibly the province of supervision.

Nature. Respects in which the nature of modern supervision differs from earlier types have been implicit in the foregoing discussion. It may help, however, to make them more explicit here.

1. Modern supervision is *co-operative.* Instead of directing attention solely to the improvement of individual teachers, it enlists the co-operative efforts of the entire staff in the study of the educational problems of the school. Much attention is directed to the function and operation of group processes, and the contribution of all members, *as members of the group,* is provided for and encouraged. Leadership on the part of all members is provided for and encouraged, and not held to be the sole prerogative of the principal. Such an approach is consistent with the democratic principle that all persons shall have a part in formulating the policies which govern their daily living, but its justification is not simply that this approach is democratic. Experiment and experience have taught us that such co-operative study and decision-making result in a more fundamental understanding of the reasons for the adopted policies and procedures than a procedure which imposes methods and techniques. Furthermore, it is much more likely that teachers who have participated in such democratic methods of working in their professional relationships with principals and supervisors, and have experienced their effectiveness, will be more inclined and able to use such methods in their classrooms. This in itself would mean a tremendous stride forward in our efforts to develop an education well suited to a democratic state.

2. Modern supervision is considerably *broader in its scope* than were earlier concepts and practices. Its functions are much more diverse. The usual types of supervision have been so much engrossed with the study and improvement of the individual teacher that the supervisory visit and follow-up conference have come to be known as "the supervisory act." This one technique loomed large in the supervisory picture, and most of the other supervisory functions derived from it. In the newer approach, the supervisory visit is different both in nature and in function. Because "the teaching-learning situation" is coming to be so broadly construed, its improvement now includes concerns and activities which formerly were considered to be outside the scope of teaching and supervision. The functions of supervision, including visits to the classroom, derive from the group's study and appraisal of problems in the local situation; therefore, the functions are unpredictable in their specifics, and are most varied. They encompass as many as possible of the conditions and influences which affect the learning and growing of the pupils.

3. The relationship of the modern supervisor to the teaching staff is a *peer relationship*. Instead of being considered as the authority who "teaches" the teachers and determines the policies which they shall carry out, he is considered as a person who is freed of teaching responsibilities so that he may serve the staff in co-ordinating and facilitating their efforts to improve the work of the school. He is not, as in the past and currently prevailing conception, a superior; he is an equal charged with the responsibility of unifying his staff and releasing their human resources in a common attack on common problems. Under this conception the supervisor does not educate the teachers; he offers specialized skill in helping them to educate themselves, and in the process is himself "educated."[5]

4. The emerging concept of supervision is *experimental* in nature. The authoritarian philosophy, in its assumption that the curriculum and the methods of teaching it are fixed, frowns upon deviations from the established order of things. In the more extreme expressions

---

[5] For excellent discussions of the role of leadership in group processes see Association for Supervision and Curriculum Development, *Group Processes in Supervision*, National Education Association, Washington, D. C., 1948; Association for Supervision and Curriculum Development, *Leadership Through Supervision*, National Education Association, Washington, D. C., 1946; A. Miel, *Changing the Curriculum*, D. Appleton–Century Company, New York, 1946, particularly chs. IV and VI; K. Wiles, *Supervision for Better Schools*, Prentice-Hall, Inc., New York, 1950; W. A. Yauch, *Improving Human Relations in School Administration*, Harper and Brothers, New York, 1949, particularly ch. III.

of such a philosophy, experimentation by teachers is considered to be insubordination. This is one of the factors which have operated to perpetuate educational practices which are outmoded, and which have been demonstrated to be ineffective if not actually harmful. In contrast, the experimentalism which is discouraged by all forms of authoritarianism is the very life of the democratic approach. One of the foundation stones of the emerging philosophy and practice of supervision is the belief that current practice should always be questioned, examined, evaluated, and placed under the searching light of critical analysis, and that such analysis should be applied to supervisory practice itself. It further believes that once such an analysis has been made, something should be done about it. Any aspect of the learning situation found to be ineffective or detrimental to the achievement of a better situation is dropped or modified accordingly. Thus, the principal, instead of enforcing or attempting to bring about a predetermined pattern of educational practice, leads the staff in the constant search for better and more effective ways of doing their job, believing always that no best way has yet been found.

The foregoing characteristics clearly imply that any distinction between supervision and administration is either unrealistic or, as in this discussion, is simply for convenience of interpretation. We can say, then, that modern supervision is more clearly identified as an administrative function than ever before. This conception more or less completes an historical cycle. The earliest elementary school principals were assigned supervisory duties as a part of their function. With the expansion attendant upon the development of free public education, the distinction between the supervisory and the administrative function became greater, finding its fullest expression in those cases where separate supervisors of elementary education and of special subjects were employed to take over the greater part of the supervisory burden, implying that the principal should concern himself primarily with other administrative duties. This point of view prevailed not only in educational administration, but in other fields of administration as well. Administration came to be identified with the management and executive function, and was considered to be concerned primarily with such matters as budget, supplies, employment, administration of records, building planning and construction, and the definition of policy.

More recently there has been a reversal of this trend in administrative philosophy. This change is well illustrated by a quotation from a discussion of leadership in social work.

We now identify administration with process rather than techniques; we see administrative functions as responsibilities widely distributed in contrast with authority centered in one individual; and we place administration in its proper setting as an inherent part of the whole social work process rather than merely a tool, adjunct, or facilitating device . . . We are beginning to see that *we cannot divorce the process of administration from the content of the . . . program or service.*[6]

Kimball Wiles' most readable discussion is one of the most modern in educational literature. Some idea of his approach may be gathered from the major divisions of his book, in which he discusses supervision as: (1) skill in leadership, (2) skill in human relations, (3) skill in group process, (4) skill in personnel administration, and (5) skill in evaluation.[7]

If the scope of supervision is as broad as is here proposed, and if it enlists extensive teacher participation, the staff and the principal will be dealing with both instructional *and* administrative problems, for administrative policies and procedures are a part of the teaching-learning situation. Thus the program of instructional improvement will deal with problems which formerly were solely the prerogative of the administrator: promotion policy, method of reporting to parents, selection of textbooks, and budgeting, for example. In so doing, the efficiency of the entire enterprise is enhanced because everybody on the staff knows *what* is going on and has a better understanding of *why* and *how,* avoiding the necessity of elaborate "channels of information" and chains of command. Such a situation is conducive to efficient teaching and learning, and to good staff morale.

Summary

We have attempted to differentiate the new from the old in terms of differences in purpose, scope, nature, and methods. Perhaps it will help the reader to see these differences more clearly if the points of contrast are placed in juxtaposition to each other, as in the following arrangement on pages 410–411.

[6] H. B. Trecker, *Group Process in Administration,* The Woman's Press, New York, 1946, pp. 16–17. Italics ours.
[7] Wiles, *op. cit.*

TABLE 6. Types of Educational Supervision

	AUTHORITARIAN	LAISSEZ-FAIRE	DEMOCRATIC
Purpose	Training or improvement of the teacher into a pattern predetermined by the authority.	Teachers "let alone," except for periodic inspectional visits; those unacceptable to the authority dismissed.	Improvement of total teaching-learning situation. Seeks basic understanding of *reasons* for adopted procedures by having teachers participate in policy formation.
Scope	Limited largely to the improvement of classroom teaching.	Limited largely to teacher rating and "inspiration" of the teacher.	Inclusive of all important factors affecting the teaching-learning situation: teacher, physical plant, materials, administrative policies and procedures, pupils' nature and needs, community, pupils' home life, etc.
Nature or Characteristics	Imposed.	Little leadership, control, or guidance.	Co-operative.
	Principal assumed to be "superior."	Principal assumed to be "superior."	Principal in a peer relationship with teachers.
	Leadership prerogatives due to status, and jealously guarded.	Leadership prerogatives due to status, and jealously guarded.	Leadership shared. Authority derived from and conferred by the group.
	Functions prescribed and limited to the mechanics of the "teaching act."	Except for teacher rating, functions vague and undefined.	Functions flexible and diverse, derive from the needs of the situation.
	Random, atomistic, scattered effort. Little over-all planning.	No planning.	Unified effort resulting from careful planning by the group.
	Fixed, rigid, static.	Amorphous, indeterminate.	Experimental and flexible. Constantly seeking better methods.
	Teacher- and pupil-focused.	Teacher-focused	Situation-focused.

TABLE 6. Types of Educational Supervision
(*continued*)

	AUTHORITARIAN	LAISSEZ-FAIRE	DEMOCRATIC
Methods	Teacher evaluated by his superior for administrative purposes.	Teacher evaluated by his superior for administrative purposes.	Self-evaluation by teacher and principal, and co-operative evaluation of their functioning for the purpose of improving the total teaching-learning situation.
	Training in "correct" teaching methods through telling, bulletins, demonstrations.	Let teachers alone and supply their needs.	Identification of needs for improvement. Continuous group appraisal.
	Class observations, followed by conference to point out errors and better techniques.	"Encouragement" and "inspiration."	Provision of consultative service at teacher's request. Observation of new teachers and discussion with them of their problems.
	Work largely limited to individual teachers.	No work with teachers.	Work with teacher groups in study and analysis of total teaching-learning situation. Group study of specific problems. Individual conferences by request.
	Coercion via rating and withholding salary increases.	Dismiss mediocre and poor teachers.	Incentive salary schedules to encourage additional study; in-service workshops, leaves-of-absence for study; recognition for good work.

SUGGESTED READINGS

See page 438.

CHAPTER XXVII

THE TECHNIQUES OF MODERN
SUPERVISION

The reader will readily appreciate that the newer philosophy of supervision will make different kinds of demands on the principal than did the old. Barr, Burton and Brueckner make the following differentiation between the two concepts.

The term "training in service" connotes teacher-centered and imposed supervision. The teacher is *given* devices, techniques, skills, and *trained* in their use. The teacher is *corrected* in his detailed techniques through *handing out* ready-made procedures. The modern concept holds that teachers (and all educational workers) should have *opportunities for growth* through the *co-operative analysis* of problems and from *choosing* from among several techniques or *devising* new ones based on the situation confronting the teacher. Teachers (and educational workers) are not ordinarily to be *given* limited specifics but are to *develop* judgment in choosing or devising techniques which fit the situation. The teacher is to be aided in studying the significant factors in the situation, in evaluating the strength and weakness of his present procedures, and in the choosing or devising of techniques.[1]

Another way of saying this is that the usual concept of supervision has attempted to improve the classroom situation by training and improving the teacher, while the new concept believes that a teacher's growth takes place best through his participation in co-operative study and improvement of the teaching-learning situation, and the self-evaluation which is attendant upon such study.

This change in emphasis necessitates techniques and ways of working

[1] A. S. Barr, W. H. Burton, and L. J. Brueckner, *Supervision,* D. Appleton–Century Company, 2nd ed., New York, 1947, pp. 6–15.

on the part of the principal which are considerably different from those which have been customary in supervision. It may help further to clarify the newer concept if we discuss some of these techniques briefly. The practices discussed are in no sense to be considered an exhaustive listing; they are simply illustrative of the type and range of modern supervisory practices.

Group Techniques

The techniques of supervision could be classified in several different ways. For convenience and simplicity, however, they will be divided into *group* and *individual* techniques, with an additional discussion of evaluation.

Co-operative study of instructional problems. One method which is proving most successful is co-operative staff study of such problems as classroom discipline, mental health considerations in teaching, use of community resources in the learning program, provisions for retarded readers, adaptation of instruction to the needs of mentally retarded and mentally gifted children, and the like. This may be done in various ways.

The former principal of the Scotch Plains School No. 1 (New Jersey) describes the use of faculty meetings to conduct a sort of "course" in problems important to the teachers.[2] The teachers defined those problems which they wished to have discussed, and helped to plan the meetings on those topics. At appropriate times the principal was the discussion leader, particularly at the outset; at other times a teacher would take over the leadership. This principal observes that "The in-school course has been quite effective in the improvement of school services . . . In the matter of professional growth for individual participants, the results have been even more significant . . . Through their participation in organizing and contributing to the in-school course and through carrying out research for the benefit of the faculty as a whole, they have learned that there is greater stimulation in active creative thought than in the passive reception of the wisdom of authorities."[3]

This suggests that the faculty meeting need not be the dry and dull routine that it has been in all too many schools. Instead of being devoted

[2] P. H. Van Ness, "Noncredit Courses at Faculty Meetings," in Department of Elementary School Principals, *In-Service Growth of School Personnel,* Twenty-first Yearbook, National Education Association, Washington, D. C., 1942, pp. 421–425.

[3] *Ibid.,* p. 425.

to routine announcements and the discussion of routine details (much of which can be accomplished through a bulletin) it can deal with matters vital to the staff. Certain important conditions should be kept in mind.

1. The problems to be discussed should be important to the entire staff, and should be chosen by the teaching group (including the principal).

2. Meetings should not be much less than one hour, and probably no longer than an hour and a half.

3. The frequency of such staff meetings should be decided upon by the staff.

4. The meeting place should be as pleasant, comfortable, and informal as possible. Avoid classrooms with fixed seats; they are formidable barriers to good group discussion. In small schools the meeting might very well be held in the homes of the participants.

5. Teachers should participate in the planning and organization of the meetings, and the wishes of the staff should govern the decisions made.

6. Insofar as possible, members should be so seated that they can see one another without neck-craning. A circle or hollow square is a good arrangement.

7. In very large schools, the staff should be broken into smaller discussion groups; the large meetings should then be reserved for making staff decisions, as a forum and clearinghouse for committee proposals, and for all-school planning.[4]

A most helpful and specific discussion of the staff meeting is that of Wiles.[5] In it he discusses the planning and organization of staff meetings, roles of participants, record keeping, and the like, and lists twenty-four specific suggestions for improving such meetings.

Co-operative study of administrative problems. Not only can staff study of instructional problems contribute to instructional improvement and teacher growth; co-operative analysis of administrative functions can serve the same purpose. Principals who enlist their staffs to help them improve administrative procedures find that ideas are developed through

---

[4] See W. A. Yauch, *Improving Human Relations in School Administration,* Harper and Brothers, New York, 1949, ch. IV, for a modern discussion of the teachers' meeting.

[5] Kimball Wiles, *Supervision for Better Schools,* Prentice-Hall, Inc., New York, 1950, pp. 150–176.

the group process which they would probably never have developed alone. Furthermore, the policies and procedures so formulated are carried out much more intelligently, willingly, and efficiently than when they are formulated by the administrator and imposed upon the staff.

The former superintendent at River Forest, Illinois, reports how group planning by the staff and community members developed a new method of reporting, a new salary schedule, a code of professional ethics, and a procedure for the evaluation of teaching. He states that "group planning by the entire personnel during recent years in the River Forest Schools has more than justified itself . . . There have been numerous occasions when the administration has despaired of reaching even an approximate goal set up by the faculty in group planning; however, most of those who have experimented over the past three or four years would probably agree that the most successful method of realizing worth-while objectives in modern teaching is through group planning in all areas."[6]

In the Washington School of Sacramento, California, the principal provided for a faculty advisory committee to assist him in administrative decisions. The committee, which changes membership annually, has helped solve such problems as a basic instructional reorganization to provide for improved reading achievement among migratory workers and otherwise underprivileged children, the salvaging of a foundering parent-teacher association, and the co-ordination of the supervision of children outside the classroom, all of which the reader will recognize as knotty problems of a school administrator. The principal states, "Teacher co-operation of the type described may seem a slow and cumbersome process for formulating and executing important school plans. On the contrary, it is surprisingly efficient . . . Because every teacher has a voice in newly projected plans and understands them thoroughly, each one tries to make them work to the best of his ability . . . Teacher participation has been an excellent means of in-service training for all . . . Our plan also discloses unsuspected administrative ability of a high order on the part of some teachers and broadens the horizon of them all."[7]

[6] V. M. Rogers, "We All Plan," in Association for Supervision and Curriculum Development, *Group Planning in Education,* National Education Association, Washington, D. C., 1945, p. 115.
[7] R. E. Learned, "The Co-operative Solution of Administrative Problems," in Department of Elementary School Principals, *op. cit.,* Twenty-first Yearbook, p. 439.

Amarillo, Texas, is but one of a number of school systems which have enlisted the teachers in the formulation of a teachers' salary schedule. A "Teachers' Interest Committee" worked out and recommended to the administration and board of education a new salary schedule, which was adopted. The result was that "it was a valuable educational experience for all, and each member of the committee now feels a personal responsibility for the success of the program."[8]

The foregoing are illustrative of the characteristics and values of the concept of supervision as democratic professional leadership. They serve well to demonstrate the inseparability of the supervisory and administrative function in the modern methods of instructional supervision.

Study groups. There are some problems in the teaching-learning situation which are not the immediate concern of all members of the staff. In such cases, it is desirable for those members who are concerned to study these problems as a group. For example, the problems attendant upon the admission of pupils to the first grade might be studied by a group of primary teachers, with the principal as a member of the group. The same procedure might be followed in a consideration of the problems of initial instruction in reading. Study of the desirability of departmentalization or of the development of skills in the use of reference materials are illustrations of concerns which might be similarly handled in the intermediate grades. In many schools the principal has provided for small volunteer study groups on topics in which a number of teachers have expressed interest, such as "Classroom Procedures Conducive to Good Mental Hygiene," or "Child Study." In other cases, such study groups are the natural outgrowth of a study by the entire staff of some school problem (such as discipline or curriculum revision). In the development of the salary schedule in Amarillo, for example (referred to above), the teachers divided themselves into five subcommittees, each of which worked upon a different aspect of the problem.

This emphasis on co-operative working together in groups is spreading rapidly. Increasingly, efforts are being directed toward means of enlisting as wide as possible a degree of participation among teachers and other staff members in group study of problems of their schools. In this respect, members of the Commission on Teacher Education of the American Council on Education make a pertinent statement.

[8] A. B. Lewis, "Teacher Participation in Salary Scheduling," in Department of Elementary School Principals, *op. cit.,* Twenty-first Yearbook, p. 477.

Our experience as field co-ordinators has convinced us that there is an integral relationship between group activity and individual performance . . . The school systems (in the study) seemingly testified to a conviction that effective group work is of major importance in school and staff improvement . . . But we also believe that responsibility for the profitableness of in-service efforts is widely distributed. It is not one which must be acquired in the first instance by school executives and at a later date by other members of the professional staff. It can be acquired gradually as classroom teachers and executives attempt to learn together.[9]

Group study of the community. With the developing emphasis on a life-centered curriculum, attention has naturally been directed to the importance of community factors in the education of children. Numbers of school staffs have conducted co-operative studies of community factors to assist them in their teaching. Such activities as the development of a card catalogue of human resources for education in the community, and a handbook of places of historical interest have proven profitable. Other staffs have studied the home and community backgrounds of their pupils so as to understand better how to operate a learning program which is suited to the children's needs and interests. It is evident that the possibilities for study of community factors are rich, and that such a study will contribute to better teachers, better teaching, and a better learning program.

Local Workshops. During the past fifteen years, the term "workshop" has come into common usage in educational parlance. Loose usage of the term has clouded its original meaning, so that it is applied to many situations which are not workshops at all in the original sense of the word. There is nothing mysterious about the operation of workshops; they are basically groups of people working together on their own problems. In this sense, the group study techniques mentioned above are workshops, for they have many workshop characteristics. Some of the major identifying characteristics of workshops, which distinguish them from other co-operative group study situations, are:

1. Attendance is voluntary.
2. Participants work only on problems they wish to work on. There is no pre-planned program (although there *is* pre-planning), no arbitrary schedule of activities.

[9] C. E. Prall and C. L. Cushman, *Teacher Education in Service,* American Council on Education, Washington, D. C., 1944, pp. 30–31.

3. The planning of the schedule and activities is done by the members. Leadership is placed as swiftly as possible in the hands of the workshop members.

4. The staff of the workshop work in the capacity of guides and consultants, not as "teachers" or determiners of policy. They represent resources for the group to use as it sees fit.

5. Usually the workshop is held at a spot away from the school. The workshoppers live, eat, work, and play together for the duration of their stay, which may be but a few days or as much as six weeks.

6. There are no requirements other than those decided upon by the group. Evaluation of the individual members is avoided if possible, although it is desirable for the group to evaluate the workshop.

7. The program is divided among meetings of the whole group, meetings of subgroups, personal interviews with staff members, and recreational activities.

Practically all the local in-service workshops of which the writers are aware have been system-wide workshops, and have met in the summer. Some of them—as in Denver, Colorado; Des Moines, Iowa; Springfield, Missouri; and Philadelphia, Pennsylvania—have been operated in close co-operation with colleges and universities; others have utilized only staff resources from their own system, or supplemented these with other resource persons, such as members from a state education department staff. In some situations where a college of education or teachers college is close at hand, a co-operative arrangement has been worked out between the college and the school system. The college and system staff a workshop jointly, the college administers it, and the "content" of the workshop is the problems of the school system. Such a workshop has been operated by Lehigh University in Pennsylvania for a number of summers, attended by teachers of the Bethlehem, Pennsylvania, schools.

Whereas it may not be feasible for the individual principal to operate a workshop for his school alone, he can himself participate actively in workshops of the school system. Prall and Cushman remark on the fact that the participation of principals in the workshops of the Teacher Education Study was disappointingly small.[10] Principals should be right in the middle of activities such as this. Workshops have been proving powerful instruments in stretching and changing ideas, in stimulating

[10] Prall and Cushman, op. cit., pp. 236 and 237.

members to new ventures, in developing skills in human relationships and democratic processes, in developing leadership, and in making progress toward the improvement of educational procedures. Furthermore, if the experience of the writers and others who have attended and worked in workshops serves well, no principal will ever regret having attended.

This much will, perhaps, serve to help the reader gain some insight into the meaning of group processes in supervision and administration. The evidence is clear and unequivocal that these methods of working are most fruitful and effective, *provided one gives the group process a chance*. Such methods demand a faith in the ability of everybody to do good thinking and to make a valuable contribution, a faith that it is difficult for one to hold until he has experienced the remarkable effectiveness of truly democratic group procedures. The trend toward this method of working is now strong, pointing to the necessity for the principal to take steps to improve his own abilities as a group leader and group member.

Individual Techniques

The recent emphasis upon group procedures in supervision has led many unthinking persons to repudiate individual supervisory techniques. This by no means follows. There are occasions when the best way to help a teacher is to help him individually. Under the new orientation, however, such help is not imposed. Imposed advice is ineffective, for, as the old saying goes, "those that need it won't heed it, and those that will heed it don't need it." In the emerging pattern of supervision, individual techniques are outgrowths of and adjuncts to group methods such as those described above.

The individual classroom visit and conference. What, then is the place of the classroom visit? As it has usually been employed, it was not in answer to a felt need on the part of the teacher; its purpose was to tell him what his weak points were and how to improve them. The newer approach gives the classroom visit a different emphasis. For the most part, it should be an outgrowth of the group study being carried on by the staff. One of the purposes of the principal is to identify the classroom problems that the teaching group is struggling with, so that he too may discuss them in an informed manner. Furthermore, if he is to be the over-all co-ordinator of the work of the staff, it is important for him to be able to see the instructional program in its entirety. It is also likely that in visiting all the classrooms he may be able better to identify those problems which will be of concern to the entire group. Frequently a teacher is unaware that a problem he is facing is also bothering others.

Another example of such visits growing out of group work is the request of a teacher to have the principal come to see how well the plans developed in the group are working out in his class. Such requests are evidence of the existence or development of a fine atmosphere of human relations, a consideration which is tremendously important for good education. In fact, the casual types of visits mentioned to this point can be made only when a good human relationships atmosphere exists. The writers have seen delightful examples of these fine relationships in schools where the principal is always welcomed by the teacher and pupils as a friend, largely because he never enters those classrooms as an overseer.

There is also the visit made at the request of a teacher who wants help on some problem. In these cases, the principal should discuss the nature of the problem with the teacher beforehand, then plan with him the best timing of the visit. Following his visit, the principal may have a talk with him in which he attempts to help the teacher reach a solution to his problem, or in which he refers the teacher to helpful sources. It is also to be noted that in the modern classroom visit the principal suits the manner of his entrance to and exit from the classroom to the wishes of the teacher and the nature of the class situation. Usually, instead of entering and leaving in the surreptitious manner portrayed at the outset of this discussion, he will greet teacher and pupils upon his entrance, and perhaps excuse his interruption if his visit is, indeed, an interruption. During a story hour or other quiet activity his visit probably would be an interruption, but during some more active situations his entrance might go virtually unnoticed. At any rate, it would be foolish for any "authority" to prescribe the manner of his entering and leaving classrooms.

It is also likely that more frequent visits will be made to the classrooms of new and inexperienced teachers for the purpose of helping them adjust to their new position more easily. New teachers are usually greatly in need of reassurance, and of an opportunity to talk over with someone the things they are trying to do. Practically all new teachers are anxious to do a good job, and would like to have the principal tell them in what respects they are doing well, and how they might improve the quality of their teaching. Some of this may be accomplished by asking a sympathetic and experienced teacher on the staff to act as a professional companion to the new teacher, but it is still desirable for the principal to visit and talk informally with the new teacher, for there is no substitute for such a friendly, helpful relationship between teacher and principal.

It is well to remember, too, that young teachers fresh from a modern teachers college are likely to have a great deal to contribute to the vitality of the staff's efforts. The neophyte should be encouraged and helped to teach as he has been taught to teach. Too frequently the attitude has been taken that, "Now you can forget all that stuff they taught you at college; it won't work here." Such an attitude is destructive of good human relationships, detrimental to the mental hygiene and morale of the new teacher, and wasteful of the resources he brings to the school. Why not help him to translate into practice the theories he has learned? What is there to lose? Much may be gained, for, as someone has said, nothing is so practical as sound theory.

The modern classroom visit, then, differs in significant respects from that of older conceptions. Its purpose is more than ever before determined by the teacher himself, rather than by the principal. Consequently, the purposes vary, and are no longer restricted to those of instructing, correcting, or rating the teacher. This concept is not in itself new. Some supervisors and principals have used it as part of their approach for years. Only recently, however, has there been sufficient clarification of the newer pattern of instructional improvement so that it can be seen more clearly where and how the classroom visit fits into the total picture.

Observation visits by teachers. Because we are coming to realize that there is no one best method of teaching which can be "demonstrated," the use of the demonstration lesson is fast giving way to the observational visit. These may be intraschool visits by teachers to see other members of the staff at work, or they may be interschool visits within one's own school system or to schools in other systems. The purpose of these visits is quite different from that of the demonstration lesson, in which one person usually demonstrated *the way* to teach a given subject. Observational visits, on the other hand, serve to emphasize (among other things) that there are numbers of "good" ways to use similar subject matter. The visiting teacher is not expected to *adopt* the methods of teaching he observes, but to gather suggestions for ways of working, and to *adapt* them to his interests and abilities, and to the needs and conditions of the learning situation with which he works.

One interesting method of handling such visits is reported by Kenneth Lant (*Teacher Growth Through Planned Visitation,* Metropolitan School Study Council, New York, 1950, mimeographed). He and his staff identified aspects of teaching in which they felt they needed to improve. Then, through the files of the Metropolitan School Study Council (comprising seventy-two school systems in the metropolitan New York area) schools were located in which teachers were reported to be doing well those things Lant's teachers were trying to develop. Arrangements were then made for one of Lant's staff to spend a day or two in the selected school, and upon his return he reported the interesting aspects of his visit to the rest of the staff in a staff meeting. The staff then considered how the information brought back by the visiting teacher could be used in the improvement of their own program. In this manner, each teacher's visits were made of benefit to the entire school.

Visits within the school may be outgrowths of group study and discussion on the part of the staff. Teachers may wish to see creative teaching methods other teachers have developed, or become acquainted with the nature of the learning program at other age levels within the school. It is helpful for primary grade teachers to learn what kind of learning program their classes experience after they leave the primary grades. Intermediate grades teachers may have their eyes opened by the problems faced and the procedures used by the teachers of the younger children. In these ways the observational visit may contribute to the breadth and depth of the teachers' educational understanding, and to their skill in suiting their learning programs to the needs and abilities of the pupils.

Child study. A most fruitful activity for the improvement of a teacher's understanding of his job is concentrated study of a child in his class. This may be launched as a school-wide program, as in the child study program of the Commission on Teacher Education,[11] or it may be under-

---

[11] Commission on Teacher Education, *Helping Teachers Understand Children,* American Council on Education, Washington, D. C., 1945.

taken as an individual project by one teacher. In the latter case, the occasion for starting it may be a child who is a "behavior problem" who has become too much for the teacher to handle. At the suggestion of the principal, an effort may be made to seek the causes of the child's behavior, a procedure which usually turns up interesting findings which add to the teacher's understanding of how he can be of help to the pupils in his classes. (See, for example, the anecdote of Jack, on pages 217 and 218.)

The child studied need not be a "problem," however. In the Teacher Education Study mentioned above the teachers studied "normal" children intensively, as well as children considered to be problems. By so doing, the teachers came to understand that:

> Children who are successful in conforming to the learning and behavioral demands of the school usually are not studied carefully. Many of them leave school with important undiscovered or underdeveloped abilities, with various mistaken or warped attitudes, with selfish social goals and aspirations, with uncorrected habits of dominating or exploiting others, or with undetected personality cleavages. Many of these children will become unsuccessful or maladjusted later, others will actively retard the amelioration of current social problems, while still others represent a needless waste of important social resources.[12]

The teachers themselves evaluated the results of this study. In commenting on what the teachers said, the commission remarks that:

> The effects . . . were described in terms of improved emotional climate in the classrooms, of reduced strain and tension among teachers, and in terms of increased friendliness between teachers and children and between teachers and parents. Both the school staff and the pupils were reported as being happier and as finding more satisfaction and significance in their work together. The schools ran more smoothly, and were marked by greater freedom and spontaneity as well as by more effective co-operative planning and wider participation in carrying out plans.[13]

If such intensive individual pupil studies are to be made, it will be helpful for the principal to enlist the assistance of a specialist in child development, provided one is available. It is to be noted that this procedure is different from the usual gathering of information which the teacher should do for every pupil in the class. It is an attempt to find out

[12] *Ibid.,* p. 457.
[13] *Ibid.,* pp. 399–400.

all that the teacher can about the child: his fears, motivations, interests, aversions, leisure activities, home conditions, physical condition, peer relationships, abilities, and the like. Such concentrated study of one child, however, is likely to improve the nature of the information the teacher will gather about other children in the class.

Another procedure which has had considerable success is the pupil guidance conference. When a teacher identifies a child as having abnormal emotional or behavior problems, he can consult with the principal, and schedule such a conference. To the conference are invited all those who are concerned: teacher, special teachers, supervisor, principal, parents, and—if available—the guidance counselor or psychologist. If a social worker has been involved in the case previously, he, too, should be present. If it seems desirable, the child himself may be a member of the conference for a part of the discussion. Each member contributes what he knows about the child, and the conditions affecting his behavior, in a joint attempt to determine the causes of the child's problem. The group may decide on the direction of further study and immediate steps, and meet again at a future date. In this manner, each member of the group, particularly the teacher, has his understanding of children increased, a result which cannot help affecting his classroom teaching favorably.

Child study should not be restricted to the study of individual children. Study of the dynamics of children's relationships in groups is a most revealing and rewarding undertaking. By the use of sociometric techniques and directed observations, teachers can come to understand much better the reasons for the behavior of a pupil group and for the behavior of individuals within the group. Understanding of the nature of the *group process* is vital to modern teaching.[14]

This area of child study has been much neglected in our educational programs. Understanding of the dynamics of children's behavior should be one of the foundations of a teacher's preparation. This is particularly true within the modern concept of education, which requires not so much that teachers be experts in subject-matter fields as that they be experts in children's growth. For this reason, any procedure, such as

[14] For a better understanding of this, see such writings as the series of articles in the *Journal of the National Education Association,* vol. XXXVII, September (pp. 350–352), October (pp. 436–438), November (pp. 502–503), December (pp. 578–579), 1948; and vol. XXXVIII, January (pp. 34–35), 1949; Association for Supervision and Curriculum Development, *Fostering Mental Health in Our Schools,* National Education Association, Washington, D. C., 1950.

those described above or others, which increases teachers' understanding of children's growth and behavior is a most important contribution to the improvement of the success of the school's endeavors.

Encouraging teachers' interests. Teacher growth is not simply an intellectual or academic concern. One of the most important aspects of the problem, as principals can well attest, is the personality and emotional adjustment of the teacher himself. While this problem may have aspects patently impossible for the principal to deal with effectively, he sometimes can do much to help. One principal describes instances in which the principal's capitalization of teachers' interests served to improve the morale and teaching performance of teachers who were considered apathetic, troublesome, or incompetent.[15]

This "technique" is only one aspect of the larger problem of improving human relations. When the human relations in a school are poor, it is a tremendous barrier to the operation of an improving program. Under such conditions group endeavor has little chance to operate successfully, and the efficiency of the teachers is certain to be impaired. The mental hygiene of individual teachers and the morale of the staff as a group are most important, therefore, for the principal to consider.[16]

Organized professional experiences. The opportunities offered through universities and teachers colleges can be utilized by teachers for their individual growth. Frequently a principal can be of help to a teacher in the planning of such work. This is not to imply a practice which is all too prevalent: that of *telling* a teacher what he should take. It might happen, however, that the group of teachers will face some problem that course work at a center of learning might help solve. If there is a teacher interested in the problem who intends taking part-time or summer session work at college, he may be willing to include courses pertinent to the school's problem.

In other cases, principals have been instrumental in persuading a nearby college or university to give an extension course in the neighborhood, so that teachers would find it convenient to attend. In some situations, principals have had the opportunity to nominate a person

[15] Department of Elementary School Principals, *op. cit.,* Twenty-first Yearbook, pp. 410–416.
[16] W. A. Yauch, *op. cit.* Part V is an excellent discussion of this topic. It deals with teachers' personal problems, relations among teachers, relations of teacher and parents, and relations between the principal and the staff.

from their staffs to represent the school at a summer workshop. (In such cases it is usually desirable, for obvious reasons, to have the staff select the representative.)

In many systems now, of course, the taking of advanced course work is "motivated" by legal requirements for maintenance of certification, or by incentive salary schedules. Whereas these means are effective in enforcing periodic academic refreshment, it is more likely that the learning experiences will be more meaningful and valuable if teachers take advanced courses to get help with problems which they have identified, rather than for the sake of credits to renew certification or to make them eligible for the next step on the salary schedule.

Summary

These are a few of the methods of an individual nature which may contribute to the growth of teachers and to the improvement of the school. It is evident from the discussion that one seldom starts with the objective of "improving" the teacher; the focus is primarily on the improvement of the teaching-learning program. Group and individual study of the problem involved in that improvement contribute directly to the growth of individual teachers. Furthermore, the reader probably has noticed how difficult it is to draw a line between individual and group methods of achieving this end. They are closely interrelated, and it is only for purposes of discussion that it is profitable to separate them.

SUGGESTED READINGS

See page 438.

CHAPTER XXVIII

EVALUATION IN THE IMPROVEMENT

PROGRAM

An important characteristic of modern supervision is its emphasis on evaluation. That is not to imply that supervision has not always concerned itself with evaluation; it is simply that the type, emphasis, and use of evaluation in the newer approach differ quite sharply from those in the more authoritarian types of supervision. The older forms evaluated the teacher in terms of the degree to which he conformed to some preconceived notion of what a good teacher should be. To achieve this, check lists and rating scales, containing more or less detailed lists of the desired traits, methods, conditions or outcomes were employed in an attempt to render the principal's judgment objective. As a result of the application of these scales, a rating was usually assigned to the teacher. It was also recommended that a copy of the rating sheet be given to the teacher, and a supervisory conference held to discuss the ratings. For reasons which the reader may surmise, many supervisors and principals ignored this latter recommendation, their teachers remaining ignorant of the ratings assigned them.

In recent years, sentiment has been building up against the rating of teachers. After the close of World War II, however, some states made teacher rating a legal requisite to a school district's receipt of state aid, and have established minimum salary schedules which made salary increments dependent upon the level of the rating. Because of this resurgence in rating practice, it may be profitable to review here the purposes assumed to be served by rating, and the degree to which rating serves them.

Why Do We Rate?

While there may be other more or less defensible purposes which it is assumed are achieved by rating, the case for rating rests largely on the belief that the following three objectives are facilitated:

1. It assists us to eliminate incompetent teachers.
2. It improves teaching by motivating teachers to improve their work in service so as to get high ratings, and thus qualify for salary increments and promotions.
3. It facilitates the administration of salary schedules, and helps the administrator to identify those who merit promotion.

These assumptions merit brief analysis.

Rating to weed out poor teachers. The increases in taxes made necessary by increases in teachers' salaries (as well as increased expenditures for other aspects of education) have caused citizen groups to demand evidence that they are getting their money's worth, and that incompetent teachers be weeded out of the schools. There are many who seem to believe that this can be accomplished by a system of rating. Such a belief is naive. Teachers who are incompetent—*truly* incompetent— will become known to a reasonably alert principal in a short time, and no system of rating is necessary to reveal such teachers. If such a teacher is on tenure, more than a simple rating is necessary to justify firing him. He has the right to appeal his case to the courts, and only concrete and objective evidence will suffice to justify his dismissal. Such evidence can be gathered without resorting to the rating of all teachers.

To a certain extent, the same holds true for weak teachers who are not on tenure. The principal's responsibility is to help such teachers as much as he possibly can. If, after two or three years of working with them, he is convinced that they are most unlikely to become reasonably satisfactory teachers, it is again unnecessary to rate all teachers in order to dismiss these weak ones.

It is the opinion of the authors, therefore, that the rating of teachers is unnecessary and unjustifiable for the purpose of identifying and dismissing teachers whose work is unsatisfactory.

Rating to improve teaching. Under the laissez-faire philosophy of supervision, it was apparently assumed that the teacher's desire to get a good rating was in itself an effective motivation to the improvement of his work. It must be admitted that such rating probably did have such motivating power, particularly when salary increases were determined by the rating. The question to be raised, however, is whether this is the most effective method of improving the teacher's classroom teaching. It may very well be that the teacher does not know *how* to improve his teaching, in which case the most powerful motivation to improve is worthless.

The training and guidance concept recognized this. It utilized various methods of analyzing a teacher's performance, and in conference with him the supervisor told him wherein his work was unsatisfactory, and suggested how he might improve. In other words, there was a sincere attempt at diagnosis, followed by a prescription of the cure. While this was a long step forward from the laissez-faire approach, it can be objected to on several grounds.

Rating is basically an authoritarian approach. The necessity for the supervisor to assign a rating, however diagnostic, helpful and friendly he may attempt to be, will raise a barrier between him and the teacher. It is inevitable that the teacher will do his best to place his best foot forward when the supervisor is present, and to conceal as much as possible those weaknesses which the supervisor should know in order to help him most effectively. In this respect, rating becomes a positive handicap to the improvement of teaching.

Administering salary schedules and promotions. The statement of this purpose raises the question of the desirability of "merit" salary schedules. It has been widely attested by teachers and others that such schedules are destructive of staff morale. Jealousies and rivalries among teachers are encouraged, and hostility to the supervisor may result when a rating is unsatisfactory. Thus there is a negative effect upon the human relationships within the school, which is certainly not of benefit to the teaching-learning situation. Some merit schedules provide for an increment, beyond the normal maximum on the schedule, for "super-teachers." This increment is awarded to but a small proportion of the staff in a commendable effort to recognize the worth of those dedicated teachers who become true master teachers. Even this is fraught with pitfalls, however. Many teachers who do not receive such recognition will believe that they, rather than the ones who did receive the honor (and the money!) were deserving of that recognition, while numbers of those who do receive it will be uncomfortable about it. Under the plan, there will also be the suspicion, and the possibility, that the person responsible for doing the rating "plays favorites." Again the effect on human relations is bad. And what about the parents? It has happened that in such situations the principal has been badgered with requests by parents to place their children in the "super-teacher's" section of the class, rather than in that of their present teacher, who isn't recognized as being outstanding.

Thus it can be seen that rating is not the effective device that it appears at first blush. The objections to it are formidable, and in the opinions of the authors they far outweigh whatever advantages may inhere in the system.[1]

Many principals, however, are required by law or by regulations of the local school board to rate their teachers for salary or other purposes. In such cases they should seek methods of rating which are least harmful and most helpful. The example of co-operative planning in River Forest, Illinois, which was mentioned earlier, stated that the teachers themselves evolved the procedures to be used in evaluating them. Whereas this does not eliminate the objections to rating, such co-operative planning of how it shall be done does serve to improve the human relations aspects of the process, develops better understanding on the part of the teachers of the purposes and problems involved, and undoubtedly contributes to their better understanding of what good teaching is.

Evaluating the Total Teaching-Learning Situation

In contrast to the philosophy which places emphasis on the rating of the teacher by an authority is the modern concept which takes the spotlight off the teacher, so to speak, and puts the floodlight on the total teaching-learning situation which includes the teacher, of course, and the supervisor as well. This type of evaluation has several aspects. There is evaluation of the learning program by the entire group, self-evaluation by members of the group, and evaluation of the processes being used by the group in the program of improvement.

[1] Association for Supervision and Curriculum Development, *Better than Rating*, National Education Association, Washington, D. C., 1950.

Evaluation of the program. Evaluation of the program is the heart of the modern program of "instructional improvement." It is the expression of the experimental philosophy which undergirds and permeates the modern approach. Principal, teachers, and supervisors take the point of view that nothing in the educational program is sacred, fixed, or final, and they subject all aspects of it to searching and critical analysis. The organization of the learning program; the grouping of the pupils; the organization of the school; the methods of evaluating, reporting and determining pupil progress; the content of the learning program; the teaching methods; the philosophy and practice of discipline; the time schedule; the time, place, and procedure of staff meetings; the procedures used in parent conferences; the study and use of community resources; all these and others are questioned, evaluated, and thoroughly discussed in the attempt to improve the learning and growing of the pupils.

This evaluation may take a number of forms. It may be simply a study of one of the aspects mentioned above, or of some other. Such a study may be initiated at the suggestion of the principal, or of a teacher, or at the instigation of parents who question the procedure in use. Once the staff has agreed that the practice or problem in question merits study, planning sessions are held to determine the method of study. The group may decide on the appointment of a committee to study the matter and make recommendations, to invite an outside consultant to assist them, to study what current authorities have to say on the matter, to have individual staff members make studies in their classrooms and then pool their findings in a general discussion, or resort to any one of almost innumerable possibilities. In this way, the area in question is studied intensively, and a new procedure or plan is evolved by the group. This new policy is put into practice (either on a school-wide basis or in one class or one part of the school) for a trial period, after which it is reevaluated, and either continued, extended, modified, or abandoned in favor of another plan evolved by the group.

Another possible approach is to conduct an over-all study of the school to identify those aspects of the situation which are unsatisfactory, obsolete, inconsistent with the over-all philosophy of the school, or in need of further study. In making such a study the group may wish to use evaluative instruments which have been prepared for that purpose.[2]

[2] H. G. Shane and S. Rovner, *A Selected Annotated Bibliography of Evaluation Instruments and Related Materials,* Northwestern University, Evanston, Ill., 1950 (Mimeographed).

Other groups have found it valuable to develop their own criteria for evaluating the school program. It is important to note that these evaluations are not (or should not be) "one-shot" affairs. The evaluation, if it is done well, will probably consume a considerable amount of time. The development of the criteria alone may take a year or more.

In other situations, outside agencies have been employed to make a critical evaluation of the school and its program: the so-called "school survey." Such a survey is particularly valuable if the staff of the school participates with the survey staff in making the appraisal. This may be a "comprehensive survey," in which all aspects of the school program are appraised, or a survey of some aspect of the school, such as the plant, or the curriculum. In such surveys, the survey staff is expected to make its own appraisal and recommendations for improvement; in co-operative surveys, the survey staff assists the staff of the school in arriving at recommendations.

Evaluations of the total situation will not of themselves produce the desired changes, although co-operative surveys may bring about changes while the survey is being made. Surveys and other evaluations are primarily "springboards" to further work. They reveal the aspects of the program in need of change, and indicate the probable direction in which the changes should be made. Further co-operative action by the staff itself should be the outcome of these evaluations.

Self-evaluation. Self-evaluation is another procedure characteristic of evaluation in the modern program. The group activities described earlier are in themselves productive of self-evaluation, and that is one of their greatest recommendations. A teacher participating in group discussions of what desirable educational practice is, and helping to arrive at decisions on that score, cannot help comparing his own ways of working with the methods that he and the group set up as recommended procedure. Thus, constant group study of the educational program of the school is motivation to constant self-appraisal by members of the staff. Barr, Burton, and Brueckner place this type of "self-supervision" on the highest level on a scale of "Supervision Principles and Practices."[3] In many ways such self-evaluation and self-supervision are analogous to the self-discipline we strive to help pupils develop. The teacher who

---

[3] A. S. Barr, W. H. Burton, and L. J. Brueckner, *Supervision,* 2nd ed., D. Appleton–Century Company, New York, 1947, pp. 66–67.

achieves this level of insight and performance is the one who, paradoxically, most welcomes the criticisms of others for the assistance it can be to him in the improvement of the work he is doing.

It is unrealistic to propose any one method of self-evaluation for teachers. The chief objective is to help teachers to develop an *attitude* of self-evaluation, for without the teacher's own disposition to evaluate himself, no self-evaluation is possible. One of the values of group study is, as we have mentioned, that it stimulates such an attitude. When a teacher has such a point of view it is highly probable that he will welcome assistance in the process. Under such circumstances, profitable use can be made of the check lists and rating scales, and of the classroom visits and conferences which are used so differently in the methods of imposed supervision.

Self-evaluation may be a most informal process, or it may be made systematic and controlled. These two types actually are extremes on a scale, and the one shades almost imperceptibly into the other. With most teachers the informal type is going on all the time. It becomes more systematic as they are helped to identify specific problems and work upon them, making appraisals of their progress. The most systematic and carefully controlled type is, of course, controlled research, in which relatively few staffs or individual teachers engage.

The task of the principal is to help the members of his staff, as individuals and as members of the group, to identify weaknesses and problems in the school program, and to develop effective methods of working on them. Such an approach will be considerably more systematic than the usual casual appraisal, but will avoid the rigidity and formality of controlled research in most cases. Within this orientation it is difficult to distinguish individual self-evaluation from group self-evaluation; it is an organic part and a natural outgrowth of group methods. A phase of the role of the principal as leader of the program of instructional improvement is to provide opportunities for, and to encourage, evaluative procedures, and to give all possible assistance to individual teachers in their evaluations of their own work.

Evaluation of the improvement process. Another frequently misunderstood characteristic of the modern program is the participation of all members of the group in the process of evaluating the program of instructional improvement itself. This is not a separate part of the evalua-

• tion program, of course; it is implicit in the program of group analytical study of the entire teaching-learning situation, for the improvement program is itself a part of that situation. Nevertheless, unless specific attention is given to the making of a critical appraisal of the work of the staff in its efforts to bring about desirable change, much of value will be lost, for such "process evaluation" will not be done automatically.

To make such an evaluation, the group must first identify the purposes which the program is to serve. Then they should formulate criteria for ways of working which will be consistent with these purposes. Yauch[4] presents some of the thinking of one staff which apparently worked in this manner. The importance of such evaluation in group process activities cannot be too strongly emphasized. It is only by continuous appraisal and critical examination that the program of instructional improvement (and, consequently, the instructional program of the school itself) will be kept alive and vital. Without such critical evaluation the dead hand of complacency and crystallization rests heavily upon the entire enterprise.

One of the finest and most comprehensive discussions of evaluation in the program of instructional improvement is that of Wiles. He discusses how both the individual teacher and the group may be helped to evaluate their work, and emphasizes the importance of co-operative procedures.[5]

Evaluating instructional leadership. The evaluation of the leadership of the program is actually a part of the evaluation of the improvement process itself, but it is such an important part that it merits some separate attention. As a matter of fact, this part of the process has somewhat of a "man bites dog" aspect. Under the programs of imposed and authoritarian supervision it was practically unheard-of to have the teachers evaluate the leadership methods of the supervisors; the entire evaluation process was in the other direction.

Adherents of the more modern point of view, however, believe that it is important to the effectiveness and vitality of the leadership to have the leadership procedures subjected to the searching light of critical evaluation by all members of the group. Whereas there are check lists and rat-

---

[4] W. A. Yauch, *Improving Human Relations in School Administration,* Harper and Brothers, New York, 1949, ch. XIII. The criteria on p. 240 are particularly illustrative of the kinds of criteria referred to above.

[5] Kimball Wiles, *Supervision for Better Schools,* Prentice-Hall, Inc., New York, 1950, chs. 12 and 13.

ing devices available for such evaluations,[6] it is probably more profitable for a school staff to develop its own criteria of desirable leadership.

Principles of Evaluation

The foregoing discussion of the place and nature of evaluation in the program of instructional improvement has necessarily been brief, with no attempt at exhaustiveness. The purpose has been to present a point of view with some general suggestions for its implementation. Interest in the problem will lead the reader to more thorough discussions.[7]

Before leaving the topic, some of the major aspects of the foregoing discussion can be emphasized, perhaps, by restatement in the form of principles, which may also be looked upon as desirable characteristics of good evaluative procedure in the program of instructional improvement.

1. Evaluation should be *comprehensive*. Instead of being limited to the usual procedure of observing and rating the teacher, or rating the teacher on the basis of tests of his pupils' achievement, the evaluation should include (as far as possible and practicable) all factors in the teaching-learning situation: teaching, organization, administration, supervision, materials and equipment, curriculum, and any other pertinent factors.

2. Evaluation should be *co-operative*. This is closely allied to the principle of comprehensiveness. If the evaluation is to be made of all aspects of the program, it is only reasonable to suggest that all persons in the program should participate in it co-operatively. The learning value of such co-operative evaluation is inestimable, for it helps to develop insights and understandings far more effectively than any method of imposed rating or authority-conducted evaluation.

3. Evaluation should be *based on valid criteria*. In other words, the criteria which are used in the evaluation should be consistent with the *accepted* philosophy and objectives of the staff. This suggests that the criteria themselves should be developed by the staff, and implies that previous attention should have been given to activities to develop some common agreement in educational viewpoint among the staff. The criteria

[6] Barr, Burton, and Brueckner, *op. cit.,* pp. 792–802; W. A. Yauch, *op. cit.,* pp. 243–249.

[7] Barr, Burton, and Brueckner, *op. cit.,* Part IV, and Department of Elementary School Principals, *Appraising the Elementary-School Program,* Sixteenth Yearbook, National Education Association, Washington, D. C., 1937; Kimball Wiles, *Supervision for Better Schools,* Prentice-Hall, Inc., New York, 1950, chs. 13 and 14.

for appraising the classroom situation, for example, would be quite different for a staff believing in a graded subject-matter curriculum and an imposed type of discipline than it would for a staff believing in a life-centered problem-type curriculum, with discipline the function of common planning and group standards of behavior.

4. Evaluation should be *diagnostic*. Any program of evaluation which stops at the making of judgments will be barren indeed. Unless one goes back of opinions, ratings, and value judgments, and attempts to identify reasons and influencing factors, the evaluation can be of little real help to the teachers. For this reason, the group should strive to document each evaluation, and think through to the implications of the causes.

5. Evaluation should be *continuous*. The usual program of evaluation has been sporadic and periodic. Teacher rating was done at intervals; reappraisals and revisions of curriculum were made every five, ten, or twenty years; whirlwind school surveys were made by outside specialists, after which the system gradually and gratefully sank back into its routine and complacent security. In contrast, evaluation in the modern program permeates the program of improvement, and is continuous. Gradual and continuous change is recognized as desirable and characteristic of a modern educational program. Although different techniques and procedures will be used at different times, and all phases of the educational program will not be appraised at once, the program itself will be an ongoing process, with a continuity derived from its integration with the entire improvement program.

6. Evaluation should be *functional*. If, as here advocated, evaluation is part and parcel of the total supervisory plan for educational growth, it cannot help being functional. Under the programs of imposed supervision, however, it was not uncommon for tests to be given or ratings to be made, the results reported to the higher administrative authority, and then filed away. In many cases, the teachers never learned the results of the appraisals. Such a procedure is most inefficient and wasteful. The only justification for evaluation is its use to improve the existing situation, and unless this is the result it might just as well not be done. In the modern program, evaluation is undertaken with the full expectation that something will be done about it. It is largely for this reason that all persons concerned are enlisted in the appraisal, for under those circumstances all persons concerned will know what changes should be made, and why.

In Conclusion

It will be noted that in supervision, as in the other aspects of the educational program discussed in this volume, there is (or should be) a close relationship to the philosophy of the educational program of the school. In a school which believes and practices an imposed curriculum, imposed discipline, imposed marks, and imposed failure and promotion, it is consistent to practice imposed supervision. If, on the other hand, the school is one which believes and practices a life-centered learning program, co-operative planning of learning experiences by pupils and teacher, authority derived from and conferred by the group, and democratic human relationships, then a co-operative program of instructional improvement is a natural corollary. Furthermore, if a staff wishes to modernize its learning program, there is no more effective way than to use co-operative techniques such as have been touched upon here, with the democratic leadership of a person skilled in human relationships. Experience has indicated that teachers who experience this type of instructional leadership are very likely to modify the conduct of their own classrooms in the direction of more co-operative, democratic, and lifelike procedures.

It is also to be noted that the modern concept of supervision demands different characteristics and abilities of the principal. In fact, most authorities in the area of supervision are suggesting that a term other than *supervision* be used to describe the modern function. To date, no term has succeeded universally in supplanting *supervision,* although *instructional leadership* has attained wide popularity. *Co-ordinator* and *consultant* seem to be the chief contenders to take the place of *supervisor.* Whatever the term used to describe this function, the fundamental changes which are taking place in it have considerable implications for the way in which the principal will work; much of the change is directly related to the changing concepts of supervision.[8] Instructional leadership is coming to be looked upon as the principal's chief responsibility.

It should be evident that a program of instructional leadership of the type described and advocated in this discussion will require a different type of leadership than will a program of the more conventional type. It demands greater skill in human relations; a thoroughly democratic

[8] Department of Elementary School Principals, *The Elementary School Principalship—Today and Tomorrow,* National Education Association, Washington, D. C., 1948, pp. 85–132 and 263–276.

philosophy, including faith in the potentialities of the staff and a deep conviction of the effectiveness and values of group processes; skill in group discussion techniques; a broad general scholarship in education (rather than a narrow specialization); a willingness to share authority and credit with others; and an emotional stability and maturity which stems from faith in himself as a leader, as an educator, and as a person. When such leadership characterizes the profession of the elementary school principalship, the future of elementary education will be bright indeed. It is most encouraging that more of such leadership is evident today than apparently has ever been the case in the past.

SUGGESTED READINGS

Association for Supervision and Curriculum Development, *Better Than Rating,* National Education Association, Washington, D. C., 1951.

————, *Group Planning in Education,* National Education Association, Washington, D. C., 1945.

————, *Group Processes in Supervision,* National Education Association, Washington, D. C., 1948.

————, *Leadership Through Supervision,* National Education Association, Washington, D. C., 1946.

————, *Fostering Mental Health in Our Schools,* National Education Association, Washington, D. C., 1950.

Barr, A. S., Burton, W. H., and Brueckner, L. J., *Supervision,* 2nd ed., D. Appleton–Century Company, New York, 1947.

Commission on Teacher Education, *Helping Teachers Understand Children,* American Council on Education, Washington, D. C., 1945.

Department of Elementary School Principals, *In-Service Growth of School Personnel,* National Education Association, Washington, D. C., 1942.

Miel, Alice, *Changing the Curriculum,* D. Appleton–Century Company, New York, 1946.

Prall, C. E., and Cushman, C. L., *Teacher Education in Service,* American Council on Education, Washington, D. C., 1944.

Wiles, Kimball, *Supervision for Better Schools,* Prentice-Hall, Inc., New York, 1950.

Yauch, W. A., *Improving Human Relations in School Administration,* Harper and Brothers, New York, 1949.

CHAPTER XXIX

THE CHALLENGE OF THE
ELEMENTARY SCHOOL PRINCIPALSHIP

The story is told of the nine-year-old lad who, until his mother should appear, was dutifully entertaining the visiting minister in the parlor. The minister, attempting to find out how well-versed the youngster was in his religious creed, asked, "Johnny, do you know who made you?" To which Johnny replied, somewhat startlingly, "No, but I'm not finished yet, and I'd like to help!"

Johnny's insight into the fact that he will have a large part in determining what he is to become is most pertinent to the elementary school principalship. What the emerging pattern of the principalship will be is something to be determined largely by elementary school principals themselves. It was mentioned at the outset of this book that the principalship is young as this world's professions go. Basic changes in educational theory and practice, and in the general culture, are bringing about redefinitions of the principal's functions and responsibilities, so that the position is now in a period of transition. It is emerging from its former conception of being simply a clerk or manager, or an officer-of-the-line to carry out the wishes of the superintendent. Increasing recognition of the critical importance of a child's early years, and consequently of elementary education, is investing the office with new dignity and responsibilities demanding a high type of professional leadership. Whether such leadership will come to characterize the office is something to be determined largely by principals themselves. The manner in which elementary school principals conceive and discharge the responsibilities of their office will be the most important single factor influencing the evolving

439

nature of the position, for it is what principals do that principals are. As long as they permit their time to be consumed by petty details, by matters of office routine, by carefully patterned routine "supervisory" visits, by the handling of innumerable "discipline" cases referred to the office, and the like, so long will the position remain that of petty practitioner, and not that of a person of truly professional stature.

The challenge to elementary school principals in the next few decades, then, is to make of the elementary school principalship an office of true professional leadership, leadership characterized by democratic operation and increasingly harmonious and effective human relationships. Such a development cannot result simply from principals thinking great thoughts or developing splendid intentions, although these are undoubtedly commendable. It is only as individual principals do their best to apply co-operative methods with their staffs to the study of educational problems, utilizing the findings of research and experience and the thinking of educational leaders to help them arrive at well reasoned decisions, that true professional leadership will be realized.

The importance of such leadership to the improvement of elementary education is not to be underrated. A moment's thought will indicate the strategic position of the principal in the school system. He is the administrative agent closest to the teachers and pupils in the school. He is the educational agent in position to be in closest and broadest contact with the community. Consequently, he is the educator in the best position to exert personal influence on the nature of the local school and its program. Tritely, but with much truth, it is often quoted that, "It isn't the school; it's the principal of the thing." Or, as McClure has said it, "More than any other person, the principal sets the tone of this living, growing, feeling thing—the school."[1] It should be obvious, then, that if the changes so urgently needed in education are to be made, the elementary school principal bears much of the responsibility for their making.

These changes cannot be brought about singlehandedly by any one person. However, one person *can* supply the leadership necessary to help groups of people to make the most of their combined resources in solving the problems and making the advances which are desirable. How else can there be evolved the new patterns of school organization that will facilitate modern conceptions of a good educational program? Where

[1] Department of Elementary School Principals, *The Elementary School Principalship—Today and Tomorrow,* National Education Association, Washington, D. C., 1948, p. 263.

will the refinement of a really functional and educative curriculum be developed? From whence will come the solutions of the problems of individualistic versus group instruction? Who will develop better processes of educating children for American democracy in the latter half of the twentieth century? These developments will have to come from the individual schools themselves. Certainly the help of specialists can be enlisted; the facilitating policies and materials will be needed from the superintendent's office; the suggestions and guidance of educational authorities will be helpful; but it is the principal and his staff who are the key to progress. Policies, methods, educational theories, instructional practices all may be developed and proposed by administrators, curriculum committees, state department officials, and professors; but unless they are understood and concurred in by the principal and his staff and put into practice in the local school, it is obvious that they can have little effect on educational practice.

For these reasons the elementary school principalship is today becoming more interesting, more difficult, and more challenging than ever before; the demands made upon the person holding the office are varied and somewhat imposing. On the other hand, the opportunities for educational service and leadership are unique. It is not a job for little men or little women; it demands stability, maturity, intelligence, and personal and professional stature.

How can such leadership be developed? Certainly careful selection by boards of education and superintendents is an important step. Too frequently appointments to the principalship have been made without appreciation of the potential importance of the position. When a vacancy occurred, the superintendent may have chosen the person he considered as the best teacher he had to fill it, indicating that he still looked on the office as that of principal teacher. In many cases, a male high school teacher with a reputation for ability to "control" pupils was appointed to the job, indicating, probably, that the superintendent considered the job to be primarily one of school management. Sometimes the office has been given to a veteran teacher as a reward for long and faithful service, even though the person was obviously not a leader, indicating that the superintendent had no appreciation at all for the possibilities of and need for leadership that inhere in the position. The trend, however, is away from these practices toward more careful selection of principals on the basis of successful experience, demonstrated leadership qualities, and adequate professional training for the position. "When superintendents maintain low and unsystematic local standards, they provide a crumbling keystone which may destroy all efforts to build the principalship upon ever higher levels of professional preparation and skill. When the superintendent himself maintains high standards, 'the arch of improvement' can be reared with some assurance that it will not tumble in the dust."[2]

Moreover, principals need not sit back and wait for local school systems to establish suitable standards. By participating in local, state, and national principals' organizations they can exert a strong influence on the standards established and maintained for the position. The Department of Elementary School Principals of the National Education Association has been active for many years in working for higher professional standards for principals. The Editorial Committee of the 1948 Yearbook makes the following recommendations:[3]

1. That every school system should have a written statement of the basic personal and professional standards to be required of all persons appointed to the principalship. These standards should be formulated by the superintendent and his staff in co-operation with local principals' organizations.

2. That these standards should require at least two years of successful elementary school experience, part of which includes direct classroom responsibilities.

3. That the professional preparation should not be less than the master's degree including special preparation in educational philosophy, administration and supervision of elementary schools, child psychology and development, curriculum, and instructional methods.

4. That in selecting new principals, discriminations should not be made on the basis of sex, residence, or other irrelevant factors. However, it is to be hoped that future local standards for the principalship will be so clearly stated and so courageously applied that the proportion of the young people who undertake the principalship as a life career will be greatly increased.

5. That there should be, in addition to physical examinations, a series of tests of emotional stability, intelligence, professional knowledge, and cultural interests. The minimum points on these tests, below which no appointments will be made, should be set in co-operation with the local principals' association.

6. That likely candidates for the principalship should be interviewed by committees of principals as well as by the superintendent and his staff. These committees should have authority to indicate those candidates who, on the basis of the evidence, are qualified for listing in the records from which the superintendent makes his appointments.

[2] *Ibid.,* p. 133.
[3] *Ibid.,* pp. 148–149.

Improvement in Service

While improved standards and procedures in the selection of elementary school principals can contribute materially to the professionalization of the position, we cannot rely on that alone. Many principals will be in their positions for a number of years to come. These men and women have a challenging opportunity and responsibility to develop in themselves, if they do not already have it, the type of leadership ability implied throughout this book as being desirable in the elementary school principalship.

Like any other learning, this will not come about without effort on the part of the learner. The most effective method of improving one's group leadership skill is to seek all possible opportunities to exercise what skill one has, while familiarizing oneself with the characteristics and methods of good democratic leadership as proposed by students of the subject. Such opportunities are abundant. For example, principals can try out co-operative leadership methods in teachers' meetings. They can attempt to lead teachers through the study of school problems, such as reporting to parents, without trying to tell the teachers, (and, we hope, parents) to try to find a better method than that currently in use. They can accept offices in principals' organizations where there will be opportunity to refine leadership ability through practice. Community organizations of various types offer many opportunities for the principal to participate in both leadership and followership roles.

Such exercise of leadership in the working out of educational problems will give rise to other activities which might be classified as professional growth activities. Some principals might decide to enroll for study at a college or university to find out more about the school problem under study. Undoubtedly, group study activities will lead to the reading of professional literature. Deep concern for some of the problems of the principalship may lead to activity in the local or state principals' organization in an effort to bring about constructive results. Plans evolved by the principal and his staff, which they consider to be unusually successful, may become the subjects of articles written for professional publication. These and other similar activities can contribute materially to the professional competence of the principal.[4]

[4] *Ibid.*, pp. 165–181; Department of Elementary School Principals, *The Public and the Elementary School*, National Education Association, Washington, D. C., 1949, ch. I.

What Is Ahead?

The discussions in the preceding chapters indicate the direction in which the elementary school principalship is evolving. If the past is any clue to the future, the major characteristics of tomorrow's elementary school principal can be predicted with some confidence.

Professional leadership. Perhaps the most distinguishing feature of the "new" principalship will be its conception of leadership. Instead of the coercive, controlling, paternalistic, or ineffectual laissez-faire types of leadership which seem to have prevailed up until now, principals will exercise positive leadership in democratic group processes. Instead of assuming that the authority for decision-making must be theirs because of the responsibility of their positions, principals will recognize that shared authority is more effective authority, and that the authority which comes from being recognized as a capable and emotionally mature leader is more functional than authority imposed on others by reason of the status of one's position. Under this conception the principal will conceive of his position as that of a professional person who is not assigned teaching duties so that he may employ all his time to make his leadership ability and training of service to the other professional people on his staff, to the pupils, and to the community.

Training. The "typical" elementary school principal in 1928 did not hold even a bachelor's degree; in 1948 he held a master's degree.[5] It seems likely, then, that five years of training will become the minimum requirement for appointment to the principalship. As was mentioned previously (page 10), this is already true in several states.

Furthermore, the nature of that training is likely to change significantly. While specialized training now concentrates on topics called administration and supervision, future training will very likely broaden out considerably. Certainly if the principal is to be a skilled leader, some training in leadership skill, group processes, and human-relations skills seems to be desirable. If he is to deal extensively with his school community as a result of a life-centered curriculum emphasis, he will have to learn something of community sociology and community study. It

[5] Department of Elementary School Principals, *The Public and the Elementary School,* ch. I.

seems reasonable to assume that he should have some specialized knowledge of school plant and business management. Some study of public relations would seem to be desirable, with, perhaps, attention to improving his ability as a public speaker. A broad acquaintance with research and thinking concerning modern educational practice would not be an unreasonable expectation. This breadth of training is an entirely different conception from that of the principal as the "best teacher" in the school. To attain such a background, it is likely that the principal will need more than simply one year of additional training beyond the bachelor's degree. Of course, some of this training can be obtained on the job or through extension courses. However it is obtained, it does seem likely that a broader training and specialization will characterize the elementary school principal of the future.

Prestige. It was mentioned in Chapter I that certain factors had operated in the past to give considerably more prestige to workers in secondary schools than was enjoyed by workers in elementary schools. These factors have been changing slowly to the benefit of those in elementary schools. The enhanced position of women in society, the trend toward equal salaries for elementary school and secondary school workers, and an increased respect for the importance of the elementary school period in the child's life, all have worked in this direction. It seems likely that with the influence of these factors, with increased training, with more careful recruitment and selection, and with the exercise of more positive and democratic leadership in school and community on the part of elementary school principals, the principal will be highly respected for the key position he holds in the educational system.

Autonomy. There seems to be a strong trend in education, particularly in the larger cities, to place much more responsibility upon the local school unit. This is the natural outgrowth of the developing life-centered educational philosophy. If education is to deal with the problems of living of the pupils, it is obvious that it must differ from place to place. No longer will it be desirable for the state, or for the school district central office, to prescribe in some detail just what the curriculum shall be for all pupils.

Furthermore, increasing emphasis is being placed on the desirability of school-community co-operative planning of aspects of school policy.

If parents and other community members are to help the school staff develop the policies for the school, it is clear that the local school must be left relatively free to develop in line with these co-operatively formed decisions.

Hence, it seems likely that the principal of the near future will have considerable responsibility for the operation and leadership of his own school, vastly more than has been common practice in our schools. This lends emphasis to the point made earlier: that the principal must be or become an able leader of people.

Educational Venturer. It was mentioned above that if new and better methods, policies, and procedures are to be developed, they will have to be developed in the local schools. The day of the private "hothouse" experimental school seems to have passed. The job now is to develop types of organization, methods, materials and processes consistent with, and outgrowths of, what we have learned about child development, learning, and sociology. To do this there is pressing need for principals and staffs who are experimentally minded; that is, who will not be satisfied simply to keep school running smoothly, but who will be constantly re-evaluating the educational program in the school, and devising better methods to enhance the quality of living and growing going on there and in the community.

The foregoing characteristics are not simply idealistic wishful thinking. Able and dedicated principals in numbers of schools are now working in the manner of the true professional leader, and their numbers are growing. Their example, and the exciting possibilities to contribute to educational thought and practice, to help a staff do a better job of guiding child growth, and to help improve the quality of living in the school communities of the country constitute a challenge to the kinds of men and women who, it is hoped, will typify the elementary school principalship of the future.